THE BEARING
OF RECENT DISCOVERY
ON THE TRUSTWORTHINESS
OF THE NEW TESTAMENT

by

W. M. RAMSAY

BAKER BOOK HOUSE
Grand Rapids, Michigan

Reprinted 1979 by
Baker Book House Company
from the 1915 edition published by
Hodder and Stoughton, London

Originally given as
The James Sprunt Lectures for 1911
Union Theological Seminary, Richmond, Virginia

ISBN: 0-8010-7677-3

This volume is part of the ten-volume
William M. Ramsay Library
ISBN: 0-8010-7685-4

PHOTOLITHOPRINTED BY CUSHING - MALLOY, INC.
ANN ARBOR, MICHIGAN, UNITED STATES OF AMERICA
1979

PREFACE

THE following pages have been almost wholly re-written since the Great War began, and in one respect show the influence of the situation. The very existence of our country was staked on the uncertain issue ; and the individual could not hope or wish to survive the nation. I felt that this book might be my last will and testament, and attempted to put into it the gist of what I had learned in the struggle of life and the study of books.

I describe no striking discoveries. My aim is to state certain principles that result from modern discovery, and to illustrate their bearing on the New Testament. The method is to show through the examination, word by word and phrase by phrase, of a few passages, which have been much exposed to hostile criticism, that the New Testament is unique in the compactness, the lucidity, the pregnancy and the vivid truthfulness of its expression. That is not the character of one or two only of the books that compose the Testament : it belongs in different ways to all alike, though space fails in the present work to try them all.

A great discovery has resulted from modern investigation, viz. the wide and familiar use of writing in Western Asia as furnishing the basis on which the

Roman bureaucratic administration was able to rest. That is really a great principle ; and yet how little is its importance understood! I adhere to the inferences drawn in the first chapters of the " Letters to the Seven Churches " and in the paper on " The First Written Gospel " in " Luke the Physician and other Studies in the History of Religion". Yet many of us will wait until some German scholar has stated the same conclusions before accepting them.

The only way, the necessary and the useful method, is to go over the New Testament sentence by sentence, and to show how great principles and big ideas form the texture of the thought everywhere.

Carrying out the view stated twenty years ago in "St. Paul the Traveller," pp. 303 to 309, I see in the earliest Church history the religion of freedom engaged in a conflict with the Imperial power. Luke shows the conflict beginning at Christ's birth. The strange situation in which He was born was caused by an order of Augustus, a world-wide order express- ing a vast force that moves through many centuries of history and always makes for slavery. The worse side of Imperial policy, as embodied in that order, drove Mary from Nazareth to Bethlehem. And what was the result? Only the fulfilment of the ancient truth and prophecy that in Bethlehem, the humble village which was the centre of old Hebrew tradition, there must be born, when the fulness of the time was come, the King of the Jews and the Saviour of the world. Autocracy compasses its own destruction, and the freedom of the Divine Will works out its perfect expression through the autocrat's error.

The episodes in the first and third Gospels, describing the circumstances of the Saviour's Birth, are of the highest importance ; Luke sets that event in relation with the tides and forces of Imperial world-history ; and Matthew describes how the traditional wisdom of Asia recognized the new-born King. On the other hand, John says nothing about such mundane matters, because his thought moves on a far higher plane, and his eye is fixed only on the infinite Divine nature; while Mark restricts himself to recounting what he had learned about the public career of Jesus as a Teacher.

It is necessary to insist on the immense importance of these episodes, and to illustrate this from various points of view, pp. 145 f., 248 f., 272 f. No one can comprehend Luke or Matthew, so long as his mind is clogged with the old ideas about the puerility and untrustworthiness of those episodes. Yet I am wrong in calling those ideas old ; here is what was said only a few years ago by one of the most distinguished and famous of Scottish theologians in his commentary on Luke's narrative, II. 1 f. :—

"One could almost wish that v. 2 had been omitted, or that there were reason to believe, as has been suggested by several writers, that it is a gloss that has found its way into the text, and that Luke is not responsible for it—so much trouble has it given to commentators."

These words were written by Dr. A. B. Bruce in the maturity of his career, after a life devoted to the exposition of the Gospels. They crystallize in a gem of criticism the inadequate method and the falseness of view, which could result in the thought that the convenience of the commentator should be put as a test of truth.

The breadth and dignity of the ideas in the New Testament are such that its outlook over human history must be ranked on the loftiest level. For example : " Not merely are all the statements in Luke II. 1-3 true. They are also in themselves great statements, presenting to us large historical facts, world-wide administrative measures, vast forces working on human society through the ages," see p. 304. Those who miss this may delude themselves with the fancy that the passage is a legend or an invention. Those who have eyes and historic sense to see know that nothing but truth can be so grand and so simple.

In the prefaces to several books, I have referred to the charge brought against me of having slighted the opinions of the Germans. I have learned much from the greater German scholars in my own subject ; but their teaching was to judge for myself and to accept no man's dictum on the credit of his name and fame. In 1885 Mommsen spent a week in Oxford as my guest, and among many memories I will quote one : we were speaking of English translations of German books, and he said, "you should not translate our books : you ought to write history from your point of view : we need to see the past from your point of view as well as from ours ".

I do not follow the prevailing tendency of German criticism of the New Testament. It is wrong because it is narrow, and because it judges from erroneous premises and unjustifiable prejudices ; and one welcomes any signs of a return to a saner and better informed judgment. Many very learned scholars have been blind to the grandeur of the thought in the New Testament ; and the cosmic ideas which inform it throughout have generally passed over their heads. Where they dimly caught the meaning of a cosmic idea, they called it "eschatological". This mirage of the "eschatology" of the New Testament arose from fettering great moral truths, expressed in terms of the infinite, with the precise hard and wholly inadequate expression of dull logical conception.

In the few cases where questions of text are concerned I give no details, but simply state the verdict of Westcott and Hort and my own arguments. No reading is adopted which they do not print as resting on good authority. Any one that wishes to go behind them ought to investigate the evidence for himself. It must, however, be added that the work of those two great scholars seems to me far from being final, and their method results in establishing the text of a fourth or late third century school ; but the school contained men of real learning, whose text was a great achievement. Now, however, it is necessary to go back behind that text to an older period.

It was not easy to complete the book amid the many duties and the mental strain imposed by the Great War; and I apologize for many deficiencies whose existence I dread. They will rise before me when it is too late.

I owe the photographs to Lady Ramsay, and the indexes to the Rev. Principal Perry, Coates Hall, Edinburgh. It is an honour to be able to speak of the latter as one of my own pupils at Aberdeen.

W. M. RAMSAY.

CONTENTS

PART I.   PRELIMINARY

PART II.   THE LECTURES

xi

PART III. ASSOCIATED QUESTIONS

LIST OF ILLUSTRATIONS

PLATES

CUTS IN THE TEXT

PART I. PRELIMINARY

CHAPTER I

EXPLANATION OF METHOD AND ORDER

HISTORICAL criticism is subject to great variety of judgment. With obviously equal honesty some critics will praise the trustworthiness of an authority whom others decry as prejudiced and utterly untrustworthy. Even in regard to an author who is so carefully and so dispassionately studied as Thucydides, the most contradictory opinions are maintained. Most scholars regard him as the greatest of historians and a model of impartial judgment and dispassionate statement, but a few go to the opposite extreme, and pronounce him a skilful perverter of historical truth.

It is therefore not to be wondered at that, in a sphere where the feelings of mankind are deeply engaged, where opposing emotions and tendencies are concerned, and where dispassionate consideration is hardly practicable—as is the case in the domain of religion—similar diversity of opinion should reign in an equal or greater degree. Hence the long dispute about the trustworthiness of the New Testament, and about the authenticity of the books contained in it. Did Luke write the Acts of the Apostles, and, if so, can what he says there be accepted as trustworthy?[1] Such is the character of the problem; and many on both sides of the discussion seem to enter on it with their minds already

---

[1] It may, of course, be taken for granted that, if Luke did not write the Acts, it could not possibly be accepted. The case for belief rests on his personality.

made up on crucial questions and with their feelings deeply stirred.

As the variety of opinions in these typical cases proves, arguments regarding the trustworthiness of the ancient authors generally cannot be dissociated from a certain element of subjectivity, and made purely scientific. Human beings always have judged and will judge diversely in such matters, according to their varying idiosyncrasy, and will come to opposite conclusions on the same evidence. Even about contemporary history, where the facts in their superficial outlines are known and admitted, diametrically opposite judgments are pronounced by skilled and educated onlookers. Taking the verbatim report of a speech delivered on any question of public affairs, some will condemn it as trifling with truth and glossing over the facts, while others praise it as an impartial and correct statement of the critical points in the case. People decide in accordance with their predilections and prejudices, and in general one could tell beforehand which of one's acquaintances would praise the speech and which would condemn it.

We must therefore frankly acknowledge that a thoroughly scientific character cannot be given to the present or to any similar argument regarding historical trustworthiness; the same reasoning which convinces one, will fail to convince another; each reader will estimate according to his own character, and every statement of the argument will vary according to the quality of the writer. On this account it seems better to give to these lectures a form that is in accordance with the elementary conditions of the case. The personal qualities of the author must influence his statement of the reasoning. Let us admit at the outset the subjective element in the present treatment of this subject. The case is stated as it appears to the writer, and others will judge for themselves; but it seems then necessary to premise a statement regarding his bent and attitude of mind, so that readers may be in a position to judge what allowance to make for his prejudices and proclivities and personal bias. The writer, of course, cannot describe his own personal quality; and yet the readers, if any be found, ought to have in their hands some means of gauging and correcting the reasoning according to his tendencies.

While it would obviously be impossible for him to make any useful estimate of his own character and bias, it is possible to mention the stages in the growth of the plan which guides the writer's work, keeping the statement as objective as can be; and this is attempted in the following chapter. Such an attempt must, from its nature, be personal, and may be condemned by some or by many as impertinent and egotistical. Those who so judge are begged to omit the rest of the introduction, and proceed to Part II, where the course of lectures begins. Some, who are likely to be in sympathy with the method that governs the book as a whole, will find that the introduction is an essential part of it.[1]

In the main part of the book there is no attempt to follow a strictly scientific order, because, as has just been said, the subject is not susceptible of strictly scientific treat-

---

[1] The following chapter was not part of the actual lectures, but was given as an explanatory statement in a different place. People frequently asked how it had come about that I had been exploring in Asiatic Turkey for thirty-four years; what first led me there? what made me continue to go there? It seemed unusual that a teacher in a Scottish University should spend much of every year's vacation in Asiatic Turkey. In trying to answer the question I came to see that it was entirely pertinent, and was prompted by a right instinct of intelligent curiosity; the answer is an integral and proper part of the book.

ment. It must partake of the author's personality; and therefore the order followed is the order of discovery, i.e. the order of the growth of opinion and belief in an individual mind. The introductory chapter states the growth of opinion in the same mind from an earlier point, and makes the later stage of life and work more intelligible and the writer's prejudice more easily estimated; but nothing is described unless it seems to have in some degree formed the judgment and determined the opinions of later life.

A certain idea of work and plan of life took possession of my mind at an early age. The idea was at first vague and misty. It did not control my life, because it was unformed and therefore weak. The stages by which it grew were not determined by me; they were forced on me in the struggle of life; and they can be described as they arose.

Sometimes it will be necessary to dwell at some length on a slight and apparently trivial incident, because it proved to be typical and determinative in the future: especially is that the case with the genesis of the idea. Often an interval of several years offers nothing worth recording in this view: the purpose did not apparently develop during that time or become clearer; rather it seemed to recede and fade away, and if external circumstances had been unfavourable, or the indwelling desire weaker, it might have died. Yet it was always there beneath the surface, waiting for the favourable moment where outward conditions should give it strength.

CHAPTER II

INTRODUCTORY STATEMENT

In March, 1868, at the end of my second year at the University of Aberdeen, I was feeling every day that college work had been an unalloyed happiness, and every moment spent in class-work or in preparation a delight. Even the details of syntax and word-formation had their fascination, and the inflection of the Greek verb was interesting. True, we never passed one throughout two years of class-work without some student being called on to conjugate it, though years before I entered college I could and did often write out the parts of every common verb without an error, and the best of my class-fellows I do not doubt had done the same. Yet the unexpectedness of the parts made this work like voyaging on an unknown sea: in that primitive period no explanation was given us how those strange vagaries were all obedient to more deep-lying laws; but one was vaguely beginning to feel that some hidden principle lay under the apparent caprice.

The idea was simmering unconsciously in my mind that scholarship was the life for me: not the life of teaching, which was repellent, but the life of discovery. Why should I not continue to voyage on that adventurous sea, where one always as it were had one's life in one's hand, where no slip or omission was ever pardoned, where the smallest fault in grammar was a deadly sin and a *maximus error*, where there was the excitement of continual exploration and the finding of the unknown? Ideas of history, too, were beginning to shape themselves in my mind, not taken in cut-and-dry form from a text-book, but gathered fresh out of the difficulties of Sophocles and Juvenal. I was learning for myself out of Greek and Latin grammar and the sentences of great authors, that, as Plato expresses it in the "Theætetus," word is spoken thought, and thought is unspoken word. But all was in embryo, I could not have told what was in my mind in those days, as we waited for the declaration of results in the class examinations.

At that time in Aberdeen the prizes and places in each subject were not announced until the final day, when they were declared publicly for each of the four classes in separate session. The old class-system was still in full force, the same system which about 1760 was carried to Philadelphia and introduced into the University of Pennsylvania by William Smith of Aberdeen, first Provost of the University,[1] and which spread thence over the whole of the United States, being accepted by all the older Universities except the University of Virginia, and adopted by almost all the new foundations. Every student belonged to the class of his own year, studied the regular subjects in a fixed order, and passed through the curriculum among the same body of associates. He belonged for life to that "class," and in Aberdeen many of these classes kept up the custom of meeting once a year, and occasionally publishing a record of the fortunes of each individual. The annual meeting of the classes is in America associated with a public function of the University, and officially used as a powerful engine for preserving its unity and its connexion with former graduates. In Aberdeen the meeting remained

---

[1] This interesting fact of University history is given on the authority of the present Provost, who told the whole story to the present writer in 1913.

always a private gathering of any class which chose to hold such a re-union, and the University took no part in it and no notice of it. Occasionally some Professor was invited to the meeting, but as a rule it was purely a students' gathering of a single class.

The class-system at Aberdeen, now much destroyed by the Royal Commission of 1894,[1] was then a power in University life and exercised a strong influence on every student. That was the case with us, although our class was one which has never held any re-union or met in any general fashion after the fourth year ended ; and this explanation of the system is needed to explain why that meeting of the class to hear the declaration of the prizes was felt as a momentous occasion for young students.

On the final day we of the Second Year gathered in the Latin class-room. The feeling was in my mind that morning that something determining was going to happen : I rose with a vague anticipation of some event, and walked with a dreamy half-consciousness of an impending change. The subjects in the Second Year were a class of mathematics, two distinct classes of Greek, and two of Latin. The mathematical declaration put me fourth, Greek twice first, and Latin the same. The Professor of Greek, who knew every student by face and position, glanced round the room before beginning to read his list, until he saw me ; and as I caught his eye, I knew before he spoke that I was

---

[1] Royal Commissions rarely do the good that might be expected ; but that of 1890-94 was peculiarly unsuccessful. Hardly any member of it had been educated at a Scottish University, or showed any sympathy with the national tradition of college life ; and Aberdeen was represented on the board of fifteen by a retired professor, eighty years of age, who lived far away in his own country, and knew the University only during his very efficient professoriate. The students now still struggle to maintain the old custom in spite of adverse circumstances.

the outstanding figure in his mind.   The Professor of Latin
mentioned that I stood apart in the list.   In that room
my life was determined : I formed the resolve to be a
scholar, and to make everything else subservient to that
purpose and that career.

In the class-room, also, one other matter settled itself.
The border-land between Greece and the East, the relation
of Greek literature to Asia, had already a vague fascination
for me ; and this was to be the direction of the life that I
imagined in the future.   As it has turned out, that thought of
the relation between Greece and the East was an anticipation
of my life ; but the form developed in a way that I did not
imagine until many years passed.   I thought of work in a
room or a library, but it has lain largely in the open air
and on the geographical frontier where Greek-speaking
people touched the East.   I thought of Greek literature in
its relation to Asia ; but the subject widened into the relation between the spirit of Europe and of Asia through the
centuries.

The difficulties in this career I did not count, because I
could not know them.   How was one to live ? I knew
enough to judge that the only path lay in an Oxford Fellowship.   That was arranged before the meeting ended, and
always was before my mind in the following two years, but
it was never mentioned to my most intimate friends.   I
was intended by my family to compete for an appointment
in the Indian Civil Service ; and, as instability was a
deadly sin in the eyes of some of my relatives, I did not
speak of the change.   For the time, the ordinary Aberdeen
course was the path to either goal ; and the new plan was
not spoken of at home, until the end of the curriculum in
March, 1871.   Then there was strong disapproval, not in
my mother's household, but outside, for many thought it

foolish to turn to an Oxford course with its vague uncertainties. That path was then untrodden, though it has become a common one since for Aberdeen students.

A scholarship was necessary ; and as I was now over twenty, the limit at that time in most Oxford Colleges,[1] opportunities were few. I had only one acquaintance at Oxford, who recommended me to enter for an exhibition at his own College, New, where nothing would be open till the following spring, 1872, and I spent a year in apparent idleness. It might have been more profitably spent : but I had no advisers, and muddled on in my own ignorant fashion.

In March, 1872, it chanced that the University Intelligence in the " Times," which I read every day in the public Reading-room, contained one Friday an " amended notice" issued by St. John's College : one of the two scholarships previously announced for competition was now stated to be open without age-limit. Here was an opening. The examination began on the ensuing Monday at 9 A.M. in the College Hall, and names with proper documents had to reach the President not later than Saturday. There was barely half-an-hour to catch the mail ; I posted a letter from a shop, saying that the needed documents would be sent later ; and then went to the rooms of an intimate college friend to discuss whether or not I should risk the journey. He confirmed my wavering resolution. My name and all the proper documents were already in the hands of the Warden of New College, where the competition was to begin a week later ; but my friend undertook to procure copies, while I packed and started for Oxford, a long journey at that time. I arrived on Sunday at 1.30 P.M. ; had lunch, found the

---

[1] In some the age was nineteen, as it soon afterwards was fixed generally.

Post Office and the College, and returned to my hotel, where I slept as one sleeps after spending twenty-two hours in the train.

One of the Fellows at St. John's took some interest in me ; and on Thursday at the end of the paper-work I learned that the scholarship lay between a man from Trinity College, Dublin, and myself, and that the loser would be offered an Exhibition of almost equal value, created for the occasion. The decision was made on Saturday morning on *viva voce* translation at sight ; this was my strong point at any time, but in the elation of success after a tedious year I could have made something of Lycophron at sight, and Aristotle, an author new to me, seemed simple.

A thing that impressed me was that my New College friend chanced to meet me in the street after the final test ; and when I told him what had happened, he explained that it was fortunate he had not known, as he would have warned me not to try at St. John's, because this Trinity man (whom he knew by reputation) was considered certain of anything he might try for in Oxford ; if St. John's had remembered in time about the unlimited nature of that single scholarship (which was open only once in five years), my adviser (by whom I was in this matter guided absolutely) would have prevented me from trying. My competitor came to St. John's, took his First, and soon afterwards was made Principal of a colonial University.

The importance of this scholarship lay in its size (£100 a year as compared with £60 at New), in its tenure for a fifth year, which as things turned out was invaluable for me, and in the free position that it gave me. At New they would have dosed me with teaching, for which I was too mature ; and I should have grown sick of college work. At St. John's they let me alone to take my own course in my own way—often a wrong way, but I had to learn to take the chances and trust myself. With this and an Aberdeen graduate scholarship I was started for five years.

Carrying out my old dream about the contact between Greece and the East, I began in 1874 to study Sanskrit, thinking that in this speech of an Aryan people who had melted into Asia one could best approach the historical problem, and spent three months at Göttingen during the long vacation,[1] studying with Benfey, who gave up his usual autumn holiday in Switzerland to continue the lessons. In Benfey I first came in contact with a really great scholar of the modern type, and learned something of German method. He opened to me a new world, and gave me fresh courage and hope, telling me that he looked to me to continue his work on the Rig-Veda. The way of scholarship had been hitherto arid in my education, the sense of discovery was never quickened, and the power of perceiving truth was becoming atrophied. Scholarship had been a learning of opinions, and not a process of gaining real knowledge. One learned what others had thought, but not what truth was. Benfey was a vivifying wind, to breathe life into the dry bones, for he showed scholarship as discovery and not as a rehearsing of wise opinions. From him I returned to Oxford, and there my eyes were opened by another teacher.

In October of that year work for the Final School of Literæ Humaniores began, embracing classical philosophy, history and scholarship—the typical Oxford school and a wonderfully stimulating and educative course, in spite of the fact that an examination is its goal. Now in philosophy I had been brought up at the feet of Professor Bain, whose

[1] Immediately after the First Public Examination in June, 1874.

ability stood out conspicuous in the University of Aberdeen, and whom I regarded as having said the final word in the subject, viz. that all philosophers had been mere jugglers with phrases, who succeeded in bamboozling the world into the belief that there was some meaning under their words, whereas in reality there was none. Bain's class of Logic had been the one class at Aberdeen in which I eagerly aimed at gaining the first place ; and it had been a severe blow when I came out twenty-first.

As it was now necessary to know something about one of those jugglers with words, named Plato, and I was perfectly ignorant as to his particular way of deluding people, I felt bound to attend the lectures of Mr. Bidder on the Republic. Going across the quadrangle to the first lecture I remarked to a friend that I should now have to spend two years in learning how Plato had been able to delude mankind.

The lecturer walked up and down the room with his thumbs in his waistcoat pockets talking lightly and easily about the development of thought and language in Greece before Plato. He put a question to me at an early stage, which I answered from the lofty level of a devotee of Bain. He airily tore my reply to tatters and explained clearly what I ought to have said. Thereafter, he continued every few minutes to put a question to me and to exhibit the helpless inadequacy of my reply. In one hour I learned what a fool I was—a very salutary lesson for a young man —and at the end of the hour I remarked to the same friend : " Bidder is evidently a man of ability, and he seems to think that Plato had some meaning in his words : I must try to find out whether that is true ". One hour had changed my whole attitude towards philosophy, and made it possible for me to begin to understand Greek thought.

In Oxford there were many other able lecturers on philosophy, and at St. John's in particular there was an excellent man, from whom I learned much ; but Bidder with his incisive speech was the one man that could have opened my eyes. I shall always remember Aubrey Moore with deep gratitude but his words would have passed me by and made no impression on my unopened mind. He could never have unsealed my eyes, though he taught me more than Bidder after my eyes were open.

It was a great step to make in that first hour with Plato. If you want to understand the relation between Greece and Asia, you must begin by understanding Greece ; but I remained blind and deaf to the true spirit of Hellenism, however much I might admire and love Greek literature, so long as the mind was closed to Plato.

Benfey recommended me to Max Müller, who took a generous interest in my scheme of studying Sanskrit, and gave me the opportunity of meeting at his house people from the greater world ; but he strongly advised me to finish the Final Schools before spending serious labour on the language. A visit to Cambridge, and interviews with Peile, the master of Christ's, author of a book on the young science of Comparative Philology, and with Cowell, the Professor of Sanskrit, confirmed Max Müller's warning that there was no career in Sanskrit except as a sequel to the regular schools. Then Benfey's attempt to procure for me a presentation from Government of the vast Commentary of Sayana on the Rig-Veda proved unsuccessful. Like many later disappointments, it was a blessing in disguise. Had the book been given me, honour would have bound me to justify the gift and to labour at Sanskrit. As it was, I was free to act on Max Müller's advice, and thus was

rescued from a *cul de sac.* The path of Sanskrit had nothing
for me : the men who wrote Sanskrit cared nought for
mundane things, and the history of action would have become no clearer from its study. I shut the books, intend-
ing to return to them after twenty-two months, and have
never opened them again.

In 1876 the Final Schools were approaching, and with
them a Divinity examination, involving either the Thirty-nine
Articles or some substitute. I could not with years of
labour pass an examination in the Articles : to read them
was as impossible as to fly to the moon. In childhood I
could have committed them to memory like the Shorter
Catechism, without understanding what I repeated ; but at
the age of twenty-four that was impossible. I took refuge in
the Epistle to the Galatians, and communed with Lightfoot,
whose transparent honesty was invigorating and delightful.
My mother's love for Paul began to move in my mind ; and
she and I read together Conybeare and Howson's Life and
translation of the Letters, a thoroughly scholarly book.
I was now full of Aristotle's most advanced treatises, and
came to Paul with a new mind, finding him the true successor
of the Stagirite.

The letter to the Galatians I was free to regard as the
work of Paul, for it was admitted in the Tübingen School,
which at this time was my guide in criticism. The logical
skill with which Baur and his associates carried out their
premises to their foregone conclusion had impressed me
deeply, and I did not inquire into the premises, which in
fact were accepted as necessary by a follower of Bain, but
should not have been accepted by one who was beginning
to think that he might succeed in understanding Plato. I
was still under the domination of schools, and accepted the
principles taught by such great writers and teachers as had

first caught me, and as yet I had not learned to go back to first principles for myself.

In the summer before the Final Schools I spent two months near Robertson Smith, and under his care read everything recent that he thought most worth reading on the Old Testament, worshipped Wellhausen, dipped into the study of comparative religion and folklore, and fell in love with J. F. MacLennan's anthropological researches. Most advisers would have regarded this as a reckless and insane throwing away of chances in the Final Schools, and they are right as regards some students, but wrong as regards others. I had been hesitating about a Special Subject in addition to the prescribed work, and was ready to offer either comparative philology with the elements of Sanskrit, or the metaphysical " Trilogy " of Plato, or the Metaphysics of Aristotle ; I had read them all with equal care, with equal interest, and doubtless with equally little understanding, and two months spent on the Old Testament was health-giving ; probably a Second Class might have been my lot, if I had not wandered on to the solid ground of history for two months. That ground was slippery : Wellhausen and others were reconstructing Hebrew history after their own free will ; but they were at least free and they were con-structing, though after a fashion which seems to me now to ignore vital conditions of the problem.

There is some truth in a remark that I heard Walter Pater make : talking of a college tutor's work he said, " I prefer pass students to honours students ; you occasion-ally find a passman who can take an interest in the subject for its own sake ; but honours men are so entirely occupied with their next examination that they have no time to think about their subject ". I think there are now probably some honours men who would escape the censure.

I had not such good fortune in the lectures that I heard in Oxford on Greek history as on Greek philosophy, and I heard none on Roman history. The new men had not begun, and the old lecturers (so far as I heard them) were hardened in the narrowness of an older school. In 1913 an Oxford historian read a paper fixing exact dates in primitive Greek history. I listened, and reflected with intense amusement that every sentence in it would have been regarded by Oxford opinion in my undergraduate days as sheer lunacy; yet here in 1913 an audience of the best lecturers in Oxford regarded it as the serious work of a serious historian. One draws a moral for the study of New Testament history. Perhaps the next generation may draw a moral for Old Testament history (as some already do).

At the end of the fourth year the problem of a livelihood confronted me. I had come to Oxford to be a scholar; there was no other path open to that life, so far as I could see, except a fellowship; and a fellowship was as far off as ever. I was not on good terms with my own College, partly from my own fault, partly from the fact that the College, accustomed to boys fresh from school, was puzzled by an incomprehensible student who aimed at being a scholar, and could not believe that he was genuine. This again was fortunate. Had the College approved of me, it would have found a place for me ; and circumstances would have forced me into the life of a College lecturer and tutor, for which I was not suited. The College acted for my best interest, and for its own also, I am sure.

I was on the outlook for any opening, and was ready to go off to English Literature, if there had been any places in that line of University work, such as now exist in fair number. The subject interested me, and there were no examinations to prepare for, which would prevent one from serious work. I had read pretty widely, subscribed to the New Shakespere Society from its foundation, and made addresses to Students' Societies on subjects of English literature. Nothing however presented itself, and the prospect was dark.

Then, as it appeared, the stroke of fate fell, and I was ordered by a doctor to go abroad and wander for a year, reading nothing, but keeping my ears and eyes and mind open, living in the open air, and reversing all the course of my life. To go down from Oxford at that stage was to go down for ever : the absent is forgotten, and new men come up :—

> To have done is to hang
> Quite out of fashion like a rusty mail
> In monumental mockery.

And so I said farewell to Oxford, and " went out sighing," thinking never to see the fair city again. I had learned much there, though not in the conventional way.

I had just enough with the last year of my scholarship at St. John's to pay all I owed, and start on my travels with nothing. I did not pay all I owed till several years later, and never regretted it, for I found that accounts presented to an undergraduate going down were charged on a lordly scale ; but some were afterwards rendered on a distinctly humble grade.

Those of my friends and relatives who had disapproved my Oxford venture, now found that their disapprobation had been fully justified : I had made a disastrous failure, none the less a failure that it had been nearly a success.[1]

---

[1] Many incidents, which are omitted because they have no bearing on the present plan, show that the phrase, " nearly a success," is justified. Other colleges had Fellowships : but, as has been said, a Fellowship of the ordinary type would have ruined my aspirations in life.

Those who had approved were now my helpers ; and my uncle Mr. Drake told me that £100 was at my disposal at any time. I went off to Germany, Switzerland, and Italy with £25 in my pocket, to which a second £25 was soon added. I had the fortune to make new friends, to get a valuable part of my education, to earn some money, and at last to return with as much in my pocket as when I started. Always since then I have cherished a warm feeling towards Americans, because it was from Americans that much of the enjoyment and profit of that year came, and it was they that taught me to live in the world of Europe.

In leaving Oxford I had the fortune to propitiate one who was not a friend, and to make a new friend. I called on the President of St. John's, who had not liked me and made no secret of his dislike. He never hid his opinions in such matters. If he thought that a man was a fool or a knave, he told him so "in good round terms". I often said in those weary years of undergraduate life at Oxford, that if we had met at some house in the country we should have got on very well ; for I always admired his blunt directness and honesty of language ; but in a college with its schoolboy rules, he was puzzled and annoyed with my views, which had been expressed to him with a directness and honesty like his own. Now that I was going down, I felt free to explain the reason of some things, and he said, " If your time here were to begin over again, I should act differently towards you ". This was about as near as Bellamy ever came to making an apology to an undergraduate. When the Asia Minor Exploration Fund was started, Professor Pelham, who managed it, found that the President of St. John's was the readiest of subscribers every year.

The day before I went down I received an invitation from the Master of Balliol, Dr. Jowett, to call on him. It happened that, while I was in Göttingen two years before, a young Balliol philosopher, now Professor J. Cook Wilson, came there to study with Lotze; and he afterwards spoke of me to Jowett. T. H. Green, one of the Examiners in the Final Schools, had also mentioned me to the Master: he had himself invited me to call on him after the examination was over, an honour that I valued very highly.

Jowett said he wished to learn whether he could help me in any way; and when he heard that I was going abroad next day, he said, " If you come back to Oxford, call on me, and I will do what I can to help you ". Seven years later, in January, 1884, I called on him and reminded him of this promise, as having been always a support to me in a time full of uncertainties. He had not forgotten; and not very long afterwards, being (as it chanced) one of the electors to the newly instituted Professorship of Greek Art and Archæology, he wrote inviting me to dine with him five weeks later, on the night after the election, " to meet Sir Charles Newton," another of the electors. It was a remarkable act, one of those bold and unconventional things that few men would dare to do, and which can be pardoned only when they have been justified by success; and we took it as a proof that he hoped I should feel in good spirits two hours after the electors made their choice. The Professorship was a small one, and candidates in that subject were few and already well known. We said nothing to anyone about the invitation until after the event. As Jowett had the reputation of caring only for Balliol men, this seems worth mentioning as a trait in the character of a noteworthy personality.

Professor Bywater, a very fine scholar and a great Aristotelian, also invited me to call on him, hearing of my interest in Aristotle; and it was refreshing to converse with him, or rather to listen to his epigrammatic talk. By a coincidence translation from Aristotle, which had decided the entrance scholarship, played a part also in the Final Examinations; the "Metaphysics" was my Special Subject, and among the unseen translations was a piece from the "Physics". Of this I gave two renderings, one straight and the other treating the passage as an unintelligent mixture of the notes made by two different pupils who heard the same lecture and wrote what they could understand of it, these separate notes having been put together by a third pupil, who edited the lecture. This theory, caught from Trendelenburg, I had in private study applied to some other parts of Aristotle; and it was excellent training for the treatment of similar theories as applied by some scholars to the Acts of the Apostles and the Epistles of Paul.

At Max Müller's house I had met Professor Sayce, and afterwards saw him pretty often. He was the first person who treated me frankly as a scholar, not as an undergraduate. The examinations that divided me from other dons did not exist for him. He saw only the interest in scholarship and the love of truth; and my inclination towards the Asian borderland was much stimulated in talking with him. He was for several years the only correspondent that I had in Oxford to keep the connexion living.

So far as work in life, or even the way of earning a livelihood was concerned, the outlook was darker than ever. In Oxford after the Final Schools, a friend and I had planned to make an edition of the Nicomachean Ethics, and that work was just begun when my Oxford life was brought apparently to an end. The deciding event was now at hand; but it came very slowly. At Rome in January, 1878, when talking with a young Oxford graduate, a Modern

History Fellow who was learning Italian for his special work, I chanced to mention what my aim had been in life, a thing which I never mentioned to any one in Oxford, after it had led to trouble in my own college, and that now no path seemed open except a place in the British Museum. He at once said that he could get for me an introduction to Mr. Stuart Poole, Keeper of Coins there ; and in due course he procured a letter from Mr. R. Lane Poole (now Fellow of Magdalen and Lecturer in Diplomatic in the University) to his uncle at the Museum. On my way home to Scotland about the end of March I presented this letter. Mr. Poole received me very kindly, and asked me to lunch to meet Sir Charles Newton, Keeper of Greek and Roman Antiquities, who, as it turned out, was to play a determining part in my life. At the time there was no opening in the Museum. Mr. Poole said that, if he had known sooner, he might have got me an opening in his Department : but he had already advertised the place for public competition, and could not withdraw from this. He suggested, however, that I should enter the competition, and said that he felt sure about the issue. I replied that I had resolved to enter no more examinations, and moreover could not compete against candidates so much junior to myself.

In Scotland sixteen months later, July, 1879, I received a letter from Mr. Poole, telling that a Studentship of £300 a year for three years had been instituted in the University of Oxford for Travel and Research in the Greek lands, and advising that I should come up to the Museum and study there in preparation for it. He said that some candidates were spoken of, but the outstanding candidate was a young graduate who had the reputation of being extraordinarily able, but who in his opinion would not be a good appointment. By this time I was married, and my wife and I were spending the vacation at my sister's house in Sutherlandshire. Next morning we started for London.

We were under no illusions as to the financial side of the case. My brother-in-law advised us to go, but pointed out that it would take £500 a year to do the work in Greece. However, as we had married on a salary of £100 a year for one year, the need of earning the additional £200 was merely a restatement of the present problem. Robertson Smith was giving me work for the "Encyclopædia Britannica," and we hoped to send letters to the newspapers from the Greek world.

The next three months were spent at the Museum, a time of unalloyed happiness, thanks largely as before to the kindness of Mr. and Mrs. Drake, who gave us the use of their house in town, while they were away in the country.

Of the other candidate, who was two years junior to myself, we saw little. His name and fame I had heard as early as 1874. He was of Trinity College, Dublin; and my Trinity rival and friend had heralded his coming to Oxford, describing him as a man of quite extraordinary ability. He finished his Oxford course with a most brilliant reputation : it was the smallest item in his fame that he had got his First with less work than any other man in the memory of history. As scholar, critic, dramatist, poet, he was the man of the future. I refer to Mr. Oscar Wilde. He occasionally appeared at the Museum, and admired the art. One would see him rapt in ecstasy before a statue ; but, as Newton was quick to see, the statues that he most admired were Roman ; and Newton could not look at anything that was not of the finest Greek period and style. Personally I thought, and still think, that something could be said on Wilde's side in this dispute ; but it was not, and is not now, my business to say it.

In October, 1879, we had to return to Aberdeen, where I was assistant to the Professor of Greek ; and Sir Charles Newton remarked that it would be necessary to hold an examination to decide between Wilde and myself. " In that case," I replied, " I am not a candidate." He asked the reason. I said I had long resolved that I would not compete against men junior to myself, and also that I did not like the examination system. " But," he replied, " what is to be done when two candidates are nearly equal ? How are we to decide ? " " If you have any doubt, prefer the junior man." And so we went off to Aberdeen, understanding that this door also was closed against us, as I knew that his colleagues the four Oxford electors were sure to prefer a man of Wilde's deservedly high reputation, and it was evident that Sir Charles Newton desired to hold an examination ; now he was a man that liked to get his own way.

Late in January, 1880, a letter came from Sir Charles Newton saying that I was elected to the Studentship, asking when I should be ready to enter on the duties, and inviting my wife and myself to live in his house and talk Greek with him for some time before going out to Greece, so as to learn in this way something about the country and the work. I could not get away till the latter part of February, when the advanced senior class which I taught in Aberdeen came to an end.

We dreamed now of Athens ; but Newton said " Don't go to Athens, which is pre-occupied by the Germans and the French ; go to the west coast of Asia Minor, where the great Greek cities offer a better field to a new man ". Accordingly in early May, 1880, we landed in Smyrna ; and

it happened that, on the same day Major (after 1881
Sir Charles) Wilson, Consul-General for Anatolia, came
down to Smyrna for one day ; and Mr. Dennis the Consul
(afterwards Sir George Dennis) invited us to meet him at
lunch. Sir Charles Wilson, hearing of Newton's advice,
said "Come into the inner country of Anatolia. The
coast-lands are open to explorers ; any one can go there,
but the inner country is unknown. People think that it is
difficult to travel in the centre of Turkey, but it is not
really so. Come and make a journey with me ; and you
will soon learn how to travel."

The presence of Sir Charles Wilson in Smyrna for one
day to see Lady Wilson off by the steamer to Europe, was
the cause that directed us to the upper country.[1] Every
other person in Smyrna warned us against this : the English
were disliked by the Government, all officials would be
hostile to us, troubles and dangers would confront us.
After some weeks the Consul informed me that he had
written to the Foreign Office clearing himself of all
responsibility for our movements and our fate, as we had
persisted in going on dangerous excursions in defiance of
his prohibition. The truth was that the danger, such as it
was, was almost confined to the brigand-haunted neighbour-
hood of Smyrna ; and we consulted good authorities before
we started on any excursion in that region.

The Consul, a very well-meaning person, would have liked
to keep us as in a sheepfold, safely tucked in every night ;
he knew nothing about the state of the country, and he
did not wish to be troubled by any incidents in his province.
Had we listened to his orders, we should have remained
in Smyrna for the three years of the studentship, except when

---

[1] Acts XIX. 1, τὰ ἀνωτερικὰ μέρη.

he went out himself with a guard of armed servants, police-men, and soldiers : in which case he was most courteous in inviting us to accompany him. In the spring of 1881 I rode with Sir Charles Wilson from Smyrna zig-zag across country to Sivas and Samsun, and got a first glimpse of the real Turkey.

Thus it came about, with no conscious choice and after many vain essays in other directions, that in October, 1881, we found ourselves starting on our first larger venture into the Phrygian country, "weird with fable," the enchanted land of Midas the King.

It had been a long apprenticeship to live through before we found ourselves at last started to explore on the borders between Greece and the East, between Europe and Asia.

In 1881, when we began our more extended journeys, the Ottoman Railway was in process of extension from Aidin, the old terminus, towards the East, and rail-head was at a village called Kuyujak. There we had our first experi-ence of life in our own tent at the uncompleted station : there was a considerable difference from travelling in Sir Charles Wilson's company, with tents and well-trained ser-vants ; but that experience had been useful in many ways. We learned what were the indispensable accompaniments of life, and how much we could do without.

We began to travel in the old Turkey of caravans and mediævalism. We have lived and travelled and observed through the years of transformation ; and now we are still travelling in the half-modernized Turkey of railway trains and French-speaking officials.

The expedition begun in October, 1881, more by luck than good guidance, resulted in the discovery of many Phrygian monuments. That gave us a start ; but the Studentship was coming to an end rapidly.

In June, 1882, a letter from Professor Bywater reached us at Iconium (Konia), offering a research fellowship at Exeter College, tenable for five years, the conditions being two years' exploration followed by three years' study and publication at home. The letter also promised that in case of acceptance an Asia Minor Exploration Fund should be formed to provide the means of exploration, and requested a reply if possible before the College meeting in the end of June. The telegraphic reply cost five francs, which implies brevity. In work such as we had drifted into, three years is nothing ; it took three years to learn what the problems of Asia Minor are, and how one should start to seek the evidence.[1]

This is an example of the way in which our exploration of inner Anatolia progressed. Something always turned up, when travel seemed to be reaching its end. My "last journey" to Asia Minor became a family joke : I often said good-bye with ceremony and pathos to inner Anatolia— there was no more money—and ever the means to return offered themselves. It was always the unexpected that happened.

Even the Three Years' Studentship which took us out to Asia Minor came to an end, when we no longer needed it, and was not renewed. It was created by Mr. Montague Bernard who expected that the commission for reforming the University (of which he was a member) would make it a permanent institution. He died before the three years ended, and the Commission made no foundation of this

---

[1] It is astonishing that in this country people now regard a Fellowship of £150 or £200 for one or two years as the endowment of Research. In America more reasonably they call this sort of thing " Post-graduate study " ; and the hideous character of the word " post-graduate " should not blind us to the truth that the Americans are right in principle and we are wrong.

kind.[1] The Montague Bernard Studentship seemed to have been made for us, and then to cease.

Thus our exploration has lasted during thirty-four years. Only in the nine years after 1891 I stayed at home, except in 1899. An attack of cholera, contracted in a ship coming from Alexandretta, incapacitated me for some years ; and I aimed at finding and financing a successor rather than continuing field-work myself. The successor, J. G. C. Anderson,[2] did much excellent work, travelling for a number of years very widely in Asia Minor ; but he was appointed to office in Christ Church, and travelling was not for a Senior Student and lecturer. Then the opportunity of returning for a summer was offered me by a friend in Birmingham ; and in 1901 we found ourselves again resident in Konia as a centre for exploration.

Even after we settled to explore in central Asia Minor, my ideas about a sphere of work still needed to be altered in one respect. My inclination was entirely towards Greek, in literature and in art ; and I spent no time willingly on Latin. In the spring of 1886 I was a candidate for the Professorship of Greek in Aberdeen, a position where the long summer vacation from April to October promised the free time needed for travel ; but was not appointed by the Crown. Several weeks later came a letter from a friend in Aberdeen saying that the Chair of Latin would be vacant within a few days, and urging me to be a candidate : he stated that certain misapprehensions had led to my being ruled out in the previous candidature, and explained how they could easily be dispelled. Had I learned about this vacancy in Latin through the newspapers, it would not have

[1] The University itself made some provision in other ways for travel in Greece.

[2] A pupil in one of my earliest years at Aberdeen.

occurred to me to be a candidate; my mind was set on Greek; but, when the idea was put into my head, it fastened itself there and took root, and in a few hours became a resolve; and I was made Professor of Latin, not dreaming what the result must be.

The reading of the Roman authors turned inevitably, owing to my bent of mind, to a study of Roman society and administration. One can spend a lifetime in Greek literature, taking only the faintest interest in the government of the Greek cities, and never looking towards the Hellenistic cities of the larger Greece in Asia. But the Roman literature clings closer to the actual conditions of life. Unless one is blinded by a habit acquired in Greek literature, one cannot study Virgil and Horace without being plunged into contemporary history and forced to understand the policy of Augustus and the glory of Italy and Rome. Thus I was led on to work at the relation of the Græco-Roman literature to the life of the Empire, and to fill my mind with the Roman idea. I had found my proper work, the study of Roman institutions in Asiatic Greece, and the influence of Asia on the Græco-Roman administration. If I had been appointed to a Professorship of Greek, as I wished, or had remained a Professor of Classical Archæology, none of my proper work could have been done rightly.

The most important department of that subject still escaped me; but Sir W. Robertson Nicoll after many requests induced me in October, 1888, to send him a long article on "Early Christian History in Phrygia" ("Expositor," Oct., 1888, to Feb., 1889); those papers caught Dr. Fairbairn's attention, and led to an invitation to give six lectures at Mansfield College, which were published under the title of "The Church in the Roman Empire before A.D. 170".

In every case the course was marked out by the judgment and will of others. In each step I had no thought of the succeeding step, but drifted without plan as fate chose. In the few cases where I formed a plan, and started on my own initiative, I was usually disappointed, and afterwards found that the disappointment was a necessary stage in education, and that success would have been a calamity.

I had gone to Oxford with the aim of getting a Fellowship as the way towards a life of Research. If this aim had been successful at the time and in the way that at first I anticipated, I should have inevitably sacrificed my dream and ambition and drifted into some other line. I left a failure; and was invited to come back successful in my own fated line of life. Nature and the world were wise and kind, and always guided where I was erring and ignorant : or dare one venture to use a more personal form of the idea, and speak of Providence ?

The story of those long years has been told, not because the writer's history is of any account, but because the following chapters stand in relation to a human being ; and those who care to weigh their value scrupulously and accurately will take into account the mind which wrote them and was moulded by the facts stated in them.

This was the way that brought me to the study of Luke and Paul and the New Testament generally, when I found that my prepossessions and pre-formed opinions were wrong. The following chapters will show how the discovery of new evidence, partly by others, partly by myself, changed the judgment and formed opinions of one who had aimed at truth and lived for truth.

PART II.

THE BEARING OF RECENT DISCOVERY
ON THE
TRUSTWORTHINESS OF THE NEW TESTAMENT

CHAPTER III

(MAP ON P. 64)

THE work that marked itself out for me in Asia Minor was to study the art, history, and antiquities of the country. Everything that fell between the dawn of history and the final conquest by the Turks lay within my period. The methods were to be determined by experience; and, under the impulse of Sir Charles Wilson's advice and example, it was quickly borne in on me that historical study must in a country like this be founded on geography and topography.

On this last point a more definite and complete statement is needed to make my present intention clear from the beginning. There did not exist at that time any trustworthy map of the country in its ancient or even in its modern state. The situation of a few important ancient cities in inner Asia Minor was known, such as Dorylaion, Colossæ, Laodicea, Antioch of Pisidia, Cæsarea of Cappadocia, and some others; but occasionally doubts were expressed even as to the correctness of the site ascribed to one or other of them. About their history, their foundation, fortunes, and decay, hardly anything was known. The evidence had not been collected and weighed. The accounts of the leading ancient cities, given in geographical and historical works, were scanty and often untrustworthy in details. True and untrue statements were placed side by side, and, as a whole,

(35)

the generally accepted and (so to say) "official" statements were quite uncertain.[1]

The inadequacy, the inaccuracy, and the frequent lack of information in the modern works on ancient geography made it necessary as a first step to read afresh all the original authorities, and to find others hitherto unnoticed. Into this programme of work New Testament subjects did not enter. It was generally understood at that time, in 1880 and the years immediately following, that these fell under the heading of "Religion," and should be kept apart from the kind of historical study on which I was engaged. Everything in the department of "Religion" ought to be reserved for theologians, and mere scholars kept aloof from it. In 1880-3 I considered the time almost lost that was spent in copying Christian inscriptions; they were outside my province, and while a sense of duty made me take copies of them, yet I grudged the moments thus spent.

In truth, it must be acknowledged that the Christian inscriptions which then were already known and published contained the absolute minimum of historical information. They were of a late period, and with hardly any exception were valueless in almost every respect to any kind of students, whether theological or non-theological. This naturally produced a prejudice against the whole class; but in the progress of discovery, new groups of Christian inscriptions gave a different character to the subject; and

---

[1] The same remark applies to some of the latest accounts given in Pauly-Wissowa, "Realencyclopædie"; the articles on Eastern geography are far below the standard of other departments. The brief remarks in Marquardt's "Staatsverwaltung," though much older, are usually right, because Marquardt confines himself to positive statements on explicit evidence; but even he sometimes misinterprets, and his few negative statements should usually be set aside, as the evidence was not sufficient to justify a negative.

many were found of the highest historical and religious importance. In a few cases the newly found proved that certain epigraphic documents previously published were Christian, though their religion, being studiously concealed, had not been detected until many similar ones were discovered.

The earliest Christian epitaphs belonged to the period when the religion was proscribed and forbidden, and when it was necessary to avoid drawing public attention to the Church by the use of language that was patently and explicitly religious. Yet even in that period certain forms and turns of expression were employed which conveyed a meaning to those who were in the secret.[1] The investigation of these private signs was at first entirely conjectural, and the way was uncertain and unmapped; but most of our early conjectures have been confirmed in later discovery.[2] In this way the realm of Christian epigraphy began to be included in the domain of Græco-Roman social and political history.

Among other old books that described journeys in Asia Minor the Acts of the Apostles had to be read anew. I began to do so without expecting any information of value regarding the condition of Asia Minor at the time when Paul was living. I had read a good deal of modern criticism about the book, and dutifully accepted the current

[1] Monsignor Duchesne was perhaps the first to publish the discovery of one highly important class of Christian epitaphs, though more recently he has apparently abandoned his opinion, and dates one of the most remarkable epitaphs of this class in the fifth century; see Part III, p. 416.

[2] The entire body of evidence will appear in Professor H. Grégoiré's collection of the Christian inscriptions of Asia Minor, the publication of which at Brussels was hoped for soon (beginning with Part I in the end of 1914), but the development of politics and war has indefinitely postponed it (see also below, last chapter of Part III).

opinion that it was written during the second half of the second century by an author who wished to influence the minds of people in his own time by a highly wrought and imaginative description of the early Church. His object was not to present a trustworthy picture of facts in the period about A.D. 50, but to produce a certain effect on his own time by setting forth a carefully coloured account of events and persons of that older period. He wrote for his contemporaries, not for truth. He cared nought for geographical or historical surroundings of the period A.D. 30 to 60. He thought only of the period A.D. 160-180, and how he might paint the heroes of old time in situations that should touch the conscience of his contemporaries. Antiquarian or geographical truth was less than valueless in a design like this : one who thought of such things was distracting his attention from the things that really mattered, the things that would move the minds of men in the second century.

Such was the commonly accepted view in the critical school about 1870 to 1880, when I had been studying modern opinions. It is now utterly antiquated. There is not one point in it that is accepted. Everything is changed or discarded. But about 1880 to 1890 the book of the Acts was regarded as the weakest part of the New Testament. No one that had any regard for his reputation as a scholar cared to say a word in its defence. The most conservative of theological scholars, as a rule, thought the wisest plan of defence for the New Testament as a whole was to say as little as possible about the Acts.

I began then to study the Acts in search of geographical and antiquarian evidence, hardly expecting to find any, but convinced that, if there were any, it would bear on the condition of Asia Minor in the time when the writer lived.

If he knew the country at first-hand, the knowledge might
show itself in his narrative ; but any knowledge that might
appear would be what the writer knew by experience: he
would not dream of spending energy on revivifying forgotten details of long-past history and antiquities.

The first thing that made me begin to doubt the judgment which I had formed, or rather, had accepted from
others, about the late origin of "the Acts of the Apostles"
was a discovery regarding the geographical statement in
XIV. 5 : "They fled (from Iconium) to the cities of Lycaonia
and the surrounding region ".[1] In these words it is implied
that Paul and Barnabas fled over a frontier into Lycaonia,
i.e. the border of Lycaonia lay between Iconium and Lystra,
and Iconium was not in the country called Lycaonia.
This piece of information is purely a matter of geography :
it has no bearing on religion and on the Church questions
of the second century.   It is technical, narrow, and in a sense
external to the narrative, which as one might think would
run equally well although this detail were absent.[2]

As the point is a technical one, it needs some technical
explanation, which leads us amid the minutiæ of Anatolian
topography ; but here at least the soil, though dry, offers
firm footing, when one takes the trouble to get hold of the
facts.   The technical argument is stated in chapter IV.
apart.   At present it need only be said that the main
facts are : (1) Iconium is described in the modern treatises
on ancient geography as a city of Lycaonia ; (2) we were

---

[1] $\dot{\eta}$ περίχωρος is a noun, the region that lies round (the cities) : i.e. Lycaonia
contained two cities and a stretch of country around, where there were no
cities but only villages organized after the Anatolian style, not according to
the Hellenic municipal fashion.

[2] In further study, however, one finds that the matter is essential and
carries much weight in the purpose of the book, although at first it had seemed
almost accidental and unnecessary for the author's purpose.

assuming that this description was true in A.D. 50, whereas a little investigation would have shown that it was false (see ch. IV.).

One authority, familiar to every schoolboy, describes Iconium as the last city of Phrygia. That authority is Xenophon, who in the Anabasis tells how the ten thousand Greeks (among whom he himself was marching) reached Iconium on their way from north-west to south-east and after leaving it crossed the frontier into Lycaonia. Now the author of the Acts had read a good deal of Greek literature, and could appreciate it ; and beyond doubt he was influenced by it. There is no improbability in the supposition that he may have read the Anabasis, and remembered this fact.

What was true, however, about the period described by Xenophon, 400 B.C., was not necessarily true about the period described in Acts, A.D. 47. In that long lapse of time many changes occurred in the boundaries of countries and regions of Asia Minor.

The evidence of Cicero, who visited Iconium, seemed clear. He speaks of Iconium as being in Lycaonia almost exactly a century before Paul visited it. Some other authorities agree, but the testimony of one witness like Cicero seemed sufficient. Then to speak of fleeing from Iconium into Lycaonia, when we take Iconium as the chief city of Lycaonia, is as if one were to speak of going from Richmond into Virginia, or from London to England. The expression does not ring true. Suppose a tramp came to ask help and told a pitiable story of his sufferings at the hands of an infuriated crowd of rioters in Chicago, and said that he had barely succeeded in boarding a freight-train and getting away into the State of Illinois, you would feel at once that he was inventing a story, and that he never had been in that part of the world, or he would know that Chicago was itself in Illinois ; and you would conclude that his story as a whole was false, because he was evidently inventing the story of the train ; and you would probably dismiss him as an impostor, unless you were extraordinarily compassionate and slow to wrath.

Just in the same way it was understood that this detail of the journey of Paul and Barnabas was deliberately invented by the writer (who was under a false impression about the situation of Iconium and the frontier) with the intention of imparting to the story plausibility and the interest of personal experience ; and the writer of the book was condemned as an impostor attempting to rouse the readers' sympathy and thus to trade on their credulity. I adopted this argument from others : but I made it my own by believing it and judging accordingly. We are all equally condemned for bad critical method and wrong judgment.

It seemed, therefore, to others and to myself then, that the author of the Acts, knowing the testimony of Xenophon, had attempted to impart the semblance of local exactitude to a story which he was writing up: he had not before him any narrative of the facts resting on real personal acquaintance : yet he does assume the show of first-hand knowledge. He sometimes uses the first person, as if he had been present at certain incidents of the history. He does, beyond all question, convey the impression that his story depends throughout on the very best and most unimpeachable evidence.

Here in Acts XIV. 5, we have a test case: at this point it seemed to me, when I began this study of Anatolian geography, that the story had been proved to ring false. The author of the book imparts a piece of topographical information incidentally, as his narrative hurries on ; but the

information is false and results from his applying a piece of
schoolboy knowledge, true in regard of 400 B.C., to the
different circumstances of A.D. 47. Not merely did this
statement seem to us to be wrong : it is given in this
incidental fashion as part of the travel narrative, so that it
appears as if it were part of the actual experience of the
wandering Apostles.

But after all, as is shown in the following chapter at length,
Iconium was not in Lycaonia at that period. It belonged
to a different region or district of Asia Minor.[1] Its people
were of a different stock, and they did not speak the
Lycaonian tongue. The proof of this statement involves
the quotation of many ancient testimonies and the results
of exploration and excavation, and this whole investigation
will be better kept separate. Here it need only be said
that the proof is complete, certain, and (as I think) no
longer a matter of dispute, but universally accepted by
scholars.

Now read the narrative of the residence in Iconium and
in Lycaonia from this new point of view. How luminous
it becomes as a story of personal experience ! The Apostles
heard people shout their appeal to the gods in the Lycaonian
tongue (XIV. 11): this impressed Paul, because he had heard a
different language spoken familiarly in home life at Iconium.
There they spoke Phrygian : in Lystra they spoke Lycaonian. The contrast struck him, and afterwards in telling
the story to the author, he almost unconsciously introduced that slight detail ; and Luke—let us call him so
for brevity's sake, because it is the right name, though I
shall not found any argument on it for the present—why,
Luke remembered it and gave it a place in his book, because

---

[1] Xenophon and many later writers say that the region was Phrygia.

it fulfilled a purpose in his conception of a luminous historical narrative.

It is, from one point of view, a matter of indifference whether those Lystrans called out in the Lycaonian language, or in the Greek, or in the Phrygian. The important matter is that they uttered this meaning, "The gods have manifested themselves to us in the form of human beings," and that they applied the words to Paul and Barnabas. To us, reading the words in Greek or in English, they are just as effective as if a Lycaonian version were printed or read alongside of them ; but to Paul it was not so. He had been used to hear the Iconian speech, and the new language struck his ear and remained in his memory. This small detail remains as a sign and proof that the ear of Paul plays a part in the narrative. We listen with him, and hear the shout in Lycaonian, and are struck with the strangeness of the sound, and remember this when we tell the story. In my book, the "Church in the Roman Empire," it is argued that visitors to Iconium must have heard the Phrygian language spoken there, and that therefore there remain so many testimonies by visitors to the Phrygian character of the city.[1] As those visitors remembered the sound of the Phrygian in Iconium, so Paul remembered the Lycaonian at Lystra.

In XIV. 5, it is stated that the two Apostles crossed the frontier into Lycaonia. That was correct alike in the time of Xenophon and in the time of Paul. Possibly there may have been a boundary stone on the road by which they travelled, and the exact frontier line will be known when this stone shall be discovered at some future time. It has fallen down, and been covered by the soil of that level

---

[1] That book was published in 1894 ; and it was only in 1910 that the proof of the use of that language in Iconium was discovered : see p. 72.

plain ; and it will not be found until cultivation and deep ploughing may perchance reveal it. Similar boundary stones are well known. I found one in 1882 lying on the road-side between Apameia and Apollonia : it marked the boundary between those two cities (and incidentally between the provinces Galatia and Asia). This stone is not covered up, because it was erected at the top of a lofty steep slope, where the road going east reaches the pass level, and on those bare and arid mountains there is no dust or loose soil to cover the stone ; but it has fallen on its side. It is a very large stone in shape like an altar, about five feet high, bearing the inscription : "On behalf of the salvation and everlasting continuance of the Emperor Cæsar Hadrian, son of the god Trajan, grandson of the god Nerva (then follow the titles, giving the date A.D. 135), the senate and people of the city Apollonia, settlers from Lycia and Thrace, (dedicated) to the Frontier-gods."[1]

The sight of such a frontier stone would remain fixed in Paul's memory,[2] as the discovery of a boundary like that Apolloniate stone remains in the memory of any modern traveller.

A certain emotion is stirred in the mind of the modern ; the stone is a mark revealing much history and topography ; he has been long on the outlook for historical evidence, and at last finds it after toil and hardship. The sight of it and the pleasure of deciphering the worn and difficult letters scratched faintly on the hard stone and conveying so much information, make the memory last for life.

Paul had no stimulus of that kind, as we may assume,

---

[1] Published in " Historical Geography of Asia Minor," p. 172.

[2] Similarly Luke noted the boundaries of the territory of the city Rome far in the south of Latium (XXVIII. 14), and distinguishes between this wider Roman territory and the city proper : " St. Paul the Traveller," p. 347.

to make him mark and remember the boundary; but there was another cause equally effective. He and Barnabas were fleeing from a hostile mob, and the boundary meant safety. They now passed beyond the limits of Iconium, and were under a different administration. It would be a crime, not merely against law, but against the Frontier-gods, for any Iconian to lift a hand against them after they had passed the boundary stone. Piety and religious feeling restrained the mob and forbade pursuit. Paul rejoiced here to be safe, because his work in Iconium (and in Antioch) was incomplete. He had to return to consolidate the congregations there, to encourage the young converts, and to appoint presbyters (XIV. 22). The residence in Lycaonia was a time of waiting.

So St. Thekla, in the early Christian legend, fleeing from Iconium to escape from pursuit and a "marriage-by-capture," reached safety at the frontier. If we had the legend in its oldest form, we should perhaps find this detail in imitation of the story of Paul. As it is, the detail was changed, and Thekla found refuge in the mountain, which opened to receive her, as the local legend still has it, though in the Acta of Paul and Thekla it is subjected to further alteration.

Reading the narrative in this way, and imagining ourselves with Paul, seeing with his eyes the boundary plainly marked, and hearing with his ears the shouting of the mob at Lystra, and feeling with his heart the anxious care of the churches,[1] we perceive that the incident of the lame man occurred at the very beginnning of the residence in Lystra. If we follow the narrative of Luke, carefully attending to the exact force of the Greek tenses (which is neglected even in the revised version, English and American), this is clear: "they

---

[1] As in 2 Corinthians XI. 28.

fled from Iconium into Lycaonia, with its cities Lystra and
Derbe, and the region around the cities ; and there they
engaged in preaching the good news ; and at Lystra a
certain man impotent in the feet was sitting, one lame
from his birth, one who never walked : this man was listening to Paul preaching, and Paul, gazing fixedly on him (as
if reading his very soul)[1] and seeing that he has the faith
for being saved,[2] called loudly to him, ' stand on thy feet upright ' ".

In this passage the descriptive imperfect tenses—they
were engaged in preaching—he was sitting—he was listening—are followed by the sharp instantaneous perception
and cry (aorist). A scene is described : the various details
of the situation are, as usual, expressed in the imperfect :[3]
then follows the action expressed by the aorist, and the
action proceeds stage by stage, each stated by an aorist,
except the process of attempting to walk, which is an imperfect tense.[4]

The intention now seems plain to represent the first part
of the Lystran narrative as synchronous with the beginning

[1] The allusion to this fixed gaze of Paul occurs only where there is strong
emotion behind the look, where the soul of one gazes into the soul of the
other (so in XIII. 9).

[2] Salvation here has hardly the Christian sense, but is used practically in
the common pagan sense, on which see the " Teaching of Paul in Terms of
the Present Day," pp. 94 f. This is a proof of early date.

[3] This is the regular usage of the language : the imperfect shows that all
the parts of the scene are co-existent contemporaneously. Out of this scene as
background stands forth the action in its successive stages (aorist).

[4] If one takes the action more minutely in detail, Paul fixed his eyes on the
man (as something in the man caught his attention : the great orator is
sensitive to everything and appreciative of the nature of an individual in the
audience) : he saw his capacity for salvation : he called out loudly in a sharp
voice six words : the man sprang up, and set about walking (a slower and
more difficult process : he had to learn how to walk). The loud sharp voice
was needed to startle and rouse the soul and the dormant will of the man.

of the preaching : they were engaged in preaching, and he was sitting and listening. An effect is painted of marvellously rapid character. The Apostles came to Lystra, and at once this remarkable event occurred ; and they were forthwith accepted by the populace as divine beings, Hermes and Zeus, Mercury and Jupiter.

Immediately the people called out that this was a real epiphany : the gods had assumed human form and come down from heaven to Lystra. One sees that this was said about strangers who had just arrived in the town. The story would seem less natural if this aspect is neglected : if Paul and Barnabas had been in Lystra for some time, they would have become familiar to the people of that small rustic town ; and familiarity would have made it more difficult to take them as gods. But, as it is, the scene shows them as two strangers. People know every one by face in a small town like this, and perceive that these are strangers. Then the lame man walks ; and the populace, quick to appreciate divine power and disposed to believe that the gods appear from time to time on the earth like men, conclude that here before their eyes is an epiphany of their two chief and associate deities, Zeus and Hermes. Then they call out in the Lycaonian language. It was the first time that Paul had ever heard that speech, and the contrast to Iconium with its Phrygian and its Greek caught his attention and his memory.

The two gods whom the people understand to have come down among them are Zeus and Hermes (Jupiter and Mercury in the Latin names). There must have been at Lystra a tendency to believe that those two gods were commonly associated with one another and likely to appear on earth together. Zeus was the supreme god, and spoke to men through his messenger Hermes ; he sits quiet, and acts through his agent and subordinate god. We must, then, understand that Barnabas had not yet spoken; Paul had led off the preaching,[1] and Barnabas was the more statuesque figure, who sat or stood by, appreciative and marking all things from his calm superiority, while Paul delivered the message from the quiet and supreme god. The situation in every respect suits best the first appearance of the Apostles in Lystra.

That Zeus and Hermes were commonly regarded in that region as associated gods is now well known. In my first books on the subject [2] I could quote in illustration only the epiphany of those same two gods to the old couple Baucis and Philemon, as described by Ovid, "Metamorphoses," VIII. 621-719.[3] This epiphany is said to have occurred "among the Phrygian hills" (621), and the people around were the Tyriaians (722).[4] Tyriaion was a small town in south-eastern Phrygia, not far from Iconium; so that Lystra, though in Lycaonia, might share in similar religious ideas.

A better example occurs in an inscription found in 1909 in Lycaonia, south-west of Lystra, where certain devotees dedicate a statue of Hermes to Zeus; such dedication takes place only where there is a close relation between the two

---

[1] ἡγούμενος τοῦ λόγου, XIV. 12.

[2] "Church in the Roman Empire," p. 58, "St. Paul the Traveller," p. 117. In "Pictures of the Apostolic Church," p. 131, a second example is added.

[3] This quotation is mentioned rightly by most of the commentators from Wetstein onwards.

[4] The manuscripts give such forms as *tirinthius, trineius, tyreneus, thyrneius;* and the older editions conjecturally give " Tyaneius "; but this is impossible because: (1) Tyana is a city of Cappadocia remote from Phrygia, whereas the event occurred in Phrygia; (2) Tyanēĩus is an impossible form, whereas Tyriêius is a correct form, Greek Τυριᾰῖος, from Tyriaion; (3) Tyriêius is nearer the MS. reading. Wesseling on Hierocles, " Synecd. " (s.v. Briana Phryg.), suggests Brianeius, recognizing that Tyaneius is unsuitable; but objections (2) and (3) apply to this word.

gods; and here Zeus needs Hermes as his agent to speak and act for him.[1]

An even better example is mentioned to me by Dr. Sundwall;[2] it is a dedication to Zeus and Hermes, and comes from the same region as the last mentioned. He has published it in an article in the Finnish language, which I cannot read, and notes the bearing on this passage of the Acts. I have not seen this inscription, which was discovered by an Austrian Expedition to Isauria and Pisidia in 1902.

These three cases sufficiently prove that the association of those two gods was familiar in the region round Lystra and likely to occur to the people when they saw a marvellous cure wrought by two strange men entering the town. All character and life disappear if we suppose that the two men had been living for some time in that little city.

We must, then, take the plain implication of the narrative, viz. that this incident occurred as Paul was beginning his work in Lystra. What force is then added to his words (Gal. IV. 12-4) in writing to those same people: "You did not treat me ill; you know the facts; illness was the reason I came preaching to you on the earlier of my two visits,[3] and you did not despise or abhor my physical ailment—trial as it was to you—but welcomed me as a messenger of God".

In those words we have a patent allusion[4] to the sudden

[1] See Calder in *Classical Review*, 1910, p. 76 ff., and *Expositor*, July, 1910, p. 1 ff.

[2] He is one of the small, but growing, band of scholars that direct their work largely to Asia Minor. His *Einheimische Namen der Lykier*, 1913, is an admirable work.

[3] As is very common in the New Testament the construction is parataxis for hypotaxis; "you know that because of illness I preached, and you did not despise my ailment" (as in the English Versions), is equivalent to the complex sentence, "when I preached because of illness, you did not despise my ailing body, as you well know".

[4] Recognized by Lightfoot, and sorrowfully abandoned by him.

and deep impression which he had made at Lystra. A similar instantaneous impression was made at Antioch; Paul came, saw, conquered ; they received him straightway on the first sabbath as the messenger of God.[1] There was no such situation as has been pictured by many modern scholars, that Paul came into Galatia and was there taken ill, and in his illness was cared for kindly by the Galatians, and then succeeded in evangelizing them successfully. On the contrary he is welcomed at his first appearance as God's messenger, though they might well have cast him out with horror as one who was accursed by the Divine power and punished by God with the Divine fire which was consuming him without external affection of any part or member.[2]

What Paul here lays stress on, what he mentions as a fact well known to the Galatians, is the instant welcome which they gave him ; they had some excuse for supposing him to be under punishment as an enemy of God, but they welcomed him as the messenger of God ; his physical illness was a real trial and offence to them, but they paid no heed to it and opened their hearts to him, and gave him of their dearest and best.

This situation is exactly that which is described in the Acts (except that there Paul's ailment is never mentioned).[3] The completeness of Paul's success on his first journey (XIV. 27, XV. 3, 4, 12) was a great encouragement to him. It stamped his mission from Antioch onwards as under the favour and blessing of God. The work in Cyprus and in Pamphylia on the contrary was not blessed in the same

---

[1] This I did not comprehend rightly in "St. Paul the Traveller," p. 99; but it is explained in detail in the "Cities of St. Paul," p. 298 f.

[2] See the "Teaching of Paul in Terms of Present Day," p. 327.

[3] This omission is one of the notable omissions in Acts, and is to be placed along with the total omission of the name of Luke and of the personality of Titus.

way; it was not a subject of interest to him afterwards (xv. 39 f.); and it is never mentioned in his letters.

It is a striking fact that both the narrative in the Acts (when rightly read) and the Epistle to the Galatians should insist so strongly on the quick, and almost instantaneous, success of the mission in Galatia. Here was the "open door". This was the fact that most deeply impressed Paul; and it must be remembered that it is his account to Luke, transmitted to us through the latter, which lies before us in the Acts. The Epistle states his general impression, but does not describe the facts: the history simply narrates facts and leaves the general impression to be gathered from them. Hence the agreement has not been noticed as it ought to be by modern scholars. Yet this agreement and "undesigned coincidence" constitutes the most decisive proof that the two written authorities are what they claim to be, and what they have been accepted as, viz. the work of Paul and of his disciple, coadjutor, and personal friend.

How completely this agreement is ignored can be gathered from the words used by the Bishop of Ely (Dr. Chase) on this subject:[1] he simply expresses definitely the general attitude of those who think with him. According to him Paul and Barnabas "entered the 'Galatian district' . . . they halted at Pessinus . . . Paul had no plan . . . he was bewildered: he allowed himself to drift . . . he intended so far as he had a plan at all to pass through the cities in the west corner of Galatia and so to journey farther north to the cities in the east of Bithynia and of Pontus: but the wanderer became once again an evangelist . . . an attack of illness brought him to a standstill . . . before he recovered, he learned to feel an interest in the Galatians

[1] *Expositor*, Dec., 1893, p. 415.

. . . he stayed in Galatia for a time, 'doing the work of an evangelist'".[1]

There is in this no quick effect, only drifting of a traveller without a plan, who does not even begin to evangelize until he has learned in the course of an illness to like the people who were caring for him and nursing him.   The writer thinks of modern conditions, in which the homeless invalid is tended by " warm-hearted Galatians ".   There is nothing like that in paganism : the want of it is conspicuous, as is pointed out below in chapter IX.   Such care of the sick stranger is the creation of Christianity.[2]   Moreover, this fanciful account takes no note of the one important word " received" or " welcomed" : it was a newcomer whom the Galatians received as a " messenger of God" (Gal. IV. 13), when he first appeared among them.[3]

Acts rightly understood is the best commentary on the letters of Paul, and the letters on the Acts.   If Luke had never known or read those letters,[4] then all the more remarkable is it as a proof of the truth and historicity of both that the agreement is so perfect.   But personally I am disposed to think that Luke knew the letters, though he does not make them his authority, because he had a still higher and better, viz. Paul's own conversation.

[1] As I read this interpretation of Paul's journey and method of work twenty-one years after it was written, I am struck with wonder. It could not be written nowadays. It is as un-Pauline in its ideas as it is impossible in its geography.

[2] Below, p. 120 f., and " Luke the Physician," pp. 352, 404 f.

[3] The force of the Greek verb δέχομαι is free from all doubt : when Paul writes to a distant people, among whom he had been, his words cannot mean " I was living among and you came to regard me as a messenger of God " ; they must imply " you welcomed me as a messenger of God, when I came to you ".

[4] It is the general opinion among modern scholars that the letters were unknown to him, or at least never read by him.

CHAPTER IV

ICONIUM AND THE FRONTIER

(MAP ON P. 64)

THE matter which formed the subject of chapter III. forms, in a sense, the foundation on which the views which the writer holds were gradually built. Each new detail rested, or seemed to rest, on suitable evidence; but the beginning lies in Acts XIV. 5. It will therefore be well to state the evidence in this first case minutely, more so than is done in the remainder of these lectures: and this detailed investigation is placed here in a chapter by itself, so that this whole discussion of authorities may stand separate, and the effect may not be weakened by working it into the general argument, while any one that desires to proceed with the argument may pass over the minuter discussion.[1]

The purpose of this chapter is to prove that to the ancients of the Roman period Iconium was, (1) not a city of Lycaonia, but (2) a city of Phrygia. The first assertion is, as I think, now admitted generally, though the inevitable inferences from it are not considered. The second is stubbornly resisted by many, but it is of very great importance for the proper interpretation of the Acts and of the Lukan picture of early Christian history.

As was stated in the previous chapter, I accepted at first the statements current in modern treatises on ancient geography: Iconium was a city of Lycaonia. So far as I looked for evidence, that was supplied by Cicero, an ex-

[1] The result, so far as it adds to Chapter III., is stated on p. 60.

(53)

cellent witness, a man of the highest education, who
travelled across Asia Minor from Ephesus to Tarsus, and
spent ten days at Iconium, and wrote many letters to his
Italian friends from the country. What better witness
could be found ? I was, as it happened, familiar with the
letters, which are on many grounds exceptionally interesting
and valuable.

Cicero in one place says that Iconium was in Lycaonia,[1]
and on a superficial view certainly any reader gets the impression that he thought of Iconium as a Lycaonian city.

The geographical impression is the same. Iconium lies
on the edge of the great Lycaonian plain : true, it is under
the shadow of the mountains that fringe the plain on the
west,[2] and the mountains are not classed as Lycaonian ; but,
though near the limiting mountains, Iconium is distinctly
in the level plain. So far as geographical considerations
are concerned, the city belongs to Lycaonia.

When the question is raised, however, it must be acknowledged that the impression which we gathered from
ancient writers is largely moulded by modern opinion and
text-books, for we read the references already convinced
that Iconium was in Lycaonia, and interpret the words
according to our preconceived idea. In one letter[3] Cicero
speaks of his intention to hold the Lycaonian and the
Isaurican assizes for his own convenience exceptionally at
Laodicea. Every commentator explains that ordinarily
the Lycaonian assizes met at Iconium ; but the truth is
that the Lycaonian assizes were held at Philomelium[4] and

---

[1] "Fam.," xv. 4, 2.

[2] They rise very steep and sharp from the level plain about five miles
west of the city.

[3] "Att.," v. 21, 9.

[4] Pliny, "Nat. Hist.," v. 95, writes under the influence of the same feeling
(i.e. he quotes an authority under its influence) about Philomelium as part

the Isaurican at Iconium. This clears up the situation: Cicero classified Iconium in the purely geographical view to Lycaonia, but in the Roman administration he regarded it as the centre of Isaurican business to which the Isaurian people resorted:[1] he was a Roman, and careless of Anatolian nationalities:[2] Iconium must be whatever Rome chose that it should be: racial facts and reasons had ceased to exist under Roman rule: the Roman unity disregarded and trampled on mere national distinctions within the Empire.

Cicero, therefore, ceases to be an authority on either side: he must be set apart as unconcerned with such minutiæ, unworthy of Roman consideration.[3] This, however, was unknown to me, when my studies in this department were beginning.

The first perception of the truth came from the "Acta

of the Lycaonian diocesis (assize district), transferred to Asia after Cicero's time. The passage is quoted and translated fully in a later note, p. 57. It is unnecessary to go more minutely into the name of the assizes, as the opinion stated in the text above will at once convince any one who studies the map and the possibilities of the situation. The matter is so simple that either on the one hand it requires no further explanation, or on the other hand it would need a very detailed discussion of topography.

[1] In the one case where Cicero speaks of Iconium as in Lycaonia, "Fam.," xv. 4, 2, he is giving a careful geographical description of his journey in a report to the Senate. Where he is writing about administrative matters, "Att.," v. 21, 9, he speaks of the Isaurican assizes, meaning the conventus meeting at Iconium. In a report to the Senate, xv. 2, 1, he describes his march across the province towards Cilicia as being through Lycaonia (Philomelium and associated towns to the east) and the [country of the] Isauri (Iconium, etc.) and Cappadocia.

[2] Strabo, p. 629, speaks very strongly about the way in which the Romans disregarded racial distinctions in arranging their assizes.

[3] One other trace of the "Isaurican assizes" may be found in Ptolemy v. 4, 12, where he puts Savatra in Isauria: that cannot be explained except as due to the fact that Ptolemy used as his authority a list of the cities meeting in the Isaurican conventus.

of Justin the Martyr ". Justin was tried with several other Christians at Rome in A.D. 163. One of these, a slave named Hierax, when asked who his parents were, replied : " my earthly parents are dead ; and I have been brought here (a slave) torn away from Iconium of Phrygia ".[1] So strange did this appear to that excellent editor Ruinart, that he proposed to correct " Phrygia " to "Lycaonia," in order to keep Hierax right. This is the only case in which the testimony of a native of Iconium is preserved ; and to change his testimony would violate the most fundamental principles of criticism. When I read this passage I remembered Acts XIV. 5, and saw that it was correct. Alike Xenophon in 394 B.C. and Hierax in A.D. 163 knew Iconium as a Phrygian city. This evidence supports and confirms Luke : Iconium was not in Lycaonia, and Paul, when going to Lystra, crossed the frontier into Lycaonia.

There is abundant testimony to the same effect. Firmilian, Bishop of Cæsarea in Cappadocia, was present at a Council held in A.D. 232 at Iconium of Phrygia.[2] An Eparchia of Lycaonia was formed before A.D. 150 ;[3] but Iconium was not included in it, remaining part of the pro-

---

[1] As a slave he had a nationality : slaves and sailors of the fleet and foreigners were in Roman usage ranked together : they were all classed by nationality. The sailors Classiarii originally had been servile, and the custom of servile naming was official in their case, as Mommsen has pointed out in his beautiful article on the designation of Roman soldiers in " Hermes," 1884 (especially p. 33). Hierax was probably a foundling (θρεπτός), brought up by foster-parents for purposes of slave-trade : on this side of Græco-Roman life, see Pliny, "Epist.," 65, 66, and " Cities and Bishoprics of Phrygia," II. p. 546 f.

[2] See Cyprian, " Epist.," 71.

[3] It was part of the large province of the Tres Eparchiæ, Cilicia-Isauria-Lycaonia. In 295 the cities of the Eparchia Lycaonia were attached to the new province Isauria : that is the case in the lists of the Nicene Council, 325, which has caused some difficulty to modern scholars (e.g. Harnack, " Verbreitung," II. pp. 187, 193).

vince Galatia, and therefore in close relation with Antioch, the secondary capital of that province. About A.D. 295 a province Pisidia was formed with Antioch and Iconium as its first and second cities, and on that account Iconium is called by Basil, writing in 372, a city of Pisidia.

Pliny, " Nat. Hist.," V. 41 (145), mentions Conium (i.e. Iconium) as one of the ancient and famous Phrygian cities ; this may be set against his other seeming statement in V. 25 (95), that it was in Lycaonia ; but, as we see on closer reading, he in the latter passage denies that the Lycaonian connexion was true in his own time.[1]

Ptolemy V. 6, 16, whose value as an authority [2] on such a point is small in this region, was evidently puzzled by the testimony, for he separates Iconium and a part of Lycaonia from the province Galatia [3] and puts them in Cappadocia, a patent and absolute blunder.

Strabo also has been read as assigning Iconium to Lycaonia ; but this is not quite clear. On p. 568 he describes Iconium vaguely as being " somewhere in these

---

[1] " The Pisidians are bounded by Lycaonia, which has been transferred to the jurisdiction of the province Asia, with which gather (*in conventus*) the people of Philomelion, Thymbrion, etc. Further a tetrarchy (division of the province Galatia) has been furnished out of Lycaonia on the side where it touches Galatia (i.e. the three tribes), consisting of fourteen cities, Iconium the most famous. Of Lycaonia proper the following cities are celebrated, Thebasa, etc." Here three parts of Lycaonia are distinguished, one a conventus handed over to Asia, one a tetrarchy added to Galatia, and one non-Roman, the true Lycaonia of king Antiochus. On the Lycaonian tetrarchy see " Studia Biblica," IV. p. 46 ff. The history of that Philomelian conventus has never before been rightly explained. On the Antiochiane see " Histor. Geogr. of Asia Minor," p. 372.

[2] He is full of errors of detail in this whole region.

[3] Including several towns which continued to be in province Galatia till A.D. 295. The Lycaonian cities which were in the new province of Tres Eparchiæ he assigns to Antiochiane. In V. 4, 10, he gives another part of Lycaonia in the province Galatia. In truth Ptolemy was utterly puzzled by the contradictoriness of his authorities of different ages.

districts," but he has just enumerated " these districts " as
being the bare, cold, dry plains of Great Phrygia and of the
Lycaonians, viz. Tatta and the districts round Orkaorkoi
and Pitnisos (all Phrygian) and the plains of the Lycaonians.[1] This passage affords as much apparent authority to
infer that Strabo called Iconium a Phrygian as a Lycaonian
city; and at least it is evident that his words are vague ;
now Strabo, when he makes a vague statement, has always
some intention in his vagueness : usually he is very precise.

At last in 372 a new province of Lycaonia was instituted
by Valens, and Iconium was made its metropolis ; and this
has been its place in the ecclesiastical lists ever since.
Stephanus, therefore, mentions it as a city of Lycaonia ;
but in his notice he quotes the legend of Annakos or Nannakos, king at Iconium, in the days of the Flood, whose
subjects were Phrygians ; and other authorities call Annakos a Phrygian king.

It remains, therefore, plain and certain that the writers
of the Imperial time do not as a rule assign Iconium to
Lycaonia, and that the most authoritative of them call it a
city of Phrygia, or a city whose people were Phrygians.
The legend of Annakos which was widely known in Hellenistic times and is mentioned by Herondas in the third
century is quite clear regarding that racial character. The
Lycaonian connexion can hardly be definitely supported by
any author of the Imperial time before A.D. 372, when the
province Lycaonia was formed. The most definite state-

---

[1] ἐνταῦθα δέ που καὶ τὸ Ἰκόνιον ἔστι, p. 568. He defines τοὺς τόπους
τούτους twice in the immediate context, once as quoted above, once as
the districts where Amyntas's flocks were pastured : now it is beyond doubt
that the plains west of Tatta up to Pitnisos and Orkaorkoi (all in Great
Phrygia) were part of his sheep-runs. Mr. Calder and I have been studying
this region and its Imperial estates (inherited from Amyntas by Augustus and
his successors).

ments regarding the Lycaonian character of Iconium are all later than 372, viz. Stephanus, Eustathius's note on Dionysius *Periegesis*, and the *Etymologicum Magnum*.

I refrain from relying on Joannes of Damascus, who in his "Life of Artemius," says: "having traversed all Phrygia and come to its last city, called Iconium". This might quite fairly be attributed to his memory of Xenophon ; the same expression is used that occurs in the "Anabasis " ;[1] and it might be supposed (as we all used to think about Acts XIV. 5) that recollection of Xenophon and a desire to display antiquarian knowledge influenced this writer. But, at any rate, the statement is in perfect accordance with Acts, and the verbs used are favourite terms with Luke.[2] It is not derived from the facts of Joannes' time, but was drawn from older authority.

Phrygian invaders from the north-west had captured the city many centuries B.C. This marked the limits of their power : it was the last city of the Phrygians. In the presence of other nationalities the Phryges maintained their national feeling and speech. Iconium was a Phrygian city ; and many of its people spoke the Phrygian tongue in home life, though Greek was the language of all educated people ; and it was, of course, in Greek that Paul addressed his hearers. Greek was, so to say, the sacred language of the Christian Church in the first two centuries, and even the Roman congregation was Greek-speaking. It was the

---

[1] τῆς Φρυγίας πόλιν ἐσχάτην is the expression of Xenophon.

[2] διελθὼν ἅπασαν τὴν Φρυγίαν καὶ πρὸς τὴν ἐσχάτην αὐτῆς πόλιν τὸ καλούμενον Ἰκόνιον καταντήσας : διέρχομαι with accusative is almost a technical term with Luke, and is rare elsewhere than in Acts or imitators : καταντᾶν occurs nine times in Acts. The expression of Joannes can best be understood as a deliberate imitation of Luke's style and thought with a Xenophontine touch added, which is in perfect agreement with Luke's statements.

influence of Christian Greek that gradually killed the native languages of Asia Minor.

The truth is that those ancient writers who had actually visited Iconium call it a Phrygian city, although strangers and Cicero sometimes call it a city of Lycaonia. The writer who composed this history, which we call the Acts of the Apostles, must therefore be ranked along with those who had visited Iconium.[1] No proof exists that he personally had ever been there, but his narrative rests on the first-hand testimony of men who had visited the city, and reproduces their correct way of describing it. So far the statement of Luke is found to be fully justified; but there is more to say.

We have failed to find any authority in the Roman Imperial period for classing Iconium as a city of Lycaonia. Ancient authority of the highest and most varied character assigns it ethnically and linguistically to Phrygia. The question, however, arises: how was it classed administratively under the Empire? As has been said above, the Romans under the Republic and the earliest Empire persistently and, as one might almost say, intentionally, disregarded national considerations, and arranged their administrative and judicial divisions in utter violation of ethnical affinities. In Cicero's time Iconium was the meeting-place of the Isaurican *conventus* (see p. 54); but no trace of *conventus* in this region is known under the Empire; and it must be concluded that that system of division (which continued in the province Asia) had fallen out of use in the province Galatia. The reason obviously was that the Imperial Galatia was not a survival of the Republican administration, but an adaptation of the

---

[1] Xenophon, Luke, Hierax, Firmilian, constitute a chain of evidence of the strongest character, running through the centuries, confirmed by local legend and municipal pride.

Galatian kingdom of Amyntas. Augustus took over this realm, and made it as it was into a Roman province with the least possible change: it was contrary to Roman method to alter existing conditions more than was necessary.

Now in this Roman province Galatia a part is often mentioned under the name Phrygia or Mygdonia. Pliny[1] speaks of Mygdonia as bordering on the southern side of Great Phrygia and as being alongside of Lycaonia and Pisidia. This description would remain obscure, and would be taken as probably referring to some more ancient facts which Pliny had not quite correctly appreciated,[2] had it not been for an inscription found at Pisidian Antioch, in which a "regionary centurion" who had acted as guardian of peace and order (in the region), is praised by Mygdonia for his success in perserving peace and saving human life.[3] There can be no doubt that this region is here called Mygdonia, and that it lay around Antioch, and that, as other considerations show, Antioch was the capital of the region. Mygdonia is a poetic equivalent for Phrygia, derived from the name of the old Phrygian chief Mygdon: and the use of this form is natural in the rude metrical epigram of that inscription; but the occurrence in Pliny shows, further, that there was some recognized appropriateness in that name. No other reference to the name is known except that this must be the Mygdonia which is mentioned by Stephanus as a part of Phrygia.

[1] Pliny, "Nat. Hist.," v. 145.

[2] He has, however, given at least unmistakable evidence of the geographical situation: Mygdonia was on the south side of the large Phrygia (included in the province Asia), and adjoining both Pisidia and Lycaonia. There can be no doubt what this indicates.

[3] Published by Professor Calder in "Journal of Roman Studies," 1911, p. 80 f. It is on two sides of a large altar, one side in ordinary prose, one which mentions Mygdonia in very rude metre.

The name Phrygia often occurs in inscriptions, as designating one of the parts or regions composing the large province Galatia.[1] Dr. Brandis remarks that the name in such cases applies only to a part of the Great Phrygia (most of which was in the province of Asia), viz., the part lying between Pisidia and Isauria and Lycaonia,[2] and containing the cities of Antioch and Apollonia. This definition is fairly correct.

Moreover, we notice that Strabo calls Antioch a city of Pisidian Phrygia, so that he recognized the existence of this separate portion of Phrygia and the need for making the distinction clear by a limiting epithet. His Pisidian Phrygia is equivalent to Pliny's Mygdonia, i.e. Phrygia of the province Galatia.

In this sense Phrygia (i.e. Pisidian Phrygia or Mygdonia) has to be classed as one of the parts or regions of the province; and, as Professor Calder says, these *regiones* are the administrative divisions of the province Galatia.[3] In the inscription just quoted the " regionary centurion " commanded all " the *stationes* of soldiers who kept the peace along the main highways of trade and administration " in the region Mygdonia or Phrygia.[4]

Now Iconium under the earlier Empire before A.D. 295, is persistently assigned to Phrygia, and it seems beyond doubt that this city also must be regarded as part of the

---

[1] Examples are C.I.L. III. 6818 and 6819; Fränkel, "Inschriften von Pergamos," No. 451; Cumont, "Bulletin de la Classe des Lettres," etc., Bruxelles, 1905, p. 205.

[2] In these words Dr. Brandis comes very close to the words of Pliny v. 145, as quoted above; yet he evidently was not thinking of Pliny's testimony, for he adds needlessly and vaguely the name Isauria.

[3] See his very full commentary in the "Journal of Roman Studies," 1911, p. 80 f.

[4] Calder, loc. cit.

Galatic region Phrygia. There are only two possible alternatives. It must belong either to the administrative region
Lycaonia of the Roman system or to the administrative
region Phrygia ; now the authorities are clear that it does
not belong to Lycaonia until after A.D. 295, and that it does
belong to Phrygia.[1]

Judging from the accepted handbooks this result is not
what we should have expected, and the earlier modern
scholars did not dream of it ; yet the ancient authorities
compel assent, and justify Luke's account in the most
complete way. It may be supposed that, when Amyntas
held that large kingdom, he discontinued the Roman
arrangements (as we see them in Cicero), and revived the
old national divisions, Pisidia, Phrygia, Lycaonia, combin-
ing them in some way as yet undetermined with the three
tribes of Gauls.[2] Then when in some year about A.D. 138,
Lycaonia was assigned to the newly created province of
the Three Eparchiæ, Iconium did not so pass,[3] but continued to be part of *provincia Galatia, regio Phrygia.*

---

[1] Isauria was perhaps not one of the regiones, but was included in
Lycaonia : it is once mentioned, C.I.L. III. 6818 (next to Lycaonia, and
perhaps regarded as joined to it by *et* understood) : it is possible, however,
that Isauria was a *regio* of the province, which, being the smallest, was not
often mentioned. I assume that in northern Isauria the Lycaonian language
was spoken.

[2] The Romans, taking over the kingdom of Amyntas as the province
Galatia, continued all the good arrangements that he had made. There is,
as Gardthausen says, no hint that any reorganization took place ; but the
record is scanty.

[3] Imhoof Blumer, " Kleinasiatische Muenzen," II. p. 415, published in 1902,
differed on this point ; but conclusive proof has been discovered to justify the
opinion that I maintained long previously. Imhoof's statement and list are
probably due to a mere slip of memory, as he gives not only Iconium, but
also Laodiceia and Parlais and Lystra as cities of the Koinon of the Lycaonians all wrongly.

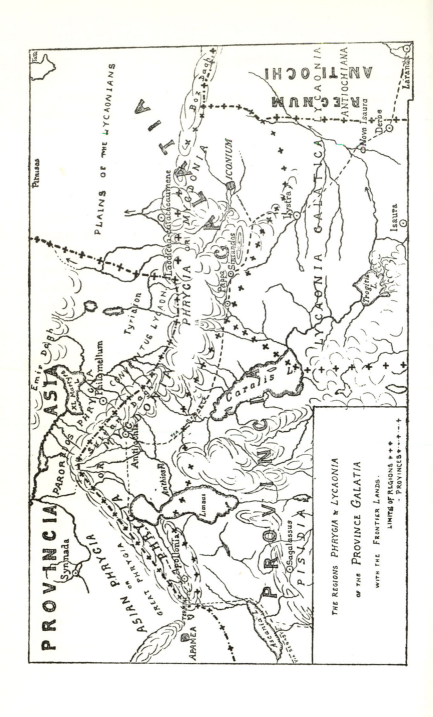

THE REGIONS PHRYGIA & LYCAONIA
OF THE PROVINCE GALATIA
WITH THE FRONTIER LANDS.
LIMITS OF REGIONS +++
" PROVINCES +·—·—·+

CHAPTER V

THE LANGUAGE SPOKEN AT ICONIUM

AS a last stage in the demonstration, it may be asked why visitors felt that Iconium [1] was Phrygian. Geographically, its situation would mark it as Lycaonian. There is no possibility of mistaking the limits or ignoring the character of the Lycaonian plain. Von Moltke in his "Letters" from Turkey quotes from some authority the statement that it is the most level plain in the world : certainly none can be more level.

A visitor, therefore, recognizing the obvious character of the great plain, would naturally regard Iconium as a city of Lycaonia. Later, he became aware that it was a city of the Phrygians, and this perception came in such a way as to abide in his memory, and make him call the city Phrygian when he spoke of it. There can be only one way to explain this. Anyone who stayed in the city heard the Phrygian speech of the people : he knew in this way that it was a city of Phrygians from their tongue. [2]

Those who study the history of Asia Minor know how ethnical and national distinctions persist there. In the same little valley one finds villages of three or four different nationalities. The people live side by side. They never

---

[1] It is quite remarkable how often this memory of the language and the racial character persists in the references quoted: " of Phrygia " is added needlessly, natives were proud of it : visitors remembered it.

[2] This was pointed out in the " Church in the Roman Empire before 170," p. 38, as long ago as 1893 (lectures of 1892).

intermarry. An observant traveller will detect the difference of racial character, but only if he is on the outlook
for ethnographical distinctions, because all speak the same
language, viz. Turkish, all are Moslem of one kind or
another, and only the women have any noteworthy difference
in dress.[1] First Christian Greek, and then Turkish, have
been levelling languages in Asia Minor.

In ancient time the local dialects lasted long. Neither
Hellenism nor Roman civilization could obliterate or even
seriously weaken national characteristics. The Romans at
first attempted to make their "provinces" supreme over the
national distinctions; but after a century they found that
nationality was a far stronger power than "provinciality".
The unity of the Roman province was external: the unity of
each nation was deeper. Yet for nearly a century the
Romans tried to impose the "provincial" unity, and the
people seemed, in their enthusiasm of gratitude for the peace
and order of the Empire, to accept whole-heartedly the
Roman unity of the province. Iconium, a Hellenistic city,
called itself Claudeikonion, i.e. "Imperial Claudian Iconium": and so Derbe called itself Claudioderbe, while
Antioch was apparently Roman to the core; Coloniæ
were, so to say, isolated fragments of Rome itself.

Yet this appearance was only on the surface. The racial
character continued, and outlived the "provincial" character.
Hellenism was a stronger power than Romanism in the
East: but strongest of all was the old language in a town
like Iconium. The people did not cease to speak Phrygian
in their home life. Greek was the speech of education and

---

[1] I do not take into account the difference which is emphasized by religious
diversity, Christian, Yezidi, etc.; but only the variety of Moslems, Osmanli,
Turkmen, Yuruk, Kurd of the western clans (different in many ways from
the Eastern Kurds), and so on.

public intercourse, for the city was a Hellenistic organization, but Phrygian survived. This language the visitors to Iconium heard, as in Lystra they heard the Lycaonian.[1]

More definite proof, however, than this general probability was naturally desired by the world of scholars, who are disposed to be a little sceptical about such statements as this regarding the language of Iconium, statements resting on a general estimate of the local conditions. Even those scholars who were maintaining against me that the people of Iconium would prefer to be addressed by their racial name (which those scholars believed to be Lycaonian), and not by the Roman provincial designation as "Galatian," were doubtful or incredulous when I maintained that Phrygian was the home language of the ordinary Iconium population in the first and the second centuries.

There is only one proof that is conclusive, and that is the discovery of epigraphic evidence that the Phrygian tongue was actually used in Iconium in the first and second centuries after Christ. This proof I did not venture to hope for owing to the position of the city.[2]

As is shown more fully in the "Cities of St. Paul," p. 317 f., Iconium is marked out by nature as a centre of population, and as a great city throughout the history of organized society; the abundant water-supply and the

---

[1] Prof. Holl of Berlin has proved in an excellent article in "Hermes," 1908, that the native languages persisted for centuries after the Christian era. Quite independently he reached the same conclusion which I have maintained for thirty years, that it was only the Christian Greek, and not the Greek of the old civilization, that was strong enough to eradicate the Phrygian and other native languages.

[2] It is, of course, beyond question that Paul and Barnabas addressed only the Greek-speaking population; they spoke to the common middle class people, the tradesmen and artisans, though with an intermixture of the higher classes, Asiarchs in Ephesus, the Council of Areopagus in Athens, Roman officials in some places, as well as local magistrates.

favourable surroundings ensure this. Hence it has been a large city, sometimes capital of an empire, throughout mediaeval times down to the present day. Much popular feeling is attached to it, and a good deal of native pride gathers round it. " See all the world, but see Konia," is an old saying about it; and every visitor is told that "those who go once to Konia always return there seven times ". As, in the East, every strong feeling tends to take religious form, Konia ranks as holy.

Iconium has therefore been a difficult place to explore. Systematic excavation would tax the resources of a millionaire, for the whole surface would have to be bought; and even the unoccupied land on the outskirts of the modern town [1] is protected by official and popular jealousy, and by the feeling that Konia is a holy city.

There was hardly any chance of finding new evidence except when a house was being built on the outskirts or rebuilt in the heart of the city. Then it appeared in preparing the foundations that the soil a few feet below the present surface is full of ancient stones; and every new house yielded some inscriptions.

Hence the gradual discovery of the complete proof lasted through a long series of years. The time from 1880 to 1890 was occupied in acquiring the first-hand knowledge of the country which made the ancient narratives more intelligible, and thus enabled me better to understand and appreciate Luke's history, and strengthened my confidence in my own judgment.

In two books that were published in 1893 and 1895 [2] the

---

[1] The modern town is not so large as the mediaeval city, and excavations on the outskirts show the wider extent.

[2] " The Church in the Roman Empire," 1893; " St. Paul the Traveller," 1895.

meaning of the narrative whose scene lay in Iconium and Lystra was explained in a way that seemed convincing to some, but not to others. Only in 1910 did a fortunate conjunction of circumstances place in our hands the opportunity of unearthing the final proof. Every year from 1901 onwards Konia had been our headquarters and centre of exploration ; but we could only put ourselves in the way, so as to be ready when influences which we could not control opened the door before us.

The principle on which I have worked has been stated often from 1883 onwards : the evidence is there : one has only to search long enough and it will be discovered. Patience is needed. The life of the explorer in such a land consists of nineteen disappointments to one discovery. Knowledge is needed. Without thorough acquaintance with the problems and the whole range of evidence little can be learned by the explorer. Money is needed. Travelling to be effective is expensive,[1] and excavation is triply expensive.

That principle should be made the rule of the explorer's life. The evidence to test all important history, and especially the Old and the New Testaments, exists and can be discovered with patience, knowledge, ingenuity, and money.

It was not until 1910 that the final proof was discovered. Only one kind of evidence in regard to a question of lan-

---

[1] I have tried every way. I have travelled for weeks with a single Turkish servant and one led horse carrying all our baggage ; and I have gone with tents and servants and horses and waggons. The traveller who goes with an imposing accompaniment gets far more from the Turks of all classes. The traveller who goes with one servant is troubled and may often be stopped. In the Greek regions it is different, for the Greeks welcome the archæological explorer quite as heartily, if he is poor, as if he bears the external signs of wealth.

guage is perfect and unanswerable : and that is epigraphic proof of its use.

In the beginning of May of that year we came to the city at an interesting moment.[1]   The municipality, desiring to get stones for building purposes, had recourse to the usual kind of quarry in Turkey, viz. the ruins of the ancient city.   In the modern town there is a low hill, on which stands the Mosque of Ala-ed-Din, also the old church of St. Amphilochius,[2] the modern Greek church of the Transfiguration, and the Armenian church.   Here also are some scanty remnants of the once stately palace of the Seljuk Sultans.   In this hill the municipality proceeded to dig, and at once began to find inscribed stones.   These were seized by the Imperial Museum, which, however, declined to pay any part of the expense of finding them.   The Municipality then refused to dig for the benefit of the museum and stopped the excavation.

At this moment we arrived and heard of the situation. I called on the Pasha, the governor of the Province (Vilayet) of Konia, and offered to conduct the excavations at the expense of the Fund, giving to the museum all the inscribed stones and to the Municipality all the rest.   The offer seems to us fair and even generous : but to the Turks it seemed to hide some subtle plan [3] for getting possession of gold (which must of course be there, but which was not mentioned in the proposal).   Were the infidels to get all the gold ?   Some

---

[1] My companion in that year was Professor Calder of Manchester, an old pupil in Aberdeen, and Craven Fellow in Oxford.

[2] Taken by the Turks long ago, and transformed to a mosque, but, as every one who went to pray there died, they abandoned it ; and it stands empty and unused, and is called Sa'at, " The Clock ".

[3] This difficulty always has to be faced in Turkey.   There is an ingrained suspicion regarding one's motives, partly caused by some really unfair action on the part of Europeans, partly due to the Oriental belief that the ultimate reason for action must be gold, and the settled disbelief in ideal motives.

negotiation was required ; and we proposed the condition that the town engineer should conduct the excavation, fix its limits, take possession of all finds, and distribute them between the different interests concerned. Thus it came about that we had the opportunity—which I had never ventured even to hope for—of digging in the hill of Ala-ed-Din. We could not go very far as there was said to be some danger to the buildings on the centre of the hill ; and after four weeks the engineer announced that the digging must stop.

The walls which we uncovered were the basement of the old Seljuk Palace ; and it is evident that the hill, though doubtless in part natural, is largely the accumulation of soil and dust over ancient or mediaeval walls. The wind-blown dust is caught and detained by every eminence, and thus heaps are formed under the protection of the walls.[1]

These basement walls of the Seljuk Palace contained a number of inscribed stones, about forty-five in all. They belonged to the century between 150 and 250 A.D., and among them were two inscribed in the Phrygian language. Now Phrygian inscriptions of that period are rare, not because the language was not spoken, but because it was not a language of education. Greek was the educated speech. All who got any education received it in Greek. Almost all who wrote, wrote in Greek. Hence even epitaphs in the Phrygian tongue are rare, and a number of these are bilingual, written partly in Greek and partly in Phrygian. The writers were able to use both languages, but for some reason preferred not to abandon wholly the non-literary Phrygian tongue. Even in country districts where there is reason to think that the use of Phrygian was customary and general, epitaphs in that language are not numerous : such

[1] We had the opportunity of observing the results of this process on the long-deserted site of Pisidian Antioch during the excavations of 1913.

districts would make a poor show in a map of ancient civilization.

Both the Phrygian inscriptions at Iconium are engraved on altars. The longer and more important is here added. In the translation the uncertain Phrygian words are left untranslated. The monument belongs to the period between A.D. 150 and 250.

The inscription has been published by Professor Calder (who copied it in 1910 along with me) in his "Corpus Inscriptionum Neophrygiarum "("Journal of Hellenic Studies," 1911, p. 188 f.). It is written in a mixture of Phrygian and the Greek of the Koine dialect, showing the way in which the old language was being supplanted by the colloquial Greek. This process is natural in an old Phrygian city, in which the language of education and of government had been Greek for more than two centuries. One could hardly say with confidence whether this should be called a Phrygian inscription modified by Greek influence, or a Greek inscription modified by Phrygian influence ; it is predominantly Greek, but yet Phrygian words, even prepositions, are mixed up with the Greek ; lines 11-14 are in real, though bad Greek ; 1-10 are in a Phrygian patois.

Ἥλιος Γάϊος αγο- ρανι αχανες τό- πον Καοανια πραγματικ- 5 όν, ατ ω κα εἰστάνι π- έλτα κα ηλι- α διθρεψα σα πριεις [᾿Α]ὐρ- 10 ηλίαν Βασ[αν· ὅστις ἐπ[ιβιά- σηστε, δώ[σει τῶ φίσκ[ω 14 (δηναρια) d.	Helios Gaios pur- chases an empty ? place in Kaoania state-sanctioned ? on which also he places a base- ment and super- structure for his sister ? Aur- elia Basa : whosoever shall forcibly enter, shall pay to the Fiscus one thousand denarii.

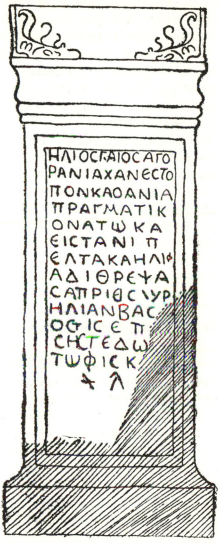

Fig. 1.—Tombstone in the form of an altar with epitaph in the Iconian Græco-Phrygian patois. The shaded part is broken off, and the form is restored conjecturally on the analogy of similar tombstones.

The general sense of this epitaph is clear; but there are many difficulties which cannot be discussed here. Some of them are explained in Mr. Calder's elaborate commentary.

The only doubtful reading is in line 9, where ϵι is far from clear, and as regards the [A ?] I made the note that A was not engraved, also that the second last letter could not be X, but γ was certain (differing in form from Y elsewhere). See Note on p. 78.

I follow Professor Calder's transcription in lines 9 f., though on the stone I convinced myself (I think with his agreement) that there never had been an A. I am disposed to think that Helia, not Aurelia, was the sister of Helios. Prieis certainly denotes some female relationship, and is commonly used as a woman's name in East Phrygian inscriptions. The legal penalty at the end is expressed intentionally in the Greek language, as it relates to a matter of law ; and Greek was the language of justice and the law-courts and municipal affairs.

The rest of the inscription is expressed in the Iconian patois, mixed of Greek and Phrygian. On the analogy of εἰστάνω (i.e. ἰστάνω) and similar forms a verb ἀγοράνω is constructed; but I incline to a different view from Mr. Calder ; it seems very probable that Keramon Agora (mentioned by Xenophon as a city of Phrygia) was, as I have elsewhere suggested,[1] the market of the city afterwards called Akmonia, and that Agora was used in the sense of "market" in Phrygian, in which case the verb αγορανω might be a true Phrygian verb. It is well known that the operations and equipments of commerce were highly developed in Lydia (and Phrygia), and that this development took place specially along the line of the Royal Road from Sardis to

---

[1] " Cities and Bishoprics of Phrygia," II., p. 595.

the East, passing through Keramon Agora. The meaning "market" in that case was adopted from Anatolia for the Greek word along with many of the devices of commerce (including coinage).[1]

Kaoania is probably the Phrygian form of the city name, which was hellenized as Konion (Pliny and some Byzantine references[2]) and modified to Ἰκόνιον or Εἰκόνιον to suggest a connexion with εἰκών an image, giving rise to a legend about a sacred statue in the city.

The stone is rather pretentious, and cannot be the grave-stone of a very poor person. The fine, too, is considerable, and fines were proportioned in some degree to the value of the property. The monument was of a common type: there was a substructure, on which stood some double erection (διθρεψα) to contain the coffin or sarcophagus. Everything points to the conclusion that the monument belonged to a household of some wealth and standing in the middle classes of the Iconian population. The Phrygian language was therefore not wholly disused even in the class of Iconian society where education was likely to have spread.

In Iconium it is remarkable that any Phrygian inscriptions should survive. The city was Greek-speaking as well as Phrygian-speaking, and Greek was the language of culture and of epigraphy. The wonder is, not that only two Phrygian inscriptions should remain in a city where that language was spoken, but that even two should exist where Greek was also in current use. This is a decisive proof that the old language still had a strong hold on the city as late as A.D. 200.

---

[1] "Cities and Bishoprics of Phrygia," II., p. 416 f.; Radet, "Lydie et le Monde Grec," p. 155 ff. The Greek word means in Homer the Council: Herodotus has it as "the market," and so the Attic usage.

[2] "The Thousand and One Churches," p. 512.

The work of years was completed. Ethnically Iconium was a Phrygian, not a Lycaonian city, and the use of the Phrygian language appeared to visitors noteworthy even in the third century after Christ. The statement of Pliny that Iconium was one of the old Phrygian cities is confirmed on all hands. Even the local mythology is markedly Phrygian in character.[1] Its heroes are Nannakos, the old Phrygian king, and Perseus as symbolic of Greek influence penetrating into an Eastern land. The goddess of the country was a form of the Great Phrygian Mother, Mêtêr Zizimmene or Zizimene, whose home was in the mountains on the north-west and north of Iconium. This title has impressed various scholars independently as a Phrygian name, a dialectic variety of Dindymene.[2] Those theological critics in this country who can accept nothing unless it is made in Germany may with clear conscience accept this identification, as it has been stated by Kretschmer, not as a mere hypothesis but as a positive fact. As his authority for the word Zizimmene he quotes the German magazine where my article appeared proposing the same identification; there was no other authority for the word when he wrote; but he does not mention that I there identified it with Dindymene. Yet he has read my comment, because he uses the same illustration which I gave (viz. Nadiandos) and no other, though many others

[1] That is shown at some length in my " Cities of St. Paul," p. 319 f. ; but much remains that has since been discovered in this subject. Such discoveries, however, are, like all mythological discussions, too speculative for the present book.

[2] I suggested this when publishing the first known inscription of this class in " Mittheil. Athen. Instituts," 1888, p. 237. Mr. Arkwright in Jan., 1914, writes me on the subject, giving new reasons for the same opinion, which came to him independently. I do not, however, regard it as anything more than a possibility, which may reasonably be mentioned; but the fact that it strikes every philologist as possible, and Kretschmer as certain, proves that this wor dhas the Phrygian character and feeling.

might be given and one has been stated by me in " Historical Geography," p. 348.[1] I am used to this way of adopting
my opinions without acknowledgment in some cases, and
of carefully specifying my name in others where the opinion
is not accepted. So long as the truth wins acceptance in
the long run I can afford to wait ; but I have repeatedly
had to plead, as for example in "The Education of
Christ," p. 66 f., that " the truth is this, and it is a truth
which will soon be discovered and emphasized by the
Germans and will then be brought over and accepted
among us ".

I would not have even alluded to the matter had it not
proved an obstacle in Great Britain to the acceptance of
obviously true statements by critics, who accept others less
evidently true, because they can quote them from a German
authority, ignorant of the fact that ultimately they are to
be found in the writer's " Historical Geography," or some
other early work.

Now, both Xenophon in the Anabasis and Strabo, p.
663, say in the most explicit way that the traveller, as he
went along the road, passed out of Phrygia into Lycaonia.
The geographer Strabo is describing in that passage a
traveller's route along the great road across Asia Minor
from Ephesus to the Euphrates ; and the traveller Xenophon is describing the march of Cyrus from Sardis to the
Cilician Gates. Strabo's evidence carries us back to the
second century B.C., for he quotes the statistics from

---

[1] Kretschmer, " Einleitung in d. Gesch. d. gr. Sprache," p. 196, where
there is a misprint 287 for 237 in quoting the authority for the existence of
Zizimmene. The perfect generosity and exquisite courtesy with which the
Austrian scholars Dr. Keil and Ritter von Premerstein have acknowledged to
the full every matter in which we agree forms a striking contrast: some
other German scholars of distinguished standing have also shown the finest
courtesy, e.g. Direktor Wiegand and Dr. Harnack.

Artemidorus ; but it gives his own knowledge, for he had himself traversed that part of the road.

Similarly, Luke is describing the victorious march of Paul across Asia Minor ; and exactly as Xenophon does, he remembers to record the passage across the frontier on the road between Iconium and Lystra.

No more striking and arresting parallel has ever been found between writers so utterly unlike, so absolutely independent of each other, yet all describing from totally different points of view the progress along a great international road, and marking the stages of the way by the nations which they traversed.

There cannot remain a doubt in the mind of any competent judge who takes the trouble to read the evidence. Paul passed the frontier between Phrygia and Lycaonia in Acts XIV. 5. From XIII. 13 to XIV. 4 he had been in Phrygia.

Note (p. 74).—One of the doubtful symbols of l. 9, interpreted in the text (p. 72) as a ligature of ε and ι, is justified by the use of the same ligature in a spelling exercise written during the first century on an ostrakon in Egypt, and published by Wilcken in Mitteis-Wilcken, " Papyruskunde," Vol. I., Pt. II., page 165. The use of ει on the ostrakon for the proper letter, which should be simply ι, is the misspelling of some careless schoolboy ; and the error is due to the unpractised hand slipping into cursive writing. So here in l. 9 the engraver degenerates from the very humble standard of the earlier part of the inscription. This may justify the reading of \ as **A.** Hence the worse form of the upsilon at the end of the line.

CHAPTER VI

GENERAL IMPRESSION OF TRUSTWORTHINESS IN THE ACTS

THE inference from these facts, as just stated, was plain. This passage in the Acts is correct: the boundaries mentioned are true to the period in which the action lies: they are not placed through the mistaken application by a later author of ancient statements to a time when they had ceased to be pertinent: they are based on information given by an eye-witness, a person who had been engaged in the action described. The reader, if he reads the narrative rightly, can see with the eyes and hear with the ears of a man who was there and witnessed all that happened.

The reversal of our judgment, then, was complete.[1] We had imagined that this detail was a blunder due to stupidity or ignorance or misplaced ingenuity on the part of the author: it has now been found to show excellent knowledge and the minute accuracy which comes from the faithful report of an eye-witness and participator in the action.

Now the condemnation which, as soon as it was tested in respect of one detail, had been proved hasty and false, evidently could not be relied on in respect of other details without being tested. Fresh examination of the whole question was needed. The reasons and grounds for our unfavourable judgment regarding the book of the Acts

[1] " Our " means those scholars whose judgment was then widely dominant, and was accepted by me as a humble and convinced follower.

must be reconsidered. Prejudice must be set aside. Ignorance of the circumstances of every event must so far as possible be replaced by knowledge through fuller study. Every condition had to be revalued. Every point had to be scrutinized again.

Of course, there is a certain presumption that a writer who proves to be exact and correct in one point will show the same qualities in other matters. No writer is correct by mere chance, or accurate sporadically. He is accurate by virtue of a certain habit of mind. Some men are accurate by nature : some are by nature loose and inaccurate. It is not a permissible view that a writer is accurate occasionally, and inaccurate in other parts of his book. Each has his own standard and measure of work, which is produced by his moral and intellectual character.

It may be said that the writer of Acts happened to have access to a good authority in one detail, and not in others. That, however, had not been our argument : the condemnation which we pronounced had been general, and it was now proved false in the first test. To try to bolster it up by such a new supposition would be wholly unscientific. Instead of trying to find arguments in its favour, we must frankly confess that it was wrong, and re-try the case as a whole.

Moreover, that way of juggling with the supposed authorities of Luke, too, has been abandoned since then by all competent scholars. The idea that the writer of the Acts had good authorities to rely on for one or two details alone would not now be suggested or tolerated. That writer had a certain general level of knowledge and information and judgment. He has to be estimated as a whole. It has probably never been suggested that he depended on an informant who was trustworthy about the twenty miles of road between Iconium and Lystra and untrustworthy or unavailable elsewhere : such a suggestion, doubtless, would always have been rejected as absurd and would certainly be rejected in modern times.

The question among scholars now is with regard to Luke's credibility as a historian ; it is generally conceded that he wrote at a comparatively early date, and had authorities of high character, even where he himself was not an eye-witness. How far can we believe his narrative?

The present writer takes the view that Luke's history is unsurpassed in respect of its trustworthiness. At this point we are describing what reasons and arguments changed the mind of one who began under the impression that the history was written long after the events and that it was untrustworthy as a whole.

In the special work on which I was engaged at the time, some fresh investigation of the case was indispensable. Good and safe evidence about Asia Minor in the Imperial time or earlier was urgently required by an explorer and discoverer. If I could find such evidence, and test it in the country, a long vista of profitable work opened itself before me. The eager desire for discovery and historical reconstruction had always possessed me and guided my life (as already described). I was finding from day to day other unused ancient evidence on a small scale ; and if Luke's narrative was trustworthy, it was for me exceptionally valuable, as giving evidence on a larger scale. There was nothing else like it. No other ancient traveller has left an account of the journeys which he made across Asia Minor [1] ; and if the narrative of Paul's travels rests on first-class authority, it placed in my hands a document of unique and exceptional value to guide my investigations. To determine

[1] Xenophon gives little more than names and distances.

the value of this narrative was a fundamental condition for my future work.

Strabo, as we know, travelled across Asia Minor from Tarsus to the Ægean Sea. He has given us no account of his journey ; but we can follow his steps, guided by the superior vividness and quality of what he says about the places which he passed through. A number of the pilgrims in the first three crusades wrote accounts of the march that they made across the country, often photographically accurate about superficial details ; but the pilgrims were uninterested in the country, unscientific in their attitude of mind, poorly educated ; they gave very little useful information, and only about a much later period, A.D. 1100-1185. A few of the Byzantine historians had seen the parts of Asia in which lie some of the incidents of their narrative ;[1] but most of them know nothing about the country and the scenes.

A word from a witness who has seen what he describes may often throw more light on the situation than a page of vague description from one who has not seen. A Pauline narrative of Paul's journeys would be invaluable for the study of Asia Minor in the first century, quite apart from the religious aspect of the case.

There was then, and there still is a strange and quite widespread prepossession that an early Christian, like Paul, must have been wholly occupied with the religious propaganda, so that he could see nothing, hear nothing, feel nothing, and observe nothing except the chance of converting some

---

[1] I include the case of historians who followed the account of an eye-witness. Nicetas describes at great length the campaign of Manuel Comnenus, ending in his defeat in the Tchyvritzi Kleisoura, A.D. 1175. Either he had seen the pass, or he used well the narrative of an eye-witness. No one can doubt this who has seen the locality. The last stand of Manuel where seven glens meet is easily recognized.

heathen individual or group of persons. This prepossession, that Christian authors lie outside the pale of real literature and that early Christians were not to be estimated as men, has been the enemy for me to attack ever since I began to look into the Christian authors with unprejudiced eyes. It may be true of some smaller figures and narrower minds. It is not true of the greater men. The wide variety of interest and information contained in the Cappadocian writers of the fourth century is illustrated in another work ; [1] and I have for more than twenty years been maintaining the same truth in respect of the writers in the New Testament and the greatest of their successors. " In becoming Christians those writers did not cease to be men : they only gained that element of thoroughness, sincerity, and en-thusiasm, the want of which is so unpleasing in later classical literature." [2]

When the Acts is read from this point of view, as the real travels of real men along roads or over seas, it be-comes vivid in the highest degree. Yet in spite of the direct statement of Luke in Acts, XXI. 15, that a large party of travellers used horses, a statement interpreted and confirmed by Chrysostom, it has seemed almost sacrilegious to some modern scholars to suggest that Paul ever made a journey except on foot.

He was probably able to swim (2 Corinthians XI. 25), and the impossibility of any other mode of travel made it necessary to admit that he often voyaged on shipboard. Why should he not ride, when friends gave him a horse ? It is a question of evidence; and Luke says that the party used horses, Acts XXI. 15.[3]

---

[1] " Pauline and other Studies in the History of Religion," pp. 369-406.
[2] " The Church in the Roman Empire before A.D. 170," p. 176.
[3] The passage is discussed in " Pauline and other Studies," p. 267.

Again, Paul expresses in the most emphatic way his gratitude to the Galatians for their kindness;[1] they were ready to give him anything, however dear and valuable, so far as physical possibilities permitted. When that was the case, why should we assume that they allowed Paul and Barnabas to walk from Antioch to Iconium? why not furnish their two guests with a waggon for the journey? I cannot feel any doubt in this matter (as is maintained in the "Church in the Roman Empire," p. 68)[2]. His deep gratitude to the Philippians for sending him money, even though it was contrary to his custom to accept any money from his congregations, is paralleled by his profound gratitude to the Galatians for giving him every kind of hospitality and for facilitating his journeys, even though he ordinarily travelled on foot and kept himself by his own labour. It seems also probable that when Paul made the land journey from Troas to Assos, while most of the company went by sea, he was riding: the word used ($\pi\epsilon\zeta\hat{\eta}$) implies only "by land" as distinguished from the other travellers who preferred shipboard, but gives no basis for inferring that he walked and did not ride.

It is singular that commentators seem not to have thought of any other possibility in this case : yet the contrast is here expressly drawn between sea and land travel, and it is a recognized principle of the lexicons and of classical and ordinary Greek, that, where that contrast is clearly in the writer's mind, $\pi\epsilon\zeta\acute{o}\varsigma$, $\pi\epsilon\zeta\hat{\eta}$, and $\pi\epsilon\zeta\epsilon\acute{v}\epsilon\iota\nu$ cannot be taken to imply travel on foot. Even where horses are actually at hand, Homer says "if you prefer to go $\pi\epsilon\zeta\acute{o}\varsigma$, by land not by sea, here are horses and a car" (" Od.," III. 324).

The facts stated in the two preceding chapters showed that

---

[1] Galatians IV. 15.   [2] See p. 313.

it was necessary to read again chapters XIII.-XX. of the Acts without any prejudice as to the origin, in order to see what could be learned from the book for my special subject, viz. the topography, social conditions, political divisions, municipal institutions, etc., of Asia Minor. A new authority of the highest value for the first century was thus placed in my hands. In many details Luke's narrative is confirmed by other evidence, some previously known, some more recently discovered. In other details no confirmation is known, but no contradictory evidence exists that will stand investigation; and the supposition of his accuracy ought to be admitted universally, at least as a " working hypothesis ".

One could not but notice that the ordinary non-theological scholars quoted the writings of Luke without hesitation for facts of Roman antiquities. Scholars who aimed simply at collecting facts, and had evidently no bias either for or against him, seemed to regard him as a sufficient authority, whereas the theological scholars, who came with a strong bias on certain issues, looked on him as utterly untrustworthy. Only on one point of Roman antiquities all were agreed, from all sides, in denouncing his statements as incredible: this was the famous passage in the Gospel of Luke II. 1-3, which every one regarded as a tissue of blunders of the most marked and worst kind. To this passage we shall return later in this book and for the present deal only with the Acts.

Further study of Acts XIII.-XXI. showed that the book could bear the most minute scrutiny as an authority for the facts of the Ægean world, and that it was written with such judgment, skill, art, and perception of truth as to be a model of historical statement. It is marvellously concise and yet marvellously lucid.

What I was at that time in search of beyond all else was

some authority for the constitution and relation of the parts in the great Roman province of Galatia. Mommsen in his volume on the "Provinces of the Roman Empire," sums up together in one chapter all the provinces of Asia Minor, and describes them after the analogy of the most thoroughly Grecized parts of the province Asia. This proceeding, however, is not admissible. It is certain that a wide diversity existed between the Greek cities of the Ægean coast in the province Asia and the general character of the province Cappadocia, where Greek and Roman manners hardly began to touch the population in Imperial times. It is also certain that the province Galatia was in some ways and in some parts almost as Oriental and non-Hellenic as Cappadocia: the cities were in part Hellenized or Romanized, but only in part, while the country regions round the cities remained almost purely Oriental. Among the cities the Roman Colonies stood on a higher rank in all respects, being, so to say, parts of Rome itself.

In the Acts then there was a considerable amount of information about the province Galatia, far more than in any other source or even in all other sources put together. The inscriptions, few as they were, made it possible to criticize, to control, and to understand the evidence of the Acts. With this book as a basis of investigation a general conception of the province Galatia during the first century was gradually formed and stated in outline in "St. Paul the Traveller," pp. 102 ff.; and all subsequent investigation has confirmed that beginning.

One of the first results of this study was rebellion against the old and dominant "North-Galatian theory". Beginning to write an introduction to the volume of "Mansfield College Lectures" above referred to,[1] I attempted to describe

---

[1] "The Church in the Roman Empire before 170."

the state of Asia Minor as Paul found it, and did so on the basis of the dominant opinion. As the description proceeded, I realized that it was hopelessly incongruous with the narrative in the Acts, and gradually the whole had to be rewritten. Then the character of the provincial organization stood forth clearly outlined in the pages of Luke ; and this vitally affects the history and the chronology of Paul, in his travels and his letters.

In the light of this new view, old in a way, but rejected in later criticism, the whole of the action in those chapters of travel is natural and probable. It is in perfect accord with all that we know about the society of the eastern provinces under the Roman Empire. We have been learning a great deal on that subject in the last thirty years; and since 1890 the accumulating results grow clearer every month through the illumination which they supply each to the other.

In an earlier period it was possible for scholars with a fixed idea prepossessing their minds to maintain that the action described in those chapters was often improbable, because little corroboration or illustration could be found. Since 1890-1900 that period has come to an end. The comparative dearth of illustrative examples was due solely to want of knowledge, and to the failure to comprehend the real character of the recorded illustrations. Incidents and passages in the previously known documents began to assume a new aspect in the light of recently discovered facts. Everything had to be studied afresh. So far as this branch of the subject was concerned, the older commentators, useful in other respects as their work was, and deserving of high respect and praise, had no longer any value and were misleading. The same must be said about Blass's commentary on Acts, an excellent and splendid work, but written by a Greek scholar of the old type, who studied literature and paid the minimum of regard to the circumstances and facts of social life (except so far as these expressed themselves in words).   For grammar and sense his commentary is most suggestive and valuable ; but for society and history it is misleading.   The commentaries of Professors Bartlet and Knowling belong to a new and better period.

In his work in the cities Paul is brought into contact with a great variety of people in all ranks of life, kings, and Roman governors of provinces, the Asiarchs (who were chief men of the province Asia and high-priests in the Imperial worship), members of the high Council of Areopagus in Athens, priests of the local gods at Lystra, Roman citizens like Gaius Titius Justus at Corinth (who hospitably entertained Paul and all Christian visitors to the city),[1] leading women in many cities (some as opponents, some as friends and helpers), tradesmen, magicians, and sorcerers and fortune-tellers and exorcists.

The variety is remarkable.   The propriety of the references, and the naturalness and suitability of the incidents, are perfect.   The more one knows about Græco-Roman society in the east, the more deeply is one impressed with the life-like character of the scenes described in rapid succession, so briefly yet so pregnantly, in those chapters of the Acts.

Everywhere Paul is the centre of the action : he beckons with his hand, he opens his mouth, and all listen to him. Where Paul is, every one else is secondary in the picture that Luke paints.   With what boldness and freedom, and yet with what courtesy and respect, Paul addresses Festus

---

[1] Acts XVIII. 7 ; Romans XVI. 23.

the governor, and Agrippa the king ! He perhaps loses his temper once and blazes forth in indignation at the callous command of the high-priest ; [1] but immediately he recovers himself, and apologizes with perfect politeness and self-command, when he learns that the person who had issued the brutal order was a ruler of the people.

The more I have studied the narrative of the Acts, and the more I have learned year after year about Græco-Roman society and thoughts and fashions, and organization in those provinces, the more I admire and the better I understand. I set out to look for truth on the borderland where Greece and Asia meet, and found it here. You may press the words of Luke in a degree beyond any other historian's, and they stand the keenest scrutiny and the hardest treatment, provided always that the critic knows the subject and does not go beyond the limits of science and of justice. Too often, when one reads some foolish criticism, the words of Shakespeare rise in one's memory, that here is " folly doctor-like controlling skill ".

Contrast with Luke's history the tale of Thekla, composed by an Asian presbyter in the second century, and condemned by the Church. It contains many details that are historical and many that are not, some good geography and some bad ; but the religious teaching is hysterical and false, and the story is only a legend, the heroine being a christianized form of an ancient Iconian mythological-geographical figure. There is a groundwork of fact and truth, but the superstructure is unhistorical. [2]

---

[1] Acts XXIII. 2.

[2] On the historical details see " The Church in the Roman Empire before 170," ch. XVI. A study of the origin of the Thekla-figure is much needed.

CHAPTER VII

TRIAL SCENES IN THE ACTS

TAKE, for example, that scene which is alluded to in the paragraph almost immediately preceding (Acts XXIII. 2 ff.). It has been much criticized. How could Paul, it is asked, be ignorant that it was the high-priest who issued the order to smite him on the mouth ? The dress and insignia of the high-priest were unmistakable, also his position in the meeting as the president of the Council. If you start on that line of thought and inference, either you must conclude that Paul told a polite fiction when he said, " I did not know it was the high-priest," and (as some do) you moralize about the lower standard of truth that was accepted and acted upon among the ancients and the Jews generally ; or you infer that Paul was too blind to recognize the insignia and rank of the president (though he blazed out in indignation against the person who had spoken) : or that the scene (as many say) is invented and unnatural. When we consider the circumstances, however, it is clear that this was not a formal meeting of the Council of the nation, it was an assemblage of leading men hastily summoned as advisers by the Roman officer in command at Jerusalem. The officer was in authority : he was the one man that could judge and give a decision : the rest were only his assessors. By no means could a proper meeting of the Council be called in the way followed on this occasion. He summoned " the chief priests and all the Council " ; they were the

persons whom he would naturally ask for the information
he needed ; but this does not constitute a proper meeting of
the Council for its own business.

Accordingly, instead of either cavilling at the inaccuracy
of the incident, or going off on wrong lines of reasoning
about the possibilities at a meeting of the supreme Council
of the Jewish nation, we should take the scene as a picture
of what would happen when the Roman officer hastily called
together the chief priests and the members of the Council :
the officer was the president : with him rested the authority
to stop the business and break up the meeting when he
pleased ;[1] he therefore presided. A moment's consideration is sufficient to show that it was not possible for the
Roman to stand apart, as a mere outsider. The dignity of
Rome would not permit such procedure. Either the officer
must be in authority at the meeting, or he could not be there.

The objection may be advanced against our view that
the Roman officer himself in his report to the Governor of
the province calls the meeting "the Council" (XXIV. 28).
It is, however, evident that the officer in this report is not
very accurate: thus he asserts that he interfered at the
riot because he had learned that Paul was a Roman,
whereas the truth (as Luke has it) is that he interfered first
on other grounds and afterwards learned about Paul's right
as a citizen. Moreover, Westcott and Hort regard the
words " I brought him down unto their Council " as being an
alternative reading, and place them within brackets in their
text.[2] Perhaps then they do not belong to the report ; and
the omission would make the report consistent with the
truth, for the words are inconsistent with Luke's account

---

[1] As he practically does in XXIII. 10.

[2] This implies that they are probably right, but some good authorities omit
them.

of the facts. The officer's report however is designed to set his own conduct in the most favourable light as a careful and well-informed administrator; and in carrying out his design he does not allow himself to be hampered by pedantic considerations of minute accuracy. Here, as always, safety for us lies in the most careful reading and interpretation of Luke's own words. He fully understood that the officer misrepresented facts; but it is part of his literary art to state the precise truth, and let his readers see for themselves how the Roman officer treated the case. The officer's report is, if anything, a more complete justification of Paul than the facts narrated by Luke are; the Roman takes the most favourable view, and practically says "there is no case that I can find against the prisoner, but these Jews hate him so much on religious grounds that his life is not safe here". Roman policy at the beginning favoured the free teaching, as Luke loves to show.

At the meeting Paul took the initiative. This course was unexpected, and it annoyed the high-priest. Moreover, Paul used the Hellenic and wholly anti-Hebrew expression, " I have lived the life of a citizen ". The very word was an offence to the stricter Jews : the thought expressed in such a word was Hellenistic and not Palestinian. One can hardly imagine that a man like Paul, so sensitive to the atmosphere and emotion of the audience which he addresses, would use the term " citizen " in apostrophizing a Jewish Council ; but here he is speaking with the officer as his judge, and he has to make his defence so as to convince the Roman. Nominally he has to address the Jewish notables ; but his real audience is the officer. The last words which he had spoken to the latter contained the word " citizen," and he now continues on the same key, " I have lived as a citizen ".

Everything that seems at first sight difficult in the description finds its natural place and function as illuminating the whole situation, as soon as we imagine the actual circumstances, Paul with the officer and his assessors, the accusation which the latter are to make, and the sudden stroke by which Paul anticipates and wards off what they are about to say.

Not even in Jerusalem would it be imaginable that the Council should be both accusers and judges. The officer wishes to learn what accusation is made against Paul, and summons the leaders and the Council as the accusers; but the decision and future action rest with the Roman. We must imagine the scene. Paul is set before the Jewish leaders;[1] i.e. over against them. He is not in their midst (as he is in the Council of Areopagus, XVII. 22 and 32). Paul is on one side, the Jews on the other, and the officer between. But in the confusion of the following dissension, the relative positions change; and the change is clearly marked in the Greek, though not in the English Version. After Paul's words in v. 6, the crowd of Jews was split into two parts. It was customary in Roman meetings for those who approved of a speaker's opinion to go over and stand beside him. The scribes of the sect of the Pharisees stood up and took part with Paul, and fought for him, asserting that he was right. Then Paul was like to be torn asunder between the two factions : his supporters were on one side of him, i.e. behind him, while the Sadducees, his opponents, were over against him as before ; and he thus was in their midst. Accordingly the officer ordered the guard to snatch Paul out of the midst of them.

The relative positions have changed during the proceed-

[1] εἰς αὐτούς.

ings, and at the end Paul occupies the same position in regard
to the Jews that he occupied among the Areopagus Council
from the beginning to the end of the meeting in Athens.[1]
Thus the very brief description becomes lucid and reveals
the course of the meeting, if the reader places himself at the
right point of view.

So it is everywhere with Luke.   The reader must see the
incident, keeping its successive stages before his eyes.   In
some cases it may make all the difference whether or not
you have in imagination placed the interlocutors in their
proper positions relative to one another.   If you have got
the wrong idea even on such a matter as their place on one
side or other of the hall, you may go wrong in interpreting
the action.   Get them right ; then apply the successive
verbs describing the action, and you see the whole incident
run its course stage after stage.

The effect of misconceiving the situation is perceptible
in Prof. Vernon Bartlet's discussion of this scene in his
Commentary (which is as a general rule so excellent and so
informing).   He is forced to the conclusion that " the
account seems to suffer from the fact that Luke was no
longer an eye-witness ".

It seems to us infinitely more probable that Luke was in
the " circle of bystanders," which was a marked feature of
every such meeting in the Roman world.   All readers of
the Roman literature of the first century know how important was the *corona adstantium*.   Prof. Bartlet says that an
essential part of the action has been omitted, viz. the state-

---

[1] No one who wishes to interpret rightly the scene in Athens will delude
himself with the fancy that Paul stood "in the midst of the hill," XVII. 22,
and then "went out from the midst of them," v. 32.   He stood in the midst
of (the Council) Areopagus, and went out from their midst.   All round stood
the *corona adstantium*, a great crowd of Athenians, as the description implies.

ment of the case against Paul for the officer's information. It is, however, apparent that the officer was as much bewildered at the end as he was at the beginning of this meeting, hearing in the mêlée only that nothing but obscure matters of the Jewish Law and belief were involved.[1] If any formal statement of the case against Paul had been made for the information of the officer, the charge would have been of provoking a riot and causing profanation of the Temple, as we know from XXIV. 5, 6. It is evident that "the statement of the case against Paul for the officer's information" never was made at this meeting.

Luke's account is quite clear, and omits nothing essential. The officer called together all the leading Jews, viz. "the chief priests and the whole Council," and he "brought Paul down, and set him before them". The action of "setting before them" implies a few explanatory words from the officer, stating the situation and asking definite information as to the charge that was brought against the prisoner.

Then Paul intervened, fixing those glowing eyes of his on the councillors as they stood in a body massed over against him.[2] We know the look of those eyes from other allusions, XIII. 9 in indignation, XIV. 9 in sympathy and insight that pierce to the soul.

Examine the scene as you please, pull it about, try it detail by detail; but do this with proper knowledge and insight. It all hangs together: every part contributes to the whole effect. This sort of account cannot be invented. It is real life and action that stand out before the reader's eyes and mind.

---

[1] So he reports in XXIII. 29.

[2] If he had been at this time in the midst of the Council who were acting as his judges, he could not have fixed his eyes on them. They must have been in a body over against him, as Luke implies.

Another feature of this book must now be mentioned. Even the language changes according to the situation. As we have mentioned the scene before the Council of Areopagus, it may be added that there the very words are Attic. Norden in his recent book, in which he studies the scene and the speech which Paul delivered, infers from the style and language that this passage cannot be written by the same author as the rest of the book. Evidently this distinguished scholar (whose work lies usually in another realm of letters) has not studied the Acts very thoroughly. Hence he has not rightly considered the work of Luke. In Jerusalem and Palestine Luke's language designedly is far more Hebraistic in type : in Athens it has an Attic flavour : in the Greek world generally Luke uses the general dialect.

The whole description of the Athenian incident, and the action of Paul, are Athenian in tone. He discusses philosophic questions in the market-place with all comers, like another Socrates; whereas in Ephesus he lectures regularly in the school of Tyrannus. A vulgar word of Attic slang is used by some speakers who had lost their temper. The entire incident is bathed in the light and brilliance of Attica. What is most specially characteristic of Luke is selected by Prof. E. Norden as a reason for condemning the whole passage as a scrap of late second century composition.

That the Acts contained and described a series of improbable incidents was a view that has not been tenable or possible since 1890 except through total disregard of recent advance in knowledge. It had by that time become evident that every incident described in the Acts is just what might be expected in ancient surroundings. The officials with whom Paul and his companions were brought in contact are those who would be there. Every person is found just where he ought to be : proconsuls in senatorial provinces, asiarchs in Ephesus, strategoi in Philippi, politarchs in Thessalonica, magicians and soothsayers everywhere.[1] The difficulties which the Apostles encountered were such as they must inevitably meet in ancient society. The magistrates take action against them in a strictly managed Roman colony like Pisidian Antioch or Philippi, where legality and order reigned ; riotous crowds try to take the law into their own hands in the less strictly governed Hellenistic or Hellenic cities like Iconium and Ephesus and Thessalonica.[2] Lystra is an exceptional case ; but in Lystra the Roman element was weak from the beginning and quickly melted into the older population.[3] Yet how differently does the catastrophe proceed in Antioch and in Philippi, or in Iconium and Thessalonica and Ephesus. The variety is endless, as real life is infinitely varied. A work composed in late time for hortatory purposes would have no such variety, and no such local truth.

Legal proceedings are taken against Paul and his friends in many places, and accusations have to be made in each case according to the forms of the Roman law. The accusation varies in each case ; it is nowhere the same as in any other city ; yet it is everywhere in accordance with Roman forms.

It was a novel case, this teaching. In itself the mere

[1] I lay no stress on the Areopagus Council at Athens, for even the humblest writer of history knew that it was typical of that city ; but the chapter about Athens is filled with the Attic spirit and the scene could be nowhere else.

[2] On the difference of Greek and Roman municipal administration see Statius, " Silvae," III. 5, 85-94, especially ll. 88 and 94. See below, p. 101.

[3] Colony Lystra was founded 6 B.C. ; and Latin was dying out there under Trajan, a century and a half earlier than in Antioch the Pisidian. This character is seen in the incidents at Lystra described by Luke. Still the four Pauline cities were centres of Romanism in this half-Romanized province (p. 86) ; whereas Apollonia rather maintained its Hellenistic memories.

teaching and lecturing was quite permissible by Roman law and practice ; and therefore an accuser had to elicit some crime out of Paul's conduct and to make a charge against him accordingly. In Philippi he had interfered with the livelihood of a small private firm ; in Ephesus he was hindering the trade of a powerful corporation ; in Thessalonica he was preaching about another sovereign, and was thereby guilty of treason to the sovereign (*maiestas*) ; in Corinth he was tampering with the law of the Jews ; in Athens, the University city of the world, he was encroaching on the privileges of the corporation of recognized professors in philosophy, i.e. the four schools.[1] Here again the variety is infinite ; each new case is different from the old, and yet each is natural, each is typical of the society and the period, each rises necessarily out of the preceding situation.

In one case the accusation was blundered badly. At Philippi the accusers appealed simply to the common prejudice against the Jews : this was the weakest form legally that was ever given to the accusation against Paul, and the tardy perception of this weakness made it necessary for the magistrates to apologize on the following day. It was not simply the Roman citizenship of Paul and Silvanus that weighed with them (though that of course was very important) ; it was the fact that after all no real crime, such as would be accepted in the view of the Roman law, was charged against them, but mere anti-Jewish prejudice was deliberately excited. The Imperial policy disapproved that prejudice.

---

[1] Only two of the four schools are mentioned : the Academic and the Peripatetic philosophers take no part. Such variety is natural. The heads of the four schools had a salary from the Emperor, and must be Roman citizens ; Mommsen, "Gesammelte Schriften," Jur. III., p. 388 f.

Again, it is characteristic of an early period in the history of the Christian faith that the religion itself is never made a charge. Beginning from the Flavian period,[1] Christianity was treated as in itself a crime ; the very name constituted a grave charge whose penalty was death. There was never any difficulty in regard to the form of the accusation against any Christian teacher from about A.D. 78 onwards. After that time no accuser would stop to formulate small charges, when this great and capital charge was ready to his hand. Why trouble to get witnesses in support of a less serious accusation, when the great accusation required no witnesses, and was proved by the mere acknowledgment of the accused person, " I am a Christian," and was followed forthwith by the death penalty ?

On this one consideration the argument for the early date of the Acts, and its absolute truth to the circumstances in which the action occurred, might be rested quite securely. Now this is fatal to the theory of a second century date, in any form in which that theory has ever been advanced ; for every form of the theory presupposes that the writer was trying to make a work which would influence his own con-temporaries, and that he was content to use poor authorities or mere oral tradition, distorted by fabricated and miracu-lous accompaniments. The miraculous accompaniments, according to every form of the theory, formed the sufficient proof that the authorities used were poor.

There is one delicacy of terminology—so delicate that it has never been sufficiently noted—which characterizes the language of Acts. We are too apt to think and speak of the population in all those Anatolian cities as Hellenes

---

[1] Some would say " Beginning from the time of Nero," but I have no change to make in my expressed opinion on this subject, " Church in the Roman Empire," p. 242 f.

when we desire to speak accurately; but that is really inaccurate. There was a certain generic character in the population of those cities, if we set aside the Italians, i.e. Roman citizens; but in a Romany colony this native population was the *plebs* (ὄχλος),[1] while in a Hellenistic city like Iconium it was called the Hellenes.   Luke is right in this: he uses the term "multitude" (ὄχλος, *plebs*) at Antioch and Lystra, but Hellenes at Iconium.

Now, as to the motives actuating Paul's accusers, how different they are in different places! how naturally they arise out of the incidents and circumstances! how characteristic they are of Eastern Græco-Roman society!   People are moved to dislike Paul, to regard him as an enemy, and to accuse him of some crime, with the intention of getting him expelled or cut off; but they are moved in diverse ways.   In Cyprus the magician Etymas Bar-jesus feels that Paul is endangering his influence with the Roman governor. In Ephesus the guild of Shrine-makers perceive that Paul is lessening the demand for shrines of the goddess, and destroying their trade.   At Philippi the owners of a fortune-telling slave girl find that she has lost her power when she has stood over against Paul, and that their livelihood is ruined.   In Athens the professors of philosophy discover that Paul is tempting away their auditors, a very trying experience for the ordinary professorial mind.[2]   In many places the Jews cause the trouble, because Paul was a thorn in their side, partly hurting their self-esteem because he placed the despised pagans on the same level of religious privilege

---

[1] The term ὄχλος is used of the native population on the Imperial estates in this part of the province Galatia; "Cities and Bishoprics of Phrygia," I. p. 283.   In a colony the population consisted of (1) the *coloni*, brought in from Rome, (2) the *incolæ*, who are native and non-Roman.

[2] *Experto crede :* I speak as a professor in two Universities, and have seen it in many cases.

with them, partly interfering with the standing and income of the synagogue by drawing the God-fearing Gentiles away to follow himself: these persons, who formed a fringe of believers attached externally to the Jewish faith, must certainly have constituted a source of income to the synagogue as well as of social influence to the "Nation of the Jews" in the city.[1]

There is, however, one case in which the forms of the Roman law are not observed. What is the reason for that? The exception is Athens, and Athens was a free city which governed itself according to its own laws in its ancient fashion through its own courts. Here Paul appears before the old Athenian Court of Areopagus which had been highly important in the old Athens of early Greek history, and which became again very important in the University city of Imperial times.

The proceedings here have no analogy to the stricter procedure of a Roman court. Things are done in an easy-going fashion. There appears in the scene what Statius calls the *libertas Menandri*, the free life of a Greek city which Menander knew and expressed in his verses. We praise in Statius the correct appreciation of the difference between the Hellenic spirit of city life and the spirit of a Roman municipality; and we comprehend his love for Naples, a city of mixed origin, half Greek and half Roman, where the stricter Roman spirit was tempered with the freer Greek tone:

"What need to praise the 'sea-born city,' where the freedom of the Attic Comedy prevails, where Roman dignity is mixed with the Greek capriciousness?"

[1] The term " nation of the Jews " was technical as designating this people in the Empire, forming part of it, yet distinct from all the rest and recognized as distinct by the administration. No other " nation " was permitted within the Empire. The national distinction was non-Roman, servile and hostile, p. 56.

Quid laudem litus libertatemque Menandri
Quam Romanus honos et Graia licentia miscent ? [1]

We should equally admire the delicate truth with which Luke in his narrative catches the soul of both Roman and Greek life, and exhibits them to us in the account of what befell Paul at the various cities that he visited. Here you have real life in all its truth and variety, expressed with a vividness which can spring only from the eye-witness telling what he saw and heard.

Yet, instead of appreciating this exquisite picture of Athenian life, many scholars persist in misinterpreting Areopagus as the Hill, instead of the Court. It is really astonishing, sometimes, to see how commentators prefer the darkness to the light, and error to truth.

As the visit of Paul to Athens has been referred to, and as the true interpretation of the incident depends on the meaning assigned to the term Areopagus,[2] it will be well to add a few words on this point. The leading teachers of two out of the four great philosophical schools " brought Paul before the Areopagus," i.e. the Council of Areopagus, and set him in the midst of the Council. These words are commonly interpreted " brought him to the hill called Areopagus, and set him in the middle of the hill ". Which is right? It is not intended here to discuss this matter as a whole; it has been treated in " St. Paul the Traveller"; but merely to add a fuller discussion than is there given of one point, viz. the meaning of the term Areopagus. This discussion is intended to illustrate the importance of noticing dialect and even colloquialism in studying the Acts and the narrative of Paul's journeys.

A familiar example in English usage will illustrate and

---

[1] Statius, " Silvae," III. 5, 93 f.   [2] Ἄρειος πάγος.

explain the importance of this point. We commonly use the term " the House," when we are speaking of Parliament. This is a colloquialism, which has become almost admissible in literature. In Oxford familiar usage " the House " means Christ Church. To some " the House " is the Stock Exchange, to others the poorhouse. One can tell a great deal about the experiences of a stranger by noticing his use of technical terms peculiar to certain places. In the Athenian scene Luke uses Attic terms with perfect naturalness and correctness.

It shows how carelessly statements are made in denial of the new and reasonable interpretation of Acts that even Blass, a scholar who in respect of Attic usage is usually most accurate, denied that the term Areopagus could by any possibility be used in the sense of the Council; and as-serted that it is used only to mean the actual hill.[1] The denial is unjustifiable and incorrect. There are at least two cases in which the word Areopagus ("Ἄρειος πάγος) desig-nates the Council, and cannot possibly mean the hill : these are an inscription of Epidaurus,[2] and Cicero Att., I. 14, 5.

The latter case shows the character of this usage : it is colloquial Attic : Cicero heard it in Athens when he resided there, and he used it in familiar speech and letters. The man who employed the word in this way knew the current way of talking in Athens. In ordinary conversation the formal expression " The Council of the Areopagus "[3] was cumbrous ; a vivacious people like the Athenians would not spend so much time on a name ; and in ordinary conversa-

---

[1] In his Commentary, p. 190, stating reasons against this interpretation, he concludes : *quod maximum, non dicitur* "Ἄρειος πάγος *nisi de loco.*

[2] Cavvadias " Fouilles d'Epidauros," I., p. 68, No. 206.

[3] ἡ ἐν Ἀρείῳ πάγῳ (or ἐξ Ἀρείου πάγου) βουλή : τὸ ἐν (or ἐξ) Α. π. δικαστήριον or συνέδριον.

tion they shortened the designation to the simple form " the Areopagus ".

Cicero, a stylist and a purist in language, would use no vulgar term. He is a perfect witness that " Areopagus " in educated Athenian conversation was used to mean the Council in the first century B.C. The other example belongs to the period A.D. 50-100. This usage was heard in Athens by Paul and his friends. The whole account is expressed by Luke in the tone and style of language in which the action was transacted. That is a fair specimen of the marvellous lifelike and truthful character of the book in even such small details. This scene is bathed in the light of Attic suns.

The preceding two examples were quoted in my first discussion of the subject.[1] I think that there are others, though the Lexicon of Pape-Benseler goes too far when it says that " Areios pagos designates sometimes the hill, but mostly the judgment-hall or the Council itself". Many of the examples which it quotes for the latter sense might be explained as cases of synecdoche, the hill being used for the Council that met originally on the hill. Some of the examples, however, would perhaps pass muster ; and, obviously, such a figure of the formal literary speech would naturally and inevitably pass into the colloquial usage, as described ; but we may leave it to students of the Attic dialect to inquire more nicely.

The two examples quoted already are sufficient proof of Attic colloquial usage ; and to them may be added Seneca, who in " de Tranq.," v., speaks of Athens as " the state in which was Areos pagos, a most revered judgment-council ". Though Seneca is writing Latin, he quotes the Greek word,

---

[1] " St. Paul the Traveller," p. 261.

spelling it in Latin letters,[1] so that he is a witness for the Greek usage, contemporary with Paul. Valerius Maximus speaks in pure Latin of " that most holy Council the Areopagus " ;[2] it might indeed be argued that what is true of a Latin term may not be true of the corresponding Greek term in Greek usage ; but it seems probable that Valerius would not have used Areopagus thus, if the Greek term was incapable of bearing the same sense.[3] He also is of the first century after Christ.

These examples prove the Attic usage as belonging to the educated colloquial speech of the Pauline period. We hear with Paul's ears and see with his eyes in Athens, just as we do at Lystra (see chapter III.).

---

[1] *In qua civitate erat Areos pagos, religiosissimum iudicium.* The Latin term is Areopagus, but the single word is practically never used in Greek.

[2] " Val. Max.," II. 64, *sanctissimum consilium Areopagus.*

[3] None of the four examples are quoted by Pape-Benseler, though they are so strong on their side. The last two are in Wetstein's Commentary.

CHAPTER VIII

THE MAGICIANS IN THE ACTS OF THE APOSTLES

A MARKED and interesting fact in the society of that period was the influence of magicians and soothsayers. They were extraordinarily numerous. It may be confidently said that in the Græco-Roman world there were few cities, if any, even of moderate size that did not possess several of them. They were to be found everywhere, for they catered to the taste of a large portion of ordinary pagan society.

Very few in that age were wholly superior to the belief in magical power, and not many could refrain throughout their life from recourse at some time and in some crisis or trouble to the help offered through magical arts. It is true that many, including all the more educated and thoughtful and respectable part of pagan society, believed that sorcerers were dangerous, disreputable and maleficent; they warned young people against having any intercourse with them;[1] but the reasons which actuated the wiser and more religious or philosophical section of society, and caused this antipathy, betray a general belief in the powers which the sorcerers could exert. People disliked the practisers of magical arts, not because they were mere impostors whose claims were false, but because they really possessed powers which they misused for evil purposes. They were hated,

---

[1] An example of this can be found in the early part of the Pseudo-Lucian's "Onos," where the reckless young man is portrayed as eager to see some examples of magical powers, and as warned vainly by a good friend.

(106)

because they were feared. Such incredulity as Lucian professes, such frank and sweeping ridicule of magicians as mere quacks, was rare; and in truth, while Lucian describes individual impostors as mere cheats, he does not express disbelief universally in the real existence of such powers.

The current conception of magical powers was that they were means of interfering with the order of nature, non-religious and illicit; and people resorted to magicians mainly in the hope of procuring what they could not obtain, or were unwilling to seek for, through prayers and acts of religious character. Religion could work wonders; magic could work wonders; the marvels wrought by magic, however, were unnatural and involved a secret and illicit tampering with the proper and moral government of the universe. Magic loved secrecy and darkness; religion was open and fair.

The ancient art of magic has been much studied in recent times, and forms the subject of a large number of treatises. The discovery of new documents has been less important than the fresh study of those which had long been known, chief among which was a most important manuscript in Paris, full of magical records. The discovery of the new documents—some of these being in themselves of a very foolish character, mere charms and spells intended to avert evil expressed in a meaningless jargon, or senseless repetition of formulæ, for puerility is a general characteristic of the magical writings—directed attention to the old, as the new had to be published and the old had to be studied to throw light on them.[1]

---

[1] The Bibliography is very fully given by M. H. Hubert in Daremberg and Saglio, " Dict. des Antiq. Grec. et Rom.," under " Magia," III. 1495 ff.; more recent literature in Professor H. A. A. Kennedy's " St. Paul and the Mystery Religions ".

Moreover, the deeper and more intelligent study of ancient religion has incidentally led to the study of ancient superstition and magic as throwing light on religion. Pagan religion and superstition are allied, and the transition from one to the other is easy ; witness the difficulty in determining whether Deisidaimonia and the cognate adjective in Acts XVII. 22 are to be understood in a good sense as religion or in a bad sense as superstition :[1] witness also the teaching of many, stated most pointedly to us by Lucretius, that there was no distinction between the two, that religion was the cause of infinite evils, that it dominated and distorted the minds of men, tormenting them always with unreal terrors and leading them in their fears to seek to save themselves by hideous crimes and even by sacrificing their own children.   All men were praying or wishing for Salvation ; they tried to win it through religion, and they tried to gain it by magical arts and superstitious practices [2] (see chapter XIII.).

Magicians could make the moon come down from heaven, raise the dead, make animals and stones speak, change men into animals and animals back again into men, and do other marvellous things.[3]   These things proved the magicians'

---

[1] I do not doubt that Paul had the good sense uppermost in his mind ; but the bad is always close at hand ; and many educated hearers in ancient times, especially the Epicureans who were prominent among Paul's Athenian opponents, had the double sense always before them and in truth consistently held that all religion was superstition.   See " The Teaching of Paul in Terms of the Present Day," p. 279 f., and above in Chapter VII.

[2] On the nature of their conception of " Salvation," and on its relation to the Christian conception expressed by the same word, the present writer has written in " The Teaching of Paul in Terms of the Present Day," pp. 10, 94 f., etc.: also in Chapter XI. of the present book.

[3] This paragraph is only a statement in brief of the description given by Monsieur H. Hubert in Daremberg and Saglio's " Dict. des Antiq." s.v. " Magia," III. p. 1895.   See also E. Le Blant on Artemidorus in " Mémoires de l'Acad.," XXXVI. pt. II. ; and Cumont, " Astron. and Religion," Index.

power ; but the populace resorted to them mainly for help in the difficulties and troubles of life. Lovers sought charms and means of enslaving the minds or possessing the person of the objects of their affection. People in general sought protection against thieves, or recovery of lost property, or rain in drought, or calm weather at sea, or the prevention of hail-storms dangerous to the corps, or the cure of diseases, or prosperity and fertility in farming and in business generally, or any of the thousand things that men desire ; and where they shrank from praying the gods for these objects, if illicit and likely to be refused by the divine power, or where they had prayed and prayed in vain in the way of religion, they tried to obtain them by magical arts. Especially where people desired to injure or hurt those whom they disliked, they could not hope that the gods would aid them, and they had recourse to magic.

Magic was in close relation to astrology, though the two domains must be distinguished. Strictly speaking, magic aims at modifying the course of events, which astrology predicts ; but the modification is effected by knowing and misusing the forces and powers through which the motions of the heavenly bodies affect the life and fortunes of individuals.

Similarly, magic rules a realm distinct from alchemy. The magicians made use, or tried to make use, of the processes taught through alchemy and discovered by alchemists. Yet, inasmuch as the methods and aims of the latter were commonly wild and unscientific and their processes were expressed in forms that partook of the secrecy and mystery of magic, the relation between the two was close.[1]

Again, divination in all its forms, the art of prophecy, the

[1] See the extracts from Zosimos in Notes to Reitzenstein's "Die hellenistischen Mysterienreligionen ".

interpretation of dreams, necromancy, etc., are more or less closely allied to magic. Necromancy especially must be directly classed as a branch of magic.

Yet divination and prophecy, in their origin, are both religious, and their magical employment comes through the eterioration of religion.

There was a widespread and deep-seated feeling in the pagan mind, that the divine power was always ready and even desirous to communicate its will to men, and that the signs which reveal the divine intention either are clearly visible around mankind, if men have only the will and the skill required to read the signs (divination), or are revealed to the mind and soul of men (prophecy).

Intimations of the divine will were conveyed especially through phenomena occurring in the atmosphere or in the heavens, such as the flight of birds, thunder and lightning, etc., and through the appearance (external and internal) and behaviour of the victims offered by men in sacrifice. The art of reading all those signs was the pseudo-science of divination, which was very liable to be tortured into forms nearly allied to magic, because that element of "the secret, the incomprehensible, the marvellous, and the absurd or unnatural," which is essential to and characteristic of magic,[1] is rarely wanting in any of the forms of the elaborated divination.

Prophecy was of a higher order, and spoke more to the reason and the spiritual nature of mankind ; but even prophecy tended to be stereotyped in certain forms, and to be localized at certain places called oracles or prophetic centres, and thus to become almost professional and pseudo-scientific, being subjected to the caprice and ultimately to

---

[1] Hubert, loc. cit., p. 1495 A.

the cupidity of men : where a fee or reward was at stake, the answer must be given, whether or not the prophet was ready to speak.   In this way it came to be often harnessed under the yoke of magic.

It would be an error to regard those magicians as mere pretenders and impostors.   They varied, of course, very greatly as regards character, intellectual power, and the degree of knowledge that they possessed.   A satirist like Lucian may have been ready to look on them all as impostors making money out of their dupes by trickery and sham ; but that simple formula is insufficient to explain the almost universal belief in, and influence of, those persons.

In the first place, some of them had a certain knowledge of the powers and processes of nature : these were the " scientists " of their time.   Such knowledge of natural and physical science as existed at that time they possessed.   In a similar way the alchemists of the mediaeval world were the founders of modern chemistry.   Until within the last few years the problems which the alchemists proposed to themselves for solution (such as the transmutation of metals) were considered by modern chemists to be impossible and delusive ; but the transmutation at which they laboured and experimented, has been brought back within the purview of modern chemistry, as some of the most distinguished scientific investigators hold.   In an American city in 1913 I received a letter from an eminent chemist, who confused me with my more distinguished namesake the Professor of Chemistry in London University : he reminded me of a former visit which I had paid to his laboratory, and invited me to come again to see how much progress he had made in the problem of transmutation since I had last visited him.

Those men practised research with a view to acquiring power and wealth ; but we need not deny that some of them may have become interested in the pursuit of know-ledge, and that this nobler aim may have come to play some part in their lives and interests. Science has raised itself gradually from humble beginnings, humble morally as well as in other ways. Some magicians were, after all, one genus of the "wandering scholar," seeking for a career and a livelihood in the line that they had chosen, and yet liable to become so enamoured of the knowledge which they had at first regarded as a means that they ended by looking on it as an end in itself. Such is a common fact of life.

We should never blind ourselves to this possible side of the ancient magician's character, though we must acknow-ledge that the influence of scientific study on the nobler side of human nature grows stronger as knowledge increases and as the acquisition of it absorbs more completely the faculties of the mind. The love of knowledge has become a far stronger motive as the range of knowledge has widened ; but it was not absolutely wanting in that time, unscientific and superficial as the age was.[1]

In the second place, some (perhaps many) of those magicians in the first century seem to have been the pos-sessors in some degree of that knowledge which has been traditional in the East from remote ages, regarding certain mysterious and obscure powers and processes of the nature of mesmerism, psychic influence, thought-reading, and so on. The character and limits of this domain are too obscure to be more than alluded to ; but probably it is not possible to understand the position and influence of such persons as Simon of Samaria and Elymas Barjesus without assuming that they had some knowledge in this realm as well as in the one described in the immediately preceding paragraph.

---

[1] " Teaching of Paul in Terms of the Present Day," pp. 242 ff.

Probably Simon was more powerful in this occult domain, while Barjesus had more of the character of a student of the powers and processes of nature, in which aspect he was an object of interest to the judicious and philosophic Roman governor of Cyprus.

Yet, in the third place, after all is said that can be said in explanation of the many-sidedness and the possible virtues of the magicians in the Græco-Roman cities, the fact remains that they were a noxious growth, condemned by the educated part of society as evil in action and intention, making a living out of the worst tendencies in human nature, its greed and its fears and its malevolence. They had to live on the credulity of others; they were fighting for life, and did curious things. In this position they had to be always ready, and it was necessary to dupe their devotees by the practice of tricks and mere imposture.

The use of magic rites in the casting out of devils is an important side of this subject, which will come more suitably in the following chapter.

It is needless to enumerate any more of the manifold species of arts and practices that come under the general title of Magic; enough has been said to show its very varied character, and the many diverse types of individual practitioners who would be found among this general class, so widely spread in the Græco-Roman world as we see it portrayed in the Acts. There is no class of opponents with whom the earliest Christian Apostles and missionaries are brought into collision so frequently, and whose opposition is described as being so obstinate and determined, as the magicians. They play a very considerable part in the book of the Acts. At Samaria, at Paphos, at Philippi, and repeatedly at Ephesus, wizards of various kinds meet and are overcome by Peter and Paul. Their diversity is endless. No one is of the same type as another.   They show the infinite variety of nature and truth.

Those scenes of conflict are picturesque; they throw much light on the character of society in the cities; but Luke does not describe them so often and at such length merely because they were picturesque, or because they illustrated the character of contemporary society.   It is not on such grounds that he apportions the space in his highly compressed history.

The magicians possessed certain powers; but the Apostles are exhibited as always possessing far greater. Luke was not averse from recording such instances of the great power which true faith and inspiration conferred; but it would be an error to suppose that this consideration alone furnishes sufficient explanation of the attention and space allotted to encounters with magicians in the Acts. That motive, taken alone, is beneath the level of this historian, who moves and writes on a higher plane.

These incidents, numerous as they are, find a proper place in Luke's history, because he is refuting an accusation that was commonly brought against the Christians.   Like the magicians, so the Christians also were stigmatized by the populace as maleficent, malevolent, and haters of the human race.   The violent antipathy which the mob cherished towards the adherents of the new religion was justified to the world on the pretext that these Christians were like magicians, practising secret rites, unlawful arts, and abominable hidden crimes.   Lucian describes the impostor and quack Peregrinus (who was of the genus, though almost too silly and pretentious for a proper magician) as having been in close relation with the Christians and actually one of their company for a time; but the satirist, true to his purpose of portraying Peregrinus as untrue in everything, makes him out to be even a false Christian and a false magician.

The supposed letter of the Emperor Hadrian to Julius Servianus (Consul III, A.D. 134) is a good witness attesting the popular belief that the Christians dealt in magical arts : " there is no presbyter of the Christians that is not an astrologer, a diviner, and a professional carer for people's physical condition ".[1] Though the letter is fictitious, it none the less shows what was the popular belief about the Christians, and it is quoted by Vopiscus as a proof of his statement to that effect.

Luke makes no direct answer to this or any other charge against the Christians. He merely exhibits in history the Christians as inevitably in conflict with all magicians and as invariably superior in power to them. The magicians are set over against the truth of Christianity, as having neither part nor lot in the faith, as causing evil and bitterness all around them, as children of the devil, enemies of all righteousness, distorters of the truth, and also as feeble impostors who shrivel into nothing in the light of the sun and the pure reality of life. Such are the actual words that the persons in the narrative use, and the facts that the historian relates.

For this purpose it is necessary to show the Apostles frequently in contact and contrast with the magicians and wizards and soothsayers and exorcists and practisers of

---

[1] *Nemo Christianorum presbyter non mathematicus, non haruspex, non aliptes.* Deissmann prefers to render *aliptes* " quacksalver," " Bible Studies," p. 336 (" Bibelstudien," p. 18 f.) ; but I think that the original and proper sense of the word was not wholly lost here (compare what is said in the following chapter on the interest shown by Christian missionaries in the physical health of the people). Vopiscus himself, in quoting the letter, renders *aliptes* as *medicus;* the letter of Hadrian is in " Script. Hist. Aug. Saturnini," 8.

curious arts, and thus to demonstrate completely the invariable antagonism between them, and the immeasurable superiority, even in superficial acts of power, that belonged to all who were really possessed of the Spirit.

There was, of course, a certain generic character, a sort of family likeness, that attached to all magicians and to the practice of magical arts, and this generic type would be familiar to any late compiler of past history. Such a compiler in a later age might have introduced specimens of the genus magician in his narrative; but the mere inventor or repeater of stories about collisions in long past time between his religion and the power of evil could never attain the infinite variety of real life and truth. He had a didactic object which would control the narrative and impart a generic sameness to the incidents.

The incidents described in the Acts, however, are so individual and so varied that they must come from actual life. The stories are true to life because they are so diverse, while all belong to one generic type. No one magician was exactly like any other, and no one magician in the Acts is like another. They varied widely in their degrees of knowledge, in their command of the occult Oriental power, and in the extent to which they admitted mere trickery and legerdemain to supplement their knowledge and powers.

It is proposed, therefore, in the next chapters to look at each of the encounters from this point of view, and to show very briefly how individual each is, amid the generic type. Every one of these stories derives light from the recent study of ancient magic, and is far more full of meaning to those who are most familiar with the results of that study.

Note.—The possible existence of the higher type of magicians is illustrated on page 139.

CHAPTER IX

SIMON THE MAGICIAN

THERE is a marked analogy between Simon of Samaria and Alexander of Abonoteichos in Paphlagonia, whose career of imposture is described by Lucian. There is, of course, a certain difference in individual character. Simon makes the impression of having been in rather less degree than Alexander a mere impostor and quack, and in rather greater degree a real possessor of power; but Lucian aims at effect rather than at truth, while Luke aims at gaining effect through absolute truth. Yet those who would understand the position of Simon should read the account of Alexander.

Simon had gained great influence through certain wonders and miracles that he had wrought in Samaria. These struck the people with astonishment (vv. 9 and 11), and they were so deeply impressed that they regarded the magician as a manifestation of the divine power in human form. He was an epiphany (to use the Greek term), or avatar (to use the Hindu), of that Supreme Power, of which even the gods themselves are only partial and inferior envisagements and embodiments. The Samaritans called him the "Power of God which is called Great," a very remarkable title. An excellent parallel occurs in a Lydian inscription : "There is one God in the heavens, great Mên the Heavenly, the great power of the ever-living God ".[1]

---

[1] Keil and Premerstein, "II Reise in Lydien," p. 110, μεγάλη δύναμις τοῦ ἀθανάτου θεοῦ.

The word " power " (δύναμις) was technical in the language of religion, superstition, and magic, and was one of
the most common and characteristic terms in the language
of pagan devotion. " Power " was what the devotees respected and worshipped ; any exhibition of " power " must
have its cause in something that was divine.[1] The wonders
that Simon could perform were exhibitions of the power,
through which he was marked out as being no ordinary
magician, but the epiphany of the supreme power of God.
The term " power " in plural was used to denote actions
exhibiting power like that of God. The goddess who
" makes impossibilities possible " is thanked in a Phrygian
inscription.[2]   The nearly synonymous term " authority "
is mentioned later in this chapter.

The word " great " also was in religion one of the most
characteristic.   Men prayed to any god whom they worshipped as " great " and they revered his " greatness ".[3]
The " greatness of God " was equivalent to the " power of
God ".

Simon in his turn was struck with astonishment at the
effect exercised in Samaria by Philip, who swayed the minds
of men in a way that any magician would have longed to
equal.   Such influence over the human mind was what
magicians aimed at ; through such influence men became
their slaves and devoted servants.   Simon's attention was

---

[1] It is unnecessary to give examples of the use of δύναμις bearing on this
subject in writers and inscriptions. See Buresch " aus Lydien," p. 113, a
dedication to the goddess, ε(ὐ)λογῶν σου τὰς δυνάμις.

[2] " Cities and Bishoprics of Phrygia," I. p. 153 f.

[3] Examples in " Church in the Roman Empire before 170," p. 141 ff., and
" Cities and Bishoprics of Phrygia," I. p. 151.   On gems we find μέγα
τὸ ὄνομα Σαράπιδος, and in Aristides, I. p. 467 (Dind.), μέγας δ 'Ασκληπιός, an
important parallel justifying the accepted text of Acts XIX. 28, where I inclined to follow the reading in Codex Bezae.

arrested, and he came over to join the company of Philip, and believed, and was even baptized. He thus had the opportunity of observing in detail the proofs of Philip's power in the exhibitions of it which took place.

In short, Simon recognized the power of God. The powers of this world recognized the true power of God. Even the devils believed and trembled. It is a universal feature in these encounters with magicians, that the latter with their sensitively organized physique always recognize the divine power inherent in the Apostles and messengers of God; they feel themselves in the presence of a power greater than their own. They are astonished, and the astonishment shows itself in different ways in the various incidents of this class.

Simon for a time was apparently one of the faithful followers of Philip; but it appeared after a little that he was only a disciple and pupil anxious to learn the secret of this power and the way in which it could be wielded. He was eager to improve in his own line of life. He felt that he was in the presence of a more powerful magician, and he was ready to become a pupil in the hope of attaining to be an Adept.

All the wonders which Philip wrought were in the way of healing; people possessed with evil spirits and afflicted with palsy or lameness were cured. The want of all medical attention, and the utter ignorance of nursing and the care of the sick, constitute a most painful feature in the life of an eastern village or town at the present day. In Asiatic Turkey there are nowhere, except in a very few of the greatest cities, any trained doctors, or any one possessed even of rudimentary acquaintance with nursing or the art of medical attention; that whole side of life is left to the Christian missionaries; and even those who have no special training have learned in civilized life some small degree of medical knowledge which is useful and which helps to give them influence. Mere living in a rational and sanitary fashion may seem to us to require no medical skill ; but, when one beholds the character and consequences of the rude village life in Asiatic Turkey, one learns that it is the result of skill and the practical embodiment of science and experience.

There is undoubtedly no surer or quicker way to the hearts of men than through some small help given to them or their families during sickness.

Although Philip treated the sick, so far as we are told, only through their soul and their minds, and is not said to have given them any medical care in the strict and proper sense, yet there is implied in VIII. 7 some kindly attention to, and thought for, sufferers ;[1] and this is always a passport to the hearts of an uncared-for population. Amid the suffering caused in an Asiatic Turkish village through ignorance and the utter lack of attention or nursing, nothing has more deeply impressed the present writer than the fact that a word of interest and kindliness with a letter of introduction, or even the simple advice to go to some American missionary or some British consul's wife, trained as a nurse and able to advise, has elicited the warmest gratitude, shown in both deeds and words.

The position of Philip in Samaria is best comprehended by those who have seen such social conditions as those which have just been described.

This character was given to the Christian teaching and life from the outset. The Saviour's compassionate care for

[1] Mr. F. C. Eeles mentions to me a book by F. C. Puller, "The Anointing of the Sick in Scripture and Tradition," London, 1904, which I have not seen.

the physical health of all sufferers is a remarkable trait—
remarkable when we consider how unprecedented it was.
The careful study of physical health is, in truth, a feature
of, and a factor in making, the higher civilization.   It belongs to the most progressive races, and is almost wanting
in the unprogressive nations.   The Turks, in some respects
a very kindly people, have generally treated their own sick
and wounded with a callousness that seems to us brutal ;
but it does not really imply that the intention is brutal :
it is rather akin to the spirit that makes birds kill any
sickly neighbour of their own species : the invalid cannot
be tended and its existence weakens the whole community.

The ancient Greeks gradually raised medicine to the
rank of a true science, and among their achievements in
the development of knowledge, the enthusiastic study of
medicine by many of their race is perhaps the greatest.

The same character can be observed throughout the early
centuries of Christian history ; see the remarks on the subject in " Pauline and other Studies in Christian History,"
pp. 380, 402 ; " Luke the Physician and other Studies in
the History of Religion," pp. 352, 404 f., and above all
Harnack in " Texte und Untersuchungen," VIII. ; also
" Analecta Boll.," XII. p. 297,[1] and Puller quoted already.

In Asia Minor and Greece proper, especially in the
former, early religion was not wholly devoid of this interest.
The importance of medicine is recognized in the medical
skill of the god Asklepios, in the personification of Health,
Hygieia, as a goddess, and in the attribution to many gods
of a certain healing power.   At the great religious centres
of Asia Minor some sort of primitive medical advice and
even medical care was imparted.   The advice was often

---

[1] On treatment of diseases, see Prof. Macalister in Hastings' " Dict. Bib.,"
s.v. Medicine.

addressed to the mind and designed to work through faith, and it was sometimes of a puerile or even of a merely superstitious character; but there are traces of better things. The statements of cures recorded by the sufferers [1] rarely mention any treatment that partakes even in the smallest degree of rational curative discipline; they usually record only puerile forms of medical agency; but such narratives, written by untrained and superstitious persons, must not be taken as fully trustworthy and complete. Those ignorant people would record all that seemed to them to attest the direct work of the god or the goddess, and would pass over anything in the way of mere ordinary medical treatment or advice as unimportant, because it did not glorify the divine power. To us the medical attention seems the really important matter, but to those devotees it was a negligible detail.

That side of the early Greek and Anatolian religion tended to degenerate in the later age; but the Greek medical authorities caught it up as a science, took it out of the domain of religion, and carried it to a high level of scientific achievement.

There is no authority in what is recorded, and not the smallest probability, that Simon had hitherto been appreciative of this side of life; but he now was struck with it when he saw the position and influence that Philip acquired. As the sequel proved, he did not understand that it was the appeal to the soul and spirit, and to the higher nature, of his hearers, that gave Philip his power over the people. He thought that Philip possessed an art and a system of knowledge which could be acquired and used by others. Moreover, it is not in itself improbable, and it is even suggested

[1] The records have been found at Epidaurus, and published by Cavvadias.

by what is said, that at the beginning Simon was really affected in some degree by the sympathetic and human aspect of the situation in Samaria, though he was not able to maintain himself on this higher plane of conduct, but gradually relapsed to the ordinary level of the struggle for existence. It is very far from rare to find individuals and whole peoples who in the enthusiasm of a great crisis are able to rise to a high level of self-denying action ; but the hard thing is to live permanently on that plane. Considerations of a lower class come in ; one must live ; it is a matter of life and death for us ; and gradually or suddenly there ensues a relapse to the old level and below it ; the last state is worse than the first.

When Peter and John came to Samaria, and through their prayers and their hands the Divine Spirit was communicated to the Samaritan Christians, Simon perceived that the marvellous powers which he had wondered at and admired when he saw them exercised by Philip could be readily transferred to others. He imagined that the visible process of the laying on of hands was the way of transferring the powers. He had no perception of the spiritual change, the transformation of heart and soul, that had occurred in the recipients. He had himself undergone no such change, and he did not know that it had taken place in others. He fancied that the Apostles, being possessed of such remarkable powers, were able further, by mere imposition of hands, to make these powers pass into those to whom they chose to impart them.

Now the acquisition of power like this had always been Simon's object. He thought that these teachers belonged to the same class as himself, and that they aimed at influence and a career, with wealth as the ultimate reward. They possessed a knowledge and a power that he coveted, and he proposed to learn from them at a great fee,[1] so that they might pass him rapidly over the earlier stages and carry him quickly to the highest stage of initiation. He regarded this as a fair business proposal. He was willing to pay well for all he asked. "Give me too this power (literally, position of authority),[2] that on whomsoever I lay my hands he may receive the Holy Spirit." He had caught the language of the new teaching; but he had no conception what was the meaning of that term, "Holy Spirit," which he used. His employment of the term "authority" proves this: the point is important, and needs careful notice.

This Greek word, rendered variously as "authority" or "power" (ἐξουσία)[3] is frequently used in magical documents, and Simon employs it precisely in the same fashion as a magician would, when he asks Peter and John to give him the same authority and power that they possessed (VIII. 19). This same Greek word was used to translate both the annual *potestas* that was entrusted to the Emperors (containing the whole authority and power of the Roman tribunes), and the *imperium* of the Roman consuls: it indicates the full powers granted by the ultimate sovereign authority to an individual. The Roman tribunes were entrusted with that extraordinarily wide and overriding power: any single tribune could step in and arrest by a word

---

[1] The Greek says only χρήματα, moneys; but the sense of the context implies that the sum was large in proportion to ordinary fees paid by pupils to teachers.

[2] The word ἐξουσία is used here and universally in the same sense: so for example in 1 Corinthians XI. 10 the veil is the authority of the woman. A veiled woman is a power in the East: unveiled, she is a thing despised whom anyone may insult; see "Cities of St. Paul," p. 203.

[3] In its more characteristic usage, especially in Roman time, it denotes legal and constitutional power; but Thucydides has it in the sense of might as distinguished from right.

the action of the highest magistrates in order to guard the rights of the humblest citizen : only in certain circumstances the *imperium* could, in its turn, override even the tribunes. Such was the "authority" of a great magician.

Peter's reply, which is too familiar to need quotation in all its length, and which must not be weakened by excision of parts, was almost incomprehensible to Simon. That it was a refusal and an indignant refusal, and that nothing could be gained by offering a higher fee at this moment, he understood clearly ; but the nature of his fault and the reason for the Apostles' indignation he utterly failed to comprehend. Their thought and their life moved on a plane to which he could not rise. As before, so still he thought that the power lay entirely in the Apostles ;[1] they could help if they were willing ; the authority to bind and to loose was with them ; the people with whom they dealt were mere automata to be moved hither and thither as they chose. "Pray ye for me to the Lord, that none of the things which ye have spoken come upon me." His own soul and nature did not matter in his estimation ; the prayers of Peter and John were all-important ; and there can be no doubt that he thought of their prayers as similar in nature to the charms and incantations of his old magic.

The relation of Simon to the really Christianized converts among the Samaritans recalls to my memory the experience and testimony of a friend, a foreigner, a Catholic, and a distinguished scholar, who spent a considerable time in the Belgian Congo investigating the facts of the rubber

---

[1] Though Peter alone speaks, as the leading spirit of the pair, yet action and power were common to both. The plural is used throughout, both in verses 17 to 19 and in 24 f. Indeed we must always remember that John was still very young : this is an essential factor in the situation, too often forgotten.

trade. Expressing high admiration of the Baptist missionaries, he said that the Catholic missionaries made a hundred
converts where the Baptists made one ; but the one was a
real convert, a man of changed character, while the hundred
remained savages as they were before. Simon the converted
remained in his innermost nature exactly the same as he
had been before.

In this first recorded collision with a practiser of magic
arts, the strongest stress is laid on the utter incapacity of
the magician to understand the nature and character of the
Christian teaching, on the essential and inevitable antagonism between him and it, and on the indignant contempt with
which his proposals are rejected and he himself practically
expelled from the Church.   Not merely was it advisable to
give strong expression to this antagonism on the first occasion : it was necessary also to do so for another reason.
At the first general meeting of the Church the outward
phenomena accompanying possession by the Holy Spirit
(Acts II. 3 f., 8, 11-13, 15-18) show unmistakable analogy
to certain phenomena that occur at a " spiritualistic séance " :
the sound as of a wind pervading the house is characteristic,
and the other phenomena are similar.[1]   In such phenomena
as those of " spiritualism " lay the powers of the magicians
(as has already been said).   The analogy in certain external
respects should not be denied, but also it should not be
misunderstood or exaggerated.

The incident of Simon the Magian furnished the means
to correct any misunderstanding.   The analogy is practically acknowledged in the narrative, for Simon finds that
the Apostles do far more effectively what he would like

[1] I take this from a letter which Andrew Lang sent me on the subject. I
doubt not that he has said the same in some of his books, but cannot quote.

to be able to do himself. Then this fancied similarity is shown to be external and unreal.

It is, however, characteristic of Luke's method that this acknowledgment and antagonism are not formally expressed in the way of reflection or exposition by the historian. They appear only in the acts and words which he records. He does not obtrude his own opinion and judgment. He leaves the facts to speak for themselves.

In the second place, Simon's full recognition of the superior power of the Christian teachers must be noticed. Other magicians recognize the same fact, but they behave in very different ways and give expression to it in diverse forms, as we see in the remaining cases (on which see the following chapter).

This acknowledgment by the magician of the Christians' power, however, had a dangerous side. The populace saw that the magicians recognized an analogy between themselves and the Christians, acknowledging the superiority of their rivals. On this was founded the popular idea that all Christian teachers were "astrologers, diviners, and physicians ".[1] Hence in this case where the analogy is most fully recognized by belief and baptism, the antagonism is most pointedly expressed.

Simon, as a believer and disciple, tries to buy the teaching. None of the other wizards and soothsayers take this attitude. Each tries a different way: one fights vainly against it, some try to steal it, one gently submits.

As the magical use of the Greek term has been touched on in this Chapter, a misconception ought to be guarded against. It is not to be believed that in 1 Corinthians VIII. 9 this word ἐξουσία carries with it any implication of

---

[1] " Script. Hist. Aug. Saturnini," VII. 4, *mathematici, haruspices, medici :* compare *ib.*, VIII. 3 quoted and discussed in the previous chapter.

magical influence or stands in any relation to magical usage;[1] and in this opinion Prof. H. A. A. Kennedy entirely agrees and confirms me. This is one of many cases where Christian expression used as convenient and even necessary for its purposes a word which was involved in one or several pagan connexions and usages. One might as well say that the salvation of which Paul spoke was the same thing that the pagans were praying for and trying to secure by magical rites, as that the " power" which enabled a strong-minded brother to eat without harm of meat offered to idols was in any way the same as the power given through magical arts. Paul means the moral power of the strong mind. How completely the modern scholars who bring him down to the level of pagan superstition and magic fail to comprehend the quality of his thought![2]

The same holds of many other cases in which the same Greek word ἐξουσία is used to indicate the power over evil spirits, as in Luke IV. 36. There is a notable analogy between the Christians' power and the magicians' over those evil forces, but the differences are equally marked : it is only the immediate and external purpose that is the same, viz. exorcism, while the means are different in kind and in manner of operation.

The belief in demoniac possession is here brought into relation to the magicians. It was evidently the cures wrought in cases of this class that were most likely to affect and astonish Simon. This belief was a strong factor in social life in western Asia, and it still is a factor in the life

[1] It is rendered "liberty" in the Revised Version, but this is a mistranslation of the Greek ἐξουσία. The margin has " power".

[2] On the use of such pagan terms as salvation, etc., in a new Christian sense by the earliest Christian writers, see "The Teaching of Paul in Terms of the Present Day," pp. 95, etc., and below, Chapter XIII.

of inner Turkey at the present day. There is much need
for a discussion of the whole subject by competent authority,
which is impossible without medical training. It is beyond
doubt that many ailments which seem to the Orientals to
be of an unusual or abnormal kind are explained as due to
possession by a devil or by devils, though physicians would
certainly class them under some recognized category of
disease ; but the question must be raised whether it would
be safe or justifiable to hold that all cases of so-called demoniac possession could be explained in this way.

Deafness, dumbness, and other defects of the senses, seem
to be classed as possession in Luke IX. 39, Mark IX. 17 and
25, Matthew XII. 22 ; but although an individual case of
dumbness is so classed, it is not clear that every dumb man
would have been declared by the popular voice to be
possessed by a devil. That seems highly improbable
a priori, and quite inconsistent with the account given by
Mark IX. 17 : it is also not confirmed by anything that I
have learned about current beliefs in Asiatic Turkey. The
essential feature in the case described by Mark was not the
dumbness, but the abnormal behaviour of the boy.

While I do not presume from the little I have seen to
make any positive statements, yet on the ground of what I
have heard and what I saw in the one case that came under
my own observation, I should be inclined to think that the
essential feature is an effect produced on the mind and
nature of the sufferer, whereby he seems given over wholly
to the dominion of wickedness, doing and suffering evil
without any good impulse striving to counteract the wicked
intent, abandoned absolutely to the sway of maleficence and
malevolence and apparently lost to all human feeling, and
bereft in an extraordinary and appalling degree of even the
outward appearance of humanity, and at the same time

himself suffering pain in his own person from the power of evil in many ways. In the case that I saw, the demoniac (as he was called) had probably suffered injustice, and he was ultimately cured (as was said) by a strolling magician; but we learned later from the magician that he had cured the sufferer through rousing the hope of vengeance in his mind. Thus he taught the man to prefer the future to the present, and restored the sway of reason in his mind. Even though the effect came through a dangerous and malevolent motive, yet at least the result was that the man could balance one consideration against another, and endure the present evil in the hope of compensation hereafter. He was restored in this way to human semblance, and ceased to be wholly under the dominion of one single hideous impulse which would not even have been vengeance on the wrongdoer.[1]

Cases of abnormality, like those described, are specially open to treatment addressed to the mind; and many surprising cures, such as astonished Simon, might be wrought in this way by a powerful and impressive benevolent personality like Philip. Whether this is the whole, or even the most important part of these cures, I would not venture to dogmatize; but at least it puts us on the right way to understand the subject, as I venture to think.

Exorcists were an order in the early Church, and the name lasted long, but their functions were gradually restricted to mere ceremonial of a general kind without reference to the curing of individuals.

The people then believed, as they do now, in the frequency of demoniac possession. At that time the magician's trade

---

[1] The demoniac was trying to tear away a young girl, his daughter, from her mother, and as the villagers said and believed, he was going to carry her off to the hills and murder her.

as a practical business lay to no small degree in this class of cases.   At the present day the two chief lines of business for a magician in a remote Turkish city are said to be in love-charms and exorcism.

The prevalence of the mental phenomena that produce this belief is caused by the ill-balanced nature of the sufferer.   The almost total lack of home training for the child is in fault.   So long as he does not annoy his elders too much, he is left to the freedom of his own caprice. When he does provoke them, he is punished with extraordinary incapacity.   At Djenin in Palestine I looked down over a garden, in which a father was trying to chastise a little boy, and failing to inflict on him any suffering.   The boy screamed and writhed, but only from passion, not from pain.   He was being punished, not for wrong-doing, but because his father was cross ; and he knew that this was so. A child grows like a weed untended, as nature ministers the power of growth.   He is taught no self-control, until it is forced on him in the school of poverty and hard work. Those of better nature, who after all are the great majority, learn for themselves in a remarkable way.   Those who are unbalanced or evil by nature degenerate often until they are said to be possessed by the devil, and seem to be in fits of passion wholly given over unresistingly to the domination of evil.

Note (pp. 114, 127).—It is possible that the same danger was guarded against by the Saviour, when he forbade the devils to recognize him publicly, Mark I. 34, III. 12, Luke IV. 33, 41.   See below, p. 310.

CHAPTER X

PAUL AND THE MAGICIANS

THE germ of all that has been said in this present book regarding the magicians in the Acts was stated formerly in discussing[1] the conflict between Paul and the Magian Etymas Bar-Jesus at Paphos ; and it is not necessary in this chapter to repeat any part of the study of that scene, as there given. All that was there said may be assumed ; but something may be added.

This is the only case in which the natural antagonism between the Christian teachers and the magicians is carried to a direct conflict and trial of strength. Bar-Jesus pits himself against Paul, and forthwith his strength is withered up. The power of the Spirit, looking through the eyes of Paul, pierces him to the soul and temporarily paralyses the nervous system so far as vision is concerned.[2]

That a stroke like this, though marvellous, is physically possible, I cannot doubt. We may be sure that a person who made his livelihood in such ways as Bar-Jesus, possessed a sensitive temperament, and was peculiarly susceptible to the influence that flashed through the gaze of Paul. Those who have studied the range of psychic phenomena could certainly quote cases quite as wonderful.

What was peculiar about this case was that Paul and the other Christian teachers made no claim to have any power

---

[1] " St. Paul the Traveller," pp. 73-81.

[2] A physician would express this in a more scientific way.

in themselves : it was the Divine Spirit that spoke and
acted through them.   Unless we apprehend this fundamental fact clearly, and hold to it throughout, we shall never
understand the Acts of the Apostles.   Pagan contemporaries, and the populace especially, never grasped this : they
thought that Paul was here performing a feat similar in
character to the wonderful acts by which magicians astonished the crowd, but surpassing even the most marvellous
of their deeds.   They ignorantly regarded Paul as the
greatest of the magicians.   Out of this popular fancy
grew the legend of the anti-Pauline party, identifying Paul
with Simon of Samaria, who played such a mean part in
contact with the Hebrew Peter.

Also, we shall never understand the personal achievements of Paul, unless we appreciate the power of his eyes,
through which his soul and the Spirit spoke.   The scene
in the Council, as described above,[1] cannot be properly
conceived until we feel how much is implied in the statement that Paul "fixed his eyes on the members of the
Council".   The memory of Paul's eyes lasted in Asia
Minor, and the tradition there during the second century
described him as having at times the face of an angel :[2]
an angel is the bearer of the Divine power.

To the ordinary pagan observer at that time the scene
would undoubtedly appear like an exhibition by Paul of his
own marvellous command of magic power.   This was a real
danger to the Christians ; and Luke guards against the
consequences (which as he knew had occurred in some
degree before the time when he was writing) by bringing
out so strongly the essential antagonism between the Chris-

[1] See p. 90 f.
[2] The description (quoted in " The Church in the Roman Empire before
170," p. 32) is from the Acta of Paul and Thekla.

tian and the magical intention and spirit.   It was, however,
not easy to disabuse the people and the government of a
fixed idea.   To them both Paul and Bar-Jesus belonged to
the class of "wandering scholars"[1] who were so numerous
in the Roman time, often men educated in the Universities
of the East, who sought a career and a livelihood in the
world and went about till they could find or make a place
for themselves.   The University of Tarsus, in particular,
sent out a large number of scholars, aspiring youths from
the Eastern provinces, especially Cilicia, Cappadocia, and
Syria, who could find no career at home, where culture was
backward and education had hardly touched the masses.
As Strabo tells us, many students from the countries which
furnished the clientele of the Tarsian University went abroad
to study and often they remained abroad.[2]   Paul was understood to be one of those scholars, and those who knew
about his birth and early life would call him one of the
many Tarsian aspirants, and would think that he was seeking to play the same part in the entourage of the Proconsul Sergius Paullus that Athenodorus the Tarsian did with
Augustus.[3]

It must be set to the credit of the Governor that he did
not retain this view permanently.   He wished to know the
truth and to keep his mind open ; and his intelligent curiosity led him to send for the two "wandering scholars," and
to hear what sort of teaching they had to offer.   He began
then by holding the ordinary popular view ; but he soon
changed when he listened.   Precisely how much is im-

[1] "St. Paul the Traveller," p. 75 ; " The Cities of St. Paul," p. 218.

[2] The account which Strabo gives is usually mistranslated, as if he said
that Tarsus was superior to Athens and Alexandria.   On the right interpretation see the " Cities of St. Paul," p. 232 f.

[3] The typical example of Tarsian wandering scholars is Athenodorus, the
tutor and friend of Augustus : " Cities of St. Paul," pp. 216-28.

plied in saying that "he believed" it is not easy to say; but at least it must imply that a very marked impression was produced on his mind and character. Luke does not waste words. On this point more is said in the following chapter XII.

This was the person that Luke introduces as "a man of understanding," i.e. an educated, intelligent man, who did not judge from superficial appearance alone, like the unthinking crowd. The fact that he considered Bar-Jesus worthy of a place among his friends and companions must be taken as a sufficient proof that the latter deserved to be ranked among the higher class of magicians, who had some interest in science and the investigation of the normal processes of nature. So much we may say with confidence : all beyond that is matter of conjecture. Bar-Jesus was regarded by the Paphian populace as one of the magicians, and Paul was classed as another of the same type after his striking exhibition of power. The populace does not usually make delicate distinctions. No serious effect is said to have been produced on anyone at Paphos except the Roman Proconsul, "a man of understanding". So far as the people are concerned the visit to Paphos must be regarded as practically fruitless in Luke's estimation.

At Ephesus many Jews, including the sons of Sceva, of a leading priestly family, were aware of the power which Paul had, calming the passions, and curing the diseases, of many sufferers. It was a situation like that in which Philip and Peter were placed in Samaria. Yet how different is the working out of the entanglement! The sons of Sceva watched Paul to discover the secret of his influence, and detected that it seemed to lie in naming the Name of Jesus over the poor sufferers. They tacitly acknowledged the power, but they were not, like Simon, willing to pay a fair market price (as he thought) for the knowledge; they tried to steal it. They thought they had found the secret; but the Name was valueless without the faith that lay behind it; and when they tried to use the power of the Name, they only exposed themselves to disgrace and discomfiture.

Other magicians in Ephesus frankly confessed their fault, abjured their practices, and burned their books of formulæ. They resembled Simon in his first stage of conduct, and we hear no more about them. Did any of them go on to believe and to seek baptism? We know not; but their action is quoted mainly to reinforce the contention of Luke, that Christian teaching was the enemy of magic.

An instructive account is given in the Acts XVI. 16-18 of the slave-girl, who brought much gain to her owners by sooth-saying. There is little to add to the considerations stated in an earlier work.[1] The slave recognized forthwith the superior spiritual power that breathed through Paul. Her naturally sensitive temperament,[2] trained to even greater sensitiveness by the daily experiences of her life, was aware of Paul's character and influence.

— Here, again, the same danger confronted Paul. The populace would at once interpret the relation between the sooth-sayer and him as the competition between two of a trade. The very words which the slave-girl used suggested this to the people: "These men are slaves of the Most High God, who proclaim to you a way of salvation". All those pagans were praying and making vows and offerings for salvation;[3] their religious acts, their superstitions, and

---

[1] "St. Paul the Traveller," pp. 215 ff.

[2] Only a person with a highly sensitive nervous system can make any success in her way of life.

[3] "The Teaching of Paul in Terms of the Present Day," pp. 94 f., etc.; see also chapter XIII. below.

their recourse to magic rites,[1] were very often directed to attain salvation ; various methods of attaining were pointed out to them in reply to their requests. The sooth-sayer indicates that Paul and his companions are declarers of "a way of salvation ". She speaks of them, too, as "slaves of the Most High God," a title for the Supreme Divine power used among the pagans, and specially characteristic of that mixture of Jewish and pagan religious custom which was common at the time.

The cries with which she followed Paul through the streets were, therefore, troublesome, and constituted an impediment to his success. As he was obviously not a priest of any recognized religion, her words were by the mob taken to show that he was a minister of superstition or of magic. Accordingly, after she had done this "for many days," Paul in vexation turned on her, and spoke, not to her, but to the evil spirit that possessed her, " I charge thee in the name of Jesus Christ to come out of her ". Instantly[2] the spirit and her power left her.

The story is reported by Luke for several reasons, but especially it serves to disprove the charge of magic made against the Christians.

This poor girl was aware of Paul's power; but she neither tried to steal it like the sons of Sceva, nor sought to learn it as a pupil, like Simon. She had the simple mind of a

---

[1] M. H. Hubert in the article quoted at the beginning of the preceding chapter mentions " Salvation " as one of the objects of magic.

[2] Literally " the same hour " : the ancients had no shorter division of time than the hour, viz. the time that the shadow on the dial took to pass from one mark to the next (i.e. one-twelfth of the sun's visible passage across the heavens) : hence this phrase is used (as in XXII. 13) where we should say " on the instant ". Compare Horace, " Sat." I, I. 7. A good example lies in the comparison of Rev. XVII. 12 with the expression of the same thought by Paul in 2 Cor. IV. 17 ; see " The Teaching of Paul in Terms of the Present Day," p. 57.

young girl : she spoke what her sensitive nature perceived. She sought nothing for herself. She was only the slave and the chattel of others. Had she learned any way of greater power, it would have benefited only her owners; but it was apparently no such consideration that weighed with her. She is represented as simple and direct in conduct, acting without ulterior aims. One cannot but feel strong sympathy for this poor benighted soul in her helpless and hopeless condition as the slave of greedy owners.

The suggestion has been made that the owners of this slave-girl were a man and his wife. This seems to be inconsistent with ancient custom and with the situation as Luke describes it. The owners lodged a charge against Paul and Silas. They seized the two missionaries, and dragged them before the magistrates. They claimed to be Romans, who were being wronged by contemptible Jews. Action like this is quite inconsistent with the part that a woman would play in a Roman colony; and we must suppose that the owners were a small company who had clubbed their money to carry on a slave-dealing business.

It used to be maintained that the contest between Paul and Bar-Jesus was invented as a pendant to the story of Peter and Simon the Magian; as Peter in old legend had triumphed over a magician, so Paul also must have his own triumph. Only prepossession with a theory could make critics so blind to the higher qualities and purposes of a historian as to imagine stuff like this. All the differences between the one incident and the other are vital to the historian's purpose. He remembers the second because it was different. Had it been a mere repetition, it would have been valueless to him. Moreover, the author is not content with making his hero (according to the theory) vanquish one magician; he makes him convince a large number, and break their power. Peter does not vanquish a magician; he simply rebukes him for his inability to understand Christian truth; there is no contest of power at Samaria: Simon was a humble pupil, and an unsatisfactory one.

All these magician incidents are equally essential to the historian's purpose. Their variety in details makes their agreement in effect all the more telling; out of the great variety emerges the one invariable result that Christian teaching hated and conquered and destroyed magic, and that the popular charge against the Christians was mere calumny.

Note (Ch. VIII-XI).—The possibility that, as we have stated, some ancient magicians had a higher character and nobler aims than a mere livelihood gained by any means, is supported by the following extract from "The Periodical," Oxford, 1914, p. 90 :—

"In 'The Book of the Key of Solomon' just published by Mr. Milford—supposed to have served as the oracle of all sorcerers throughout history—occurs a paragraph showing that the magic art was looked upon as a serious occupation. It is thus translated by Professor H. Gollancz :—

"'I beg and command any one into whose hands this compilation may fall, that he will give it to no man unless he be of a retiring disposition, able to keep a secret, energetic in the performance of this kind of work ; and I adjure him by the Living God, the Creator of the Universe, that in the same manner as he would guard his own soul, he will guard this book, and not reveal it to such as are unjust. And should he not listen (to this admonition) I place my supplication before Him who has graciously imparted this knowledge to me, that He shall not suffer him to prosper in all the actions and desires which he seeks to bring about. Amen, May this be His will.'"

CHAPTER XI

THE MAGI AT THE BIRTH OF JESUS

IN one passage of the New Testament, the word Magian or magician appears in an incident where a totally different connotation is popularly attached to it from that which it bears in all the other cases. Matthew II. I says: "Now when Jesus was born in Bethlehem of Judea in the days of Herod the king, behold, Magians from the east came to Jerusalem, saying, Where is he that is born King of the Jews?" In making up their conception of the magicians in the New Testament and their encounters with Christianity, modern scholars usually omit this passage and judge of them on the other passages alone, while in this one case it is assumed that the name must refer to a different class of persons.

That procedure is unscientific. There is no ground for thinking that the word was applied to two totally different classes of persons, or that Matthew has in mind one of the two classes, while Luke thinks only of the other. The same class is meant in the New Testament in every case, and our conception of its character must be widened so as to embrace the whole record regarding them. In fact Luke uses the term Magian only of Bar-Jesus. Simon of Samaria is not called a Magian, though the verb and the verbal noun [1] are applied to his way of living and acting. In respect of the other dealers in sorcery and sooth-saying

---

[1] μαγεύων, Acts VIII. 9, μαγία, VIII. II.

none of these words is employed; but terms are used, which indicate other sub-species of the class that we have roughly called magician.

In our view it is necessary to embrace all these incidents under the same class. In Matthew we notice that the Magians were familiar with Jewish books. That is known to have been a characteristic of ancient magic: it was a mixture of ideas and forms and names caught from various religions, including the Hebrew, which was acknowledged to be specially powerful. The acknowledgment was apparently not confined to votaries of the Hebrew faith, but was general in the world where the Hebrews were known. Jews were, by natural character, likely to be adepts in the art of utilizing for their livelihood the weaknesses of human nature: hence Jews of low character, even though they were of high birth, appear among the magicians or exorcists at Ephesus.[1]

The Magians were astrologers. They watched the stars and saw the present and the future written in the heavens. This again is one of the characteristics of the class of magicians.

They were also prophets, in the sense that the divine power spoke directly to their souls. Bar-Jesus was a "false prophet," which implies that he had turned the belief that one should listen watchfully to catch the divine voice into a means of individual gain: he had degraded the best thing in life to the worst. The term "false prophet" does not mean that he did not try to do and to be what prophets did and were; but that he took away the spirit and the truth out of the prophet's life. He was a prophet

---

[1] At Ephesus ἐξορκισταί and τὰ περίεργα πράξαντες are the terms used. At Philippi the slave-girl was a sort of prophetess (μαντευομένη) or diviner (ἔχουσα πνεῦμα πυθῶνα).

who had lost, or never got, the spirit that makes the prophet ; but he wore the outward semblance of a prophet.[1]   So the false brethren of Galatians II. 3 were in outward guise and profession Christians, but lacked the spirit and the soul.

The theory that the story in Matthew is an idle, empty myth, I set aside at once as totally irrational, although it is still widely accepted, and the difficulty is to get people to regard the tale itself as worth discussion.   A myth is not idle and empty, but is well worthy of careful consideration : probably, however, those who call it an idle myth mean that it is a mere piece of popular gossip, but they do not explain how it has found its way into a book which is now regarded by every reasonable scholar as a serious attempt to make a trustworthy record.[2]

There seem to be only two views possible for an unprejudiced and rational thinker to entertain.   One is that the story is the expression of a certain belief regarding the relation of this great event, the Birth of the Saviour, to a certain class of persons who exercised a distinct influence in the ancient world, and to a certain accumulated store of ancient wisdom and teaching which was supposed to be in their possession ; and that this belief clothed itself in mythic form during the gradual growth of a body of Christian tradition in the first century, under the influence of a creative impulse due to half-conscious speculation about the cosmic importance of such an event.   Some who maintain this theory might hold that the Birth of Jesus was a real

[1] In 1 Corinthians XII. 2 Paul says, if I rightly catch the meaning, that there was a kind of inspiration in the faith of dumb idols, and that this inspiration produced a sort of prophecy, which lacked the real divine Spirit.

[2] Dr. Moffatt seems (if I rightly interpret his obscure and brief reference) to regard it as a " free composition," p. 249, having a historical nucleus in " speculation amongst Babylonian astrologers " about the " conjunction of the planets Jupiter and Saturn," which took place in 6 B.C.

event, some that it never occurred ; but that is immaterial
so far as the possible growth of a belief and a myth is concerned.

The other possible view is that the narrative is an account
of a real incident, which was remembered and recorded
because it expressed an important truth. Many things
were forgotten, as less important ; but this was remembered
owing to what was implied in it.

The purpose of the present chapter is to advocate the
second view. It is, however, evident that the meaning
which was implied in the event, and which led to its being
recorded, is open to the other interpretation ; and that the
deep truth which lay in and under the facts might very
well be regarded as a growing and creative idea in the early
Church, gradually working itself out in the myth. I do not
know at present anything that can absolutely disprove this
better form of the myth theory ; and the theory is likely to
commend itself to many, who are repelled by the fact
that Matthew alone mentions the story. In this form
the myth-theory is totally distinct from the view which we
have unhesitatingly rejected, that the story is a piece of
empty gossip. It holds that the belief in the world-wide
importance of the event sought expression in a narrative of
acts done by representative personages, i.e. personages who
exist to give expression to a true idea : the truth is real, but
the acts are only created in order to body forth the idea to
a public which preferred the concrete to the abstract, and
disliked mere philosophic statement as alien to its character
and incomprehensible to its way of thinking. The myth is
the more concrete expression of philosophic truth.

From the view which we have taken in all the chapters
on this subject, it follows that, in the Gospel of Matthew,
the Magians must be taken as representing, or rather as

being the embodiment of, the hereditary store of knowledge in the Oriental world, as knowledge was at that time.

The customary translation "Wise Men," for the name Magians in Matthew II. I, will suit the purport of this chapter well. The "Wise Men" are examples of the best type of the ancient magician. In them the devotion to knowledge and the interest in truth are the most prominent characteristics. They appear in this one incident, they show this supreme quality, and then they disappear. If the narrative about Simon of Samaria had concluded with the statement in Acts VIII. 13, that he "also believed ; and being baptized he continued with Peter," then we should have unhesitatingly classed him with "Wise Men".

Now, as we have observed in all the cases of contact with the new Faith, the magicians recognize intuitively the power of the Spirit that acts through the new teachers. Accordingly in Matthew II. I the Magians became aware, through their own previous investigation into truth, that the new power which must come had come at last into the world, and they travelled far to do homage to the king. They did not fully comprehend the truth, but they believed without understanding.

The Wise Men are the embodiment of the past : they welcome and worship the future. Their visit embodies in concrete form and action, the great truth that the birth of Jesus was the completion of past history and the starting-point of a new age. The expression is Oriental and Hebraic in type, not philosophic and abstract. The best of the extra-Judaic world welcomes its new-born Saviour, but being outside of Judaism it does not fully comprehend.

It is not right, nor is it implied by the terms of the story, to suppose (as is sometimes done) that the Wise Men when watching the heavens in their astrological pursuits saw some wholly new and unexpected star, or other astronomic phenomenon such as a conjunction of planets, and recognized that this must portend the birth of a king of the Jews. Such an explanation does not fulfil the conditions of the story. It is clearly implied in the tale that the Wise Men had other knowledge from other sources, making them expect the coming of some special king of the Jews, whose birth was an event of universal interest to the world. There is implied both a certain store of traditional knowledge, and a certain expectation of the cosmic event. It was not the birth of any common king of the Jews that roused their adoration and prompted their journey. It was some special king whose advent was looked for by them and by all that studied history.

The belief was widespread in the world at that time or earlier that the Epiphany, or coming of a god in human form on earth, was imminent, in order to save the human race from the destruction which the sins of mankind deserved and had brought nigh. The world was perishing in its crimes, and only the coming of the God Himself could save it. This belief can be observed in various forms during the years that preceded. It prompted the Fourth Eclogue of Virgil and it is seen in the Second Ode of Horace. To them it means the glory and the triumph and the permanence of Rome.[1] The West shall rule over the East. A new war of Troy shall be fought, and a new European leader shall conquer the representative city of Asia, and shall restrain the raids of the Median cavalry. That is the "Salvation" which Rome has to offer, as is shown in chapter

---

[1] On the ideas which Virgil derived from Isaiah through a Greek translation and incorporated in that Eclogue, see the last chapter of Part II in the present book.

xv., where the real nature of that paternal government is described as it worked itself out in history.

This belief in the King of the Jews, the Messiah, the Conqueror, was universal among the Jews for a long time before and after the birth of Christ, and was one of the remarkable features in that strange people, which drew the attention of the Roman historian in describing them. Tacitus speaks of the general conviction among the Jews before the great rebellion of A.D. 67-70, a conviction based on the ancient books of their priests, that the East should revive and that men sprung from Judea should rule the world.[1]

Suetonius mentions the same belief, evidently deriving it from the same ultimate source as Tacitus;[2] but points out what was in his opinion the real meaning of the prophecy, viz. that one coming from Judea, to wit Vespasian, should obtain the empire of the world. This was an explanation after the event of a prediction which had been current in the East before the event.

These Roman authorities show what were the forms in which this expectation was current in the pagan world during the century from Virgil to Vespasian. In the Hebrew prophecy the restoration of power to the East, and the end of the domination of the West, were implied; but the Romans understood, and Suetonius carefully explains, that the real meaning was the domination of the West over the East. All, however, interpret the prophecy as referring to the great struggle of East and West, that immemorial conflict which reaches through all history from the beginning

---

[1] Tacitus, "Annals," v. 13 : fore ut valesceret Oriens profectique Iudaea rerum poterentur.

[2] Suetonius, "Vesp.," 4 : esse in fatis ut eo tempore Iudaea profecti rerum potirentur.

down to the present day, and which must continue in the future.

The Magi in the East saw the star, the rising of the Morning Star [1] of hope ; and they, of course, accepted the Oriental interpretation. An Asiatic king, a king of the Jews, had arisen in the world. That the East was struggling against European domination is a great historical fact. Mithradates derived all his importance from being the champion of Asia in the long conflict. He had been destroyed ; but that was only one stage in the struggle. The Magi eagerly welcomed the child, who was born King of the Jews.

It is a narrow view, very different from the truth and the kingdom of Christ. Yet the disciples themselves cherished it, and even after the Crucifixion and the Resurrection they asked, " Lord, dost thou at this time restore the Kingdom to Israel ? " [2] The Magians were pervaded with the ideas of their age and their race ; and it would be absurd to attribute to them conceptions more universal and elevated than those of the Twelve.

They are remembered in history and chronicled by Matthew, not as witnesses to, or believers in, the true character of Christ, but as furnishing by their journey the evidence that the stored wisdom of the world was prepared for the birth of Jesus at this time, and ready to accept Him when He came according to their conception of His mission.

The incident had to be. It was necessary that the world should of itself and through its own natural instinct recognize its Lord. " Then comes the check, the change, the fall."

[1] I accept the general lines of Colonel Mackinlay's interpretation in his book on " The Magi: How They Recognized Christ's Star " (Hodder and Stoughton, 1907).

[2] Acts i. 6.

The world could not maintain itself on this high level of intuition; but for the moment the consciousness that this overpoweringly great event had happened, penetrated to the mind of the Magi.

The same truth is expressed in historical form by Luke. He is a Greek, and has the historian's instinct. In that most wonderful passage, II. 1-3, where he describes the circumstances that led to the birth of Jesus, he brings into the sweep of his conception some of the greatest forces that move through all ancient and modern history, and shows how they cross one another at one point, acting and reacting, and that point is the birth of the Saviour, the central fact in all history.

In Matthew the truth is presented to us in concrete form as a series of acts performed by individuals. There is a certain resemblance here to myth; but it is not a myth, any more than Jesus Himself is a myth. He must come. The whole history of the world leads up to Him, and finds its explanation and justification in Him. That this world with the stored-up wisdom of the past, imperfect as it is, should recognize Him was another event that must be. This is what Paul puts into the form of a "philosophy of history" in Romans VIII.

The story of the Magians appealed to the simpler heart of the Mediaeval world. Painters and sculptors loved it as a subject. Matthew, having to use words only, might omit the number of the Wise Men, but when a painter showed the scene he must represent the actual number, either precisely as two or three, or vaguely as a multitude. During the third century the number is two in a painting in the Catacomb of SS. Peter and Marcellinus; but as early as the fourth century the tradition established itself finally that the number was three; this, however, was merely a result of the artist's need.   The number three is a natural one to select, as believed to be the perfect number, and having artistic advantages : moreover, three kinds of gifts were brought by them.[1]

[1] See V. Schultze, " Christl. Archaeol.," p. 329.

CHAPTER XII

SERGIUS PAULLUS AND HIS RELATION TO CHRISTIAN FAITH

SO far as Sergius Paullus himself is concerned this episode described in Acts XIII. 6-9 seems unmotived and abrupt. He passes for the moment conspicuously across the stage of history, and then disappears. His name seemed almost to have perished, and the first edition of the great "Berlin Dictionary of Roman Biography" in 1898 had little to say about him and nothing about his family;[1] such continued to be the case until 1912 when we began the systematic excavation of Pisidian Antioch, starting with the great Sanctuary on the hill-top overhanging the city some miles away, and continuing in the city proper.

Naturally, this work gave us from time to time the opportunity of gaining access to inscriptions concealed in private houses in the modern town, near the old site. Such inscriptions are always difficult to find owing to the jealousy with which the Turks seclude their homes. In one of these occurs the name of Lucius Sergius Paullus the younger, whom we at once confidently recognized as the son of the Proconsul of Cyprus. Professor Dessau confirms our opinion on this point ; and in a letter which he kindly sent, he adds a brief statement of the family career in Roman

---

[1] " Prosopographia Imp. Rom.," II. p. 221 (1898).

Imperial history, with the comment, "evidently no member of this family was Christian". In this I quite agree, so far as the distinguished members are concerned; but in my turn I ask, "Does this disagree with, or does it confirm what Luke says about the Proconsul?"[1]

The text is engraved in good letters of about A.D. 60 to 100, on a block of stone which once must have formed part of the wall of a building. It was copied at Salir, one of the outlying quarters of Antioch, by Mr. J. G. C. Anderson and myself in 1912.

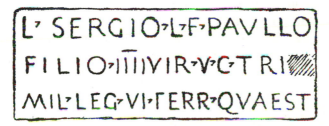

FIG. 2.—In honour of Sergius Paullus.

L Sergio, L(uci) f(ilio), Paullo filio, quattuorvir(o) v(iarum) c(urandarum), tri[b(uno)] mil(itum) leg(ionis) vi Ferr(atae), quaest(ori),

"To L(ucius) Sergius Paullus the younger,[2] son of Lucius, one of the four commissioners in charge of the Roman streets, tribune of the soldiers of the sixth legion styled Ferrata, quaestor, etc."

[1] Professor Dessau is the first authority on the subject, editor of the "Prosopographia Imperii Romani," and engaged on the new and greatly enlarged edition of that work. His experience in tracing the history of the great Roman families gives unique value to his opinion.

[2] In Latin, "son". In Greek inscriptions the same distinction between son and father of the same name is much more frequent, and is usually expressed by νέος or νεώτερος.

The rest of the career was engraved on a separate stone, which has not yet been found. The course of office is that which was regular and customary for men of senatorial rank.

The second *filio*, written in full, distinguishes this Sergius Paullus from a well-known father; and the character of the lettering shows that, as Mr. Anderson remarked, the inscription should be assigned to the latter half of the first century after Christ. L. Sergius Paullus must have served as an official in the province Galatia before he attained the consulship;[1] and the inscription was then placed in his honour by the Colony Antioch. His office was most probably the governorship of the province, because there was no other official of senatorial rank in the province except the governor; and this office was regularly held before the consulship. Inscriptions in honour of governors are very common in Antioch; but inscriptions in honour of senatorial officials other than Governors are not found there, except when the official belonged to an Antiochian family and governed another province.

From this inscription we learn that the Proconsul of Cyprus, L. Sergius Paullus (such is the correct Roman spelling) had a son who passed through the regular senatorial course of office; and the first stages in the career of the latter are recorded in this inscription. The Proconsul Paullus had also a great-grandson of the same name, who was consul about A.D. 150, and again in 168.[2]

A new aspect, however, is imparted to the whole question, when we take into consideration another inscription which

---

[1] If he had attained the consulship, this would in ordinary course be stated immediately after his name and before the earliest office of his career.

[2] The interval seems too long for the consul of 168 to be regarded as grandson of the Proconsul of Cyprus in 47.

has been published for nearly thirty years, but formerly was totally misunderstood. It was republished by Mr. Cheesman of New College, Oxford, from a revised copy in the present year. The inscription, as it remains, occupies the whole of a large block of limestone; but, large as it is, it is only a part of a much larger inscription, placed in honour of a distinguished citizen of Antioch who was in the highest course of Imperial service, viz. the senatorial, and of his wife, whose name was in part lost. Her second name was Paulla. Often as this inscription had been seen, it was only in 1913 that the full name of the lady was discovered. She was Sergia Paulla.[1]

With this discovery the inscription assumes a new interest. From a document similar to several hundreds of others, it becomes a memorial associated with the drama of early Christian history and throws a light (which, as I hope to show, is great) on the narrative of the Acts.

The full meaning and bearing of the inscription cannot be understood without considerable explanation. The marriage of a Roman lady of the senatorial nobility, like Sergia Paulla, to a mere citizen of Antioch, is in itself somewhat remarkable. We shall see that this marriage was a determining factor in an interesting episode of history. The situation was as follows.

The most prominent family in Antioch was that of the Caristanii Frontones, whose history Mr. Cheesman has traced

[1] For all details see Mr. Cheesman's article in "Journal of Roman Studies," 1913, p. 262 f. The inscription, which every visitor to Antioch must see as he walks through the streets near the Bazaar, is clear and well preserved, but parts of the stone are broken. We have often seen it and verified Prof. Sterrett's published copy; but only in 1913 did I observe that in one slight detail the type of his printed epigraphic text does not reproduce sufficiently the appearance of the stone, and that on this slight point depends the great value.

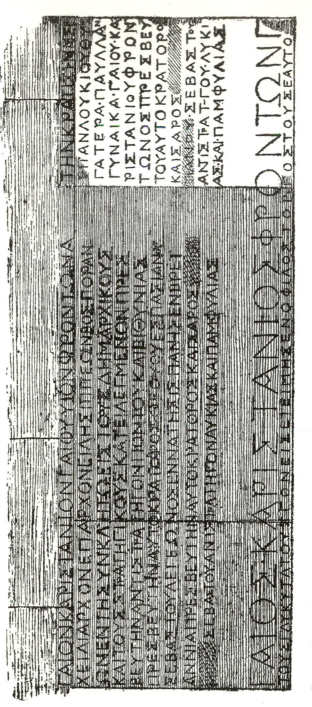

Fig. 3.—Honour to Sergia Paulla and her husband erected by their son. Horizontal shading indicates loss or break of the stones (originally part of wall of tomb?): oblique shading indicates erasure of the name of Domitian. The stones are restored as alternately long and short. γονεῖς is common in the Koine of Asia Minor for γονέας.

[GAIUS CARISTANIUS FRONTO, SON OF GAIUS, military tribune, praefect of a squadron of horsemen Bosporani, enrolled in the Senate among former tribunes of the people and former praetors, legatus with praetorian rank of Pontus and Bithynia, legatus of the deified Emperor Vespasian Augustus of the Ninth Legion Hispana in Britain, legatus of the Emperor Caesar (Domitian) Augustus with praetorian rank of Lycia and Pamphylia]

[The most excellent Ser-]gia Paulla, daughter of Lucius, wife of Gaius Caristanius Fronto, legatus of the Emperor Caesar (Domi), tian Augustus with praetorian rank of Lycia and Pamphylia

[GAIUS CARISTANIUS FR]ONTO, SON AND GRANDSON OF GAIUS, [did honour with loving duty] to his own [sweetest parents]

N.B.—The left-hand column is restored from a contemporary Latin titulus of C. Caristanius Fronto · the Greek translation of some of the Latin technical terms is not always the same.

through five generations. It was an Italian family, probably from southern Latium or the Campanian frontier, which had come to Antioch with the first Roman colonists about 24 B.C.[1] The family had only equestrian rank, until a certain Gaius Caristanius Fronto was promoted to the senatorial career and the highest course of office in the Empire. The date of this promotion is fixed by Mr. Cheesman, a very careful and cautious scholar, to the joint censorship of Vespasian and Titus in A.D. 73-4. On this date compare a special note at the end of this chapter.

Now when we consider that this Gaius Caristanius was the husband of a noble Roman lady, we cannot doubt that Mr. Cheesman is correct in attributing the early promotion of an obscure Roman knight from a city of Galatia to the influence of the family into which he had married. The wife carried her husband with her into Imperial favour. He must undoubtedly have been a man of outstanding merit, otherwise the marriage would not have been arranged; and he knew how to use the opportunities which it gave him.

Further, the marriage may undoubtedly be connected with the governorship of L. Sergius Paullus in the province Galatia. The Governor visited Antioch, and the inscription already published was erected in his honour. His attention was attracted by the young Gaius Caristanius, whose merit and wealth made him a suitable match for the sister (or daughter) of Sergius Paullus; and the governor recommended him to the Imperial notice and favour. The promo-

---

[1] As King Amyntas died in 25 B.C., leaving his kingdom as a Roman province, it can hardly have been earlier than 24 that the province was organized and the colony founded. The first of the Caristanii will appear later in connexion with the life of Quirinius, Governor of Syria in the year that Christ was born: see the Gospel of Luke II. 2, and below in chapter on Quirinius.

tion serves to date the tenure of Galatia by Sergius Paullus to the period about 72-4,[1] and the marriage falls in the same period. There seems no other time or way in which a Senator of high Roman family could be present in the colony of Antioch. Now as the father of the governor of Galatia had been only Proconsul of Cyprus in A.D. 47, a rather humble office held by persons before the consulship, it seems improbable that the son was old enough to have a marriageable daughter in A.D. 73. We may, therefore, take Sergia Paulla as his sister, and as daughter of the Proconsul who was in contact with Paul at Paphos.

The period 72-4, then, probably marks the tenure of the province Galatia by Sergius Paullus, the marriage of his sister, and the promotion of her husband to the senatorial career, first to the grade of tribune and then to that of prætor. From this we may infer that Caristanius was probably about thirty-two years of age in A.D. 74,[2] and was born about 42.

Thus we are coming closer to the Proconsul; we have found his daughter; can we now discover anything more about her?

Sergia Paulla and Caristanius had at least two sons. The eldest took the father's name, while the younger had a cognomen Paullinus derived from his mother according to a common custom in that age.[3] The names Sergianus and Paullinus, as we observe in passing, can both be observed in the province of Galatia: the latter very often; it was very common for provincials who were promoted to the Roman

---

[1] Calpurnius [Nonius] Asprenas governed Galatia from 69 to probably A.D. 72. See Dessau, " Prosopographia ".

[2] The lowest legal age for holding the tribunate was twenty-five, for the prætorship thirty, and for the consulship thirty-three.

[3] See Cagnat, " Manuel d'Epigr. Lat.," p. 66 (Ed. 3).

citizenship to take names derived from the governor whose official sanction had been given to the honour.[1]

The eldest son, Gaius Caristanius Fronto, erected this inscription to his parents. We observe that he wrote in Greek. It is remarkable that the son of a Roman senator, bound by Roman custom to the career and the language of a Roman, should prefer Greek to Latin. The very name Caristanius, too, disappears now from Roman epigraphy. The two facts must be connected. The son of a Roman senator and a noble Roman lady degenerates from Roman to Greek custom, and his family and name disappear from Roman history. He sank consciously and intentionally from Roman custom: he became a mere Greekling: the ways of Roman honour knew him not. This is a fact so noteworthy as to call for further examination.

It was, indeed, the case that gradually the Roman citizens of Pisidian Antioch forgot the use of Latin and became merged in the Greek-speaking population of the province;[2] but that is a fact of a later time. The leading families of Antioch even so late as the early fourth century still used Latin on formal occasions, though evidently Greek was more familiar to them. A careful Austrian scholar has studied the process, and dates in the third century[3] the early stages of the degeneration from the use of Latin. Even if we suppose that it began earlier, we cannot place the first steps in the process before the late second century. Here, however, we have a case which must

---

[1] The names of all the governors of this period can be traced in the epigraphy of Galatia: Nonius, Asprenas, Caesennius, Pomponius, etc. We find even Nonius Paullus and Nonia Paulla, uniting the names of the two governors, who went and came in 71 probably. We presume confidently that the governor's sanction was needed.

[2] The degeneration at Antioch is described in "Cities of St. Paul," p. 278.

[3] Kubitschek in "Wiener Studien," xxiv. 2. My dating has been the same.

be dated after A.D. 81 and not later than A.D. 83. The other cases, too, are found in mere provincial surroundings; but here we have a Roman in the line of Imperial service, son of Romans of the higher nobility.

The more carefully we observe the facts, the more we are struck with their unusual and non-Roman character.

The hypothesis forces itself on us that the reason lay in religion. As yet the suggestion that follows must remain a mere theory; but further evidence may be found in Antioch during the future excavations; and the hypothesis may guide and sharpen the search.

We recognize here the external signs of Christianity at this period. Unwillingness to take public office was a widespread characteristic of the Christians, who shrank from positions in which they were obliged to assist at pagan ceremonies and even to take a leading part in the ritual. On account of their reluctance to serve the State, they were bitterly blamed and stigmatized as unpatriotic and traitors and enemies of their country.[1] Greek was the language of Christian teaching at that time. The Church in Rome itself used Greek and ranked as a Greek-speaking Church until well on in the second century. Accordingly, if the young Caristanius was a Christian, the situation is forthwith seen to be natural and almost inevitable. His religion came to him from his mother, and it came to her from her father the Proconsul. Thus we are gradually getting closer and closer to the story that Luke relates.

It may be urged as an objection to the result stated as a conjecture in this chapter, that it seems to conflict with a general principle of the Roman bureaucratic system under the Empire: certain duties were imposed on the descendants

---

[1] "Church in the Roman Empire before 170," p. 352.

of a senator to the third generation,[1] and in particular the son of a senator was obliged to undertake a magistracy and so enter the senate.[2]   This compulsion, however, rested on the ancient principle that every Roman citizen was bound to perform any public duty which the choice of the people imposed on him, and the presiding officer at an election could compel any citizen to stand for office by placing his name against his will in the list of candidates.   In practice, however, as Mommsen says,[3] the compulsion was restricted to pressure of an indirect kind.   There would be something very unusual, but not at all impossible, in the conduct which our hypothesis attributes to the youngest C. Caristanius ; but our hypothesis is founded on the undeniable fact that there was something quite unusual in the situation, and this element must be recognized and explained.

The question will at once be put, whether this hypothesis is not disproved by the facts which we admit as practically certain.   The brother and the husband of Sergia Paulla, and the descendants of her brother, were all pagan, and engaged in the ordinary Imperial service.   Is it possible, is it in accordance with a reasonable view of the situation, that the older Sergius Paullus the Proconsul, with his daughter, should have been either Christian or half-way on the road towards Christianity, while such near relatives were pagans ?   This must be carefully considered ; and, as I believe, the discussion will prove instructive.

In the first place, consider the relation of the younger Sergius Paullus, governor of Galatia, to his father the Pro-

---

[1] Mommsen, "Staatsrecht," III. 468 f.

[2] Ibid., I. 476: see also Mommsen's paper in the "Festschrift Hirschfeld," p. 1 ff.

[3] Loc. cit., p. 1, note 4.

consul of Cyprus. Before A.D. 72-4, the younger Paullus had been prætor and then doubtless served as commander of a legion (legatus) for three years and filled some other office before he came to Galatia. Probably he was quite forty years of age by that time, unless he had risen to the prætorship in the earliest legal year of his age.

When the father was in Cyprus there is no probability that his son was with him. On the contrary it may be taken for granted that he was being educated in Italy as young Roman nobles were educated in preparation for the work of their life. An interesting and valuable picture of a school for such boys at Naples is given by the poet Statius, whose father was the principal of the school.[1] The young Sergius Paullus may quite possibly have been one of the pupils.

If the older Sergius Paullus had become a Christian, or even had acquired a leaning to and an appreciation of Christianity, there is no likelihood that a boy of the age of his son and educated like him for the Roman service, would be affected by his father's change of mind, about which he would learn only after his father's return to Rome. Whatever may have been the feeling and belief of his father, the son probably was already fixed in his Roman career. The fact that in patriarchally administered homes[2] of an Eastern

---

[1] No passage is more instructive about the best side of Imperial life than " Silvæ," v. 3, 146-90. About that side one hears nothing from Juvenal or Martial or even Tacitus, except by indirect inferences from miscoloured records. No one can understand the Imperial system who has not studied and digested the " Silvæ " in great part. He may know the facts : Statius shows the spirit, as a poet who passionately admired the beautiful in art and morals saw it.

[2] On the character of such households as those of Lydia, who came from Asia Minor, and of the jailer, something may be learned from those of Phrygia described in my " Studies in the History of the Eastern Roman Province," pp. 150, 373, etc.

town like Philippi, belonging to a comparatively humble class, the whole family were baptized with the head of the household,[1] cannot be taken as proof of what would happen in such an aristocratic family as the Sergii Paulli with a son in the circumstances usually attending that position. The son would naturally continue his own life and work, without change of religion, whatever were the case with the father.

On the other hand, a daughter was often in a very different relation to her father. Much of course depended on the character of the father ; but a certain interest in study and science was evidently hereditary in this family, and the contemplative spirit is favourable to the affection and the life of the home. The daughter would in all probability not be with her father in Cyprus : the Roman system did not favour the presence of wives with their husbands in the province or the camp ; of old that had been forbidden ; but it had become more common under the Empire, though some objected to it, and would have restored by stringent rule the old prohibition.[2] Quite probably Sergia Paulla was too young, or not even born, in A.D. 47. In Rome, in her father's house, during his residence in the city, she might naturally and probably come to think as he did about the interesting nature and noble quality of the teachers of the new faith. As to the question whether he became in the fullest sense a Christian, the answer depends on the interpretation of Acts XIII. 9, on which see the later paragraphs of this chapter.

As Lightfoot pointed out,[3] a certain Sergius Paullus is

---

[1] In passing we may remark that probably the children of those households were young and under control of the head of the house.

[2] See the debate in the Senate reported by Tacitus, " Annals," III. 33 f.

[3] "Contemporary Review," May, 1878, p. 290 f. ; Meyer-Wendt quotes also Hausrath, " N.T. Zeitgesch.," II. p. 525.

quoted in Pliny's list of authorities for statements made in his second and eighteenth books ; and in both of those books various facts are recorded regarding Cyprus ; hence probability is distinctly in favour of the estimate just stated of the Proconsul's character. Similar character belongs to his grandson or great-grandson, the Consul of A.D. 152 and 168 (as already stated). In fact, the known character of the youngest Paullus was formerly regarded by some as a proof that this philosophic and scientific governor mentioned by Luke was a sort of reflection of the second-century consul, as mirrored in the mind and memory of the supposed late concocter of the Acts. Lightfoot retorted by showing the probability that the old proconsul was a man of similar tastes to his great-grandson.[1]

So much is certain : the little that we do know gives a favourable conception of the family, as a whole, and is in accordance with Luke's account.

Moreover, we know that in that period there was a certain admixture of Christianity in some noble Roman families ; but it would be absurd to suppose that, because one member of the house was Christian, therefore all were Christian. Domitilla, niece of the Emperor Domitian, and Flavius Clemens his cousin, and Pomponia Græcina (wife of Aulus Plautius, the conqueror of Britain), were almost certainly Christians. It has never been imagined that their entire families were of the same religion. So it is with the Sergii Paulli. One must understand that there was during this period a certain informal agreement in such families, otherwise family life would have been impossible. The character of Pauline Christianity in Phrygia, and the system of mutual allowance which existed there during the second

---

[1] The relationship was not then assured. Now through the intermediate stage Professor Dessau considers it may be taken as certain.

and third centuries, is described by the present writer else-where.[1] That tolerant system was quite in the spirit of Paul, who fully contemplates and makes rules for Christian conduct in mixed households. It, however, was destroyed by the massacre of Diocletian ; the moderate and tolerant were to a great extent exterminated then in Central Asia Minor ; and a new generation arose which did not under-stand the spirit or preserve the tradition of Paul. The present writer, without being conscious of the similarity, has described the like effect produced in a much less degree by the persecution of Domitian.[2]

The Sergii Paulli belong to this period ; and if there was any Christianity among them, as Luke says, we have no reason to think either that it was universal in the family, or that it led to the total break-up of family life. The progress of discovery goes entirely to confirm this estimate of the situation.

Now comes the question how much we can infer with confidence from Luke's words in Acts XIII. 9 ; that "the Proconsul believed, being astonished at the teaching of the Lord ".

What is the force of the term "believe" ($\pi\iota\sigma\tau\epsilon\dot{\upsilon}\omega$) in the Acts? Does it necessarily imply that all who "believed" were converted and permanently became Christians in the complete and final sense ?

First let us take the general question, without prejudice due to this special case.

The example of Simon Magus seems to furnish a very strong argument. Simon believed [3] and was baptized. Yet

---

[1] The evidence, so far as known in 1894, is collected in "Cities and Bishoprics of Phrygia," II. chap. XII.

[2] " Church in the Roman Empire before 170," pp. 275 f., 296.

[3] Acts VIII. 13.

it is hard to suppose that he became in the final sense a Christian, although for the time he was a member of the Church. The language of Luke, on the whole, suggests that he fell away from the Faith, though certainly this is not distinctly stated. Simon, it is true, after his baptism "continued with Philip; and beholding signs and great wonders wrought, he was amazed" (ἐξίστατο). Yet no word is said to mitigate the final condemnation pronounced on him by Peter: "thou hast neither part nor lot in this matter; for thy heart is not right". He is not described as repenting, but only as asking, in fear of the future, that Peter should pray for him.

It seems highly probable that Luke knew the reputation which the magician afterwards acquired,[1] and that he regarded the subsequent history of Simon as the natural result of what occurred at the beginning of his connexion with the Christians.

Luke seems to regard belief as the first stage in a process. The second stage is "turning to the Lord,"[2] of which the seal is baptism, and which is consequent on believing. Later there ensues the settled Christian life of those who are styled in the perfect tense πεπιστευκότες, who are in the state of them that have come to believe.[3]

A process is here presumed which regularly and usually passed through these stages; and in various places, e.g. XVIII. 27, this process is described as a whole by mentioning only the first stage, belief, and assuming that the normal continuation followed. The context is the proof that

---

[1] Without accepting as historical the presumptions of the pseudo-Clementine treatises, one must regard them as having a certain foundation in the belief and tradition of the Church about Simon.

[2] Acts XI. 21, ἐπίστευον καὶ ἐβαπτίζοντο, XVIII. 8, cp. VIII. 13.

[3] Acts XXI. 20, 25; XIX. 18, etc.

"belief" implies all this.   But is that always the case? does πιστεύω always imply that the person who believed went on through the later stages, and became a Christian in the fullest sense?   If so, why should Luke often add a second verb, indicating one or other of the subsequent stages?   I think that the state of mind called believing (πιστεύειν) sometimes advanced no farther than intellectual assent and emotional impression ; and it would not be safe to assert that belief always was followed even by baptism.

There is no sign, and no probability, that the Proconsul was baptized.   It is not likely that Luke, who pays so much attention to the attitude of the Romans to the new religion,[1] would have omitted to say so if it had been the case.   It may reasonably be doubted whether his words imply more than intellectual belief resulting from amazement at what had been heard and seen, i.e. some very deep impression on the mind, but nothing beyond that of an openly avowed and permanently religious character.

The use of ἐκπλήττομαι elsewhere by Luke—three times in the Gospel, here alone in Acts—does not suggest that astonishment was a sure prelude to conversion.   His employment of the almost synonymous ἐξίσταμαι is equally unfavourable to that view.   Mere astonishment is not the state of mind which favours real conversion ; it produced the unreal and evanescent conversion of Simon Magus ; it made the mob of Samaria his devotees.

One piece of evidence seems strong.   Luke IV. 32 uses the same words about the people of Capernaum as about the Proconsul, "they were astonished at his teaching" ; but they were not converted.   The Proconsul was astonished at Paul's teaching ; he admired it as a moral

[1] "St. Paul the Traveller," p. 304 ff.

and intellectual display ; he was delighted with the boldness and the power of these itinerant lecturers; but this
spirit Luke does not regard as a proof of real conversion, and he adds the words, "he was astonished at the
teaching of the Lord," to show the limitations of the case.

Meyer-Wendt and probably almost all ordinary readers
consider that the Proconsul was converted ; and Blass even
connects "he believed in the teaching of the Lord, being
astonished at the miracle" (ἐπίστευσεν ἐπὶ τῇ διδαχῇ τοῦ
κυρίου)—regardless of the Greek order and of the analogies
which he quotes (Luke IV. 32 ; Mark I. 22); but he has
not persuaded Wendt to accept this translation, and is not
likely to find others ready to follow him.

Mr. Rackham, on the contrary, takes a very different
view, and has a judicious and cautious note in his edition
of the Acts, to which I may refer the reader ; and he
concludes that a real conversion of the Proconsul would
have had more serious consequences, whereas Paullus "had
no more dealings with the Apostles, who leave Cyprus".
I would ask, however, how we know that Paullus had no
more dealings with the Apostles ; we are informed here
only about the moment : there remains much to say, that is
not here said. Mr. Rackham is rightly sensitive to a certain
abruptness in the incident, regarding which see below.

Luke lays full emphasis on the highly favourable impression which Paul made on the first Roman official with
whom his mission work brought him in contact. This is
in accordance with his general plan, and illuminative of his
purpose in this history (as is pointed out in "St. Paul the
Traveller," pp. 304-9).

Some will be disposed to set no value on Mr. Rackham's
first argument: "it seems incredible that at this date a
Roman Proconsul could have been converted—it would

have made a great stir in the Church and in the world, of which some echo must have reached us ". Admitting all this, they would simply add that Luke, not being a trustworthy historian, incorrectly represents Paullus as having been converted; thus the mistranslation of the statement in the Acts would be made into a charge against the trustworthiness of the writer.

We do not, however, admit Mr. Rackham's presumption that, if the Proconsul had been converted, it would have caused a great stir in the world—any more than we should admit the reply that Luke gives an untrustworthy account of the incident. The presumption rests only on the view that the world was interested in this new religion, and watched keenly for every trace of its progress. Quite the opposite is the case. Hardly anyone except the few Christians felt any interest in the new faith. The great world was profoundly indifferent to the rise of another Oriental " superstition ": there were already a score of them, and the addition of one to the list was not worthy of any sensible person's notice. That is the spirit of the first century. It was affected in some degree by Nero's capricious and unreasonable action in A.D. 64-6, the act of a detested tyrant whose memory was condemned and whose acts were annulled; but ultimately the attack made by the despot resulted, as Tacitus says,[1] in rousing sympathy for the sufferers; and thus Tacitus dismisses the case. No permanent change was produced in the public attitude.[2]

---

[1] " Annals," xv. 44 : " unde . . . miseratio oriebatur, tamquam non utilitate publica sed in saevitiam unius absumerentur ". Tacitus shows clearly that this sympathy was misplaced, and that the Christians all deserved death ; but that knowledge arose from subsequent history, and was not in the minds of the Romans at the time.

[2] This is one of the most important aspects of Tacitus's narrative. His condemnation of all Christians as evil-minded springs from later experience, and anticipates cruelty.

The case which Luke presents to the Roman world rests on this general attitude : the State had decided, first through the action of a provincial governor (Junius Gallio, Seneca's brother), and afterwards by the formal judgment of the Supreme Court of the Empire,[1] that the government should take no heed of such matters, i.e. that teachers might teach and preachers preach as they pleased (so long of course as they did not make themselves liable to prosecution for treason or disrespect to the Emperor or any other crime).

The world of Rome, therefore, was not in the smallest degree affected by the change of philosophic or religious attitude in Paullus, if such a change occurred. His friends might remark over the dinner-table,[2] that he had taken up with a new Oriental doctrine, just as they might tell how another acquaintance had been initiated at Eleusis, or a third had fitted up a private chapel for the rites of Isis ; and this or other such tales might become public gossip for a moment at the baths. Beyond this it is quite clear that during the first century public opinion did not concern itself with the doings of individuals, except for a time under Nero and again under Domitian, both Emperors whose acts were repealed at their death. Pliny had some difficulty : he knew that the general principle condemning all Christians as disloyal and enemies of society had been established ; but the matter was not quite clear to him. When had the principle been established? Obviously no act of Domitian or Nero was valid, therefore only Vespasian remains. He had come to the opinion that State policy required the extermination of the Christians ; but he did not actually carry it out, as Domitian did. Trajan reviewed the whole

---

[1] In the first trial of Paul at Rome.

[2] Juvenal, " Satire " I. : " nova nec tristis per cunctas fabula cenas ".

case and confirmed the principle, but discouraged all activity in action against the proscribed Christians.

Thus it is contrary to everything we know about the position of the Christians to suppose with Rackham that the conversion of a Proconsul would cause any great stir in the world at that time.

Here comes in the evidence of the Antiochian inscriptions. They point probably to the conclusion that Christianity came into the female branch of the Sergian family, and therefore that Sergius Paullus must have believed in a very thorough-going way, though this could not safely be taken as implying baptism and full membership.

There is more to be found in the future regarding this governor.

Another case where the same term is used with uncertain force is Acts XVII. 34 : "certain men also clave unto him and believed, among whom was Dionysius the Areopagite, and Damaris," etc. In this case I believe that no Church was formed, and no baptism administered at the time. Doubtless the effect produced on a few persons was genuine and deep, but Paul did not then remain in Athens to follow it up. This we gather from a casual phrase of his in 1 Corinthians XVI. 15, which opens up a wide question, and cannot be treated in this place. See below in chapter "First-fruits of Achaia".

Even if we take the words of XIII. 12 in their lightest implication, the tendency and favourable opinion that Paullus felt for the new faith might very well result in his daughter at Rome gradually going farther. But certainly, while this must be admitted, the simplest sense, which practically every reader takes from that verse, is distinctly favoured by the interpretation which has been proposed for these Antiochian inscriptions ; though we fully acknowledge that the interpretation remains a hypothesis for the present. New evidence may be found if the excavations be completed ; but the completion is a work of years and much expense.

In the opening paragraph of this chapter we spoke of the abruptness with which the Proconsul is dismissed ; but this would disappear entirely if he continued to be a personage known among the Christians, for whom the historian wrote. The incident was merely the introduction of a well-known figure in their history : they knew the rest : a complete history of the work of the Holy Spirit in the world (which it was Luke's aim to write in outline) would have more to say about him.

This consideration, that Luke addressed a public to whom many personages in his story were familiar as household words, must be kept in mind when we are estimating his work, and its purpose and quality.

The same remark applies to Simon of Samaria as to Sergius Paullus. He, too, appears for one occasion in the history, and then is lost to us ; but we know that he continued to play a part in the drama of the early Christian time, though legend and invention have obscured the real facts of his subsequent career.

In both cases there remained much to tell. Luke knew, as he was writing, that he was dealing with figures of importance, and that later Christian annals would know those two persons : and there is a certain abruptness in the way they are dismissed which becomes intelligible if there is more in the future to tell.

That such abruptness indicates that there is more to say which is not said at the moment, either because it was familiar to the readers at that time, or because it was going to be stated in the course of the history, is suggested by the

abrupt dismissal of Philip in VIII. 40. He is brought to
Cæsarea and left there. There is no apparent reason why
Cæsarea is mentioned, until we come to XXI. 16, when the
purpose becomes evident. This relation between VIII. 40
and XXI. 16 was recognized even by some of the old
Tübingen School, who were not prone to see purpose or
plan in the Acts.

Note (p. 156).—It is known that Vespasian after his
accession in 69 advanced several of his personal friends
to places in the Senate; but Caristanius cannot have ranked
among these. Mommsen considers that, until the assumption of the censorship for life by Domitian, emperors exercised the right of *adlectio in senatum*, i.e. *inter tribunicios*,
aedilicios, etc., only when they were actually holding the
censorship ("Staatsrecht," II. ed. 3, p. 944). This view is
not fully justified; but exceptions were rare and are of such
a character as to suggest that they were contrary to a
usual practice. Assuredly Vespasian is not likely to have
promoted Caristanius between his act of 69 and the censorship, during which he made a large number of such pro-
motions. On the whole question see Groag in "Arch. Ep.
Mitth. aus Oesterreich," 1897, p. 49; he considers it likely
that Vespasian did not use the right of *adlectio* after 69 until
he assumed the censorship and exercised the right on a large
scale; and he points out the exceptions to the rule that
Mommsen laid down in his "Staatsrecht," loc. cit.

CHAPTER XIII

"SALVATION" AS A PAGAN AND A CHRISTIAN TERM

WHAT was the salvation which the lame man at Lystra was capable of receiving? It has been pointed out already [1] that the word in this place "has hardly the Christian sense, but is used practically in the common pagan sense"; and that "this is a proof of early date". At the same time the rendering in the Revised Version "faith to be made whole" seems strangely narrow and unsatisfactory. The Authorized Version "faith to be healed" is far better. There is no reason why the revisers should have changed the rendering, unless they wished definitely to exclude any possible wider intention than mere physical restoration to health. This narrowing of the scope must, however, be condemned as unjustifiable.

To the pagans salvation was safety, health, prosperity; but even in pagan usage "the word never wholly excludes a meaning that comes nearer to reality and permanence"; it is never wholly material and ephemeral; "there is latent in it some undefined and hardly conscious thought of the spiritual and the moral, which made it suit Paul's purpose admirably".[2] Such was the usage among the pagans. In such a context, when he is describing his first appearance

---

[1] See above, p. 46: though the noun is not used, but only the cognate verb ($\pi i\sigma\tau\iota\nu$) $\tau o\hat{v}$ $\sigma\omega\theta\hat{\eta}\nu a\iota$, yet this is equivalent to $\tau\hat{\eta}s$ $\sigma\omega\tau\eta\rho ias$, which was avoided as ambiguous and almost suggesting the meaning "the confidence that springs from salvation," cp. Col. II. 12, etc.

[2] "The Teaching of Paul in Terms of the Present Day," p. 95.

as a preacher in a pagan city, it is inconceivable that
Paul should have used the word with a more restricted
intention than the pagans attached to it, when they employed it in a religious connexion.

The lame man wished for salvation as he could imagine
it, safety and health.   Paul read his mind by a flash of insight.

This passage well illustrates the close relation between
the pagan vows for salvation, and the offer of salvation
which Paul brought to the Græco-Roman world.   He
offered them something that they wanted and were praying
for ; and in the offer he took the opportunity of purifying
and spiritualizing their conception of that salvation, which
they were trying " to purchase by vows or to extort by
prayers and entreaties from the gods ".[1]   He gave them
what they wanted, and yet something far above what they
could ask or even think.[2]

The word "Salvation" ($\sigma\omega\tau\eta\rho\iota\alpha$) was especially suited
through its pagan religious use for employment in making
the Christian Gospel intelligible to the Græco-Roman world.
The world wished and was praying for something like the
"Salvation" that Paul announced to all.   The study of
this word is peculiarly instructive in respect of the relation
between the teaching of Paul and the religious longings and
conceptions of the Græco-Roman public, and especially the
syncretistic religion of the great pagan Mysteries.   There
are striking analogies between the pagan and the Christian
use ; and in modern time some scholars have been so impressed with these analogies as to forget or ignore the even
more startling differences.[3]

[1] " The Teaching of Paul in Terms of the Present Day," p. 95.

[2] Ephesians III. 20.

[3] Loisy, catching the analogies from some German scholars, has emphasized them with extreme superficiality, being blind to everything except what

That the earlier Christians (whom Paul followed) derived their use of this word from the Greek translation of the Old Testament is, of course, certain. They did not use it because it was commonly employed by the pagans in pagan religious expression, but because it was familiar to themselves in their own Scriptures. To the pagans, however, the word carried meaning and power, not because it was in the Septuagint, but because it expressed the desire of their hearts, and was familiar to them in their own religious observances.

The general fact that this term "Salvation" was so important in the pagan mystic religions may be assumed as familiar. The evidence has been stated from different sides by several scholars, and is put prominently in Professor H. A. A. Kennedy's "St. Paul and the Mystery-Religions": those religions "may be said to offer salvation to those who have been duly initiated" (p. 199): "but it is important to note that the salvation was invariably assured 'by the exact performance of sacred ceremonies'" (p. 216)[1]: "above all, it did not necessarily involve a new moral ideal" (ibid.). Yet Professor Kennedy is fully alive to the germs of higher ethical and religious ideas involved: "no unbiassed mind can fail to read between the lines almost pathetic indications of a craving for fullness of life, for a real and enduring salvation" (p. 95). The salvation was gained through a new birth: "the initiates are fed with milk as being born again".

In paganism the association of their "Salvation" with the idea of rebirth or of death and a future life, was invari-

catches the eye on a first view of the subject; see "The Teaching of Paul in Terms of the Present Day," pp. 286, 304, etc.

[1] The last seven words are quoted from Cumont, "Les Religions Orientales dans le Paganisme Romain," p. xxii.

able. Both Paul and the Mysteries "taught the Way of
Salvation, or simply ' the Way'; but in the Mysteries the
Way was literally a path marked by a white poplar tree
and other signs, which the soul of the dead man had
learned in life through the esoteric and mystic lore ".[1] The
simple inscription on a rather elaborately sculptured tombstone of the type of a door, found at Akmonia in Phrygia,
was probably an expression of the mystic teaching :—[2]

ζω-	They
σι[ν]	live,
μέγαν κίνδυ-	great danger
[ν]ον ἐκπεφευ-	having es-
[γ]ότες	caped.

These words are incised rather carelessly and irregularly
near the edge of the stone, while the middle, where the
inscription usually stands, is left blank. The reference is
to safety gained in a future life from the dangerous situation of man in the present world with its "hard and
dreadful servitude to the power of the demonic rulers,
organized in a sort of hierarchy of evil forces, 'angels and
principalities and powers' (Romans VIII. 38) under ' the
ruler of the power of the air' (Ephesians II. 2)." [3] Such
safety and life is the "Salvation" of the Mysteries. As
Professor Kennedy on p. 95 says " the hope of immortality
is conveyed to their votaries through an elaborate ritual,"
the centre of which was formed by "grotesque myths" in
which was "embodied the return to life of Osiris and Attis".
There is a certain outward resemblance between some

---

[1] " The Teaching of Paul in Terms of the Present Day," p. 302.

[2] It is published from copies by myself and Professor Sterrett of Cornell
in "Cities and Bishoprics of Phrygia," II. p. 564 f., no. 465, among the
Christian inscriptions; but I should now prefer to assign it to the my
paganism.

[3] " Teaching of Paul," p. 304.

of this teaching, so far as it contains the germs of finer ideas, and the purely spiritual teaching of Jesus and Paul; but no true analogy exists between them.   Only those who ignore the difference between mere prescribed ritual and what is really spiritual can mistake superficial resemblance for real organic analogy.   " It is painfully evident in the writings of the school whose views we are discussing that they are so habituated to consider ritual the essence of religion as to miss the essential character of the Pauline 'Way '." [1]

Among the pagans, then, the term " Salvation " was largely material in its connotation, and salvation was gained by ritual and ceremonial.   There were three chief departments, so to say, of salvation among the pagans : the salvation gained by religious duties and vows and prayers, the salvation sought by magic rites,[2] and the Imperial salvation.   As in every other department of life, so here, the policy of the Empire enters to dominate and to guide the thoughts and acts and even the prayers and wishes of all its subjects : chapter XV.

The salvation that was sought by magic was practically the same that the devout pagans prayed for.   Magical art grows out of the degeneration and degradation of religion ; and the only difference between magical and religious salvation was that the devotees of magic were on the whole lower in moral and mental character than the other pagans, and their conception of salvation was therefore more material and more vulgar.   In the following chapter XIV. some examples are quoted of the ordinary pagan religious salvation.

[1] " Teaching of Paul in Terms of the Present Day," p. 304.
[2] Hubert in Daremberg-Saglio, " Dict. des Antiq.," under " Magia " gives salvation as one of the objects sought by magic arts.

CHAPTER XIV

PRAYERS FOR SALVATION AMONG THE PAGANS OF ASIA MINOR

WE must try to comprehend more clearly by looking both at the subject of chapter XIII. as a whole and at some typical examples, first how Paul thought about his own teaching in its relation to the pagan world, and secondly what was involved in the prayers and vows which the pagans were making.

To understand the feelings of his pagan contemporaries, and so to be able to make his message intelligible to them by showing them that it satisfied their vague and "ignorant"[1] gropings after higher religious and ethical ideas, was a necessity for Paul, and is now a necessity for us, if we are to comprehend the history of his work as contained in the Acts. Some paragraphs of the Epistle to the Romans especially,[2] and many allusions elsewhere, show that Paul was fully alive to the existence in the contemporary pagan mind of such germs of better thought. It has been the purpose of the present writer from the beginning to exhibit the close relation of Paulinism to the highest conceptions of right and good among the pagans.

By the term Paulinism it is needful to explain that I mean Christianity as expressed by Paul to the Græco-Roman world—not a development out of the Teaching of Jesus, nor a superstructure built upon that Teaching, but

[1] Acts XVII. 23.   [2] Romans I. 19 f., II. 13-15, VIII. 18 ff.

(178)

the expression of it in a form which could be readily comprehended by his pagan hearers, and become vital and creative among them. That vitality and creativeness rested first on a certain organization, which was necessary in order to knit together a really growing society, a congregation, and in the complete stage a Church, and secondly on a common teaching so expressed as to be comprehended by all.

Both conditions were fundamental, and implied in Paul's idea of the unity of the Church. No unity, no permanent harmony and brotherhood, can exist among scattered congregations, divided both by long distances and by diversity of training and blood and ideals, except through a certain machinery of organization. Such organization was necessary to maintain the vitalizing and unifying intercommunication among the separate congregations which was the life-blood of the Universal Church; it was needed also to maintain permanence of tone and ideals in the individual congregations. That such organization of the congregations was contemplated by Paul from the beginning of his mission to the Roman world, and is described to us in the pages of Luke, I have always maintained. Some modern scholars discredit and ignore all this creative side of Paul's character and work, but hardly any have gone quite to such an extreme as Professor Deissmann of Berlin in his recent "St. Paul: a Study in Social and Religious History".[1]

The fundamental forms of such an organization were floating in the atmosphere of the Roman world. They were Roman forms, but not pure Roman; they were the forms suited for the society that existed in Asia, uniting

---

[1] The concluding chapter of the present writer's " Teaching of Paul " is devoted to a criticism of Dr. Deissmann's book.

elements that partook of the genius and the nature both of Jews and of Hellenes, varying in details from Imperial province to province, yet everywhere bearing a generic type as Roman. These forms were at hand. Paul did not imitate any existing organism; he merely worked with the conceptions and used the forms of his age, adapting them to his purpose; and his successors developed them to new uses.

Along with the religious conceptions and the organizing forms, Paul (and in much smaller degree the pre-Pauline teachers) adopted the names and words of existing society. He did not attempt to create a new Christian language:[1] such an attempt must have proved vain, and would have stultified itself: he must speak to his audiences in their own language if he wished to reach their heart.[2] But the already existing words he filled with a fuller and richer and more spiritual content.[3] Thus the words of the early Christian teaching were old, and yet in a sense they were new: the sound was old, but the meaning was so much developed that they were new. Yet the change of meaning was such that they were still intelligible in a certain degree to the pagans—not indeed fully intelligible: who has ever grasped the full meaning of Paul's teaching? what pagan or what Christian theologian has ever fully understood all that is set forth in the letter to the Romans? The teaching of Paul remains always on a higher level than we can attain, and yet it is always in a degree intelligible and vitalizing even

[1] " The Teaching of Paul in Terms of the Present Day," ch. LIII.

[2] As Ennius said, he had three hearts, because he had three languages : I do not dogmatize about the meaning of the word heart. A friend who knew the Turks very intimately said that a Turk to whom you talked in French became a totally different person when you talked to him in Turkish; and this friend was a diplomatist of thirty years' experience.

[3] " The Teaching of Paul in Terms of the Present Day," pp. 285, 410.

to the simplest religious heart; and there is a power in it that is even more effective and intelligible to the simple religious consciousness than to the complex theological mind.

There are, therefore, two things which must be kept in mind, as we try to understand the history contained in the Acts. We must have always before us, first the relation of Paul to the pagan religious ideas current in society, and secondly his relation to the Imperial organization.

These two matters the present writer has always tried to state emphatically and as clearly as possible, from the beginning of his work in this department; and the present chapter is intended to serve the same purpose. In the first place I shall quote some brief typical sentences from earlier books, and in the second place I shall add some illustrations from contemporary documents of the early Christian period.

The modern world has awakened to the complexity and the intensity of the religious questionings that were then burning in the pagan world.[1] In paganism Paul saw also that there was, or rather had originally been, an element of truth and real perception of the Divine nature.[2] The regions where the new religion spread at first most rapidly were those where the people were becoming aware of the beauty of Greek letters and the grandeur of Roman government, where they were awaking from the stagnation and inertness of an Oriental people, and their minds were stirred and receptive of all new ideas, whether Greek philosophy or Jewish or Christian religion.[3] Here and always we find that

---

[1] " The Teaching of Paul in Terms of the Present Day," p. 284.

[2] " Pauline and Other Studies in the History of Religion," 1906, p. 166 (in a reprint of a paper read to the Oriental Congress about 1891 or 1892).

[3] " The Church in the Roman Empire before A.D. 170," p. 147.

the spread of Christianity was favoured by intelligence and freedom of mind in those among whom it was first preached.[1] The Asiarchs, who were Paul's friends, had no doubt held, many of them, priesthoods of the native deities before they became officials of the Imperial cultus.[2]   Paul did not make speeches at Ephesus inveighing against the goddess of the city.   In the denunciation of images he stands on the footing of the philosophers.   His teaching was introduced to his pagan audiences in the language of the purest and simplest theology current among educated men.   From this he proceeded to more advanced teaching. Hence the instantaneous and electrical effect produced on the Galatian cities.[3]

The new Empire transcended national distinctions and national religions : this new unity required a new religion to consecrate it, and to create a common idea and a tie . . . the new Empire set about creating a new religion, taking up the existing religions and giving them a place in its scheme : the Emperor represented the majesty, the wisdom, and the beneficent power of Rome, and he was in many places conceived as an incarnation of the god worshipped in that district :[4] this new Imperial religion was the expression of Roman patriotism, the bond of Roman unity, and the pledge of Roman prosperity :[5] it was the keystone of the Imperial policy.[6]   Christianity also created a religion for the Empire transcending all distinctions of nationality ; and the path of development for the Empire lay in accepting the religion

---

[1] "The Church in the Roman Empire before A.D. 170," p. 134.

[2] Ibid., p. 133.   [3] "St. Paul the Traveller," pp. 146-9.

[4] "The Church in the Roman Empire before 170," p. 191.

[5] Ibid., p. 209.

[6] Ibid., p. 324 : this expression has been quoted by Mommsen as the perfect expression of the importance of the Imperial cultus in the State : see "Expositor," July, 1893, p. 2.

thus offered it to complete its organization. Universal citizenship, universal equality, universal religion, a universal Church, all were ideas which the Empire was slowly working out, but which it could not realize till it merged itself in Christianity.[1]

A few typical dedications may now be quoted as examples of these two fundamental conditions in the relation between Pauline Christianity and the established social and religious system of the Empire. They are all selected as bearing on the longing felt, and the vows and the prayers offered, for " Salvation " by the pagans among whom Paul moved and preached. They are for the most part later than the first century, because the native spirit in Anatolia did not express itself in writing on stone at that time; but there is every reason to think that they are as characteristic of the first century as of the second. Towards the end of the third century there appears a new tendency to compete with and to outdo Christianity by adopting some of its ideas and forms.[2]

We have spoken about the frequent occurrence of the term " Salvation " in pagan vows. It is common; but there is an even larger number of cases in which it is left to be understood, and there can be no doubt what word is to be supplied from the analogy of the cases where " Salvation " is mentioned.[3] Two examples are therefore given in the accompanying cuts, and others are quoted.

I. The first was found at Dorylaion (Eski Sheher), and is published by Professor G. Radet in his " En Phrygie," p. 147.

---

[1] " The Church in the Roman Empire before 170," pp. 191 and 192.

[2] " Pauline and other Studies in the History of Religion," art. iv.

[3] In the " Teaching of Paul," p. 94 f., I have spoken too strongly, writing from memory, about the frequency of the term in dedications, and " very many " should be changed to " many "; but the words are right if one includes the cases where the term is to be understood.

It is a work of the rudest kind, and that is the reason why
it is selected. We here have the prayer and vow ot the
common, poor, and uneducated peasant. The language is
as rude as the art; but still the meaning is certain, except
that the opening word can be understood in more ways
than one. It may probably mean "To (the god) Papas,"

FIG. 4.—Vow to Papa Mên for salvation.

Παπ῀ Παπᾶς   To Papas Papas
τέκνων σωτ-   [for] his children's sal-
ηρίας Μηνὶ   vation to Men
εὐχήν [1]   a vow.

with another title Mên applied to him later in the dedication.
This seems to me the most likely interpretation; but it
is also possible to translate: "Papa son of Papa" (or even

---

[1] In line 2 Professor Radet has E and reads τέκνῳ Νεωτηρίας, "For Papas,
child of Neoteria, Papas (made) a vow to Men". This cannot be defended,
and is evidently a mere slip: the form that results is in several ways contrary
to all usage.

"the son of Papas, Papas ") made the vow.[1] The patronymic sometimes occurs before the son's name in Anatolian dialects; see a paper by the writer : " Inscr. en Langue Pisidienne" in "Revue des Universités du Midi," 1905, p. 358, no. 5.

Papas literally means " father," and this title was commonly applied to the supreme God in Asia Minor, especially in Bithynia and North Phrygia. It also was one of the commonest personal names all over Anatolia, especially in the less hellenized districts. The dedication then means " To Papas (the Father God), i.e. to Mên, Papas (the man) [for] the children's salvation (makes, or pays) a vow".[2] Another interpretation, however, is possible after the analogy of that group of epitaphs in which the making of the grave for a deceased member of the family is at the same time described as the making of a vow to the god : an example of this class is given below as no. IV. in the present chapter. In that case there would be omitted between line 1 and line 2 a line[3] containing the words καὶ ὑπέρ, and the meaning would be : " To (his son) Papas and on behalf of the salvation of the children Papas to Mên (makes) a vow ".

The form and style of this rude monument are similar to those which are described in the chapter on Luke's Name. The preposition ὑπέρ or περί is omitted in line 2 ; the formula regularly has the preposition. The two prepositions

---

[1] Papas is the usual nominative with papa in genitive and dative ; but there is reason to think that sometimes a (possibly Phrygian) inflexion, Papa, genitive Papas, may have been used : " Essays in the History of the Eastern Roman Provinces," p. 321, 10, where read ἐπὶ [πρω]τα[νακλι]του Αὐρ. Παπᾶς.

[2] The mystic identification of several different gods as varying forms of the same ultimate divine nature was widespread in Anatolia. Numerous examples occur : one of the most elaborate is No. 197 in " Cities and Bishoprics of Phrygia," II. p. 375 ; compare pp. 34, 104, 263 f., 293 f., and Nos. 98, 100 f. in the same book.

[3] The engraver was unskilful, and certainly omitted something : that he omitted a whole line is the easiest supposition.

are used in these dedications practically as equivalent.[1]
Also in the Christian form that Jesus died for man, both are
used; and in 1 Thessalonians v. 10 the true text is doubtful, as both ὑπέρ and περί have good MS. authority. On
the analogy of the Christian and the pagan forms more is
said at a later point in this chapter.

II. The following, found at Nakoleia, was copied by me
in 1883 :—

FIG. 5.—Vow to Zeus the Thunderer for salvation.

Μητρόφιλος ᾽[Ασ-	Metrophilos son of
κληπᾶ(ς) σὺν γυναι-	Asklepas[2] with his wife
κὶ ᾽Αμμίᾳ περὶ ἐαυτῶν	Ammia for their own
κὲ τῶν ἰδίων κὲ τῶν	and their family's and
κάρπων κὲ τῆς κώ-	the crops' and the vil-
μης σωτηρίας [Διὶ	lage's salvation to Zeus
Βροντῶντι ε[ὐχήν	the Thunderer a vow.

[1] Out of the equivalents ὑπέρ and περί a novel Byzantine form ὑπερί was
evolved. I have copied this twice, but doubted my own copy, or the engraver,
thinking that +περί was intended. Professor H. Grégoire confirms this form.

[2] The inscription reads: "Metrophilos Asklepas," a double name; but
probably sigma is an accidental dittography, hence I translate as above.

This vow is comprehensive. The inclusion of the family is common. It is evident that the family life was very closely united in the Ægean countries in the less hellenized circles of society. In Phrygia the family unity even included the married sons with their wives: the "brides" (νύμφαι) were part of the household.[1] Hence the salvation is besought for the family as a whole; and, when the head of a household found salvation (as in the case of Lydia and the jailer at Philippi) the entire household shared in it, and if the salvation took a Christian form, they received baptism in a body. The same, doubtless, was the case with the household of Stephanas at Corinth: see chapter "First-fruits of Achaia". The thought expressed here is typical of Anatolian and Macedonian custom.[2]

III. Another dedication found at Kuyujak, between Dorylaion and Nakoleia, was copied by Professor Sterrett in 1883. I have not seen the stone.

Ξεῦνα 'Ιάσονος	Xeuna Jason's
σύνβιος περὶ τῶ-	wife on behalf of her
ν ἰδίων σωτηρί-	family's salvation
ας Μηνὶ Οὐρανί-	to Mên the Heavenly
ῳ κὲ 'Απόλλωνι	(god) and Apollo
εὐχήν	a vow.

This dedication is given because it offers a good parallel to the case of Lydia. Xeuna acts on behalf of her family in this vow for their salvation. Apparently her husband is living, but is not interested in religious matters. The parallel, however, is not perfect, for Lydia changed the religion of her family, which it can hardly be supposed that her husband would have consented to, if he had been living

---

[1] See " Studies in the History of the Eastern Provinces," pp. 71, 82, 150, 372.

[2] Zeus Bronton is almost entirely confined to the northern part of Phrygia about Dorylaion and Nakoleia: he is also the Father, Pappas or Papas.

and near her ; but no one would wonder that Xeuna made a vow on her own account for her family, even though her husband was not interested.

Vows on behalf of the entire family, without the defining word " salvation," are quite common.[1] As was said above, it may be assumed that the purpose of the vow in such cases is the " salvation " of the family.

IV. An example of the omission of the defining word " Salvation " is added in Fig. 5, which was copied at Dorylaion by me in 1883, and was afterwards published by Domaszewski and by Radet, whose copies differ as to one of the names ; but they are proved incorrect since another dedication to a different deity by the same persons[2] has been found and published.[3]

This is an inscription of a remarkable kind. It is an epitaph in memory of Timon, and at the same time it is a dedication to Zeus[4] for (the salvation of) the household. To make the grave was a religious duty, and the erection of the epitaph over it is the record of the vow.[5] This class of gravestones is common in Phrygia. The word salvation is sometimes expressed in such cases, and sometimes omitted.

---

[1] ὑπὲρ τῶν ἰδίων πάντων. πάντων is sometimes omitted, sometimes expressed. ὑπὲρ τοῦ οἴκου also occurs.

[2] Domaszewski, " Arch. Epigr. Mitth. aus Oesterreich," 1883, p. 178, reads Απίωνος; Radet " En Phrygie," p. 149, reads Καπίτωνος; but Ἱππωνος is confirmed by the inscription in " Essays in the History of the Eastern Provinces," p. 271. Supply both εὐχήν and σωτηρίας.

[3] I read ιδιων with blank at the beginning, but both Domaszewski and Radet have the form ειδιων.

[4] In one case Zeus the Thunderer, in the other inscription Zeus of the district Dagoutta in Bithynia.

[5] On this subject see a paper in " Journal of Hellenic Studies," vol. v., 1884, on " Sepulchral Customs in Phrygia," by the writer, also " Essays on the History of the Eastern Provinces," p. 271 f. In some cases of this class the formula is " to so-and-so and to the god a vow "; the first inscription in the present chapter may be understood in that way ; and there are other varieties.

FIG. 6.—Dedication to Zeus the Thunderer on behalf of the family (Dorylaion). The top is restored conjecturally as an example of a common type of votive or sepulchral tablet. Some symbol was placed above the inscription (perhaps eagle or thunderbolt).

Μένανδρος Ἵππω-
νος καὶ Ἀμειὰς Τεί-
μωνι θρεπτῷ, καὶ
Ἀπολλώνιος
καὶ Διονύσιος συν-
τρόφῳ ὑπὲρ τῶν
εἰδίων Διὶ Βρον-
τῶντι

Menander son of Hipp-
on and Amias to Ti-
mon their foster-child,
and Apollonios
and Dionysios to their
foster-brother on behalf ot
the family's (salvation) to
Zeus the Thunderer (a vow).

It is remarkable that the idea of " Salvation " should be so closely connected with the making of the grave. Respect to the dead is a prayer for the whole family and its permanence and prosperity. The dead has gone to be a god with the gods ; the tomb is his temple ; and the worship of this new god is inaugurated with the grave and epitaph, which are the discharge of a vow to secure his blessing for the entire household. In the two dedications Timon the foundling is regarded as identified with Zeus the Thunderer and with Zeus of Dagoutta.

Evidently $\grave{v}\pi\grave{\epsilon}\rho$ with the simple genitive implies $\grave{v}\pi\grave{\epsilon}\rho$ $\sigma\omega\tau\eta\rho\acute{\iota}as$ with the genitive. Is not the same explanation to be given of the use of $\grave{v}\pi\acute{\epsilon}\rho$ in the Christian formula that Christ died for men ($\grave{v}\pi\acute{\epsilon}\rho$ and $\pi\epsilon\rho\acute{\iota}$)? He died for (the salvation of) men.

It is not quite clear whether Apollonios and Dionysios are children or only foster-children of Menander and Amias : but the form suggests as perhaps more probable that they are only foster-children. If the latter is the case, then Menander would seem to have made a trade of bringing up foundlings, who were usually well treated and who occupied a recognized place in the household ; they are sometimes distinguished from the slaves, but in other cases it looks as if they were practically slaves. The custom of selling them as slaves was certainly not infrequent.[1]

---

[1] On this subject see Pliny's well-known letter on the subject to Trajan and the Emperor's reply, with Hardy's commentary; also the discussion in " Cities and Bishoprics of Phrygia," II. p. 546. Such foundlings brought up in a strange family are called θρεπτοί, θρέμματα, even θρεπτά in one case. The parents are θρέψαντες, and this term is used about Menander and Amias in the second inscription mentioned above, but not quoted in full.

CHAPTER XV

THE IMPERIAL SALVATION

ANOTHER form of dedication, which is extremely common, is for the salvation and everlasting continuance of the Emperor and his house.

From the beginning of its history Christianity was brought into the closest relations with the state and the religion of the Emperors. Paul obscurely hints at the worship of the reigning Emperor, "him that calls himself God," and the dead Emperors in 2 Thessalonians II. 1-12. The Revelation of John is absorbed in the conflict against him that sits on the throne of Satan. After the time of Vespasian "a charge of Christianity was tested by calling on the accused to perform the ceremonies of loyalty and worship of the Emperors ".[1] From the beginning to the end of the contest with the State this worship of the Emperors was the immediate enemy of the Christians in a far more pressing way than the worship of Jupiter or the other gods. A few indulgent governors of provinces were willing to accept as the test of loyalty for accused Christians their oath by the salvation of the Emperor ;[2] and even Tertullian permitted this oath to be taken by Christians.[3]

What then was the "salvation" of the Emperor ? It

[1] " Church in the Roman Empire before 170," p. 275.
[2] Ibid. p. 323 f. in footnote.
[3] " Apologet.," 32 ; but the oath *per genium Augusti* was forbidden.

was a very vague term, and we can attempt only to describe its most prominent aspect.

This class of dedication is specially characteristic of the custom on the Imperial estates, which embraced a very large part of the best land throughout Asia Minor. Those estates were most extensive in the less hellenized provinces, like Cappadocia and Galatia, where the Roman Emperors inherited the vast properties of the kings, as well as those of the great religious centres. The population on the estates were in a specially close relation to the reigning Emperor; they were not like ordinary provincials, but stood on a different platform of rights: in fact they had no rights except such as the Imperial pleasure and the force of custom allowed them. They were not far removed from being the slaves of the Emperor, though they were not actually slaves, nor were they even serfs attached to the soil, though their status had considerable analogy to that of serfs and steadily degenerated towards it, until after the middle of the fourth century they may be fairly called in the fullest sense serfs, bound to live on and cultivate the soil and passing with the soil by purchase or inheritance to the next owner.

The cultivators of those great Imperial estates, therefore, being in a status and legal position that approximated to slavery, had the right of slaves to be considered a part of the household of the Emperor.

Hence the frequency on the estates of vows and prayers for the salvation of the Emperor and his household. The whole household formed a unity, as in private life; and the members of the household prayed for the entire body.[1] Slaves and freedmen made vows for their master; their

---

[1] Similarly, in the preceding case, a villager prays for the salvation of the village: chapter xiv., p. 186.

most sacred oath was by the genius of their lord, who stood to them in the relation almost of father and god—these two relations approximated in the mind of the common people —and in making such vows and prayers they included themselves as part of the household. They seem to have hardly thought themselves free to approach the god, except through their master, who was to them the embodiment on earth of the divine power. All those ideas, however, were fluid, and must not be treated or reasoned about as if they were definite logical principles.

Thus the vows for salvation of the Emperor illustrate the unity of the household, a feature so marked in Acts XVI. 15, 33, 1 Corinthians XVI. 15. They also show how closely the person of the Emperor was connected with the life and conduct of the people in the provinces, in the first place of the cultivators of the great estates, and in the second place of the ordinary provincials who came to imitate more and more the fashion that ruled on the estates.

The vows for the Emperor's salvation are often signed by long lists of the coloni,[1] who cultivated the estate. They present no feature of interest except what lies in the words. An example is given which was found at Saghir, the religious centre of the great Imperial estates near Pisidian Antioch, and copied by Professor Sterrett of Cornell University and afterwards by myself:—

" For the fortune and victory and eternal continuance of our Lords and the salvation of his whole household the (association of coloni called) ' Guest-friends of the Symbol' dedicated a bronze (statue of) Fortune " ; then follows a list

---

[1] The word coloni, as denoting the cultivators of the great estates, must be distinguished from the coloni or citizens of a Roman Colony. The difference was world-wide, yet in origin they were the same.

of names and subscriptions with date by the secretary of the society.[1]

This inscription was incised on the pedestal of the statue of Good Fortune, which was erected with the money contributed by the association of cultivators of the estates. An example of a similar dedication, erected by the city of Apollonia, is published on p. 44 above.

Here the Emperor and his family, who are summed up as " our Lords," are conjoined with the body of tenants (coloni). The latter are organized as a religious association uniting in the worship of the Lords Emperors. In this case the identification of the Imperial family as a whole with the gods of the association is unusually clear : the Imperial family is the divine family, the god, the goddess, and the child.

Such an association of coloni was obviously a body of servants and slaves of the god, δοῦλοι τοῦ θεοῦ, as Paul calls himself. The coloni on the estate considered themselves to be absolutely the property of the Lord God their Master. The date of this inscription is certainly a little after A.D. 200 ; and the family may be that of Elagabalus or more probably Alexander Severus ; but the constitution of the cultivators as an association goes back to Augustus, and was unquestionably an inheritance slightly romanized, without essential modification, from the arrangements under King Amyntas the previous landlord.

An institution like this is obviously inconsistent with any

---

[1] [ὑπὲρ Κυ]ρίων τύχης καὶ [νί]κης καὶ αἰωνίου διαμονῆς καὶ τοῦ σύνπαντος αὐτοῦ οἴκου σωτηρίας ἀνέστησαν Ξένοι Τεκμορεῖοι Τύχην χάλκεον ἐπ[ὶ ἀν]αγραφέος Αὐρ. Παπᾶ δίς κτλ, " Studies in the History of the Eastern Roman Provinces," p. 333 f. The construction is illogical, as the single reigning Emperor is not specified except through αὐτοῦ. Had it not been for αὐτοῦ, one might have supposed that Κύριοι were two joint Emperors.

personal liberty in a political sense.[1] The god is the father of his people according to the Roman fashion, with power of life and death over all his children. Hence dedications occur to the Emperor as the Father God (πατρὶ θεῷ). This principle was carried out thoroughly in the institutions for the government of the estate and its cultivators. As the god himself could not be present with his worshippers, he was represented by his procurator, who fulfilled the duty of priest *ex officio*. The old Asian principle that the priest is the representative on earth of the god was thus carried out in a very literal fashion.[2] Augustus, indeed, probably did not insist very strongly on the identification of himself with the god and of the Empress with the goddess; but the theory was there, and the institutions carried it out in practice.

As the divinity of the Emperor became more and more explicitly and openly a part of the Imperial system, it followed that on those great estates near Antioch the identification of the Imperial god and goddess with Mên and Selene was necessary. Since the local goddess was also regarded as Cybele, and was most frequently invoked as Artemis, various difficulties must have arisen for the logical mind ; but the worshippers were not logical, and disregarded all the difficulties of personality. Cybele, Artemis, Selene,

---

[1] The administration of the Anatolian estates is best described by the brilliant Russian exponent of the economy of the Empire, Rostowzew, in his "Studien zur Geschichte des röm. Kolonates," *passim*. He there adopts and approves everything that I had inferred from the series of inscriptions of this class in the Studies, pp. 306-70 (as already quoted). Some remarkable confirmations are given in "Annual of Brit. School at Athens," 1912, xviii., p. 62.

[2] The Anatolian practice commonly seems to have been that the priest wore the dress and bore the name of the god, disusing his personal name and assuming the sacred name when he succeeded to the priesthood, e.g. Atis at Pessinus.

Julia Domna, Tranquillina, are they not all varying aspects and titles of the single ultimate divine nature?

Finally, this Imperial association was a very convenient instrument for co-ordinating to one purpose the strength of all the members. Apparently this was done on a great scale during the struggle between the Emperors and the Christians during the third century. The association was essentially pagan. No one could belong to it who did not worship the God-Emperor. Yet any Christian cultivator on the estate must necessarily be a member of the association. What then was to be done with such a disaffected colonus?

Probably the idea of the membership was not carried out to its logical extreme before the third century, and the religious nature of the association was allowed to be ignored by those members who did not approve.[1] In the third century, however, the religious aspect was made prominent, so that membership was a proof of loyalty; and then the entrance into the association became an act of renunciation of the Christian faith, and was coupled with some rite of a novel character, designated by a newly invented word;[2] and this rite was performed in some cases two or three times in succession.

The system of the Imperial estates gradually affected the

---

[1] There is no trace of any very thorough-going persecution in Anatolia during the second century. Isolated, and perhaps fairly numerous cases of martyrdom of individuals occur; but the State forbade the hunting of Christians; only those who were denounced and caught were punished. In central Asia Minor there seems to have been great freedom on the whole at that time: see Chapter XII. of my "Cities and Bishoprics of Phrygia," and Chapters X.-XIV. of the "Church in the Roman Empire before 170".

[2] The verb τεκμορεύειν, to show the Tekmor or secret sign, is a novel word: some other words were invented in this Tekmoreian Association, see "Journal of Roman Studies," 1912, p. 158 ff.

free cities in the disorder of the third and fourth centuries
Already examples occur of freemen and burgesses from the
self-governing cities preferring the system of the estates
with their practical serfdom as early as the first half of the
third century,[1] and the customs spread. Thus serfdom
became the goal of the Imperial order,[2] and produced the
developed serfdom of the mediaeval land-system, which
lasted in Russia until about 1860.

This is the "Salvation" of the dedications on the great
estates. To explain its nature has called for a rather long
historical review; but it is impossible to understand the
nature of any human institution or of any such object of
human prayers, until we trace it in its development and its
effects. The paternal government was "Salvation" in the
estimate of the cultivators on the estates. It had its advantages. The Father God through his procurators protected his people, advised them, told them their duty,
looked after peace and order, punished them for their faults,
and in general made life easier for them. In the degeneration and growing disorganization of the Empire, freedom
lost its charm, and gradually ceased. The freeman was
more exposed to oppression and insult than the serf. He
could not protect himself, while the serf had his master to
protect him from some of the evils of life.

The logical issue of the paternal system of government,
as we see it fully carried out under the Roman Empire, was
the negation of freedom. In its opposition to the Imperial
policy the religion of Christ was the champion of freedom.
Such is its spirit in central Asia, where we can best see it,
during the second century. Such is its spirit as declared

---

[1] "Studies in the History of the Eastern Roman Provinces," p. 357.

[2] Zulueta in Vinogradoff's "Oxford Studies": there is a vast body of
literature on this subject.

by Paul to the people of Antioch, Iconium, etc. : " ye were
called for freedom," and " for freedom did Christ set us free :
stand fast therefore, and be not entangled again in a yoke
of bondage ".[1]   He spoke to nations of slaves, the Phrygians and the Lycaonians, raised in some small degree from
the condition of slavery by the Græco-Roman education,
but liable to slip back again as the Imperial system developed its paternal character thoroughly.   The " Salvation "
of Jesus and of Paul was freedom : the " Salvation " of the
Imperial system was serfdom.

The fourth century saw a gradual change.   The Christian religion was taken under the protection of the State
in the new Empire, and acquiesced in most of the evils of
the Imperial system.   That, however, lies outside of our
subject, which is the truth, not the deterioration, of Christianity.   We take it as it is set before the world at the
beginning.

[1] Galatians v. 13 and 1.

CHAPTER XVI

TRUSTWORTHINESS OF THE ACTS, CHAPTERS I TO XII

IN beginning to appreciate the great historical value and trustworthiness of the Acts, I was at first guided in some degree by old-fashioned ideas about sources and authorities employed by the author of the book, drawing on my former experiences in respect of Aristotle and my studies in Old Testament history (as described on pp. 16 f. and 18). Being very careful not to go beyond the evidence, I did not in my first book venture to argue for more than " that the narrative in Acts of Paul's journeys is founded on, or actually incorporates, an account written under the immediate influence of Paul himself ".[1]

The conviction became steadily stronger in my mind that the book was a unity, and that one part could not be separated from the rest as true, while the remainder of the book stood on a lower level of trustworthiness. The author is very emphatic about the excellence of his authorities (Luke I. 1-3), and allows no exceptions : he is trustworthy as a whole, or not at all. The quality of his work is as uniform as the style. Those parts in which the historian speaks as an eye-witness, the " We-passages," are not more or less Lukan in character, not more free from marvellous accompaniments, than the rest. This is fully acknowledged

[1] " Church in the Roman Empire before 170," p. 6.

by Dr. Harnack,[1] who concludes that Luke had a constitutional tendency towards the marvellous, and could not avoid seeing events in that light. This judgment is a matter of personal quality, and is quite in the critical style of the nineteenth century, whereas Harnack writes often from the point of view of the twentieth century. The present writer's experience leads him to feel more and more convinced, as the years pass, that the world around is full of the marvellous and the incomprehensible, if one has eyes to see rightly.

There is among many modern people a strong inclination to doubt such general statements as those in Acts V. 12, "by the hands of the Apostles were many signs and wonders wrought among the people," or VIII. 7, "from many of those which had unclean spirits they came out; and many that were palsied and that were lame were healed". Along with this doubt follows a general tendency to rate low the credibility of the book in which such statements occur, and the intelligence of the author who admits them. But we should take into consideration the character of an Oriental population, where physicians and medical attendance are almost unknown and magicians abound, where ignorance and a low standard of living and of thought are prevalent, and where that peculiar class of trouble or disease called in the New Testament " possession by devils " is rife. I feel convinced that those who can appreciate from experience the actual situation and conditions of such a state of society, will be the slowest to doubt the credibility of statements like those which have just been quoted. Now imagine that amid this Oriental population, keenly suscept-

---

[1] Harnack, "Lukas der Artzt Verfasser des III. Evang. und d. Apostelgesch," p. 60, points out that the " We-passages " are thoroughly Lukan in style : see " Luke the Physician and other Studies," pp. 4, 34, 38.

ible to religious emotions and strongly influenced already by many superstitious ideas and customs, a great religious idea is introduced and propagated widely through the degraded masses by one extraordinary personality and by a devoted enthusiastic group of followers, all themselves men and women of eminent power and magnetic influence. Take into consideration the strange and yet indubitable facts of faith-healing, and similar phenomena. No one who weighs the conditions of this question can regard these general statements in the Acts as improbable in themselves, or as detracting from the credibility of the book as a whole. The present writer can only assert his own conviction that those statements express just what would be likely to occur. Some slight account of the situation where belief in demonic influence grows strong is given above in chapter IX.

At the same time it must be frankly acknowledged that the general prevalence of such conditions must always lead to the too ready acceptance without investigation of particular instances ; and that many of the individual cases would not stand rigorous examination. Not every mendicant who pretends to be ill is really so. Imposture and trading on pretended diseases would be detected in many cases.

Yet none the less do even these examples of common delusion attest the reality of the curative influence. The public mind and body have as a whole been diseased, and they undergo a health-giving renovation. The impostor who deludes the world with his pretended disease of body is really diseased in soul ; and it is no small thing that his mind should be cured and his life transformed into a healthy one. But most of the so-called impostors are physically diseased to some extent as well as morally diseased in their whole nature. Exceptions indeed occur, in which the pretended sufferer from incurable disease or loss of eyesight or so on, is perfectly sound; but generally there is nervous or other malady of some kind as well as moral disease.

Cures effected in these cases furnish real proofs of the power which the new religious idea exerts on those whom it seizes. The medical expert would not label the disease and the cure exactly as the popular opinion does; but there is in each case a disease, and a cure is effected.

Luke, however, claims to be a good authority, because he has his narrative from the authority of eye-witnesses; and in most cases we can determine who were the witnesses. Yet the strictly scientific inquirer will not be satisfied with the evidence even of eye-witnesses in the case of every cure, or of raising from the dead. Was the witness competent to distinguish death from mere suspended animation? Did the witness really test the case? I have myself seen a man brought in from the harvest-field, washed and prepared for burial, mourned in the vehement Oriental style, carried to his grave and buried; but I should be a bad witness to his death, because the suspicion has always haunted me that the man was perhaps not dead. Of those scores of witnesses, probably only my wife and myself had any doubt as to the man's death; and in the hurry of events—for little more than two hours elapsed between the man's collapse in the field and his deposition in the tomb—everything was so convincing that it was only after all was over that we began to ask each other, " was that man really dead? "[1]

That the circumstances in all those incidents occurred as Luke relates there is not the smallest reason to doubt. The

[1] Nothing is more difficult than to be quite certain that death has occurred, even for a physician. I know well a man who, after long illness, was pronounced dead by the excellent doctors and nurses in Paris who had been attending him, yet he recovered.

inference from the facts may, however, be doubtful. That the lame man at Lystra was really lame, and not an arrant impostor, must be taken as certain : he was known from childhood as lame : he had been a beggar [1] familiar to every one in the small city of Lystra, and all believed in the reality of his lameness and the extraordinary nature of the cure. Yet, when the medical expert comes to examine the case, he will ask whether the theory of unconscious imposture might not be admissible. The physician can give many examples of mental disease simulating such bodily conditions as lameness. The case was not critically examined at the time. We have started from the assumption that mental and nervous diseases of an obscure kind must have been numerous in the state of society which existed at that time in western Asia.

Even supposing, however, that the lame man might have been an unconscious impostor, who thought he was lame and had never walked, the incident remains just as marvellous as if he were really lame.[2] His mind was cured, and he saw his real self. Such apparent lameness might be due to nervous causes ; but none the less it is lameness.

There is little to be gained for our purpose by investigating each case. That is a subject for the medical expert. The question in such an investigation would be how the facts should be labelled. What scientific name shall we apply? The facts stand recorded in their external as-

[1] The man is not stated to have been a beggar ; but what is said about him leaves no doubt in the mind of anyone acquainted with the habits of the Mediterranean peoples, that he was sitting (perhaps at a gate as a good beggar's station) a mendicant (Acts xiv. 7).

[2] The state of his ankles and feet, after many years spent without walking, would have been exactly as described in Acts. The account states as the climax, that " he never walked ". That was the outcome of the evidence as known to an eye-witness.

pect, as they would appear to unscientific witnesses. They are sufficient evidence that the individual was abnormal and diseased in some way, and that he was restored to normal existence and to happiness.

Such incidents, too, attest sufficiently the remarkable spiritual power over the minds and bodies exerted by the Apostles in the way of bringing men to a reasonable, natural and healthy condition ; but this in itself does not prove that, because a person who believes is cured, therefore his belief is truth. Belief in a delusion may sometimes produce a curative effect, though only in exceptional cases. That this was not a case of delusion has to be proved by other reasons, of which there is abundance.

A strong and general popular belief is a great power. The new idea as preached by the Apostles had this great power supporting it and pushing it forward. And there was no pretence on the side of the Apostles and of the Church. They felt and knew what a revolution they were making in the world. They saw with their own eyes that the souls and bodies of men were growing healthier around them ; and they knew that the cause was simply and solely belief in the Jesus whom they were preaching. Their own faith was made stronger by those cures, as well as the faith and character of the people that were cured.

We need not enter on the question whether the Apostles were possessed of any personal healing power, which acted independently of any faith or belief felt by the patient. For our purposes that is immaterial ;[1] but the remarkable article by Dr. Schofield in the " Contemporary Review," March, 1909, on " Spiritual Healing," may be quoted as evidence that modern medical science accepts the view that

[1] They always claimed to act and to have power only in the name of Jesus.

some people possess such personal power.[1] Still even on his showing the fact is clear that the faith of the patient is an enormously potent influence and by far the most common. Cure by the simple power of the healer must be always rare and exceptional; and the record of a cure seems more credible when it lays stress on the faith of the person cured. That was the case with the lame man at Lystra. Paul, fixing his gaze on him, saw that he had the faith which gave him the capability of being saved.

It is, however, needless, irrational, and unfair to require that Luke's narrative should be like the report of a nerve-specialist. He tells us what seemed to the spectators to happen, just as he had heard it from them, or as in various cases he had himself seen it. He is very careful in many cases to define, with accuracy unusual in an ancient writer, exactly how much was vouched for to him and how much he was prepared to guarantee.[2]

The best and probably the most scientific way is to read the Acts simply, gather from it the opinions of those who were eye-witnesses, and give this its full value, but always to remember that they were not medical experts. The general opinion and impression will prove quite good enough for a fair judgment.

It is matter for a special book to study the authorities whom Luke used for the first part of his history. The present writer's view is that Luke was careful to indicate his authorities, not indeed by formal quotation as a modern writer would, but indirectly. A good deal rests on the authority of Philip the Deacon, with whom Luke was long

[1] The fact that some people are, so to say, walking stores of typhoid infection, without themselves developing fully the disease, is not exactly parallel, for degeneration is more catching than health.

[2] In " St. Paul the Traveller " this feature is pointed out in several cases. At Lystra the disciples " supposed that Paul was dead ".

in intimate relation, first when Paul and his company landed in Cæsarea, and afterwards during Paul's imprisonment there. Those parts which describe Philip's own action are marked by great modesty: he keeps himself secondary, and speaks of Peter and John as standing on a higher rank, and wielding more authority than himself.

The episode of the Ethiopian is an exception: this figure, in short, finds a place in Luke's pages mainly for the purpose of bringing into relief the character and power and influence of Philip, and not as indicating an important direction in the growth of the new Faith towards the south. Such a story was not gathered from Philip himself, but from a warm admirer of Philip. Yet admiration does not affect the representation of the facts. The same limitation to Philip's power is observable here as at Samaria. Philip can only baptize; his influence does not carry with it the gift of the Spirit.

Our view, therefore, is that the Ethiopian episode was included by Luke rather with a view to showing the character of Philip than with the intention of describing a step in the growth of the Church. Luke appreciated the great men who had made the early Church, and was resolved that his readers should appreciate them also. He knew that no impressive view of history can be given or acquired, unless the dominating figures are set in their true light. He was writing for the congregations of the Græco-Roman world; and one of his main objects was to move them, and to affect their life. To do this it was above all things necessary to put before them in their true colours the great figures Peter, Stephen, Philip, and Paul. Luke had at the same time the Greek sense of historic truth and of proportion: he shows those figures to us in action, and never merely describes them.

For example, the scene of the voyage and shipwreck in chapter XXVII. is not directly important in itself for the development of the Church; but it is highly important as illuminating the character of Paul and showing how, even as a prisoner and a landsman at sea, he became the dominating personage in a great ship's company as soon as danger threatened; and it also draws the reader's attention to the central and critical importance of the scene towards which it leads up, viz. the trial of Paul in Rome.

So, also, the Ethiopian episode places Philip before the reader in a new light. Henceforth we realize his character and his action in a very different way; Philip now rises from the level of a second-rate figure almost to the higher plane on which Peter and Paul move. Even the Samarian episode assumes a different character, when it is read in the light of the Ethiopian incident.

Such seems to be the intention of Luke, when he gives the story of the Ethiopian eunuch a place in his history. He heard it, not from Philip himself, but from the prophetesses his daughters, one or all. It was the prophetesses who imparted the spirit of the Old Testament to the story, regarding their father after the fashion of an old Hebrew prophet, who went forth into the wilderness, to whom the messenger of the Lord spoke, who was caught away by the Spirit when he had done what he was ordered to do. The narrative impressed the imagination of Luke, and has been recorded by him in the same tone in which he heard it. It is markedly different in certain ways from the Samarian narrative.

It shows us how Philip impressed those among whom he lived; and we recognize in him the person who was fitted to write the Epistle to the Hebrews.[1] He was a great ad-

[1] The writer's view on this subject is stated in a paper in " Luke the Physician," pp. 301-28.

mirer of Peter, and yet he had the freedom of mind that fitted him to appreciate Paul. The self-suppression that characterizes the part of the Acts where he was Luke's authority is also evident in the Epistle, where the writer never mentions himself, and where the first person singular appears only as a literary form.[1] The personality of this great leader of the early Church will yet be recovered in far more complete fashion by a careful study of the Epistle to the Hebrews in its relation to the portions of the Acts which depend on the testimony of Philip.

Luke had known John Mark, and he had certainly seen and entered the house of Mary his mother. The way in which he uses evidence gathered there is studied as regards one incident in the following chapter XVII.

[1] See " Luke the Physician," p. 324.

CHAPTER XVII

RHODA THE SLAVE-GIRL

THE writer's view is that Luke has always a definite purpose in mentioning any individual—a purpose bearing on the plan of his history, and not a mere desire for literary effect. The case of the slave-girl Rhoda in chapter XII. may seem to be an exception. It may be thought that the details of her action are recorded only for their picturesque and literary value. While Luke was certainly quite sensible of this value, he has another purpose in view. He knows the very inmost feelings in Rhoda's mind, her joy as she heard the voice of Peter, her fluttering eagerness which defeated her own desire by leaving Peter in the street in danger of discovery while she ran into the inner house to tell the news, her confidence that she was right while the others disbelieved her and thought she was mad. This is the way in which Luke intimates to us that he had himself talked to Rhoda, and had her own evidence to go upon. Only from her, or from some one who took a warm personal interest in her, could he have learned these details; and there was no one who would interest himself in the slave-girl's emotions, and treasure up such information to retail to Luke. We have here personal recollection, narrated to Luke by the maid herself, and caught by his sympathetic and appreciative mind.

Incidentally, we notice here the close and friendly relation between the slave-girl and the family and its friends.

Rhoda knows Peter's voice, is full of joy at hearing it, forgets in her joy her duty as a servant, and runs in to impart the glad news to the family as a friend. She is in the most real sense a part of the household, fully sharing in the anxieties and the joys of the family, knowing the family's friends as her own friends. As has been said above, it is impossible to judge ancient society and life from the proper point of view, unless this unity of the household is fully appreciated.[1]

The story of Peter's release from prison is palpitating with life. There is nothing quite so picturesque, after a certain fashion, in the whole of Luke's work as this scene: but the fashion is not exactly that of Luke's pictures generally. This scene stands apart by itself, just as the Ethiopian scene also stands alone. Some special authority was followed by Luke in each case for one scene and no more. The ultimate authority for the facts of Peter's escape was, necessarily, himself. No other had seen the facts. No other person could tell what thoughts, and what confusion, filled Peter's mind. No one heard his soliloquy, when the angel left him in the street. But the description of the scene was not got by Luke from Peter's lips: it has all the character of a narrative by a spectator, who was present in Mary's house and listened with eager interest and retentive memory to his hurried account of his deliverance. The listener's attention, of course, was concentrated on Peter; and the Apostle's narrative was brief and confined to the facts which were most important in his hearers' estimation and his own. He had already lost some valuable minutes while Rhoda was talking with the incredulous people inside and maintaining that Peter himself was at

[1] See above, pp. 187, 192.

the door. His escape might be noticed at any moment, an alarm raised, and strict search made for the fugitive.

Accordingly, when he is relating all that had happened, neither does Peter tell, nor do the hearers ask, what the two soldiers watching in his cell were doing, what the two sets of sentinels on guard outside the cell—"the first and the second ward"—were doing, whether all were asleep. We gather later that the escape was not discovered until the next morning. As Peter had been roused from sound sleep by a blow on his side, and was as in a dream throughout the whole escape, and only awoke to full consciousness after he was clear of the prison and the angel had left him, his account would naturally take little notice of surrounding circumstances, and be restricted to the facts that had most strongly impressed him; he saw nothing else, and was conscious only of those urgent facts, and that in a dim and half-dreamy fashion. No questions were put to him by any of his hearers on those other circumstances, or, if put (which is extremely improbable), they were not answered:[1] although information about them might be useful in view of his escape from Jerusalem and the chances of immediate pursuit. It was sufficient for the little crowd of listeners to have a clear conception of the really important factors in the situation—the distress of the Church in the prospect of losing its most influential and guiding spirit:[2] the earnest prayers of its members: the wonderful deliverance by "a messenger of the Lord" at the very moment when those

---

[1] Implying that Peter either had no information to give or no desire to give it. But, considering the character of the Oriental audience, I should feel very confident that no questions were asked, and that the description of the scene is perfect and complete in all essentials.

[2] James was now evidently regarded as the head of the Church in Jerusalem; but that was probably due to the frequent absence of Peter on external duty (VIII. 14, 25, IX. 32, Gal. II. 12).

prayers were being made most insistently and distressfully in the last night before the execution. These are the features set clearly and strongly before the reader in the whole narrative, and only one of them, viz. the deliverance, belongs to Peter himself or could originate from him. His story is, in the strictest sense, only subsidiary to the greater story of the Church's need; and it is placed before us from that point of view.

In short, as has been said, we have here the authoritative statement of a Christian who listened to Peter, and had prayed for Peter. But the circumstances were such as to impress Peter's words indelibly on the memory of his hearers: we have the scene before us in all its intensity and anxiety, yet in every stage deliberate and unhurried. Even Peter's dressing is described point by point; he and his guide move on in the light, but the light shines in darkness, and all that does not concern their acts from moment to moment is shrouded in the darkness.

The narrator was Rhoda. Luke had listened to her. He had doubtless heard the tale from others, e.g. from John Mark, perhaps, when they were together in Rome [1] or elsewhere. Probably he heard Rhoda tell the story in the house of Mary, and in the presence of other witnesses who could corroborate or correct her. But she needed no correction. It was the great event of her life, and she told it in that striking fashion in which we read it. Luke recognized that her narrative gave the true spirit of the scene; and he used the narratives of others only as subsidiary.

If we are right in this interpretation of the source, the story of Peter's deliverance lies before us almost in his very

---

[1] Colossians IV.; Philemon.

words and certainly in the exact details of the facts, as they were described within an hour after they occurred by the one man who knew them. This has a most important bearing on the trustworthiness of the Acts. There is no room here for invention or for the growth of legend. People were too eager: the need was too great: no one could do anything except under the overpowering urgency of the danger. All the persons who played a part in the scene were compelled by the circumstances to be themselves for the moment, and to strip off all pretence and regard to outward appearance. *Eripitur persona : manet res.*

That this interpretation is the true one must be felt by every one who has the literary and the historic sense for reality. Luke, according to his custom,[1] gives the story of his informants with an added touch of literary skill, but never such a touch as to disturb the simplicity and the vivid rush and hurry of the original ; and Rhoda is the main authority.

Now, given this tale, based on this supremely excellent testimony, related to Luke thirteen years after the event, and, doubtless, often related in the interval, what are we to make of it ? We have here a test case of the worth of the class of evidence on which (as I believe) ultimately the whole three Synoptic Gospels rest, as well as much of Acts : the evidence is that of eye-witnesses, and absolutely honest, truthful witnesses. What is its value ? what are its defects ? It is obvious, on the surface, that we in one sense do not know exactly what happened in the prison, but that much is enveloped in obscurity, and observed almost in a dream ; and

---

[1] Harnack has demonstrated this custom fully in his " Lukas der Artzt ". Salmon has anticipated in his brief and telling fashion most of the correct views in Harnack's book ; and the very notable agreement in point after point reveals a certain kinship in nature between the two.

that in another sense we know on the very best evidence all the really important and critical facts of the case.

As has been said, Peter's escape is described to us by Luke in words closely approximating to those in which the fugitive narrated it to the group of the Saints at Mary's door within an hour after it occurred. It would be difficult to find any narrative of an escape from prison better authenticated, or related amid circumstances which exclude more absolutely the supposition either of falsification, or of the growth of legend. The description of the scene at the house must convince the unprejudiced judge, who examines the evidence critically, that Luke had listened to the story as it was related in the presence of several other witnesses of the scene by Rhoda herself, and that he intends to convey to his readers that he had been in the house and heard the story there.

In the story we hear not a word about the conduct of the guards, of whom three sets had to be passed. Were they, so to say, hypnotized by the angel, or drugged, or bribed? Did Peter and the messenger pass among them without being visible? The supposition that they were asleep naturally cannot be entertained where so many were concerned, all bound by their duty to be vigilant and all responsible for their vigilance with their life. Under the head of hypnotism we may include any and every kind of superhuman influence which prevented the guards from observing what was going on. The Divine power, if we adopt the theory that the deliverance was accomplished in a supernatural manner, acts through natural means so far as possible ; and there must have been some reason evident to an observer why the guards did not take notice of what was going on, not even of the opening of the outer gate, until the morning.

Peter's story explains in part why he observed so little, and why the circumstances are left so obscure. He was wakened out of sleep—evidently a deep sleep—by a blow on the side; but he was still in such a confused, half-awakened state, that he believed all was a dream, until out in the street he found himself alone, after the " messenger of God" had disappeared. Then at last the cold night air and the continuous exercise restored his faculties, and he began to review the situation. He was a practical man, not an observer and student of psychical phenomena. He misses out what would interest the man of scientific temper : " when he was come to himself he said, ' Now I know of a truth, that the Lord hath sent forth His messenger and delivered me out of the hand of Herod, and from all the expectation of the people of the Jews ' ". He pictures to himself the scene on the morrow, the disappointment of the people, and the annoyance of the monarch whose hand and power had proved so feeble. He was conscious of this side of the situation first ; and then later came the thought of escape, and of what immediate steps he should take to save himself. The order of his thoughts shows a calm and sane intellect, with a distinct sense of humour. A fussy or timid person would have thought at such a moment only of flight and safety. Peter, as we can gather from this scene, even if we knew nothing else about him, was a man far above the common in respect of coolness, courage, and presence of mind. He resolved that the best thing to do was to retire to some obscure spot, after first relieving the anxiety of the brethren about his safety.

We observe that Peter had to think over the situation before he came to the conclusion that his deliverer was a messenger of the Lord. He had not as yet been conscious of anything apparently supernatural in the circumstances,

except that the gate "opened of its own accord".[1]   He
knew of no agent or instrument pushing it, but saw it open
before him.   Otherwise the accompaniments were all
natural : the light was needed in the dark cell : he fastened
his girdle round his tunic, and put on his thick upper gar-
ment and his sandals, before going out into the cold night.
The chains had indeed dropped off from his hands ; but
this occurred first of all at the very moment that he was
wakened, and he had no knowledge how the fastenings
were unloosed.   The " messenger " or " angel " appeared to
him, therefore, in ordinary human form ; and Peter only
inferred his superhuman mission from subsequent reflexion
about the circumstances.   During the escape from the
prison Peter was not in a condition to think ; he simply
obeyed and acted.   When, standing alone in the street,
he collected his thoughts and reviewed the situation, he
concluded that the deliverance was the act of God.

Now, since previously the steps of the action had proceeded without his observing anything supernatural in
the appearance or conduct of the deliverer, it is not
necessary to understand from the conclusion which he
stated, that the deliverer was a supernatural being.   In the
life of such people in modern times as Dr. Barnardo, who
from small means have built up vast and beneficial organiza-
tions in reliance on the help of God, that help has come
always in apparently natural ways.   When a stranger in a
hotel in Oxford, noticing Barnardo's name in the visitors'
list, told him that he would make the first Village Home
for girls, " we need not say that Dr. Barnardo and his friend

---

[1] This is a very vague thought in the mind of an Oriental, and is perfectly
consistent with other explanations besides that of supernatural action.   At
the same time, I do not doubt that Luke understood it to imply supernatural
agency.

received this as an answer to prayer, doubting not that the
hand of God was in it". Was Peter, or were any of the
early Christians at that time, less able or likely to recognize
the hand of God in the affairs of the world than Dr. Barnardo and his friend? On the contrary, the Oriental mind
is far more prone to see the hand of God in everything that
goes on around us than the English mind is. To the Oriental God is always very close. The Oriental thinks and
speaks of God far more frequently and familiarly than we
do; and yet in his way of introducing the Divine name
and supposing the Divine presence and action in the most
common affairs of life, there is no irreverence. He does
so, because he feels that God is always moving in all that
goes on, great and small; that "not a sparrow falls to
the ground without Him". We, on the other hand, tend
to reserve the action of God for the big things, with the
result that the logical mind, which cannot see any reasonable distinction between the small and the big things, fails,
and must necessarily fail, to see that hand anywhere. Was
not Barnardo more near the truth when he saw the hand
of God in the bestowal of a needed subscription, and read
in this act the fulfilment of his prayers?

Such is the Oriental view, at any rate; and there cannot
be a doubt that, whether or not Peter actually knew his
deliverer to be a real human being, he would equally confidently conclude that this was an angel, the bearer of the
power of God. Peter's words should be judged from his
own point of view, as they were meant. The Church was
in the direst need, when its leader was on the eve of death.
The Church engaged in earnest prayers. The prayers were
answered. So much is certain; and we may safely assert
that, whether the deliverer was man or a supernatural being,
he was equally " the messenger of God," in Oriental phrase.

Further, we may take it as certain that the escape occurred in the darkest part of the night, before the moon rose. The night following the last day of Unleavened Bread was the twenty-second of the moon, which therefore rose very late. The deliverance was doubtless timed, so that Peter should have a long period of darkness to place himself beyond the reach of pursuit. All the more remarkable is it that his escape was not observed until the next morning. The dawning was not very early at that season of the year ; and several hours must therefore have elapsed before the guards observed the facts, and began to inquire what had become of Peter. It is not stated whether the outer gate closed behind the fugitive, or remained open. Peter observed only what bore on his immediate movements, and evidently never looked behind him, until he collected his thoughts in the street at some distance from the prison. But we cannot suppose it possible that the outer gate of the State prison remained open for hours, especially after the moon had risen, without some one perceiving it and giving the alarm. The gate, therefore, must certainly have been closed by the same agency which, unseen by Peter, had opened it, naturally or supernaturally, to let him go out.

Now there cannot be a doubt that the "messenger" who struck Peter on the side and guided him had human form, and had opened the door of the cell; for Peter, who described the other details so exactly, seems to assume that this door was open, and that only the outer iron gate at the top of the seven steps needed to be opened before them.[1] But, though the "messenger" had the form of a man (like "the messenger" who appeared to Cornelius),[2] he was

---

[1] The seven steps are mentioned only in the Western Text.

[2] Acts x. 30: when Cornelius tells the story he speaks only of "a man in bright apparel"; others speak of a "messenger," or "angel," of God.

to Peter merely an instrument used by the Divine power. God works through natural instruments and agents; and Peter had none of the desire which we feel to investigate and state precisely the nature of each stage in his escape. The supernatural and the natural were not separated to his mind by any clear dividing line; the one melted into the other, and he was not interested in drawing the line between them.

Luke also was not interested to divide precisely the region of the natural from that of the supernatural. On the contrary, it would rather seem that he in many cases purposely leaves a debatable ground between the two. Those who, like the present writer, assume as the starting-point of their thought, that the Divine Power does continually exert itself in the affairs of the world, must recognize that at some point the Divine intervention (which is in its origin beyond our ken) becomes knowable to us, i.e. at some point it begins to act through means and in ways that are amenable to the ordinary laws of experience and reason. But where does that point lie? To answer that question is always difficult. To answer it in the case of Peter's deliverance is impossible, because Luke intentionally or unintentionally— the present writer believes, intentionally—leaves the line of demarkation in obscurity. Does the so-called natural action in this process begin only when Peter stood alone in the street, and was it previously all "supernatural"? Or did it begin with the agent of the deliverance, in whose heart the thought was born and the means were carefully planned out? We cannot say with certainty. But we can say with certainty that every one, whether he prefers to make the "supernatural" element larger or smaller, must acknowledge that at some point that element ceases and the ordinary and "natural" begins; and we can feel great confidence that

Luke, who was generally disposed to enlarge the sphere of the supernatural, purposely leaves the transition obscure.

Now there is no doubt that at the court of the Herods, just as later at the court of many Roman Emperors, the Christians had friends, sympathizers, and even adherents. Slight references occur in the Gospels and the Acts, which may half reveal a considerable background of fact. The wife of Herod's steward was a follower of Jesus. The "foster-brother" of Herod,[1] Menahem, was one of the leading Christians, prophet or teacher, at Antioch. Others have observed and collected these indications; and it is not necessary here to enlarge on them. There is therefore nothing improbable in the supposition that some person influential in the *entourage* of Herod Agrippa I. had skilfully engineered the escape of Peter. The occasion was well chosen, as we have seen, in respect of darkness. Even if Peter had suspected or known who the deliverer was, he would not have mentioned the name at a street door; and he would equally have regarded his helper as "the messenger of God".

This case is typical of what can fairly be expected in the narrative of the New Testament, and of the limitations which must be allowed for. The essential facts and the spiritual truth are placed beyond doubt in this story, for they rest on evidence of the highest kind. But those who are bent on knowing the commonplace facts, those who regard it as the most important part of this historical scene to learn who

[1] I cannot wholly agree with Prof. Deissmann's argument in his "Bible Studies," p. 310 ff., that this term was merely a court title. I think that every one who comes into contact for a time with the life of the Levant lands, and knows how great a part in it is played by foster-mothers and foster-brothers, will be slow to accept some of the sentences in his argument. He writes like one used to German ways of life, and taking these as universally applicable.

managed the escape, and how the guards were evaded, will be disappointed : it is utterly impossible from the evidence to do more than make a vague conjecture, founded on general considerations and not on the special evidence, about these matters. The reason is that such things were indifferent both to Peter and to Luke : they are mere details, which do not in any way affect Peter's conceptions of real and spiritual truth, and the evidence does not even in the remotest way bear on matters of this class. The historian and the sociologist may long to know what was the relation of the royal court to the new Faith : it would be to such scientific inquirers a matter of real value to know whether some person who possessed influence at court managed the escape. Luke, however, did not write for them. Luke wrote for the Christian congregations of the Græco-Roman world : and he told what was of permanent value for those whom he had in mind as readers. This principle must be applied in general throughout the New Testament narrative.

In the houses of Philip and of Mary, and in other houses of Palestine and Jerusalem, Luke had learned the general tradition of the early Church at its source within less than thirty years after the Crucifixion. It is this general tradition that dictates the conceptions which are expressed in his history. The historian caught the idea as it was still fresh and young and living in the hearts and lives of eye-witnesses, and it lives for us in his pages. This gives a unique value to both the Gospel and the Acts.

CHAPTER XVIII

APPROACH TO THE GOSPEL OF LUKE

In two books already mentioned [1] the result of some years of study were stated; the opinions in the first are much less developed than in the second. In the former it is maintained that the Acts may justly be quoted as a trustworthy historical authority. In the latter the purpose is to show that Luke is a historian of the first rank; not merely are his statements of fact trustworthy; he is possessed of the true historic sense; he fixes his mind on the idea and plan that rules in the evolution of history; and proportions the scale of his treatment to the importance of each incident. He seizes the important and critical events and shows their true nature at greater length, while he touches lightly or omits entirely much that was valueless for his purpose. In short, this author should be placed along with the very greatest of historians.

It is no part of the present plan to repeat, or even to give a résumé of, the argument stated in those two volumes; but only to show how they form a step in the growth of a better, fuller, and truer understanding of the meaning and the immense value of the historian Luke's work in two parts, the Gospel and the Acts.

The second of those volumes was reviewed at some length by a distinguished foreign scholar. He gave a quite fair résumé of the book, and then disproved the opinion which

[1] " The Church in the Roman Empire before A.D. 170 " (1892); " St. Paul the Traveller " (1894).

(222)

is championed in it about Luke's rank as a historian in one
brief concluding sentence : if Luke is a great historian,
what would the author of this book make of Luke II. 1-3 ?
Nothing more was needed. This brief question was sufficient.

It was at that time fully admitted on all hands that the
statements in that passage are entirely unhistorical. Not
merely did theological critics brush them aside as incredible,
every one that had any acquaintance with Roman Imperial
history regarded them as false and due either to blundering
or to pure invention. There are in it four statements about
the action of the Roman Imperial government which the
critics of the New Testament pronounced to be incredible
and false.

Now we are bound by the principle which has been
already stated on p. 80. The great historian is great in
virtue of his permanent quality of mind. If an author can
be guilty of any such perversion of history as has been
attributed to the writer of Luke II. 1-3, he cannot deserve
the rank and name of a historian. After reading the review
I began for the moment to feel guilty of pronouncing an
opinion on part of the evidence : I had not taken the Gospel
of Luke into consideration, but had written with my eye
on the Acts of the Apostles and mainly on the second half
of the book. I had assumed that, if Luke shows himself a
true historian there, he must be so everywhere ; and the
critic retorted in crushing style that, since he showed himself
not to be a trustworthy historian elsewhere, he could not
be so in the second half of the Acts.

The retort could be answered only in one way. Either
Luke II. 1-3 is good history, or there was something
seriously wrong about my contention. If this passage is
historically trustworthy, some proof or probability must be
established in its favour.

It was not with any intention of replying to the criticism that I began to investigate this subject afresh. The review had been impersonal and unbiassed : it stated my position fairly—with a gentle sarcasm, indeed, but still with fairness —and there was no call to make a formal reply to the concluding question. When some years later I set about writing a small book on the subject, " Was Christ born at Bethlehem ? " it did not take the form of a reply to criticism, but was an investigation to discover truth.

The investigation was undertaken purely for my own satisfaction. A serious difficulty required serious consideration, and might possibly entail either modification of my opinion or other wide-reaching results in some other way. Bad history and good history could not both come from the same author. No rest was possible until I had reached some definite conclusion about the Gospel as well as the Acts ; and it was necessary to begin from those three verses, as being by universal consent the weakest in the work of Luke.

First of all, a brief recapitulation of opinion on this subject is needed ; and we shall state separately the opinion of theological critics and of Roman historians. The theological critics were far more savage in their expression of contempt for and disbelief in Luke's description of the incident than the historians ; but it may be presumed that the historians know more about the subject than the critics. I shall not quote the opinions stated by any historian of Rome except Mommsen, Gardthausen, and Wilcken.[1] If I

---

[1] Wilcken is not strictly a historian, but he is one of the foremost authorities on the economics of the Empire in the East, and mainly in Egypt. Gardthausen's " Life of Augustus " is the largest and most ambitious study of the history under that Emperor. I lay no stress on Rostowzew (quoted later), the most brilliant and suggestive writer on Roman economics ; the critics do not recognize a Russian scholar.

were to mention the opinions of English historians, the objection might be advanced that they were prejudiced [1] in favour of Luke, or that they were English.

None of those three distinguished authorities has any prejudice in favour of Luke. Wilcken speaks of the passage Luke II. 1-3 as "the Lukan legend" (das Lukas-legende), and the expression is in exact agreement with the spirit of the other two. Yet we shall find that, when details are examined, the historians differ markedly from the theological critics in respect of historical values.

A number of the German critics, followed by many outside of Germany, used until recently to say without hesitation that Augustus never issued any decree ordering a census, that there never was under the Empire any regular system of census, that where any casual census was held the presence of the wife was not required but only of the husband, and that his presence was never required at his original home. Here are four distinct and separate points, in regard to each of which accuracy is demanded from any historian, and in regard to each of which Luke was declared confidently and triumphantly to fail. Certainly he flatly contradicts the assertions of the modern critics; but, as we shall see, he is right and they are wrong.

The reason for that feeling of triumph on the part of many critics lay of course in the desire to discredit the superhuman element in the history. Their hostility to Luke arose out of their refusal to admit the superhuman element in the government of the world.

Further, in respect of the dating by the governorship of Quirinius, it was asserted by a large number of critics, (1) that Quirinius never governed Syria until A.D. 5-6, nine years

---

[1] " Instar theologorum " is the expression used about them by Mommsen,

after the death of Herod, and (2) that the census which he then made in Palestine was transferred by Luke's simple blundering to the reign of Herod, who died in 4 B.C.   Then, when this transference had been made in defiance of historical truth, the circumstances and manner of a Roman census (which as a matter of fact were unknown to the critics) were manipulated and misrepresented by Luke so as to make it appear that Joseph of Nazareth came to Bethlehem to be counted (which there was no need for him to do), and that Mary also came to be counted (although, even if her husband had for some reason been required to appear at Bethlehem, there was no possible cause why her presence should also be called for).   The theory of the critics was that these fictions were concocted by Luke in order to explain why and how the son of persons who lived at Nazareth came to be born in Bethlehem.   Then to give dignity to this whole series of inventions, Luke, according to the critics' theory, added that the census was universal for the Roman world, and that the decree ordering a universal census was issued by the Emperor (who was the only authority able to issue such a universal regulation, and who therefore was introduced for the purpose).

Luke has already been proved in the process of discovery to be correct in almost every detail of his statement.   Nowhere in the whole range of historical study has there ever been such a complete revolution of opinion and of established knowledge as in respect of this statement, which brings into its sweep so much of the general principles of bureaucratic government and so many details of administration.   The story is now established, and the plea now is that Luke's story is a legend because it is true to facts (ch. XX.).

In this supposed series of errors and fabrications concocted by Luke, we are struck with the fact that most of them are entirely unnecessary. Why should Luke introduce any reference to Augustus, or to the universality of the census, or to Quirinius, or to this census being the first, unless he had some ground for the statements? Gratuitous and needless blundering was the crime charged against him. No explanation was given why he inserted such a tissue of falsehoods in his history, except perhaps the desire of an ignorant person to show off his scraps of learning, without the ability to put them correctly.

The journey of Joseph and of Mary, however, was a necessary and integral part of the fabrication. The other details might have been cut out, without affecting the Evangelist's purpose—those critics would not allow him the title of historian—but the journey of the parents was a necessary invention in order to bring about an agreement with old Hebrew prophecy.[1] Those few critics who have regarded Jesus as a mythical and unhistorical figure, considered the entire set of details as equally fictitious. Those who admitted that a real Jesus had once existed, maintained that he was born at Nazareth of parents who lived there; and that the birth at Bethlehem was a fiction of later time, unknown to the Evangelist Mark and to the author of the Fourth Gospel.

Such was the general state of opinion among the so-called "critical" theologians; and it was not easy to make any headway in opposition to the strong tide of opinion. There was hardly any attempt to show up the fallacy, ignorance, and pretentiousness of the "critics". As an example of the attitude which was maintained over against them by those theologians who refused to accept their

---

[1] The whole value of the agreement with prophecy lay in its being natural and unsought. A fabrication to produce the agreement destroys its importance entirely: see chapter on "Analogies and Fulfilment".

reasoning, take the words used by Dr. Plummer in his Commentary on Luke (in the International Critical Commentary series), 1896, p. 50 :—

" We must be content to leave the difficulty unsolved. But it is monstrous to argue that because Luke has (possibly) made a mistake as to Quirinius being governor at this time, therefore the whole story about the census and Joseph's journey to Bethlehem is a fiction. Even if there was no census at this time, business connected with enrolment might take Joseph to Bethlehem, and Luke would be correct as to his main facts. That Luke has confused this census with the one in A.D. 6, which he himself mentions in Acts v. 37, is not credible. We are warranted in maintaining (1) that a Roman census in Judea at this time, in accordance with instructions given by Augustus, is not improbable; and (2) that some official connexion of Quirinius with Syria and the holding of this census is not impossible. The accuracy of Luke is such that we ought to require very strong evidence before rejecting any statement of his as an unquestionable blunder."

We cannot, however, be content with any such partial and conditional correctness as Dr. Plummer argues for. In this matter either Luke is correct, or he is untrustworthy. It is not a case in which some degree of correctness in some parts of the story is of any value. It is all or nought.

Some attempt was made to improve the conditions for Luke by the theory that Quirinius governed Syria twice, and that the census at the birth of Jesus occurred in his first governorship, while the census mentioned by Josephus was held in his second governorship. Dr. P. W. Schmiedel, however, will have none of this.[1] He dismisses this first governorship of Quirinius as a mere groundless fiction,

---

[1] The historians of Rome agreed with him to a certain point; see below.

ignorant apparently that the best modern historians regard it as a fairly certain fact. Although he writes in the "Encyclopædia Biblica" for a general public, which could not be expected to know the opinion of Roman historians, Dr. Schmiedel does not warn his readers that such unprejudiced and high authorities as Mommsen and others were dead against him on this point; and he could hardly have expressed himself as he has done, if he had been aware of the state of educated historical opinion. His words are as follows ("Encyclop. Bibl.," II. 1780): "Quirinius was governor of Syria A.D. 6, *ten years after this time.* The most plausible explanation suggested is, perhaps, that Quirinius was *twice* governor of Syria; but there is no direct, and scarcely any indirect evidence to justify the belief. There is also no proof that Mary's presence was obligatory." [1]

As was observed before in another context, p. 85, we remark here that the mere commonplace historians of Rome are much more merciful to Luke's account of the census than the theological critics. We have just seen what a host of errors the latter find in those three verses. Contrast their criticism with Mommsen's remarks: [2] " if we have been right in the demonstration that Quirinius governed Syria for the first time in 3-2 B.C., then Luke, when he fixes the date of Christ's birth about 2 B.C. under the government of Quirinius, [3] has made no assertions that are not probable, except that he has wrongly introduced Herod and has transferred the census from the second to the first administration of Quirinius ".

---

[1] The italics in this extract are Schmiedel's, who is apparently so excited in the contention against Luke, that mere words are too weak to express his stern resolve, and he has recourse to such typographical devices to obtain additional emphasis. Or should we understand that the italics are due to the editor, whose zeal is said to have led him into taking liberties with the articles of contributors? Schmiedel's objections are both false.

[2] " Res Gestae Divi Aug.," p. 176 f.

[3] Mommsen fixes that date for Quirinius' first governorship.

There will be more to say regarding the matters in respect of which Mommsen condemns Luke for inaccuracy; but for our purpose at the moment it is highly important to note that, in Mommsen's opinion, all the other points which come up in Luke's account are correct.   Can we press Mommsen's words to their legitimate issue? or must we say that he has written a little hastily?   If we can venture to assume that he meant all that lies in his words, then it follows that according to the highest single authority on such a matter— in a work published in 1883 and never retracted: it is a second edition and represents his most mature and long-considered judgment—Luke's other statements are probable, viz. that Augustus issued the decree ordering a world-census, and that every person, man and woman, had to go to the proper domicile in order to be counted.

Some might argue that it is doubtful whether Mommsen fully meant this, and that probably he thought only of the instructions issued by Augustus to Quirinius ordering a census of Syria and Palestine; those instructions would be comprised in the general *mandata* stating what Quirinius as governor should do.   Those of us, however, who have studied Mommsen most carefully and deeply, and have kept company with him and his work day after day and year after year, know that he means what he says, and that a definite historical judgment like this was not stated in a loose fashion by him.   We must remember that the quotation is from a second edition of his work, almost wholly re-written; and that he had carefully considered and reconsidered his opinion on all these matters and modified them in some respects.[1]

<hr>

[1] He had in his earlier life denounced the famous Venetian inscription mentioning Quirinius as forged in the interest of theological orthodoxy; but he recalled that opinion immediately when part of the actual stone was found

We are bound to accept his words as stating his mature judgment: all that Luke says about the institution and manner of the census is according to him probably correct. Yet the critics continued for many years later to take no notice of his opinion, but to reiterate their confident assertion that all the details of the manner of taking the census were false. Mommsen's personal friends will feel all the more bound to insist that he meant what he said in this sentence, because now it is completely proved that what he said there is true. Luke is correct in every detail, and Mommsen was right in admitting so far the probable truth of his statements.

Mommsen, as we see, has no prejudice in favour of Luke. He thinks that Luke was all wrong about Herod, and about Quirinius; and he has nothing but condemnation for those who would suggest that Quirinius twice made a census of Palestine, during his first and again during his second tenure of office in Syria. He declares in the most emphatic terms his opinion on this point; it is not possible that Quirinius could have held such a census when he first governed Syria, for it is an inadmissible supposition that Palestine could have been subjected to a census by the governor of Syria, before it was incorporated in the province; and only theologians or persons like theologians, whose reason is fettered, would advance such an opinion. As he adds, those who know anything about Roman history will assert unhesitatingly that Luke made foolish use of Josephus, and mixed truth with falsehood in his account of the census; and Tertullian rightly saw what a blunder Luke had been guilty of, for he throws Quirinius overboard and states that Jesus was born during the census which was held in Judea

after having long been lost, and the genuineness of the inscription could no longer be doubted.

by Sentius Saturninus, 8 B.C. (obviously on the ground that the latter governed Syria while Herod was still living).

As to the other prominent authority on the reign of Augustus, Gardthausen, in his very large work, Vol. I, p. 921 f., takes a distinctly less favourable view of Luke than Mommsen does, without being nearly so harsh to him as the theologians were. Besides those faults which Mommsen stigmatizes, Gardthausen also declares that Augustus never ordered a general census, for if he had done so he would certainly have mentioned this in his review of his own achievements ; also that there never was any census-system under the Roman Empire, though isolated census were made sporadically in all the provinces of the Empire.

All that Gardthausen says beyond Mommsen's assertions may be disregarded ; but two remarks are needed in regard to the latter.

In the first place, evidently Mommsen has read Luke rather hurriedly and therefore has not rightly apprehended his assertion about the census. Luke does not say (as Mommsen declares) that Quirinius conducted the census in the year of Christ's birth ; he asserts only that the census was made during the time when Quirinius was governing Syria. Mommsen has transformed a mere date, given after the common ancient fashion by a governor, into an assertion that the governor made the census in Palestine. Tertullian, it is true, understands the matter so, and asserts that Sentius conducted the census ; but Luke is more careful. We must not attribute to him statements that he does not make.

In the second place, there followed from this another incorrect charge against Luke. Mommsen says that no census of Palestine could possibly have been held by the governor of Syria before Palestine was incorporated in that province. Now, under Herod the king, Palestine was, so to say, an independent and extra-Roman kingdom, where a Roman census by a governor of a province could not take place. This whole charge falls to the ground when we remember what Luke does actually say about Quirinius, viz. that the first world-wide census was made while Quirinius was governing Syria. Obviously Quirinius is not stated here to have made the census anywhere except in his own province. He had nothing to do with the census which was assuredly made in Egypt, and in Asia, and elsewhere, in that year.[1]

The argument brought forward by Mommsen under this head reduces itself automatically, then, to the assertion that a census of the Roman world did not apply to Judea, which was an independent kingdom not amenable to the orders of the Emperor Augustus. This is a very bold statement, and Mommsen would hardly have cared to commit himself to it, had he not been carried away by his misapprehension about the control attributed to Quirinius over the census.

We know very little about the relation of those so-called independent kingdoms to the Roman State. They were not independent, but in the strictest sense dependent kingdoms. It was pointed out in my book on the subject that they formed part of the Roman world, and were understood in the Roman system to be outlying countries, which were not yet sufficiently well trained to be capable of receiving the more honourable rank of provinces, but were in process of being trained in obedience and educated up to that level. Strabo, who knew the Roman world widely under the rule of Augustus, states this in quite clear and emphatic terms.[2]

Augustus's order ran in Judea, when he wished it. Herod had to obey, when Augustus ordered, and to be on the out-

---

[1] I assume here the results stated in the following chapter.
[2] Strabo, final chapter. "Was Christ Born at Bethlehem?" p. 120 f.

look even to anticipate what Augustus would desire, and, if he did not wish to carry out the order, he had to be careful to send an explanation of his reasons and views and to ask for permission to disregard the Imperial command.

Whether the order regarding a census of the Roman world would apply to the dependent kingdoms was a matter for Augustus to say. His word was final.

In this case we may conclude that Augustus intended the edict instituting an Imperial census to apply to the dependent kingdoms. For this confident statement there are two reasons.

In the first place, Luke assumes that it did apply to Judea and was carried into effect there, presumably by Herod: perhaps he had Roman soldiers to help, but the details are quite uncertain.

In the second place, the census of A.D. 34 was enforced in the dependent kingdom of Archelaos,[1] on the border-land between the provinces of Galatia and Syria-Cilicia. This kingdom was in a position perfectly analogous to Palestine under Herod. What applies to the one almost certainly applies to the other.[2] The execution of the order provoked disturbance among the tribes of Taurus; and it is only on account of the disturbance that we are informed of the census.

As to the view held by Wilcken, our third non-theological witness, regarding the details of the census, we shall quote below in chapter XX. his statement of all these details, and his opinion that these are correctly described by Luke, and that, in fact, Luke evolved his " legend " out of the real facts of a census, as he saw it performed period after period around him.

---

[1] This was afterwards given to King Antiochus.

[2] " Was Christ Born at Bethlehem? " p. 161 f., and Tacitus, " Annals," VI. 41.

What Wilcken calls a legend, however, would more correctly be styled a fraudulent invention. A legend is vague and shadowy. Luke, as he thinks, worked up a falsehood so as to be true to the external features of a Roman census. As he says, Joseph and Mary had to go to Bethlehem in the legend, because at the census every one, male and female, must appear personally for enrolment.[1]

The theological critics try in one way or other to leave Luke some rag of unintentional mistake, so as not to accuse him (or the earlier authority whom he quotes) of absolute falsification and invention ; but Wilcken regards the legend of Joseph and Mary and the child as intentionally constructed with an eye on the real details of ordinary Roman procedure. According to the critics Luke, while desiring to be true, was guilty of an astonishing series of blunders in fact. According to Wilcken he tried to palm off a falsehood on the world by keeping it true in every detail of fact and accompaniment. These theories are mutually destructive. One cannot accept both : we accept neither. As in the opening chapter III. of these lectures, it has seemed best to give in this chapter a brief statement of the general position and the results of modern discovery, and afterwards to state these in more detailed fashion in the following chapters. Discovery confirms the correctness of all the facts that Luke mentions regarding the census and its manner and its date.

The final criticism, however, remains. The truth of the historical surroundings in which Luke's narrative places the birth of Jesus does not prove that the supreme facts, which give human and divine value to the birth, are true. It may be—in fact it must be—admitted as true that " the

---

[1] The same principle was observed at the Epikrisis : Mitteis and Wilcken, " Papyruskunde," I. i. p. 194.

first enrolment " really took place, that Quirinius was governing Syria during at least the first half of the year, and that the general order was issued in Syria for all to return to their own homes in preparation for the enrolment. Yet this does not prove that Mary was the mother of Christ, as Luke describes Him, and as John and Paul saw Him and believed in Him.

The surrounding facts are matter of history, and can be discussed and proved by historical evidence. The essential facts of the narrative are not susceptible of discussion on historical principles, and do not condescend to be tested by historical evidence. That truth exists and moves on a higher plane of thought. It is known through the absolute insight into the heart of human life and divine nature. It comes to, or is granted to, or is forced upon, a man as the completion of his experience and the crown of his life and the remaking of his nature. It proves itself to the soul of man. When he sees it, he knows that it is the one truth— the one ultimate truth—in a world of half-truths, a world of preparation, where he is being moulded, and fashioned, and hammered into a condition in which he can receive the truth.

This knowledge cannot be proved by mere verbal argument. It is not in word, but in power. It does not spring from any more fundamental principle. It is the fountain from which all other so-called principles flow. It is the guarantee of all other truth. There is nothing true without God ; and there is nothing true except the Divine in the infinite variety of His manifestation.

No man can make historical investigation and historical proof take the place of faith ; and it is not the purpose of these lectures to put the one for the other. The Christian religion is a matter of living, not of mere intellectual knowledge ; and " the just shall live by faith ". Yet it is not without its value to have the truth of the concomitant circumstances demonstrated. One must remember that Christianity did not originate in a lie, and that we can and ought to demonstrate this, as well as to believe it. The account which it gives of its own origin is susceptible of being tested on the principles of historical study, and through the progress of discovery the truth of that account can be and has been in great part proved. There is, however, more to do. The evidence is there, if we look for it.

CHAPTER XIX

LUKE'S ACCOUNT OF THE FIRST CENSUS

WHAT does Luke say about the census? That had never been determined. Mutually inconsistent and thoroughly unjustifiable (if one may venture to use such an adjective regarding the opinions of great theological critics)[1] interpretations of his brief statement on the subject were advocated; and the simple, natural, and obvious translation was not, so far as I am aware, ever considered seriously.

The critical question is this: what is the meaning of "first"? Why is this census called the first? Everything else depends on the answer to this question.

On the principles laid down in "St. Paul the Traveller," pp. 27 f., there could not be for me any doubt. Luke says this was "the first," in order to distinguish it from later occasions on which the census was taken. He knew of several such occasions of census-takings, and one of these he actually mentions as "the census,"[2] viz. the one which was made in A.D. 6 when Judea was organized as a province of the Empire. Now if Luke describes a census as the first, we are led on inevitably to the supposition of a series of census-takings, and something in the way of a regular census-system. See Note on p. 254.

---

[1] Such as, for example, that πρώτη Κυρινίου meant the census before Quirinius was governor of Syria. These interpretations need not be enumerated: they are all wrong and impossible in Greek usage.

[2] Acts v. 37: this practically means " *the* census," the great census.

(238)

No one thought of attributing such a meaning to Luke's words. It was too absurd even for him. Not even the harshest critic would attribute such a foolish meaning to him. Accordingly, every one had set about discovering or inventing possible meanings for his words, as the plain and obvious one could not have been in his mind.

For me, however, there was no alternative. I had declared my principles, and stated how Luke's words ought always to be taken. This passage could only mean that Luke referred to some system of taking the census from time to time, that this system was inaugurated by a decree of the Emperor Augustus, and that Jesus was born in the year of the first census-taking.

Then I asked myself whether any person could invent the story of such a system. Every contemporary would know that there was no such census-system; and no historian of any kind or class would state a falsehood whose falsity was obvious to every reader. A bad or unprincipled writer might invent a false incident, if his only public consisted of strangers who did not know the facts; but no one puts in writing an evident falsehood, which must instantly be detected.

The conclusion was evident. Luke trusted to his readers' familiarity with the facts and the census-system. He spoke of the first census, knowing how much that would imply to them. They knew the system as it was carried out in the Roman Empire.[1]

If that was so, then we might expect to find some references to such a census-system. It is not one of the things that attracted or interested ancient historians; they loved

[1] By Luke and his contemporaries the Empire was called "the world," i.e. the civilized world: see "Was Christ Born at Bethl." p. 119 f. The Roman Empire always claimed a monopoly of civilization.

to write of battles and sieges and dynastic facts, and all the
" great events of history " ; but the minute details of bureaucratic government were not a subject on which they ever
give information. Still, there are occasional references to
census-taking in various provinces ; and some of them have
been stated by Gardthausen in the chapter in which he
rightly emphasizes the importance that Augustus attached
to the collecting and co-ordination of statistics in his system
of administering the provinces in all respects as regards the
manner of taking the census, and as to the requirement of
personal presence at the original home.

Such unconnected and unclassifiable traces of a census as
these were of no use in the present state of our knowledge,
and many of them may relate to a different type of census :
but an allusion in Pliny is much more valuable. He tells
that, during the census conducted by Claudius in A.D. 48, a
man was found at Bologna who returned his age as 150.
This great age roused the Emperor's attention, and on investigating the records of previous enrolments it was cor-
roborated by his statements on those occasions.[1]

Here we have a clear allusion to a census-system. This
man had given to the Imperial officials a statement of his
age from time to time. The records were preserved, and
the officials knew at once where to turn in order to test his
accuracy. This implies a regular system, in which statistics
about population were collected and preserved, evidently
to form a basis for good administration of State interests. Such a system involves, obviously, that enrolments
must have been taken at regular intervals ; and this one
passage of Pliny taken in conjunction with Luke's term

---

[1] Pliny, " Nat. Hist.," VII. 48 (159) ; other notices of the operations of Claudius in the census when he was censor, A.D. 48, occur in Tacitus, " Annals,"
XI. 25, 31 ; Suetonius, " Claud." 16.

"first census," reveals the outlines of the system, while the details remain obscure.

The interval between the enrolments could not be recovered from the scattered references to a census. One in A.D. 35 has been already mentioned in the previous chapter. The one mentioned by Pliny occurred in 48 apparently.[1] Tacitus mentions a census held in the provinces of Gaul at the end of the events of A.D. 61. Vespasian and Titus were censors in 73-74. We now see that these correspond in a loose way to the census periods of A.D. 34, 48, 62 and 76; but the correspondence is inexact.

Even taking in, as connected in some possible fashion, the great year of census and reviewing of resources in 8 B.C., one could not possibly recover any outline or dim shadow of a system from the facts. Yet that some sort of system existed was distinctly implied by two Christian writers, who, however, were set aside as absolutely valueless by critics, just because they were Christian.

Now we grant at once that if a writer merely borrows from Luke what he tells us about the first census, he does not add in any way to the strength of Luke's statement, regarded as historical evidence; but if a later writer says something that is not in Luke, and evidently had access to some other authority, then there is added the weight of that other authority, whatever it be.

Clement of Alexandria, in the latter part of the second century, mentions that Christ was born " in the 28th year, when first they ordered enrolments to be made ".[2] This is

---

[1] Tacitus, loc. cit., speaks of Claudius as holding a census review at Ostia personally in 48; but the general operations probably belong to A.D. 49.

[2] Strom., I. 21, 147, ὅτε πρῶτον ἐκέλευσαν ἀπογραφὰς γενέσθαι; " Was Christ Born at Bethl." p. 128. The mention of year 28 leads on to the

not simply taken, or mistaken, from Luke. Clement thought of a series or system of enrolments : he was personally familiar with it, and speaks of it as a matter of Roman life. As we now know, this must have been in Clement's mind, because such was the situation in which he lived ; and on a fair estimate of his words no reasonable scholar can doubt that this is the meaning of his words.

He was familiar with the census-system as it was performed periodically around him throughout his life in Egypt ; he had filled up his own census paper, and had seen his parents and friends do the same ; and he believed that the same periodic system of census was practised in Palestine, and had begun, like the Egyptian census, under Augustus and by order of Augustus just as Luke says ; but he is not simply borrowing his statement from Luke. He is confirming Luke from his own knowledge.

That is all reasonable, natural, and simple,[1] but it was regarded as too absurd even for Clement ; and so it was not even taken into consideration ; but now we know that this system of periodic enrolment did exist, and that Clement had seen it in operation throughout his life, and recognized that Luke was speaking of the first census of this system in his Gospel II. 1-3.

One thing more we can infer from Clement. He had no

question how and why it was that the Christian era came to be wrongly calculated, and thus the Birth of Christ was placed in what we know to be the fourth year after the death of Herod. This error, originating in the second century, has caused much trouble. It is confusing to say that Herod died 4 B.C., and yet Jesus was born in the days of Herod the king. The "Christian Era" is a mere convention among chronologists, and is wrongly placed; but that is apart from the subject of this investigation.

[1] As I read the quaint arguments of the critics on subjects like this, the expression which I have often used about the Turks rises in my mind, "anything may happen in Turkey except what is reasonable and natural and possible ".

thought that the census was peculiar to Egypt: he implies that it would take place in Palestine after the same fashion as in Egypt. On this he could hardly be mistaken: it was a thing that must have been well known.[1]

The records of these successive enrolments were preserved and could be consulted, as we have learned from Pliny. If such vast records could be consulted many years later, as he says, then they must have been classified for consultation. In fact, no rational ruler would plan a system of periodic enrolments, unless the statistics were to be classified and tabulated. Without that a census has no value.

Tertullian evidently consulted the records, and he made a remarkable discovery.[2] He says that Jesus was born when the census was made in Syria by Sentius Saturninus. We have the excellent evidence of Josephus that Sentius governed Syria 8-6 B.C.

Formerly Tertullian's statement was set aside as absurd and valueless, because no one put the birth of Jesus so early as that; but, as we shall see, the first enrolment in the Augustan system coincides with the government of Sentius, and forthwith Tertullian's statement acquires unsuspected weight. He corroborates Luke as regards the time of the census during Herod's life, but not as regards the name of the Roman official. He must, therefore, derive from a different source of information independent of Luke, because on one essential point he diverges from him; and, at the very least, his statement proves that there existed different written

---

[1] Justin Martyr refers to the same census; but his words might quite well be founded on Luke alone, and do not necessarily imply any other authority or any knowledge of his own, but only his belief that records of census did exist and might be consulted.

[2] "Adv. Marc." IV. 19.

sources of information, which is an important fact for the historian.

If Tertullian had only the authority of Luke to rest on, it is inconceivable that he could have named Sentius as the officer that made the census, for he regarded Luke as a perfect authority. He therefore had access to another good authority.

Now it is evident that if this census had been a mere fiction invented by Luke, there could not be other sources of knowledge about it. There must lie behind these two statements, partly harmonious, partly diverse, some historical reality and some independent tradition. A historical process that is mentioned by only one witness might be a fabrication; but a process that is attested by two totally independent authorities cannot be set down by sane criticism as a pure invention.

We must therefore accept what Tertullian says as giving a fixed point in this investigation. He had access to records, and as we shall see they were trustworthy records, showing that the first Enrolment or Census took place in 8 B.C., and that Saturninus directed the operation. It is not necessary to understand that he got both facts from the same source. Probably he knew from one authority[1] the nature and times of the periodic Enrolments; and he consulted another source for the official's name. Finally, he depended on Luke's authority for the fact that Jesus was born at this first census.

Simply from the severe but intelligent study of the two most definite ancient authorities, any truly rational criticism must infer that the statement of Luke II. 1-3 is not an in-

---

[1] This authority would naturally be the actual recurring system, as Tertullian knew it in his own experience. Clement of Alexandria knew it as a familiar act in ordinary life.

vention of his own, concocted stupidly from half-knowledge and from misuse of the fact that Quirinius was connected with another provincial census in A.D. 6-7. Luke must have had information from some source or other about events of that period, and this information was trustworthy and of inestimable value, for it gives a picture of the beginning of that most remarkable institution, the periodical census of the East.

Why does Tertullian say that Sentius took the census when Jesus was born, whereas Luke says that Jesus was born while Quirinius was governing Syria, and Josephus again declares that Sentius was governor of Syria? It has been thought that Tertullian contradicts Luke, but that is not so. They make different statements. Luke gives a date after the usual ancient fashion (followed by him on a great scale in III. 1, 2): Tertullian makes an assertion about the official who took the census. On the officials in Syria at the time see chap. XXI.

Probably the counting of Roman citizens was performed in a different way from the counting of the subject population for taxation purposes. Augustus records the number of Roman citizens whom he counted at the census held in 28 B.C., 8 B.C., and A.D. 14.[1] The first is older than the institution of periodic enrolments ; the second agrees ; but the third is remote from agreement. Apparently, during Augustus's weak health in old age, the proper occasion, A.D. 6, was passed, and his colleague and successor Tiberius counted the citizens for him in the year of his death. Later the two operations presumably were carried out regularly at the due periods, each in its own fashion.

As to this system which Luke seemed to imply, I did

[1] He does not allude to any enrolment of tax-paying subjects ; but he writes as a Roman for Romans. (See also p. 294, note 1.)

not think, when starting on the investigation, that the design of Augustus was likely to have been successfully carried into effect and to have become permanent in the Empire. As we now know it was successful, and lasted for 250 years or more, before it stopped in the disorganized and weakening Empire; but at that time, in 1895, with only Luke's brief statement to rest on, I was quite prepared to find that a measure contemplated and ordered by Augustus proved unsuccessful; and even yet we have far more evidence about it in the Eastern provinces,[1] which had an old and settled organization, than in the west. The machinery needed for a great census-system is large; the operations are complicated; perhaps the system (as I thought) might not have become universal, for the Imperial civil and military service was certainly carried out by what seems to us a very small number of persons; but it certainly could be traced in the East.

Moreover, it was by no means certain then that later Emperors appreciated so thoroughly as Augustus did the importance of basing administration on the collection and grouping of facts. We can now say that the system and principles established by Augustus were maintained and developed by later Emperors on the lines that he sketched out.

In seeking for evidence about the initiation of the system under Augustus, we were faced with one difficulty. Information is most inadequate. The inscriptions available were not so numerous or so important [2] as for a later period ;

---

[1] This is mainly due to the fact that paper lives in Egypt for thousands of years, but decays quickly in the damp soil of other countries.

[2] Of course there are some few notable exceptions to this statement, such as the " Res Gestae Divi Augusti," the recital of his own achievements by Augustus, written by a Roman for Romans, and influenced by that fact.

and the literary authorities are extraordinarily scanty. Horace, Virgil, and even Propertius have an important political aspect in their works. Ovid has no value in that view : he saw only what concerned his pitiful self.

Hence the latter part of the reign of Augustus, in fact the whole period from about 15 B.C. to the beginning of the reign of Tiberius in A.D. 14, is almost completely hidden from our knowledge.[1] No historian illumines it. Suetonius and Velleius hardly mention anything in it except some dynastic matters. There was nothing else, from their point of view, worthy of mention ; there reigned an almost unbroken peace except for some frontier wars, and the bureaucratic system of Augustus worked, on the whole, so efficiently, that there was nothing striking to record except the German war and the tragic defeat of Varus. Had a formal history of Augustus's reign been preserved by a writer like Tacitus, he would probably have lamented the want of great events, and would have mentioned little except dynastic gossip during that period. It did not occur to the ancient historians that it was a worthy task to record—what we in modern times most desire—an account of the bureaucracy, a study of the provinces, details about the improvements whereby Augustus made the provinces contented and happy, and through which he deserved— if man could deserve—to be idolized by the nations whom he had found in slavery and misery and had made, to a certain degree, free and progressive.

[1] As an illustration of its obscurity take the following. A certain Favonius is known, from an inscription found recently, to have held the very highest offices of state in the last years of the reign of Augustus; but except from one single stone found in Phrygia, he seems to be utterly unknown, unless the conjecture be admitted—a conjecture which has nothing in its favour --that Favonius is an otherwise unrecorded cognomen, attached to the name of some known historical figure.

A glance into any account of the history of Augustus, written according to the old-fashioned type usual forty years ago, will show the obscurity of this period. Take Smith's "Dictionary of Ancient Biography". To Augustus are given fourteen columns and a half, of which eight or ten short sentences exhaust this period, and these are dynastic or touch on German frontier wars. One would not say that this is good history, or right method; but it is the old-fashioned style of history, and it is the sort of knowledge by whose standard the New Testament has been judged too often in the past fifty years and at the present day.

The extract from Luke II. 1-3 plunges us right into the midst of provincial administration with its minute details, the "enrolment" of the provinces, as it was seen in one of them, the first enrolment of a series[1] implying that there followed systematic enrolments at intervals, the action of a member of the bureaucracy, the implication that many other members of the bureaucracy must have co-operated in such a vast administrative work, which was begun by an order of the governor calling back every individual to his own city.

Luke gives a very striking picture of a splendid piece of governmental work. He tells of a bold law for the whole Empire, instituting a series of enrolments, a regular census-system. Taking into account what machinery is required to hold a census, to tabulate and use its results, to make this a universal system for the Empire, and to repeat the Imperial census at intervals, the historian is struck with admiration of the Augustan idea. The statesman who thought of making such a system universal knew that wise

---

[1] I have been criticized for maintaining that Luke distinguished in meaning πρῶτος from πρότερος; but now discovery has proved conclusively that in this passage at least "first" must mean "the first of many"; and I have nothing to retract.

government depended on the collection, classification, and registration of details; and he must have expected that his bureaucracy would prove equal to the work. If he thought of a system, he must have determined his system by regular recurrence at regular intervals: no other way need or can be thought of. If Augustus could plan out such schemes as this, it is no wonder that his great Imperial foundation lasted so long, and that his bureaucratic system of administration fixed the general type for all modern methods of government. Anyone who has a true feeling for history must be thankful to the great historian who has sketched for us in such brief and masterly fashion by a few pregnant words such a skilful picture. He has lit up the obscurity of this dark period, and given us a specimen of Imperial administrative method. The historians of the century that follows the age of Augustus were so occupied with the "great events of history" that they would not mention such humble matters as enrolment and its methods; and Luke was left to tell the tale alone. Such very slight corroboration as has been recorded by Tacitus intervenes incidentally, and is alluded to in such slight and contemptuous fashion that it gives only the minimum of information, and was not even recognized as corroborative until the whole census-system was cleared up in the gradual progress of research.

Most recent writers on the New Testament, however, had stood placidly and contentedly apart from the modern developments of Roman Imperial history, and had evolved the theory that Luke had invented this incident "all out of his own head" (in the children's phrase),[1] to ex-

[1] His starting-point (as it is supposed) lay in a blunder about Quirinius, who did actually take another census in Judea (the second of the series). According to this fashionable theory, Luke misplaced the census of A.D. 6 to a date in the reign of Herod who died 4 B.C.

plain how Jesus could be born in Bethlehem of parents who lived in Nazareth.

Assume for the moment that this is so. What genius for historical fiction is implied in the invention! Luke had no foundation in fact to go upon; his starting-point was only his blunder about the date of a totally different kind of enrolment made by Quirinius in Palestine in A.D. 6,[1] when that governor conducted the survey and valuation of the country which was now for the first time being constituted as a province of the Empire. All the rest of his story is, according to the fashionable theory, pure fiction.

How comes it that Luke could imagine all that is implied in his picture? How could he invent a vast process which hangs together so well in itself, and which puts before us a quite wonderful piece of bureaucratic administration, extremely complicated, requiring the collaboration of a great many officials, and yet all purely fictitious? Still more wonderful is this when we find from recent discovery that every detail in Luke's picture can be paralleled from administrative practice in the Empire at a later period. The historian was not merely a genius, but also a prophet. He foresaw what the subsequent Emperors were going to do; and he imagines Augustus doing it all before the death of

---

[1] It must be remembered that, if Quirinius in A.D. 6 was not making a periodic census, his enrolment would not be a model from which Luke could draw the picture given in II. 1-3. On our view there were combined in the enrolment of that year the valuation and inquisition which were required for Roman administrative purposes in a new province, along with the counting by household (ἀπογραφὴ κατ᾽ οἰκίαν) of the periodic census. It was perhaps the former part that did most to provoke the great disturbances among the Jews as recorded by Josephus. The counting by households necessitated an inquiry into home life that was offensive to the Asiatic mind and society; but the other inquisition was probably even more unpopular and detested, as implying the beginning of complete domination by the great alien Empire.

Herod in 4 B.C. The scholar who now says that Luke invented the picture which is drawn in II. 1-3 has to face these alternatives: either he must glorify Luke as a genius in fiction and a prophet in history, or he must confess that his own theory is wrong.

Let us, however, investigate more strictly what is implied in the theory of false invention. The whole procedure, according to the writers of this class, was a fiction: Jesus was born in Nazareth (only a very few go so far as to deny that he was ever born or had any historical existence); and after a legend connecting Him with Bethlehem had grown up, Luke set about inventing historical circumstances and conditions to explain and give plausibility and historical background to the legend. But observe how much this theory implies: it may be doubted whether those who hold it have ever put clearly to themselves or their readers all that they really are contending for. They are really maintaining :—

1. That Luke, without possessing any true historical instinct (such as was the heritage of the Greeks, making them seek after and value for its own sake historical truth), yet had a certain untrained craving for a historical setting to his story; that he cast about in the past, to search for something suitable as a historical background; and that finding a census recorded as occurring in A.D. 6-7, he took this and transferred it to a different time. It is not made quite clear whether the argument is that Luke committed this blunder from pure chronological inability and historical ignorance, fancying that it afforded some explanation, or that he deliberately and knowingly transferred the census to a wrong time; the commoner view seems to be that he acted through ignorance and incapacity.

2. That Luke invented without any authority the state-

ment that Augustus ordered a census or enrolment of the whole Empire to be made ; there could (as these writers assume) be no record of such an impossible act, but Luke supposed that the order of Augustus [1] regarding the Palestinian census of A.D. 6 (which he misplaced) was universally applicable to the Roman world. The argument in this case is that Luke, without any need or any authority, invented the statement. That census in A.D. 6 was, of course, taken on the instructions issued by Augustus to the Governor of Syria ; but to invent unnecessarily a general edict of Augustus, and thus transform a local process at the organization of a new Province into an Imperial regulation for the Empire, shows not merely gross ignorance about facts and methods of government, but also deliberate forgery of historical testimony performed for the purpose of imparting a false air of historicity to a legend. Carelessness in a historian is bad, but such calculated falsehood is much worse.

3. The fashionable theory implies further that Luke invented, not merely one world-wide Augustan census under Herod, but also the idea of a series of enrolments, of which this was the first. Now, why should he do this? His other inventions were hid in the far-away times of King Herod and might deceive the unwary ; but a series of enrolments was a thing that could be tested by every reader from his own experience.

One feels that this part of the accusation overtaxes one's power of belief. No rational writer could or would go to

---

[1] The instructions (*mandata*) given by the Emperor to his *legatus*, whom he sent to Syria in A.D. 6, would, of course, contain a provision for making the usual valuation, etc., required in constituting the new province. No special edict was needed for this action in a single new province. Out of this Luke, according to the fashionable theory, has evolved an edict issued to the whole Empire.

such an extreme of needless and useless invention. If this is all false it adds nothing to the verisimilitude of the narrative ; and it must have forthwith betrayed its falseness to every reader at the time when Luke's Gospel was written. We cannot admit such an incredible accusation. The theory destroys itself.

4. The fashionable theory, further, maintained that the idea of every person going to his own home to be enrolled was a pure fiction, and could not possibly have been true : it was a mere device to explain how Jesus could be born in Bethlehem of parents who lived in Nazareth : it was a false explanation of an invented occurrence : Jesus, if born at all, was born in the home of his parents. From modern discovery, however, it now appears that the order to return to the original home, though in a sense non-Roman in spirit was the regular feature of the census in the Eastern provinces, as will be shown in the sequel.

From a fair, unprejudiced and rational consideration of the evidence of Luke, Pliny, Tacitus, Clement and Tertullian, we conclude that the statements of Luke are all probable in themselves, and that the theory either of invention or of stupid error on his part is unreasonable and unjustifiable. Any theory of that form only casts discredit on the historical acumen of those who proposed or accepted it as probable ; and yet it was not merely regarded as probable, but was generally accepted as demonstrated and certain truth. Even Mommsen's plea that most of what Luke says was probably correct was ignored and remained ineffective.

This theory is an astonishing example of modern European capacity for making false judgments. From

[1] Strauss and others were, at least, stating their opinion in books of investigation, good or bad ; but Schmiedel was stating in the " Encyclopædia

Strauss to Schmiedel,[1] what a series of distinguished and famous scholars have blindly assumed that their inability to estimate historical evidence correctly was the final and sure criterion of truth. This we can now say freely, because the whole matter, so far as the census is concerned, has passed out of the sphere of speculation into the region of definite historical truth. We know that Luke was right in the external facts, because the records have disclosed the whole system of the census; but as to the inner facts, the birth and the divine nature of Jesus, there can (as said above) be no historical reasoning, for those are a matter of faith, of intuition, and of the individual human being's experience and inner life.[1]

Note (p. 238).—In "St. Paul the Traveller," p. 27 f., discussing Luke's use of πρῶτος, I wrongly admitted that in Stephen's speech, Acts VII. 12, the speaker used πρῶτον where πρότερον would be right. So it had been asserted, and I allowed it; but this is not so. Three visits were made by the sons of Jacob (as both Genesis and Stephen say): the first is expressed by πρῶτον, the second by ἐν τῷ δευτέρῳ, and the third by a changed form.

Biblica " for general use views which should have been certain and fundamental; and he states his own blunders more dogmatically than almost any other scholar. It is no wonder that this audacious self-confidence misled the less educated public.

[1] See the last three paragraphs of Ch. XVIII.

CHAPTER XX

THE AUGUSTAN CENSUS-SYSTEM

WHEN I had reached the conclusion that the balance of probability, judging on mere historical principles, was decisively in favour of Luke being correct in his description of the census, the discoveries made in Egypt offered themselves. Three scholars almost simultaneously announced that there existed in Egypt a census-system extending from A.D. 90 to 258. The incidence and nature of the census was proved by the enrolment papers that had been preserved in the dry soil. The idea occurred to me that this was the system which Luke mentions as put in action for the first time under Herod; and the periods when reckoned back gave a system originating from the completion of the Imperial authority of Augustus on 29 June, 23 B.C., and falling due for the first time in 9 B.C.

In describing the census-system, I shall ignore the variations in regard to the beginning of the new years, which varied much. I speak of the periodic census years as 9 B.C., A.D. 6, 20, 34, 48, 62, etc.; but it will be understood that in applying these years to Egypt, or to Asia Minor, one who seeks to be accurate would call those years 10-9 B.C., A.D. 5-6, A.D. 19-20, because in those countries the new year began not on 1 January, but on some day in the late summer or autumn.

It will also be remembered that the actual enrolment was almost always made in the year following, as the intention was to count every person who had come into existence up to the end of the periodic year.   Hence the actual census-taking was in 8 B.C., A.D. 7, A.D. 21, and so on, and most frequently in the later months of those years. The census papers are all carefully dated and leave no doubt on these points.

It will be convenient to give a very brief summary of Wilcken's statement on the subject.[1]   He is the most cautious and sure of scholars, and anything that he states as demonstrated fact may be accepted without the smallest hesitation.

Augustus seems to have left the old Ptolemaic system of annual census in Egypt undisturbed, when the country was brought under the Empire in 30 B.C.[2]   After some interval the fourteen-year-cycle was introduced.   Actual census papers have been found of the periodic year 62 [add also 34] after Christ.[3]   Indirect references occur to the census of A.D. 20 and 48.[4]   Grenfell and Hunt rightly argue that Augustus must have originated this cycle.   Beyond this there is no certainty, and we must await the discovery of fresh material.

Before the periodic year 62 the form of census was not quite the same as it became on that occasion and continued thereafter in unbroken series down to A.D. 258.[5]   In parti-

---

[1] Mitteis and Wilcken, "Papyruskunde," I, i. p. 192 f.

[2] Wilcken, I. p. 192, arguing from Grenfell's i. 45 and 46.

[3] Wilcken, *ibid.*   I have added the period 34 from a Strassburg Papyrus recently published in "Philologus," confirmed by a letter from Dr. Hunt answering my question about this document, which is strange in expression. This papyrus was published since Wilcken wrote: he knew no census paper earlier than 62.

[4] Wilcken, *ibid.* from Grenfell and Hunt, "Oxy.," ii. 254 and 255.

[5] No census papers of a later date have been found but no change or reason for change is attested, except that about this time the whole ad-

cular the term "household enrolment"[1] is not known until A.D. 62. That earlier period is therefore a time of transition.

At this point I would add to Wilcken that the Augustan system, as found in Egypt, could not, even on the Egyptian evidence, be taken as applying to Egypt only. The system is calculated, not on the Egyptian reckoning of the reign of Augustus, but on the Imperial reckoning. Augustus counted his reign in the Empire generally by the tribunician authority conferred on him, 29 June, 23 B.C.,[2] whereas in Egypt he exercised his sovereignty on a different footing,[3] starting from 29 August, 30 B.C.; and any device intended for Egypt alone would be arranged accordingly.

Now there are practically only two alternatives: a device like this, found in Egypt, must be either restricted to Egypt or universal for the Empire.[4] We have found that it is not confined to Egypt, therefore it is Imperial, and the decree that ordered it must, as Luke says, have gone forth to "the whole world".

This is a fair and probable inference from the Egyptian evidence, taken by itself. When we further consider the weight of authority for a wider census, as stated in Chap. XIX., there can remain no reasonable doubt. It is, however, not admitted by Wilcken, for he makes no suggestion

---

ministration of the Empire everywhere was slackening and growing weaker, and its strength was diminishing. The Christian Empire, as Mommsen says, reinvigorated the State as a whole. Wilcken, I. p. 193.

[1] κατ' οἰκίαν ἀπογραφή.

[2] This reckoning was followed by the later Emperors; each reigned as champion of the Commons, and counted the years as Trib. Potest. I., II., and so on.

[3] On its nature see the statement later in this chapter, and also Chap. XV.

[4] The supposition that the census should have been ordered only for a few Eastern provinces cannot be admitted. There is no reason to think that Augustus ever restricted his orders after that fashion,

as to the origin of the census-periods.   The inference was drawn in my book,[1] which Wilcken does not mention.   In fact he attributes to Messrs. Grenfell and Hunt the discovery that the census-system originates from Augustus ; and this he admits, only leaving a doubt whether the first periodic year was 9 B.C. or A.D. 6.   That discovery, however, as the two English scholars mention, was stated by me a year before their volume appeared,[2] containing their first statement of their opinion on this subject.   So far as I am concerned, the matter is of no consequence ; but as it relates to Luke, it has some interest.   The discovery was made by taking Luke's account as trustworthy and searching for evidence bearing on the subject.   I took as a working hypothesis that there was an œcumenical decree of Augustus, instituting a census, and the investigation was directed accordingly.   That is a procedure that is not merely scientifically permissible : it is in the present state of knowledge the only scientific method.   This is a point of supreme importance.

In every case that has been sufficiently tested [3] Luke has been proved to state, not merely correctly in a superficial and external fashion, but correctly with insight and fine historic sense, the facts of history and of Roman organization in municipal and provincial and imperial government.   Such

---

[1] "Was Christ Born at Bethl.," Chap. VII., after having been published already in the " Expositor," May, 1907.

[2] " Oxyrynchus Papyri," Vol. II, 1899, p. 207 ff.

[3] The statement about the insurrection led by Theudas in Acts v. 36 has not been, and cannot at present be, sufficiently tested.   This statement is uttered by Gamaliel, about A.D. 30, and his speech is reported by Luke. Josephus mentions a rebel Theudas, who lived and died in A.D. 44.   The little that is mentioned about these two rebels does not agree ; and there is no reason to doubt that an older rebel named Theudas may have been known to Gamaliel, but not mentioned by Josephus, who certainly did not mention every insurrection that was made in Judea against Rome.

progress as the present writer has been enabled to make in discovery is largely due to the early appreciation of the fact that Luke is a safe guide. From this follows the principle that the path of the explorer lies in the careful study of Luke's narrative, wherever it bears in any way on the subject of investigation; and it will always be found best to begin by fixing clearly before our eyes in its proper perspective a picture according to Luke.

We now resume the account given by Wilcken. The household enrolment in Egypt was subsidiary to taxation purposes, for the poll-tax was levied on all who had reached the age of fourteen, which determined the census-period. The intention of the census was to reckon completely the population according to their home (*ἰδία*), and hence the order was issued by the governor of Egypt that every man must return to his own home (*ἰδία*) for the census, exactly as Luke relates in respect of Judea.[1] Generally, and perhaps always, the edict ordering the return to the home for the census was different from and later than the edict stating the imminence of the census and the arrangements for it.[2]

The order is stated in the edict of the Prefect Vibius Maximus in A.D. 104, "that all who for any reason whatever are away from their own Nomos should return to their home to enrol themselves". By this edict, however, certain exceptions are permitted at Alexandria, in the cases of persons who are needed by the city. The only city in Egypt was Alexandria, and its citizens had the right of self-government by their own magistrates. The governor of the land of Egypt makes this exception from respect to the city. The rest of Egypt was imperial property, one vast

[1] Wilcken, I. p. 193.
[2] *Ibid.* p. 193 f., II. pp. iv., 235 f., no. 202.

estate on which the cultivators occupied much the same relation towards the Emperor as is described above in Chap. XV. The Emperor stood in the place of the old Pharaohs and of the Ptolemaic kings; and the people were his subjects and almost his slaves.

Egypt, therefore, was not in the strict sense a province of the Empire. It was the property of the Emperor himself; and the account given of the provinces and the provincials must not be applied to this unique country. No member of the Senate was permitted to land in Egypt without a special pass from the Emperor.

There can be no doubt as to the purpose of this remarkable order, which apparently was repeated regularly at every census. It was intended to bring the cultivators back to their own home, to keep them on the land, and to prevent them going off to other avocations and leaving the land without sufficient hands to cultivate it. The harvest of Egypt was of immense importance for the economy of the Empire, and no risk must be incurred that the land might pass even in a small degree out of cultivation. The order to return to the home was an economic measure intended to ensure that the supply of food should be maintained for the Empire by keeping a sufficient number of cultivators on the land. It was also a device for keeping up the value of the vast Imperial estates all over the East. Their value to the Emperor as owner depended on the high state of cultivation and productiveness in which they were maintained.

Now in the ages when freedom was valuable and valued, there was some temptation for the cultivators to leave the estates and try to merge themselves in the free population of the self-governing cities. Even if they could not easily become burgesses of a city where they settled, they could be ranked as resident strangers, of whom there were many in every city.

Later, and markedly during the growing degeneration of administration and security in the third century, the social condition of the whole Empire deteriorated, freedom ceased to have much charm, and the free citizens began to drift towards the Imperial estates. The condition of the cultivators was bad, but they could appeal to their Lord and Master, and it was to his interest not to let their state become too miserable lest their value should deteriorate. This we saw in Chap. XV. The cultivators had in some small degree a protector during that later period of decay, but the free citizens had none.

In the first and second centuries, however, all over the East, it seemed important to the Imperial policy to counteract the tendency of the cultivators on the estate to move towards the cities.

Now Rostowzew has rightly inferred from the nature of the edicts ordering return to the home for the census, that there was no law compelling the cultivators even in Egypt to remain on the land. The change of domicile was still legal; and the cultivators possessed the rights of freemen. Yet the Imperial government aimed at preventing the cultivators from leaving the land in too great numbers; and they took advantage of the census to compel return to the home once in fourteen years. This regulation clipped the wings of freedom, and served the purpose of the government for the time.

Very few scholars would have been disposed to accept as a regular Roman principle this rule that the census must be taken of each individual at his original and proper home (ἰδία). The present writer did not do so, and on this point his book on the subject was wrong. The error was not due to doubt about the accuracy of Luke, but simply to ignorance of the Roman custom, which had not become known.   Wherever the present writer followed Luke's authority absolutely and with knowledge he was right down to the last detail.   Where want of knowledge obscured the way, he was wrong.   He advanced the hypothesis that this regulation was special to Judea, and was due to the desire of Herod to conduct the census in a way that would be less offensive to the Hebrew feeling than the ordinary Roman custom.

We now know that the regulation mentioned by Luke was the customary Roman method of making the census. This is a noteworthy fact, and opens up a great vista of history.[1]

When the writer had recourse to a supposed concession by Herod to Hebrew feeling, he was groping in the proper direction.   It is quite true that the principle of the return to the home is an example of the influence of native Oriental custom on the practical administration of Roman rule in the East; but this was no mere exception due to Hebrew prejudice.   It was a far bigger and more wide-reaching principle than that.

In Greece and the East the Roman rule was applied to people with a very ancient civilization, with national customs and elaborate legal forms fixed by the usage of countless generations; and, above all, the Romans were here in contact with peoples so proud as the Greeks and so antagonistic in spirit as the Semites and other Orientals. Government could not safely be carried on in such countries without very careful adaptation to the character of the people.   The Romans never intentionally destroyed an

---

[1] It is expressly mentioned in Palestine, Thrace and Egypt, but that implies the whole East, at least.

existing civilization within the Empire (perhaps with the solitary exception of the Carthaginian): they used it, and built upon and around it.

Even in the barbarian West there can be no doubt that, while Rome imposed her own law and customs upon these provinces, she was not wholly unmindful of native custom and character. In the Three Gauls she adapted her rule to the tribal system. In southern Britain and in Narbonensian Gaul the tribal system was destroyed. This difference of treatment, due to difference in native character and circumstances, was probably accompanied by difference in the degree to which pure Roman law was administered in these neighbouring yet diverse countries.

Thus, for example, if I may diverge for the moment to a side illustration, it is quite false method to assume (as many recent writers in Germany and England have done) that St. Paul and his correspondents were familiar with the pure Roman law. The Apostle could never have seen this administered, either in Tarsus or in Palestine: Tarsus and Antioch were free cities, in which the Roman law was not applied: Palestine was governed according to Jewish law. Even in ordinary provincial cities, like Iconium or Derbe or Perga, the Roman law was (as Mitteis has shown) strongly affected by the hereditary law and custom of the Greek East. Paul in his letters was not writing to people who knew the pure Roman law; and in his legal figures he has in mind the law that was familiar to his correspondents. In Pisidian Antioch the colonists were Roman citizens, and here Paul, perhaps for the first time, experienced the strictly Roman law in a city of the East. Paul's legal references are usually to facts and ideas, such as adoption and will-making, that were common to the Graeco-Asiatic and the Roman custom; but he has a few which are not expressed in har-

mony with pure Roman law ;[1] and it is as a whole unjustifiable to illustrate his legal allusions by quoting from the pure
Roman law of the Republican period. Illustrations from
Imperial rescripts, even of later time, are much more pertinent, because, although issued later, the rescripts quoted
usually were to a great extent a systematizing and authorizing of current administrative custom in the East.

In the East, therefore, we have always to think more
about Græco-Asiatic law as developed by Imperial policy
than about the strict Roman law. It was the former that
the readers and hearers of Paul or of Luke knew ; and to it
Paul went for his illustrations and his metaphors.

If that was the case with the general rules of law, much
more must it have been true that Roman practical administrative devices were suited to the Eastern peoples, and were
as a rule only the modifications of pre-Roman local custom.
The Roman census-system was simply an adaptation of
earlier Ptolemaic custom in Egypt ; and it was not justifiable to expect (as we did) that it should be purely Western
in character and method.

No evidence has survived about the method of the census
under Augustus ; but later, as we have seen, the Prefect of
Egypt issued an edict, evidently as a regular custom at the
approach of the census, ordering every one to return to his
own home in anticipation of the enrolment.[2]   Similarly the
magistrates of Mesembria in Thrace summoned the whole
population to come into the town to be enrolled according
to the law of the city and according to the custom.[3]

---

[1] Examples are given in " Historical Commentary on Galatians," pp.
349-74 and 385-91.

[2] " Papyri Brit. Museum," III, no. 904 ; also Milligan, " Selections," no.
28, p. 72 f.   The edict is of A.D. 104.   See p. 259.

[3] Cagnat, " Inscr. Græc. ad res R. pertinentes," I. 769, from Dumont and
Homolle, p. 460, no. 111e.   Quoted by Rostowzew, " Stud. z. Gesch. d. röm.
Kolonats," p. 305.

These are examples, the only three attested by the scanty evidence, of what must have been a general custom in the East. The administrative order was issued by the proper authority, viz. in a free European city by the elected magistrates, in subject Egypt by the Prefect, who was viceroy and lord over a population of servants ; but the authority for this method comes from the Emperor Augustus, or his successor for the time being.

Such was the custom of the census at a later period after Luke was dead. It is clear that, if he was inventing this general order, he like a prophet described exactly what was going to be the method at a later time. Such an idea is absurd ! It is beyond doubt or dispute that he was describing the method of the periodic census, as he knew it in regular practice.

In the Ptolemaic period similar papers, couched in remarkably similar terms, used to be issued for the census in Egypt. There can be no doubt that Augustus only modified the old census of the country and extended it generally over the East. Probably the return to the home was a device older than Augustus.

Joseph and Mary obeyed the administrative order, and went to their own proper home at Bethlehem : in Nazareth they were only resident aliens and could not be counted there.

Accordingly Rostowzew [1] infers without any hesitation from Luke that " already in the beginning of the Imperial period all people, whether inhabitants of cities or of villages, were summoned to return to their proper domicile (ἰδία) for the census exactly as was customary in Egypt ". He considers Luke's words a sufficient proof that this was the general Augustan rule.

---

[1] " Studien z. Gesch. d. röm. Kolonats," p. 305.

This regulation about holding the census only at the original home is diametrically opposed to our modern ideas of a census.   It is destructive of many of the purposes for which a census is valued in modern administration.   It tends to prevent free settlement, to impede trade, and to put fetters on intercourse through the country.   Why should Rome impose such a condition in the East?   For the strengthening of the Empire it was urgently required that national distinctions should be obliterated in the wider patriotism of the universal citizenship ; and many of Augustus's measures show that he was aiming at a progressive unification of the whole Roman world through the weakening of the merely national or tribal unions and the encouragement of œcumenical patriotism and sense of common and universal brotherhood.   Yet here the Augustan census is, according to Luke, accompanied by a thoroughly retrogressive regulation which seems to mean that every one ought to stay at home, that no one can acquire the right to be away from home for more than a few years, and that all must be counted at their own proper home at every census, as if they were bound to that home and could only be temporary sojourners everywhere else.

Such a regulation was opposed to the general tendency and to the best side of the Augustan system ; and we had some apparent ground to rest on, when we pronounced the regulation to be non-Roman.   But we wrongly assumed that the Augustan system was perfected, and that all parts of it were carried out on the same general principles.   On the contrary, the Imperial system was incomplete, wavering, often partaking of the nature of compromise ; and so far from rejecting as non-Roman the bond of attachment to the original domicile, both Augustus and his successors seem to have used this principle wherever it seemed convenient for them.

Mr. Zulueta, in a remarkable essay published in Vino-gradoff's " Oxford Studies," 1909, p. 42,[1] states well the purpose and nature of this principle (*die Lehre von der ἰδία*, as it is called in German); and I quote his words, which seem almost like a commentary on Luke, though it may be taken as certain that the learned writer of this Essay on the later Roman law had in his mind no thought of explaining or defending St. Luke.

He points out that, while the Imperial policy rarely, and only in critical times, made any use of the old Oriental principle of the *corvée*, according to which the population might be called upon to perform forced labour for the public service, yet " The government held in reserve a more far-reaching principle, which was asserted whenever political or economic troubles threatened to bring the industry of the country to a standstill. This was the principle that every man had a [personal attachment to the home and soil of his birth] (*ἰδία*), a place of origin in which he had his proper sphere of activity and to which he could be held in the public interest. [There is] a remarkable series of texts testifying to the operation of the rule of *ἰδία* from the Ptolemaic period onwards.[2] We may quote as typical the edict of the prefect of A.D. 154 (BGU 372), which con-cludes with the following threat " : " if any person . . . is found straying on alien land, he shall be arrested and brought before me as no longer merely suspect but actually a con-fessed malefactor " ; and " the general duty is " to devote

---

[1] Zulueta, " De Patrociniis Vicorum ". Each of the two Essays in the volume has its separate paging.

[2] He quotes in illustration : OGIS 90, 19 f. ; P. Taur. VIII. 13 f., 19 f.; P. Tebt. I. 5, 7 (118 B.C.).   P. Oxy. II. 251-3 ; OGIS 669, 34 ; P. Lond. II. 260, 120 (all cent. I.) ; BGU 372 (A.D. 154), 15 ; I. 475, 902, 903 ; P. Fröhner (W. in " Festschrift Hirschfeld ") ; P. Gen. 19 ; P. Tebt. II. 327, 439 (all cent. II.) ; BGU 159 ; P. Gen. 16.

oneself to agriculture on one's proper soil.   Precisely similar terms are found in the royal ordinance of 118 B.C.   In A.D. 415 a new idea was added, viz. the protection of the interest of a *dominus* in his tenants or labourers by means of local servitude.

In the census there was a special need, and the taking of the census had to encounter many difficulties.   To make a census accurate enough to serve as a basis of administration is no easy matter ; a successful census is a triumph of skilful government and good method.   It was an accepted Roman principle to permit, and even to encourage, free intercourse through the Empire, and thus to foster a feeling of Imperial unity.   Yet the existence of a floating population and of many travellers made the census difficult.   How and where should the migratory population be counted ? These immigrants and travellers could not be numbered as they stood at any single moment, which is the modern way. The staff of administration was totally inadequate in Roman time for such a vast undertaking : even the most elementary acquaintance with Roman Imperial facts teaches any student that government was carried on with an extremely small staff, and as a matter of fact we know well that the staff was hardly capable of coping with the ordinary duties of government : for example, the maintenance of public order and security, and the suppression of brigandage on the public roads, were far from thorough and satisfactory.   For an extraordinary effort like the census the Imperial civil service was quite ineffective ; the census (like the guarding of public security) had to be largely carried out as a branch of military duty ; and the only possibility of doing the work at all was to distribute it over the whole year, and to order the household returns to be sent in by each householder at some time during the year.

To meet the difficulty the government, in Mr. Zulueta's words, asserted the far-reaching principle of the proper home or ἰδία, an old Oriental fact. Every man must return to his proper home or ἰδία for the census. This we see in Egypt, in Thrace, and in Palestine (according to Luke), as appears from the references quoted above. To judge from Luke it was not only the householder but also his family, that must return to the ἰδία, and Wilcken elicits from an Egyptian Prefect's decree the universal rule that all were ordered to return to the proper home, not merely the male householder, but the family, so that the enumeration should be really a Household-enrolment (see p. 272).

The principle of the ἰδία is based deep in human nature, not merely in the East, but also in the West. There is a tendency to distrust the stranger and the wanderer. Experience shows that only too often he has emancipated himself from the controlling power of his original surroundings and society, without substituting any other sufficient guidance in his life. Such is the danger. The overcoming of the danger produces a higher standard of thought and morality ; but that is not the invariable result, and least commonly so in stagnant and backward society.

It is too much to expect that the Imperial government should have refused to descend to the employment of such a principle. Even in modern life, and in the most progressive societies, this tendency manifests itself in various ways, often disguised. In the great international railway-station of Budapest it refuses to recognize any international language, and orders that every inscription on every door and office shall be in Magyar alone. It makes the English disbelieve every German official utterance, and the German distrust every English official statement, as devices of an enemy.[1]

---

[1] This paragraph was printed in the year 1912.

In the unprogressive countries, such as Turkey, the tendency rules supreme.   The stranger is disliked as a danger :
a partial exception is made in favour of Europeans as being
different in nature, but they are only tolerated, not liked.
Other strangers are probably hostile.   One frequently hears
the principle invoked.   You pass on the road in Turkey two
or three Circassians, and you know that there is no Circassian
village within twenty hours distance.   The inference is at
once drawn that these strangers can be after no good so far
from home.   The police arrest them, if they dare.   The
traveller flees from them, if he can.   The principle justifies
itself in most cases, because the reasoning founded on it
proves true.   Only if the stranger goes direct to a guest-
house or a khan, is it admitted that he may perhaps be
honest, although appearances are rather against him ; but
he has a claim in universal custom to hospitality " for a day
and a night and a morrow ".

Education overcomes this tendency ; and through the
growing power of education dislike and distrust of the
stranger grows rarer and weaker, and disguises itself under
the form of patriotism or otherwise.   But in countries which,
like the Roman Empire, are degenerating from a higher
plane of civilization, the operation of the tendency grows
wider and deeper as the years pass.   It had been always
strong in the Eastern provinces.   Its history can be studied
in them for centuries before Roman legions had been seen
there.   It was connected with the story of conquest and the
domination of victorious races in the regions which they subdued.   The land was treated as estates, of which the con-
querors were lords, and which the older population tilled as
subjects of the new masters.   The presence of the old population was necessary.   They had the agricultural tradition,
and without them the land would have relapsed into desert,

as the water, which generally had to be artificially supplied, ceased to flow through channels that were not properly maintained, and as other subsidiary operations were neglected.   The new lords were soldiers and not agriculturists.

There was, however, at first only a tendency to remain, and not a tie to bind the cultivator to the soil.   Neither custom nor positive law had at that time transformed the tendency into a thoroughly binding tie.   The convenience of government and the advantage of the landlord gradually strengthened it.[1]

The tie to the soil was created and strengthened by the needs of the case and by the custom of the country.   Under the legal-minded Romans the tie was stereotyped, and afterwards became a matter of formal law.   The lord of the estate established a legal right to have the benefit of the work of the cultivators on his land.   If the cultivators left the estate and went elsewhere, the landlord suffered financial loss.   When there were abundant cultivators, the loss caused by the departure of some was not felt; but when cultivators were few, as was in later times the case, agriculture suffered, the loss was serious and attempts were made by law to guard the interest of the landlord in the labour of the people on his land.

In A.D. 415 Imperial law recognized formally this right of the landowner to the work of his cultivators.[2]   They must remain on the soil to cultivate it, lest the owner should lose the value of his property.   That is the earliest and as yet hardly complete recognition in express legal enactment of what had long existed in embryo, viz. the

---

[1] On this gradual growth of the tie see Mr. Zulueta's paper, already quoted.   Fustel de Coulanges and Mommsen were the pioneers in the study of this rapidly growing branch of history.

[2] Zulueta, loc. cit., p. 42 f.

bond of custom that fastened the cultivator to the soil and deprived him of his natural freedom to leave his home. The cultivator, once nominally free, who had been in a sense joint owner of the land, degenerated gradually into a serf bound to the soil (*adscriptus glebæ*), and the bond was rivetted by the enactment which recognized the claim of the landlord to the agricultural service of the cultivators.

Here we have a historical and social force running through the centuries. Luke is perhaps the earliest historian who takes notice of it as a factor in human history. The significance of the tendency had not been observed when he wrote. Administrators used it, but did not discuss its nature. No one knew what it would become, and probably no one thought of it as a power that was remaking human society for the worse in the Mediterranean world. Luke notices it only because it produced the regulation that led Joseph and Mary to Bethlehem in order to facilitate the taking of an Imperial census.

A feature like this cannot be invented. How should a mere inventor divine the future law of history, and attach to it the fate of the puppets whose motions he was devising? A true and great historian may have the divine gift of insight into the laws that govern human history ; but this gift belongs only to those who love and study the truth, and not to inventors of airy fiction.

Wilcken has observed another important feature of the Household enrolment. Not merely were written census returns handed in ; but the entire population had to present themselves personally for inspection. This he infers from a passage in a London Papyrus with practical certainty, and rightly calls it a very important point.[1]

---

[1] Lond., ii. 55, l. 39: Mitteis-Wilcken, I, i. p. 194.

"Accordingly," as he says, "Joseph and Mary in the legend of Luke must both go to Bethlehem." The argument which Wilcken has in mind is that Luke, who knew this regulation to hold in every census, invented this detail regarding the journey of Mary in order to be true to the custom.

Luke's narrative used to be called a legend, because it was historically false. Now it is called by Wilcken a legend because every detail has been demonstrated to be exactly correct. There is no way of satisfying those people who have made up their minds. Whatever proof they advance for their opinion, is shattered; but they pluck victory out of the jaws of defeat, and in the disproof of their former argument they find a new one. One thing alone they reckon certain and necessary : Luke was an incapable and untrustworthy historian, and this must be demonstrated at all hazards and in any way that serves.

The critics ridiculed the story of the journey, because it was absurd and inconceivable that Joseph should be called to his original home for enrolment. It is now known that this order to return to the home was regularly issued and enforced.

The critics ridiculed the idea that Mary should have to return to the home, even if by any chance Joseph had to do so. The head of the house was sufficient. Wilcken has shown that every member of the household had to be present for enrolment, and that therefore Mary would have to go with Joseph. The only inference which he draws from this is that the legend arose out of the law and practice. May we not infer that it is a piece of real history, that Joseph and Mary did present themselves for the census at Bethlehem, and that Jesus was born there ? It is contrary to every canon of historical criticism that the story should be set aside as a legend, because all the details in it are true.   There is no other instance in history of an invention like this, where so many circumstances and conditions of the Imperial administrations are transferred to a false date and applied to make up a false story, yet all with perfect truth to the circumstances and conditions of a different time.

As the census involved that everyone should personally present himself or herself to the officer for enumeration, it follows that the modern method of counting every person in his actual position during one day could not be applied. A year was open for the census ; and people might present themselves at their place of origin for registration at any time during the year ; but the later months of the year were most frequently used.   We in modern time make the census for one fixed and universal moment, catching our migratory population at the given instant, as if by an instantaneous photograph.   The Romans tried to cope in another way with the difficulty of numbering people who might be far from home, viz. by bringing them at some time during the enrolment-year to their proper and original home ; and they permitted them to come for enrolment at any time during the year.   On this rule there is much more to say.

CHAPTER XXI

WHEN QUIRINIUS WAS GOVERNING SYRIA

THERE remains the difficulty connected with Luke's dating of the first census "in the time when Quirinius was governing Syria". This loose method of dating is to our conceptions of chronology extremely unsatisfactory. It does not even imply a definite year, for governors of Syria often retained office for three years continuously.[1] It was, however, quite in accordance with the ancient custom; and it is in Luke's own style, as we see in the dating of the coming of John in III. 1, 2, "in the time when Pontius Pilate was governing Judea, and Herod was tetrarch of Galilee, and Philip his brother was tetrarch of the Iturean or Trachonitic region,[2] and Lysanias was tetrarch of the country of Abila". In that case the exact year of the reign of Tiberius is stated also, a unique date in Luke's work in respect of minuteness. Such vagueness in respect of time was characteristic of ancient literary style;[3] and Luke wrote for his own time and the audience of his contemporaries, not for our modern taste.

[1] Legati of the Emperor very commonly governed for a period of three years: under Tiberius, who disliked changes, some held office in a province for a much longer time.

[2] This geographical definition is very often mistranslated and misunderstood: it indicates one region, not two regions, viz. the region which might be called equally well from different points of view Ituræan and Trachonitic. There is no geographical term Ituræa, only the tribe Ituræi and the adjective: see "Expositor," Jan., 1894, p. 52; on Lysanias, p. 297 below.

[3] "St. Paul the Traveller," pp. 18, etc., and Index III.

Such as it is, the dating by Quirinius has been a serious difficulty; and in solving it Egyptian discovery has given as yet no help. The progress of exploration in Asia Minor, however, has come to the aid of Luke, and has shown that his words give an almost exact date, certainly a date under Herod the king, which is the really important and indispensable fact. A year or two up or down in Herod's reign is a matter of modern chronological exactitude; but a date under Herod is necessary, if Luke and Matthew are right.

Here we are deprived also of Mommsen's support. It was mentioned above in Chap. XIX. that that great historian regarded all the other statements of Luke in II. 1-3 about the manner and origin of the census as probably right; but he felt no doubt that Luke was wrong about Quirinius and the date, on the double ground that Quirinius did not govern Syria until after the death of Herod, and that he made no census of Judea before A.D. 6.

In these two negative statements, as we shall see, Mommsen went beyond the evidence accessible in his time; and, in fact, his clear summary of the evidence shows that the statements are merely his individual estimate of the outcome of considerations which are far from producing certainty. It is rare for Mommsen to speak with absolute confidence where the evidence only warrants probability; but he was here carried away by the inveterate nineteenth century prejudice against the superhuman relations involved in the narrative: there must be something wrong somewhere in Luke's recital of the circumstances.

Mommsen's statements in respect of Quirinius have since been quoted frequently by the critics who were hostile to Luke; but, as has been already mentioned, none of them ever mentioned his decision in favour of Luke in all other respects. This they omitted quietly. I do not mean that they intentionally concealed either evidence or testimony unfavourable to their view; but only that they were constitutionally incapable of judging fairly and of seeing the natural import of Mommsen's words. They were on the outlook for evidence and opinions that could be quoted against Luke; and statements favourable to him made no impression on their mind, and did not remain in their memory.

Gradually the opinion of modern scholars has crystallized into the conclusion that Quirinius governed Syria twice, the second occasion being in A.D. 6-7. The reasons for this conclusion were stated most powerfully by Mommsen in 1883,[1] on which occasion he revised some of his earlier judgments. Until new evidence was discovered, there was nothing to add to his discussion of the whole subject.

Yet Prof. P. W. Schmiedel, in a work intended to be a storehouse of assured facts for the general public and for students, the "Encyclopædia Biblica," dismisses as fanciful that supposition of the two governorships of Quirinius with an airy and pretentious but quite ignorant dictum. His words are quoted above on p. 229. If Dr. Schmiedel had taken the trouble to make himself master of the history of Augustus's reign as stated by modern scholars, he would not have dared to print his assertion; but as it stands in the Encyclopædia it is regarded by credulous English and American scholars as possessing the authority of accepted historical judgment.

Mommsen's reasoning convinced the cautious and careful compilers of the great Biographical Dictionary of the Empire,[2] de Rohden and Dessau, who speak of the first government as "sine dubio". I shall follow the detailed

---

[1] " Res Gestae Divi Augusti," p. 168 ff.
[2] " Prosopographia Imperii Romani," III. p. 287 f.

biography of Quirinius as stated by them and by Mommsen, and it will be found that the simplest way is to throw the present chapter into the form of a biography of Quirinius, and thus to bring his governorship of Syria into its proper relation with the other events of his career.

We are able to found the biography of Publius Sulpicius Quirinius on Tacitus's sketch in the Annals, III. 48 (compare II. 30 and III. 22, 23), given on the occasion of his death in A.D. 21 at an advanced age. This account is invaluable, because it is in chronological order, although, as usual with Tacitus, no precise dates [1] are stated.

Publius Sulpicius Quirinius was sprung from a very obscure family in the small Latin town of Lanuvium ; and fought his way by sheer merit and hard work to a foremost position in the State. He was evidently one of those capable and energetic, but hard and unlovable, military officers, whom Rome produced in such numbers, as occasion required. He probably fought his way up in the army ; but no record of the humbler stages in his career is preserved,[2] though the words of Josephus and Tacitus clearly point to such a period.[3]

After his prætorship, the date of which is not known, he

---

[1] So his biography of Agricola has no dates, for Tacitus evidently thought dates unliterary and beneath the level of his subject. Only in a sort of appendix, c. 44, he gives the dates of birth and death, leaving the rest of the career to be apportioned between those limits. In "St. Paul the Traveller," p. 18, I illustrated Luke's custom in such matters by this biography, which soars above chronology. A reviewer retorted that the " Agricola " is one of the most certain and perfect pieces of chronological statement : he trusted to school texts where all the dates are given in the margin (not always correctly). It has taken much study and comparison of many other sources of knowledge to fix the dates, and more than one is uncertain. Many modern scholars declared that Tacitus gives a wrong date for Agricola's birth.

[2] It was not usual to record any position lower than equestrian in the career of one who attained senatorial rank.

[3] Josephus, " Ant. Jud.," XVIII. 4, 1 ; Tacitus, " Annals," III. 48.

apparently governed Crete and Cyrene, and in this position conducted the war against the nomad tribes of the Cyrenaic desert to a successful issue.[1] How difficult a matter this must have been we can imagine from the troubles which the Italians recently encountered in the same region, warring against the descendants of the same nomads, and from the very moderate success which they achieved.

The victory of Quirinius proved his ability, and marked him out for further work of a similar kind in the East. There was a war to which Augustus was in honour bound. The Homonadenses, a tribe of the Cilician Taurus region, had defeated and killed Amyntas, one of the client-kings, in 25 B.C., and Augustus as his heir was required by law and religion and duty to take up the quarrel and pay the debt, because he had accepted the inheritance. The heir was bound to accept every obligation along with the estate, viz. the kingdom of Amyntas, which was organized as the new Imperial province of Galatia.

The Homonadenses are ranked by Strabo and Tacitus in Cilicia,[2] and the command in the war against them naturally fell to the governor of Syria, of which province Cilicia formed a part. Moreover there were no legions in the continent of Asia except those stationed in Syria. Quirinius, therefore, naturally was appointed governor of Syria in order to conduct this war ; and the question is what date should be assigned to this office.

In order to govern Cilicia Quirinius must be consul ; and

---

[1] This office is conjectural. Florus says that he conquered the Musulamii and Garamantes ; but a proconsul did not usually have command of an army.

[2] Tacitus says *per Ciliciam ;* Mommsen, Nipperday-Andresen, etc., would read *super Ciliciam ;* but there can be no doubt that the name Cilicia extended to cover all this part of the Taurus country, as Appian and Strabo show. This region was excluded from the province, but the relations with it naturally fell within the purview of the governor of Syria and Cilicia.

he was appointed in 12 B.C. The next office in his career mentioned by Tacitus is his proconsulship of Asia. Between those two falls the war in the Taurus region conducted by him as legatus of the Emperor in Syria. According to Mommsen there is open for the proconsulship of Asia either 3 B.C. or the period between A.D. 2 and 5 (see p. 295). The other years are filled by known proconsuls.

Mommsen placed the proconsulship of Asia in A.D. 2-3, and the war against the Homonadenses in 3-2 B.C.; but against so late a date there were two strong arguments, which he did not sufficiently estimate : (1) It is improbable that the task of avenging the death of Amyntas would have been so long postponed. Urgent and pressing needs of the State prevented Augustus from discharging that sacred and imperative duty until 12 B.C.; but then there was more leisure, and the Emperor was free to think of the Homonadenses. It is difficult to think that this task was postponed long after 12 B.C. (2) Mommsen's theory is that between 12 and 3 B.C. nothing worthy of note occurred in the career of Quirinius, and no office was held by him ; but that between 3 B.C. and A.D. 6, there came in succession an extraordinarily rapid succession of great events, and that Quirinius was successively governor of Syria, commander in a great war, proconsul of Asia, in charge of Armenia, married to one of the noblest Roman ladies, and governor of Syria a second time. This also seems improbable.

Both these reasons are negative, and merely show that Mommsen's chronology is involved in a certain improbability; but positive reasons might be strong enough to overcome the negative. There are, however, no positive reasons. He rested his chronology mainly on the improbability of any other system; and he apparently did not consider a dating so early as we shall see cause to adopt.

In fact it is now proved that the Homonadensian war during which Quirinius held the government of Syria, must have occurred much earlier; and it may be confidently said that the consulship of Quirinius in 12 B.C. was intended to qualify him for commanding the armies of Syria, and to organize the preparation for that war. This is the outcome of a series of inscriptions found in Asia Minor in the southern parts of the province Galatia along the northern outskirts of the Homonadensian part of the Taurus region, and in the Pisidian Taurus westwards from the Homonadensian territory. This evidence was unknown to Mommsen when he was writing about Quirinius in 1883; and, as I know from himself, he saw that it affected the question. Since he died the evidence has been much strengthened and is now determining.[1]

In treating this subject Mommsen could approach it only from the side of Syria and Cilicia, where some literary evidence was at hand, mainly Tacitus and Josephus. There was also the Tiburtine fragment of the epitaph of Quirinius.[2] There is, however, another important side to the operations. The war was naturally waged from the north, i.e. the Galatian side, as well as from the south and south-east, the Cilician side. That was, of course, obvious and necessary; the Homonadenses were caught between the two Roman provinces, and operations on both sides must have been carried on; but no evidence was known when Mommsen was discussing the subject. The evidence has

---

[1] In my book " Was Christ Born at Bethlehem ? " (1898), I placed the war from 8 to 6 B.C. The latest discoveries point probably to a date so early as 10-7 B.C. Herod the king lived till 4 B.C.

[2] In that epitaph the name of the deceased is lost, but part of his career remains, including his second administration of Syria. The epitaph was restored to Quirinius by a series of scholars, culminating in Mommsen's decisive argument, " Res Gestae Divi Aug.," p. 168.

now been discovered : it lies in the purpose and the early history of the Roman Colony at Pisidian Antioch and of the other colonies in Galatia, along the southern frontier of the province. The statement of this evidence is simply the statement of Augustus's design in founding "Colonia Cæsarea Antiochea," 24 B.C.

In 25 B.C. news reached Augustus that Amyntas, king of Galatia, had been killed by the Homonadenses, and had made the Emperor his heir. Augustus accepted the inheritance.[1] The situation in the East was critical. The tribes of Taurus were free to ravage the fertile plains on the north, especially towards Pisidian Antioch, which had lost the protection of Amyntas and his army, now defeated. The death of the king proves that his army must have suffered very severely. The character of the Taurus region exposed the invaders to great peril; and Amyntas, while evidently a man of activity, seems not to have had much military experience,[2] and there is no reason to think that he possessed the caution and skill needed for pressing an invasion in such a difficult country.

The most urgent matter for Augustus was to ensure the safety of the southern regions. No reorganization of the province was, apparently, attempted.[3] It was taken over as Amyntas had arranged its various regions. For the defence of the south the city of Antioch, the old guardian of the southern

---

[1] By Roman law the heir was free to accept or reject an inheritance; but he accepted it with all the burdens of the previous owner, the discharge of which was a religious duty. Hence "sine sacris hereditas," an inheritance without any religious burdens, was a proverbial expression for a lucky windfall.

[2] He had been the secretary of king Deiotarus.

[3] Gardthausen notes that nothing is said of any reorganization; it is true that the records are scanty, and silence on such a matter causes no wonder; but other reasons show the probability that the organization of Amyntas was accepted by Augustus.

Phrygian lands, was reconstituted as a Roman garrison city, i.e. a "Colonia". We must date the foundation as early as possible;[1] for the new Colonia played a considerable part in the events of the first years of the province. We can dimly see the character of the situation, but the details elude us.

Now 25 B.C. is too early, because there was not time to send the coloni after the news reached Augustus; therefore 24 represents the actual operation.[2] There were among the coloni soldiers of the Fifth Legion called Gallica, and perhaps of the Seventh Legion; four epitaphs of veterans of the former and two of the latter have been found.

In official usage, the new city lost its old name Antioch, and was called Colonia Cæsarea for about seventy years; but under Claudius or Nero the original name was officially added. This implies that in the ordinary language of the old population, the name Antioch was never disused, and that it forced its way even into Latin official custom as early as 45-60. The name in Greek was always Antioch.

The primary purpose of Colonia Cæsarea (Antioch) was to ward off the attacks of the Homonadenses and the Pisidian mountaineers. It was on that account a place of Imperial interest; and the honour was allowed it to elect Drusus Germanicus, the stepson of Augustus, to be its duumvir, or chief magistrate, for two successive years.[3] A squadron of auxiliary cavalry was stationed at Antioch, and took the name Germaniciana from Drusus. War was the duty of the city, and its magistrates were soldiers. The

---

[1] The proof lies partly in the early importance of the Colonia and the urgency of the crisis, partly in the Latin epitaph of an original colonist, which uses twice the ending -ai for -ae in dative singular feminine (unpublished).

[2] Probably, however, 25 B.C. may have been the official date, while 24 was the actual settlement.

[3] Calder in "Journal of Roman Studies," 1912, p. 100.

Imperial hold on the southern part of the province Galatia was maintained through its military power. The Homonadenses had one broad and tempting way open for their plundering raids: they descended on the rich valley of lake Trogitis, lying deep among their own mountains, and swept north along lake Caralis, until they came up against the walls of Colonia Cæsarea (Antioch).[1]

The Roman colonists must have been familiar with the name and deeds of that tribe; they had little rest until the great war came. That the war was coming must have been known to them from the first. Their history was determined, and their importance was measured, according to a standard of the Homonadenses.

The warlike character of Colonia Cæsarea would suggest that the election of Drusus Germanicus for two years as duumvir took place immediately after his German victories in 11 B.C. He died in 9 B.C., and the title Germanicus was bestowed after his death. Probably the name was given to the ala, when news of his death in office and of his title arrived. Then Quirinius was elected for 8 B.C. (See p. 286.)

It had never been suspected that Quirinius was brought into any relations with Antioch; but, as soon as the early history of the Colonia Cæsarea is taken into consideration, we see that his operations during the war must have been followed there with the keenest interest. Yet I felt astonished when my eyes lit on his name in the following inscription at Antioch, and still more when in the following year I found a second inscription in his honour. All the importance of this evidence flashed on my mind as I

---

[1] The description given by Strabo in pp. 569, 570, 668, 680, is clear when they are read in connexion with each other. The plain with many αὐλῶνες of which he speaks is the deep gap in the Homonadensian Taurus where Trogitis lies against the indented mountain-wall.

PLATE I.—Basis of the first statue erected in Pisidian Antioch, probably 8 B.C., in honour of Caristanius, præfectus of Quirinius, honorary duumvir of the Colony while governor of Syria. The stone is now lying on its side.

read the name in the first of these two inscriptions, for the evidence had been clear before me since writing on the subject; and in this text I read the confirmation of all that I had contended for, viz. that the war and his governorship of Syria must have taken place several years earlier than Mommsen had allowed, "in the days of Herod the King ".

The following inscription was copied at Antioch in 1912 by Mr. J. G. C. Anderson of Christ Church, Oxford, and in 1913 by Professor Calder ; and by myself on both occasions. The photograph is by Lady Ramsay.

C. Carista[nio	To Gaius Caristanius
C. F. Ser. Front[oni	(son of Gaius, of Sergian tribe)
Caesiano Iuli[o,	Fronto Caesianus Juli[us,
praef(ecto) fabr(um), pon[tif(ici),	chief of engineers, pontifex,
sacerdoti, praefecto	priest, prefect of
P. Sulpici Quirini duumv[iri,	P. Sulpicius Quirinius duumvir,
praefecto M. Servili.	prefect of M. Servilius.
Huic primo omnium	To him first of all men
publice d(ecurionum) d(ecreto) statua	at state expense by decree of the
posita est.	decuriones, a statue was erected.

In 1912 I had the great advantage of stating my views about this inscription to Professor H. Dessau, of Berlin, who since Mommsen's death stands in the foremost rank as an authority on such matters as are involved. In regard to the date between 10 and 7 B.C. and the general bearing, he confirms the views which are here stated.[1]

---

[1] I am permitted to quote the words of his letter : " mit der Erklärung und zeitlicher Ansetzung der Inschrift des Caristanius Fronto Cæsianus haben Sie zweifellos recht. Nur in ein paar Einzelheiten möchte ich mir erlauben von Ihnen abzuweichen." Then follow remarks (which I adopted) about Julius and Servilius. His reading Iulio, for Iuliano, was confirmed in 1913 by the discovery of the following inscription. The three *cognomina* and the use of Julius as degraded to a *cognomen* already at this early period, he defends by quoting C.I.L. III. 551, XIV. 3606 (Inscr. Sel. 921), C.I.L. VI. 1403 (Inscr. Sel. 966), IX. 4197, and later VIII. 12,442 and III. 15,208 (Inscr. Sel. 1110).

Gaius Caristanius Fronto was either one of the original colonists or the son of one of them. In Antioch, as other inscriptions show, his family played a leading part for more than a century; his great-grandson rose to senatorial rank, and attained the consulship and perhaps also the proconsulate of Asia. The first statue which was erected in the colony at the expense of the colonial government in accordance with a decree of the decuriones, stood on the basis which bore this inscription. Now as to the facts which brought him in contact with Quirinius.

Quirinius was elected chief magistrate (*duumvir*) of the colony Antioch; and he nominated Caristanius as his *præfectus* to act for him. This sort of honorary magistracy was often offered to the reigning Emperor by *coloniæ;* but in such cases the Emperor was elected alone without a colleague. Under the early emperors, and especially under Augustus, the same compliment was sometimes paid to other distinguished Romans, chiefly members of the Imperial family. Exceptional cases occur in which the field of choice was wider.[1] This inscription is the most complete example of the wider choice: it mentions two such cases: both Quirinius and Servilius were elected in this way.

There must have been some special reason in these two cases. Quirinius was not a man of any special distinction. Why should he be elected in so complimentary a fashion a magistrate of this remote colony in south-eastern Phrygia. (i.e. or southern Galatia)? He had neither Imperial connexion nor outstanding reputation to commend him to the Antiochian *coloni*. But everything is clear when we remember that he conducted the war against the Homonadenses, with whom Antioch was constantly at strife. It was at the time of that war that they elected Quirinius a *duumvir*.

---

[1] Mommsen, "Staatsrecht," II. 814, 828.

It is not at first sight obvious why M. Servilius was elected to the chief magistracy. He was indeed a noble;[1] but of his career nothing eminent or creditable is known, except that he was consul in A.D. 3; he was, however, a favourite of Tiberius. He also must have been in some way brought into relation with the colony; and the obvious probability is that he was governor of Galatia. This would fully account for the compliment. On this view it is tempting and plausible to suppose that he was *duumvir* along with or immediately after Quirinius,[2] and that they co-operated as governors of the two Eastern provinces Syria and Galatia, in the war, operating from the south and the north respectively. The friendship lasted, see p. 296.

On the interpretation which has just been stated, the governors of the two provinces concerned both nominated Caristanius to act for them in Antioch. This would have the effect of putting all the force of the Colonia Cæsarea under the direction of one man, and would have a similar effect to the old Roman method of naming a dictator in critical times and putting the whole force of the State under his control.

Now as to the date of this event, which fixes the time when Quirinius was governor of Syria. Several reasons, stated by Mr. Cheesman, place it early.

(1) The fact mentioned about the statue of Caristanius,

---

[1] Tacitus, "Ann.," III. 48. I follow Professor Dessau's identification. I had thought of an older M. Servilius, legate of Brutus and Cassius in Asia in 43 B.C.

[2] When the Emperor was elected to an honorary duumvirate, he had no colleague. When any other person was thus elected, he had a colleague in the ordinary fashion, as Mommsen thinks ("Staatsrecht," II. 828). Mr. Cheesman, who published in "Journal of Roman Studies," 1913, all the inscriptions of the Caristanii, mentions an example of a governor of a province being elected to an honorary magistracy by a city of the province.

that it was the first erected at state cost in the colony, would in itself suggest an early date. Not many years are likely to have elapsed after the foundation of the colony, before a statue was erected in the city. The connexion of Caristanius with the glorious events of the Homonadensian war gives a good reason for the honour of a statue.

(2) Whereas Colonia Cæsarea Antiochea was founded immediately after the formation in 25 B.C. of the province Galatia,[1] the five Pisidian colonies were founded together, and at a different time from Antioch, as appears from the names which mark them as a group founded on one plan :—[2]

> Julia Augusta Prima Fida Comamenorum
> Julia Augusta Felix Cremnensium
> Julia Augusta Olbasena
> Julia Augusta Felix Gemina Lustra [3]
> Julia Augusta colonia Parlais.[4]

The first three of these coloniæ commanded the roads leading north from the Pamphylian cities Attaleia and Perga ; and they had no connexion with the Homonadenses, but were founded as part of a general plan for the peaceful administration of the whole mountain regions of the Cilicians and Pisidians.[5] Lystra or Lustra, the fourth, commanded the point where the Isaurican road issues from

---

[1] " Cities of St. Paul," p. 268.

[2] Colonia Cæsarea Antiochea was in the survey of Agrippa, before 12 B.C., and thence Pliny took it ; but none of the Pisidian coloniæ were known to Pliny or mentioned in that survey, and they are therefore later.

[3] Lustra in Latin on coins and inscriptions (evidently under the influence of popular Roman etymology) : Lystra in Greek.

[4] The names of Parlais and Olbasa may probably have been lengthened by other titles. We possess only late coins, in which the titles of these *coloniæ* are usually cut short (e.g. at Lystra).

[5] Strabo, p. 569, describes the danger from the Cilicians and Pisidians : the Cilicians whom he means are the Homonadenses, pp. 668, 679.

the hills on to the plain of Lycaonia. The fifth, Parlais, stood at the south-eastern corner of lake Caralis, and blocked the road leading direct from the Homonadensian country towards Antioch: it held the crossing of the considerable river which flows from lake Caralis into lake Trogitis : see p. 284.

That these five Augustan coloniæ were founded together is proved by the fact that they were connected with Colonia Cæsarea Antiochea by a great road-system called Via Sebaste. Several milestones of the system have been found between Antioch and Lystra, and one was found actually on the site of Comama. All give the distance from Antioch (C.I.L., III. 12217 ; J.H.S., 1902, pp. 102, 105): they are all practically identical except for the number.

The five Pisidian colonies, therefore, must have been founded at this time, 6 B.C. ; and the operation resulted from the Homonadensian war, and formed part of the pacificatory settlement. The war was completed by the system of roads and garrison cities ; and this system was so effectual that the coloniæ seem never to have been called upon to act. Their presence was sufficient to keep the peace after the war ; but only one of them was designed by its position to be a check on the Homonadenses.[1]

The war therefore falls between 10 and 7 B.C. Quirinius, consul in 12, probably came to Syria in 11, and the war would begin in 10. The description which Strabo gives of the country corresponds with that drawn by Professor

---

[1] On Mommsen's side it might be said that the coloniæ were founded to restrain the Homonadenses before the war; but the scheme is far wider than that. It relates to the whole of Pisidia ; and probably the Roman power was not strong enough in these mountain regions to maintain a colony at Parlais until after the war. If the Imperial government had been able to found and maintain this system of colonies before the war, there was no reason why it

Sterrett and with the truth; it is cut by very deep cañons, with sides rising almost perpendicularly, in which flow the Calycadnus and its tributaries; and passage across the country is slow and difficult for a small party of travellers, and much worse for armies. There were doubtless many fortified villages which had to be reduced, one by one. Amyntas had captured some of them before his death.

The war probably lasted more than two years, as Quirinius' successes were rewarded by two supplications; and the end was crowned by the bestowal of the insignia of a triumph. The triumphal ornaments were not frequently granted by the Emperors, and only for complete success in a war of real importance. This occupied the years 10-8 B.C. Then followed the general reorganization of the mountain-region in 7 and 6 B.C. This was naturally left to the governor of Galatia, in which all the garrison cities were situated.[1] The work of Quirinius was ended.

So much might be inferred from the first Antiochian inscription about Quirinius. The statue tells a tale of victory. The coloni were proud of their connexion with Quirinius and their place in the war, and the first public statue that was erected in the colonia was in honour of their own citizen who acted as præfectus of the great general.

The next inscription confirms these inferences. It depends on my own copy alone. The stone on which it is engraved is built into the wall of a courtyard in the village of Hissar-ardi, close to Antioch. The house is near the

should have waited till 6 B.C. No sufficient power was applied sooner. The war marks the beginning of a general system of safety and strength. Previous to the war all rested on Colonia Cæsarea.

[1] The territory of the Homonadenses was situated towards the northern side of Taurus, i.e. "within Taurus," as Strabo, p. 668, says. This corresponds with the situation of their mountains above and on the flanks of lake Trogitis, as already described.

mosque, in a street that runs off at right angles from the stream on the opposite bank; and when the gate is opened, it hides the stone. Moreover, the stone is below the surface of the ground, and only a few letters appear.

C. Caristani[o C. F. Ser(gia) Frontoni Caesiano Iulio praef. fabr., tribuno mil. leg(ionis) XII fulm(inatae), praef(ecto) coh(ortis) Bos(porianae), pontif(ici), praef(ecto) P. Sulpici Quirini II vir(i), praef(ecto) M. Servili, praef (ecto)

To Gaius Caristanius (son of Gaius, of Sergian tribe) Fronto Caesianus Julius, chief of engineers, tribune of soldiers of legion XII Fulminata, praefect of a Bosporan cohort, pontifex, praefectus of P. Sulpicius Quirinius duumvir, praefectus of M. Servilius, praefectus of

It appears from this second inscription that the præfectus of Quirinius became a man of some distinction in the Imperial service. Before the war he had only been " chief of the engineers," a merely titular position, forming an introduction to the career of colonial magistracy. After the war he commanded a cohort of infantry, raised in the territory of King Polemon of Bosporus, and he was also a tribune in the twelfth legion Fulminata. According to a famous tale, this was the legion which, being wholly or mainly Christian, was able by its prayers to cause a storm of rain and thus to save the army of Marcus Aurelius from perishing of thirst; and from this incident it was called the " thundering legion "; but here we have the name attached to it more than 150 years before the time of Marcus.[1] See concluding Note, p. 296.

After the Imperial offices the colonial service of Caristanius is stated; most of this is mentioned in the first inscription. The order of enumeration is not chronological; it is clear that Caristanius was præfectus fabrum, and afterwards held all the colonial offices mentioned in the

---

[1] The name means " having the thunderbolt in its insignia ".

first inscription. Then his military career in the Imperial service was continued as commander of an auxiliary cohort and tribune of the twelfth legion, which both probably took part in the Homonadensian war, and which always continued to be a part of the Eastern armies. It is probable that the cohort was sent by King Polemon for this war, and that it now was enrolled for the first time among Roman troops.

The second inscription breaks off at the most tantalizing point. It was evidently engraved on a wall, and continued on a lower stone. Caristanius was præfectus of another honorary magistrate in the colonia. His municipal career, therefore, was remarkable. He was the outstanding citizen, nominated on his merits by three distinguished Romans, who were elected titular duumvir of Antioch. Probably the name of the third noble duumvir would clear up the whole situation, if the other stone be ever found.

As it is we have the records of a typical yet eminent Antiochian colonus. The colonia was a frontier fortress in Phrygia "towards Pisidia," as Strabo puts it. Its early history was of frontier wars. Its leading citizens were soldiers. A year or more before 6 B.C. it paid Quirinius the compliment of electing him an honorary magistrate ; but this was no mere empty compliment : it was part of the organization of resources for the Homonadensian war. It is also a crowning step in the proof that the story in Luke II. 1-3 is correct, for it exhibits to us Quirinius as engaged in the war, and therefore as governor of Syria before 6 B.C. Now Servilius was succeeded as governor of Galatia by Cornutus Aquila, who still held office 6 B.C., when the construction of the Via Sebaste and the foundation of the Pisidian colonies was going on : and Quirinius governed at the same time as Servilius (or earlier).

The exact year is a matter of chronological interest; but it was in the reign of king Herod. Every circumstance narrated by Luke has been conclusively proved to be natural and probable. The circumstances are those which ordinarily accompanied a Roman census, and Quirinius was in office about that time for several years. See p. 300.

Two other matters, however, demand comment, which may be brief.

Why does Tertullian say that Sentius Saturninus held the census, if Quirinius was in office? Two answers are possible: (1) If Quirinius governed Syria part of the year, and was succeeded by Sentius, both Luke and Tertullian would be technically correct. We have seen that the taking of the census lasted a whole year, and that the method was not definitely fixed in all details until A.D. 62. It may well be, and in fact it may be regarded as inevitable, that there was a good deal of difficulty in working the first census, especially in Palestine.

(2) It might be suggested—and this is the most probable solution of the difficulty—that both Quirinius and Sentius were legati of Augustus in Syria at the same time with different duties. It would be difficult for Quirinius to attend to the purely Syrian business, when he had this war on his hands. It is well-established that, in various other cases, two legati of the Emperor were present in a province at the same time. If Quirinius commanded the legions and military resources of Syria, while Sentius looked after the delicate and complicated political relations in Syria and Palestine, both would have enough to do. When Quirinius in A.D. 6 returned to administer Syria this would naturally lead to the expression in his epitaph " legatus of Syria again " (legatus iterum Syriæ). An excellent example occurs on a milestone in Africa. Rutilius Gallicus was sent

there, probably in A.D. 75, to hold the census.[1] At the same time the ordinary commander of the African army held office. On the milestone both are mentioned, followed by the joint title " legatos Augusti ". The milestones were placed in regular course under the authority of the governor of the province. In this case both the ordinary and the extraordinary legatus are mentioned as authorizing the supervision of the road and the placing of the milestone.

Again, as to the year of the " first census " in Palestine, that is a matter of chronology, and leads into other and wider fields. We have shown that Luke's words are exactly correct. We have also pointed out on Wilcken's authority that the early census-periods were a little irregular, and that it took more than fifty years to stereotype the process (ch. xx.). Elsewhere I have shown that the actual counting might possibly have been postponed as late as 6 B.C.;[2] and the sharp criticism of this part of my theory by Messrs. Grenfell and Hunt has not shaken or altered it even in the smallest degree.[3] It stands as it was written, a possibility, not (as they assume it to be) an assertion of confident dating ; and a corroboration of the possibility of such post-ponement is stated in "Expositor," Nov., 1901, pp. 321 f.[4] The postponement remains a possibility ; but Tertullian's authority confirms the date 8 or 7 B.C. under Sentius, and

---

[1] Ad census accipiendos : the census year in the ordinary system was 75-6, and the provincials were counted in 76-7. We have stated the probability that the cives Romani were counted earlier than the provincials ; see ch. xx. We see also that the duty of taking the census lasted probably longer than a year, the Romans being counted in 75-6, and the provincials in 76-7. See the remarks on p. 245.

[2] " Was Christ Born at Bethlehem ? " ch. ix.

[3] " Oxyrynchus Papyri," Vol. II, pp. 207 ff.

[4] The operations in incorporating Paphlagonia in the province Galatia were postponed long. Even such a slight and simple matter as the taking of the oath of allegiance was performed more than a full year too late.

other considerations favour the date 8 : see ch. XI. The one argument against this early date is that it makes Jesus almost exactly 32 years of age when His ministry began, while Luke says He was "about 30".

Now if Luke could calculate the other dates so carefully, he could have stated the exact age of the Saviour; and he had probably some reason for the vaguer words "about 30". It might be suggested that the later rule among the Jews that public life should begin at the age of 30, was already known as a common practice; and that Paul's entry on Jewish public business began at that age. Thus there was a motive prompting Luke to speak of 30 approximately : Jesus fulfilled the Jewish custom : so did Paul.

Note I.—The later career of Quirinius need not detain us. He was proconsul of Asia in 3 B.C.,[1] and in A.D. 2 he married Æmilia Lepida,[2] whom he afterwards divorced.[3] She was a great heiress, betrothed to Lucius Cæsar, and the marriage must be dated after his death in A.D. 2. The Romans showed the minimum of delicacy in such matters especially where the hand of an heiress was concerned; and we may take it that the marriage occurred very shortly after the death of Lucius.[4]

Then news came of the death of Lollius, the adviser of Gaius Cæsar in Armenia; and the ability of Quirinius, combined with his experience in the East, recommended him for the responsible position of guide to their heir-apparent in his Eastern expedition. During A.D. 3 and part of 4,

---

[1] Mommsen and the Prosopogr. agree that 3 B.C. and A.D. 2 or 4 are open for this office, but A.D. 2 is too long after his consulship.

[2] Called by a slip Domitia Lepida in "Was Christ Born etc.," p. 234.

[3] His action against her in A.D. 20 was later than the divorce.

[4] Mommsen places the marriage in A.D. 4 or 5, after Quirinius returned from Armenia, and supposes an interval of 16 years; but this is more difficult to reconcile with Suetonius' expression "the twentieth year".

Quirinius was in the East. Lucius Cæsar died on the Lycian coast on 21 February, A.D. 4. It was probably on the way to or from Armenia that Quirinius paid court to Tiberius, an exile at Rhodes. This attention was not forgotten by Tiberius when he returned to power. In 6 Quirinius was sent as legatus of Syria for the second time. He remained there two years or more, and then seems to have resided in Rome as an old man who had finished his public career.

In advanced age, A.D. 20, "in the twentieth year" after his marriage, Quirinius brought a charge against his divorced wife ; this action was certainly a stage in the obscure and tortuous Imperial policy ; and his old ally in the East, Servilius, appeared as a witness on his behalf. It was regarded as a duty in Rome to support one's friends in a lawsuit by testimony ; and the acquaintance gave Servilius the means of knowing the circumstances of Quirinius' household.

Note II (p. 292).—In "Klio," XIV. p. 57, Prof. E. Groag advances the hypothesis—needless to say on good grounds —that there was a legio XII. in the west under Octavian [1] and another legio XII. antiqua in the east under Antony, and he further adds the theory—more hazardous, but still quite probable, otherwise it would not have been stated by such a scholar—that Octavian, after his victory over Antony, united the two in the legio XII. Fulminata. On the other hand Henzen and Domaszewski think that Antony's legio XII. antiqua was an old legion of Cæsar's army which Augustus retained, calling it first paterna, and thereafter

---

[1] It was, as inscribed bullets show, part of the forces that attacked L. Antony in Perusia, 40 B.C. : "Eph. Ep." VI. p. 66 f., no. 79 f. (C.I.L. XI. 6721, 28 ff.) ; it was in Sicily, C.I.L. X. 7349, and probably at Actium, C.I.L. V. 2502, 2520 (cf. Mommsen on p. 240, and Gardthausen, "Augustus," II. i. p. 216). That X. 7349 belonged to the troops on Augustus's side, however, is uncertain.

Fulminata.[1] In any case it is beyond doubt that the title Fulminata is as old as the time of Augustus.

Note III (p. 293).—Misapprehension and error were caused to some readers of my former argument about Quirinius by their confusing between two governors of Syria named Saturninus : one L. Volusius Saturninus in A.D. 4-5, and the other Sentius Saturninus in 8-6 B.C.

Note IV.—I am indebted to Dr. Moffatt's article in the "Expositor," January, 1913, for directing attention to "the discovery of a new Greek inscription at Suk Wadi Barada, the site of Abila," described with a facsimile in the "Revue Biblique," 1912, pp. 533 ff. It turns out, however, to be only a new and improved copy of an inscription known for more than a century, and published, according to Pocock's copy, in the Berlin Corpus of Greek Inscriptions, III, no. 4521.[2] While we are grateful for the improvement in the text and the confirmation of the genuineness and general trustworthiness of Pocock's publication, we must grant Pocock the credit of having got everything in his copy that was important. All that was inferred from the new copy could be elicited with almost equal certainty from the old ; but a second copy always adds to the assurance of the first ; and hence Mommsen in Vol. III of the Corpus of Latin Inscriptions mentions from time to time any new copy of previously published inscriptions.

It is the dedication of a temple, etc., " on behalf of the sal-

[1] Henzen, " Bull. d'Inst.," 1867, p. 178 f. ; von Domaszewski, "Arch. Epigr. Mitt.," xv. 1892, p. 188, 30. Legio paterna, C.I.L. xi. 1058. Veterans of Antony's legio xii. were settled by Augustus in Patræ of Achaia, C.I.L. iii. p. 95 ; Mommsen, " Res Gestae d. Aug.," ed. ii. pp. 74, 119 ; P. M. Meyer, " Heerwesen d. Ptol. u. Röm.," p. 149 f. ; Vaglieri in Ruggiero's " Diz. Epigr.," iii. p. 335.

[2] Dr. Moffatt mentions this in the later part of his short article.

vation of the Lords Imperial and their whole household" by "Nymphaios a freedman of Lysanias the tetrarch".

During the time when tetrarchs were in power at Abilene there was only one period when there could be a prayer and vow for the salvation of the Augustan Lords; and that was between the beginning of the reign of Tiberius in A.D. 14 and the death of his mother Julia Augusta in A.D. 29. How long exactly Lysanias ruled we know not; but between those two limits his freedman could offer a dedication and vow for the Augusti, Tiberius and Julia.[1] It is no great step to suppose that Luke was right, when he dated the first appearance of John the Baptist (III. I), A.D. 25, in the time when Lysanias was tetrarch of Abilene, the district of which Abila was the capital.

Why not take the step? Why not say that the reference in Luke is correct? There has been absolutely no justification for the unreasonable charge that this dating in Luke III. I was wrong. The most extraordinary suggestion was that he had misplaced a king, Lysanias, who reigned in Abila three-quarters of a century earlier. It was actually maintained that Luke had transferred that king to this much later period, and had miscalled him "tetrarch," presumably because the name "tetrarch" was commoner in that later time than it had been in the middle of the first century B.C. It was, however, known and used even then. The older Lysanias was a king: the younger was a tetrarch. That the two ought to be regarded as different persons, distinguished by title and by period, was sufficiently assured on Luke's sole authority. That is an elementary deduction from the most fundamental principles of historical criticism : any other opinion involves the holder in absurdity: the

---

[1] Augustus did not associate his wife with himself as Empress. After his death Livia was recognized as Julia Augusta, one of the Imperial gods.

authority was quite good enough to justify a highly probable inference.

In addition to this, however, we have the inscription of Abila, mentioning the tetrarch Lysanias in the time of the associated Lord and Lady, Tiberius and his mother, somewhere close to the very year when Luke asserts that the tetrarch was living and reigning. Here is the external authority of contemporary registration to confirm the natural interpretation of Luke's statement as good historical evidence. The confirmatory authority was published and well known. Why was it disregarded? There is only one sufficient reason, and that is ignorance; the critics did not inquire into such matters of Roman custom when they told in favour of Luke; they took interest in them only when something against Luke might be expected from them. It really almost looks as if that were so. This inscription was sometimes misinterpreted as a dedication to Augustus and Tiberius as associated Emperors; but no such joint inscriptions are known. Tiberius was recognized as a colleague early in A.D. 12; but there is no reason to think that Augustus associated him as joint owner of the estates, or that the people recognized him as landlord and god before Augustus died. The inscription is a dedication to Tiberius and his mother, who were regarded as joint deities.

The dedication is a good example of the prayer for the salvation of the Imperial deities, as described in Chap. XV. The freedman of Lysanias regards his master as a client of the Imperial household, and thus the freedman comes to be a part of that great household.

Coins bearing the name and title of Lysanias the tetrarch are assigned by numismatists to King Lysanias of Chalcis on the assumption that he took the humbler title on coins.

This is rather strange, and it is possible that they should be restored to the tetrarch of Abila; but that is for numismatists to consider.

Schürer maintains Luke's correctness, but that did not stop the doubts (which are repeated in Dr. A. B. Bruce's Commentary).

Note V (p. 284).—The early importance and subsequent military insignificance of Antioch and the "Phrygian region" may explain a problem of the Roman auxiliary troops. There existed at one time seven Alæ Phrygum. Of these only the seventh is actually mentioned in any known inscription; the other six disappeared. Mr. Cheesman in his treatise on the auxiliary troops connects these Alæ with the province Galatia (though five-sixths of Phrygia was in Asia); and he is certainly right. It may be conjectured that the whole seven were originally designed for the defence of Galatic Phrygia or Mygdonia against the Homonadenses and the Pisidians. With them ranks Ala Augusta Germaniciana, which is mentioned only in Antiochian inscriptions. When the need for defence ceased, all these Alæ except one ceased to be recruited. The Roman army was strong enough without them. Hereafter the progress of discovery at Antioch may prove this conjecture.

Note VI (p. 293).—The chronology is most probably as follows: all the steps have been separately established on independent evidence, and all point to the same result:—

Drusus duumvir at Antioch I and II	10 and 9 B.C.
Quirinius duumvir at Antioch	8 B.C.
Servilius duumvir at Antioch either 7 or	8 B.C.
Cornutus governed Galatia before and during	6 B.C.

Thus Quirinius and Servilius were governing the two adjoining provinces, Syria-Cilicia and Galatia, around the year 8 B.C., when the First Census was made.

CHAPTER XXII

ANALOGIES AND FULFILMENT OF PROPHECY

An ancient Hebrew view is expressed in the Song of Deborah : "the stars in their courses fought against Sisera ". To put this in modern and Western fashion takes away that vague majesty which belongs to it in its Hebrew form ; but we must try to conceive it in our fashion, which is more definite and logically precise than the Semitic cast of thought. The will of God has imposed a certain harmony on His world. Those who resist His will find that His whole world fights against them. Every reader of the Greek epic and the Greek drama, especially Æschylus, is familiar with Greek expression of the same thought : that audacity and arrogance in man outrages and antagonizes the order of nature, the purpose of the supreme God, whether He choose to be called Zeus or by any other name.[1]

The stars, the winds, the clouds, the storm, and every other phenomenon of nature, are the messengers of God and the bearers of His power. As Isaiah says, " Jehovah rideth on a swift cloud ". Such thought leads to a certain reverent observation and study of the phenomena of nature, and lends dignity to the original form of astrology : that pseudo-science, however, rapidly and generally was degraded from a handmaid of religion to an instrument of magic, but it has in its origin an element of truth and right. The stars in their courses fight against the enemies of God, therefore

---

[1] " The Teaching of Paul in Terms of the Present Day," pp. 91 ff.

their courses should be observed, and they can suitably be
used in prophetic anticipation of the Divine action in the
world.   This study, however, is not really astrology, though
analogous in some degree to it.

Something of this thought expresses itself in the story of
the Magi and their visit to Bethlehem (see above Ch. XI.):
the Magi envisage to us the relation in which the accumulated wisdom of the East stood to the expected
appearance of the Divine Saviour.   His coming was
looked for, and was heralded at the proper time by His
star—not a new star, but the rising [1] of the proper star " in
the fulness of the time ".   The time had come : the world
was ready : the wisdom of the East knew approximately
that the event was at hand : the rising of the star marked
the crisis.   What the star was I do not presume to judge ;
nor can one tell certainly without some knowledge of
Eastern doctrine.[2]

The book of the New Testament in which this aspect of
cosmic influence is treated as highly important is the
Apocalypse of John, the most thoroughly Hebraic part of
the whole, and the part which was last in obtaining canonical
recognition.   Because the Hebraic element is so strong, the
wider Christian outlook is less evident ; but that wider outlook, the Christian view which surveys from a point above
the Hebrew, seeing everything that the Hebrew sees, and

---

[1] Matthew II. 2 : " We have seen his star in the rising " : ἀνατολή, the rising of the star : ἀνατολαί, " the risings (of the heavenly bodies)," i.e. the East.
Such is Matthew's distinction in II. 1 and 2 and 9.   It is therefore a mistranslation in A.V. and R.V. to put it, " we have seen His star in the East ".

[2] Col. Mackinlay has an interesting speculation, well worth study, in his
book, " The Magi : how they knew Christ's star " (Hodder and Stoughton)
on which I have said what I think to be probable in a paper in " Luke the
Physician and other Studies in the History of Religion ".   The chronological
reasons point probably to the date which is indicated by his theory, 8 B.C.

more than the Hebrew saw, belongs after all to the Apocalypse and justifies the final inclusion of it in the New Testament. There is an element in it which is required to complete and unify the wide range of the New Testament; that element, however, is not simply Hebrew but greater than Hebrew; it is Hebraism raised to its highest power.[1]

This Hebrew view was not in accordance with Luke's Western mind; he does not include the story of the Magi in his gospel; but that does not prove either that he was ignorant of it, or that he rejected it. It appealed to the Semitic mind: Luke writes for the Græco-Roman mind, as exemplified in Theophilos.[2] Yet he expresses the same view in Western fashion: the shepherds under the guidance of the Divine messengers in the heavens express the recognition of the new-born Saviour by the general world: Simeon and Anna utter the same recognition in the name of

[1] I regret that Canon Charles is too completely occupied with the Hebrew aspect in his most interesting and instructive lectures on the Interpretation of the Apocalypse, and that he therefore becomes rather insensitive to the higher, the Christian, element in the book. After reading his work, one must wonder how the Apocalypse ever came to find its way into the New Testament: were its champions, and the general sense of the Church at last, unaware of the spirit and essence of Christianity? I see that Dr. Charles regards me as accepting and upholding the astrological interpretation of the Apocalypse (see his p. 53). Readers of my "Letters to the Seven Churches" will wonder at his statement, for the idea of astrology never occurs in that book as a help to interpretation; he depends on a sentence or two in my introduction to Dr. Lepsius' instructive but one-sided championing of that interpretation; and the introduction as a whole shows that the sentences either do not justify his charge or fail to convey adequately my view. The introduction appears in several months' issue of the "Expositor" for 1911 and 1912.

[2] That Theophilos is a definite Roman official is proved by the technical Roman title, κράτιστος. Still he is a sample of the audience which Luke had most in mind. Blass's view that κράτιστος is a mere honorary vague expression cannot be accepted, and his own examples tell against him: "St. Paul the Traveller," p. 388.

Hebrew prophecy and old Hebrew traditional wisdom (II. 32 and 34 f.).

It is noteworthy that Luke assumes, without expressly stating the Matthaic and Hebrew point of view, that the Saviour must be born in Bethlehem. He tells how it came about that Jesus was born there ; but he does not mention that it was a fulfilment of prophecy : he simply assumes this in II. 4 and II. I. 69 f. as familiar to his readers.[1]

The Lukan historical point of view, however, is expressed in II. 1-4. There, in the severest and simplest terms of history, the Birth of Jesus is set amid its proper surroundings as an event in the development of Roman Imperial relations. We have just seen what marvellous insight into great imperial bureaucratic problems is here displayed (pp. 250, 272).

Not merely are all the statements in Luke II. 1-3 true. They are also in themselves great statements, presenting to us large historical facts, world-wide administrative measures, vast forces working on human society through the ages. He sets before us the circumstances in which Jesus came to be born at Bethlehem, not at Nazareth, as caused by the interplay of mighty cosmic forces. This is not the fancy of some commonplace inventor of pseudo-romantic fiction, as the episode has been pronounced by the critics to be. It is the view of history as history is conceived by a true historian, who can look into the heart of things, and who thinks on a grand scale.

Seen rightly, of course, every event may be thus conceived. The forces of the universe make each individual man in their interplay, and unmake him when his brief span of existence is ended. But he who pictures or describes

---

[1] Similarly in II. 4 he assumes the essence of what Matthew tells more fully in I. 18 ff. I assume the accepted text of Luke here.

the process whereby the man comes to be, is a true historian in the highest sense, or a poet.

According to Luke's conception of this epoch-making historic event, Augustus formed a wonderful plan of world-survey and world-registration, and promulgated his order that all the world should be counted. The term used is "the inhabited and ordered world," which was practically restricted to the Roman Empire by the Romans; but there lies behind it the vague conception that, rightly seen, the Empire is co-extensive with civilization, that what lies outside the Empire is mere barbarism, and that it is the destiny of the Empire gradually to assimilate the outer nations and raise them up to the level of the Imperial "salvation," and then admit them into the Imperial unity.

The edict went forth, and it was followed in the East[1] by another, which directed to the service of the State a force of peaceful and contented ignorance, the force of inertia, closely akin to slavery, which we see through the ages ordering human affairs under the domination of masters and lords.[2] It suited the Imperial purpose to use this force for the enrolment; and the order that was issued affected among others Joseph and Mary, and brought them to Bethlehem. The highest rank and the humblest are brought together in this wonderful historical picture of a great bureaucratic device.

I confess that, when I see the self-satisfied and pretentious ignorance of the critical theologians miscalling and vilifying this most wonderful little gem of historical insight and word-painting, I find it difficult to restrain my indignation. These are the dull and blind savants whom the modern world has accepted as learned, and to whom so

[1] No independent proof exists about the West.   [2] See p. 267.

many have humbly bowed down and done homage and worship.

The man who cannot see the splendour of this passage, when he sets aside all theological or anti-theological bias, must be blind to the spirit of history. Augustus, the mighty Emperor, and Mary with her infant child, are set over against one another. Luke was sensitive to the dramatic character of the episode: in fact, some critics have distrusted him, because he has too clear perception of the dramatic and literary aspect of his subject. He knew what he was telling. The autocracy of the Empire, the free voluntary obedience of the Church to its legitimate orders and its freedom where the Imperial right ceased: these were the chief factors in history as Luke saw it. Here they are set side by side in this opening scene, the Birth of Jesus.

In a sense this scene is not necessary to the Gospel. It is not alluded to by John or by Mark. It can be omitted, and the Gospel remains intact and complete. Yet it is needed to place the religion of Jesus in its proper relation to human history. It is the indispensable introduction to the long struggle between the Church and the Empire.

Luke throughout his history takes care to mention incidents bringing Christ into relation with the Empire.[1] There were not many such incidents; and the other Evangelists hardly allude to them. Luke alone records that Pilate thrice pronounced Jesus to be innocent; John records Pilate's declaration twice, and the others only once. The Roman centurion and the commendation pronounced by Jesus, setting his faith above all that He had found in Israel, are mentioned by Luke and Matthew. As this Evangelist noted those matters, so he marks emphatically the relation of Jesus to the Empire even in His birth.

[1] " St. Paul the Traveller," p. 307.

For centuries the religion of freedom was destined to contend against the power of the great Empire; and it is an arresting fact that even in His birth the Founder of that religion was tossed hither and thither at the command of the Emperor. And what was the result? Only the triumph of Jesus. His poor mother must travel far to Bethlehem; and the Child was there born; but all that the Emperor achieved was to stamp the Child as the Fulfiller of prophecy and the promised Messiah. As in the death of Christ the sarcastic statement of His crime which Imperial policy placed over Him, was a placard blazoning Him to the world as the King of the Jews, so in His birth the Imperial order which drove the unborn Child to Bethlehem qualified Him to be the governor, who should be the shepherd of Israel (Matt. II. 5 f.).

Such analogies with sayings of Scripture, or with events in the life of the Saviour, lay very near the heart of the early Christians, and were always being observed by them. The Smyrnæans saw in Polycarp's death, beyond a doubt, a succession of features and conditions that marked out their great Bishop as a successor very like his Master; and they were right, for his courtesy, dignity, patience, and sweetness of temper make him worthy of being compared in his death to Jesus. But the impressiveness of the analogies lay in their springing naturally and spontaneously from the surrounding conditions, and in their being entirely unforced and not intentionally emphasized.

Such coincidences were a feature of that early Christian literature, because they are a feature of life. This leads us into the wide and difficult subject that is called fulfilment of prophecy. There was no fulfilment of prophecy, if an individual designedly got himself up to correspond to prophetic description. In order to fulfil prophecy, the

fulfilment must be unintentional. What we should call
now-a-days "undesigned coincidence" is in the truest sense
fulfilment of prophecy. If Mary, hoping that the son
who was about to be born of her should be apparent to
the world as the promised Messiah, had gone purposely to
Bethlehem in order that the child might be born there, the
fulfilment of prophecy would not have been so striking as
it was when her journey to Bethlehem was forced on her by
the constraint of external power. The order of nature, the
law of the Roman world, drove her there without any intention or plan for her son, and thus was brought about
the coincidence between the prophecy and the event.
Whether or not Luke intended it, he brings out in II. 1-3
the wholly unintentional character of the incident. The
Emperor ordered, God planned, Mary did as they willed
her to do without any design except obedience.

That there are many such unintended coincidences
between the life of Paul and the life of the Saviour was the
idea of Luke; but he never forces this idea on his readers,
or emphasizes the facts so as to impress the thought on
them. As has been pointed out elsewhere,[1] the advent of
Paul to the strange land of Macedonia was pictured by
Luke like the coming of Jesus to the strange, almost hostile
country of Samaria. Paul went out along the bank of a
stream, and sat down, and spoke to the women that were
met there; and a woman, a foreigner living there, listened,
and was moved and converted and baptized with her
household. So Jesus had sat down weary by the spring
near Sychar,[2] and a woman came for water, and He spoke

---

[1] "Teaching of Paul in Terms of the Present Day," p. 55.
[2] It is called a spring or fountain of flowing water in John IV. 6 (twice)
and 14. The Orientals always seek for running water to drink (compare IV.
10), if any can be obtained. The "well" of IV. 11 and 12 is a real difficulty

to her.[1] In each case the woman opened the way to affect the whole town where she lived; and both Jesus and Paul were pressed to remain. Those who knew the subsequent history of Lydia, i.e. the contemporary readers for whom the book was written, were aware how much is implied in this suggestion that she was influential in opening the door at Philippi. I have never been able to feel any hesitation on this point. Lydia, like Sergius Paullus and Simon of Samaria and Mnason,[2] is one of those figures in the Acts who were full of historic significance. They appear for a brief episode, and disappear from the book; but the abruptness of their disappearance was suggestive. It has always seemed to me highly probable that Lydia, i.e. the "Lydian woman," was merely a familiar name, used according to a very frequent custom in the Ægean world and Asia Minor generally. She had her own personal name, which would appear in legal documents, and wherever more formal courtesy was aimed at or was employed naturally by persons who were used to be more gravely polite. Paul was of the last class : he never speaks of Priscilla or of Silas, but of Prisca and Silvanus. Lydia was not the name by which he would speak of this lady in writing to the Church of Philippi. She is either Euodia or Syntyche of Phil. IV. 2, we know not which.[3]

not as yet solved. Probably it springs from popular speech mixing the words for " well " and " spring ". In modern Greek πηγάδι is a well.

[1] John IV. 27, ἐλάλει μετὰ γυναικός : so in Acts XVI. 13, ἐλαλοῦμεν ταῖς γυναιξίν.

[2] Mnason was the authority for the episodes of Æneas and Dorkas : hence nis place in this history. Luke thus introduces in his own way an important authority.

[3] We might perhaps suppose that Paul would name her first, because she was the earliest Christian ; but there may be a lesson and a hint here conveyed by naming her last. Syntyche is a name known in Lydia and the Phrygian borderland. The matter remains uncertain ; but something may yet be found to determine our opinion.

In the immediate sequel of the narrative regarding Paul's fortunes at Philippi, there occurs an equally clear parallel to the life of the Saviour.   There are two remarkable passages in the early part of Mark's Gospel, I. 34 and III. 12.   " He suffered not the devils to speak, because they knew Him " ; and " The unclean spirits, whensoever they beheld Him, fell down before Him, saying ' Thou art the Son of God ' ; and He charged them much that they should not make Him known ".

These two incidents cause difficulty in some ways owing to their unusual character.   In other places Jesus does not avoid coming in contact with demoniacs.   He appears also in Luke IV. 33, 41, to forbid the demons to express their recognition of Him and respect for Him.   Yet He openly confers such power on others, and speaks about it.   So in Matthew VIII. 4, He charges the leper who was healed to tell no man; but elsewhere, e.g. Matthew XI. 5, He appeals to such cures as publicly known.

Why does He act thus in these cases ?   There must be some reason for the difference of action at different stages of His career.   The two incidents are mentioned only by Mark and Luke.   Matthew, though he made so much use of Mark, omits those two passages ; perhaps he observed the difference of the Saviour's attitude in these from other places.   They all left out a great deal, and recorded (as John expressly says, XXI. 25) what seemed to them most characteristic of His life, and most instructive, or most easily comprehended by the public.   We cannot say confidently ; but for one reason or another Matthew omitted those two incidents, which are so striking in their diversity from the rest of the Gospel record, and on that account all the more valuable to us as revealing a certain side of Christ's action, less common but still a present force in

His life and thought. He did at times forbid the evil spirits, who always seemed to recognize and shrink before Him, from giving public expression to their knowledge.

Similarly at Philippi Paul felt much troubled by the slave-girl, who followed him, calling out that he and his companions were slaves and servants of the Most High God, and preachers of the Way of Salvation. He was annoyed at this public and oft-repeated recognition. He knew how it was caused, and he ordered the spirit that possessed the girl to leave her. She at once lost her sensitiveness of temperament, and her power of sympathetic comprehension of the nature of Paul and of all those with whom she had to deal professionally; and she could no longer produce any gain for her owners.

The analogy here to the passages just quoted from Mark is evident. We notice also that this case differs from the usual practice of Paul and of the Apostles (Acts VIII. 7 and XIX. 12). In this case alone he is said to have forbidden the recognition of his character; but we may fairly assume that such recognition was a common and even a regular feature: it is implied as a usual accompaniment by the language of Acts XIX. 15: "The evil spirit retorted on them 'Jesus I know, and Paul I know, but who are ye?'"[1]

An explanation has been suggested in Chap. X. of the reason for Paul's action in this case: the public of Philippi would regard the words of the slave-girl, herself a servant of magic, as indicating her recognition that Paul was a magician, greater and stronger than herself, but still a magician. Paul was at the beginning of his career in a new city and a new country; and he wished to ward off this real

[1] In this passage the power of the mere Name of Jesus is assumed to be already familiar to the public, and the knowledge is derived rather from general practice than from that of Paul alone.

danger at the moment. Permanently it could not be avoided: it was always a trouble and a hindrance and a scandal among the ignorant mob and even among the more educated, as has been stated already.

There is no reason to think that this episode in Paul's career was introduced for the sake merely of bringing out the analogy between his action and the Saviour's. It was recorded by Luke for the reason just stated; but certainly Luke loved to dwell on such analogies as they arose spontaneously and unforced amid the adventurous career of his hero, the great Apostle.

A similar analogy occurs in the story of the shipwreck, Acts XXVII. Paul suggests to the whole company to take food, in order to strengthen themselves for the escape from the ship. This was a wise and a necessary act. It was forced on Paul by the situation; yet he was the only one that preserved sufficient coolness and courage to think of preparing for the immediate future.

In this action, rising so naturally out of the circumstances, the analogy springs to light. Paul standing among the great multitude, almost all pagans, treated the meal as if it were the celebration of the Eucharist. He took the bread and gave thanks, and brake it. Compare Luke XXII. 19, where the succession of verbs is the same.

In later time the same feeling is observed. The example of Polycarp's death has been quoted above. An instructive example is the following, derived from epigraphic discovery.

It is an interesting remark of Monsieur S. Reinach that the action of Avircius, the Phrygian bishop of the second century, who travelled through the Christian world, "holding Paul in his hands," was like the conduct of the Ethiopian eunuch, who read the prophet Isaiah as he rode in his car. I have always understood the epitaph in the sense that the bishop carried in his hands his own copy of the letters of Paul, and in my translation I tried to bring this out clearly; but the analogy with Acts VIII. 27-8 escaped me.[1]

If this hypothesis, that Avircius Marcellus, composing about A.D. 190 the epitaph for his own grave according to the Phrygian custom, had in mind the incident of the Ethiopian reading as he travelled the book of the prophet Isaiah, be accepted—and it seems to me convincing, as we learned that it seemed to Monsignor Duchesne (when it was stated at the Academy of Inscriptions in Paris in July, 1914)[2]— then some interesting inferences follow from it.

(1) Avircius Marcellus probably travelled in the same fashion as the Ethiopian in his car. This had not previously occurred to me; but it is evidently necessary. The Bishop did not travel on foot, visiting all the Churches from Rome to the Euphrates and beyond it. Time and strength do not allow that an ecclesiastic whose proper sphere of work lay in the Pentapolis of Phrygia should expend his energy in such kind of work. He was sent on from congregation to congregation, as a rule, in a car (according to the suggestion made above with regard to Paul in the Galatian regions).[3] The kind of travelling car which was used in journeys along the postroads of the Danube provinces, and doubtless generally, is described by Professor M. Rostowzew of Petrograd in a paper published in 1911.[4] A Roman military

---

[1] The translation which is printed in my article on the subject in the "Expositor," 1889, p. 255, and repeated in Lady Ramsay's "Everyday Life in Turkey," p. 184, is: "I followed, holding Paul in my hands". That meaning seems inevitable.

[2] I quote from a summary in the "Figaro," kindly sent me by a courteous correspondent whose name I could not decipher, in September, 1914.

[3] See p. 84: also "Pauline and Other Studies," p. 266.

[4] "Ein Speculator auf der Reise," in "Mitt. Arch. Inst. Rom.," 1911, p. 268 ff. This relief is in the Museum at Belgrad: the inscription is in Dessau's

courier[1] is shown on his tombstone riding in a car along a road, as he had travelled in life. The two-horse car is in rapid motion ; a third horse is loosely harnessed on the near (left) side ; and all are galloping. There are two travellers in the car, doubtless the courier and his personal attendant slave. The courier, though a legionary soldier, is unarmed ; his duty was to travel, and to traverse rapidly long distances in official service at the order of the governor of the province ; and arms would have been only an incumbrance in such duties.

According to the legend, which is quite untrustworthy as historical evidence, being composed not earlier than the end of the fourth or during the fifth century, Avircius travelled with one personal attendant, a slave no doubt ; and possibly this detail may be part of a true tradition. More probably, however, it is merely suggested by the ordinary custom : people who were not wealthy regularly travelled in that way with an attendant slave.

On this sort of car the attendant sat behind. We are not informed whether the Ethiopian, as a wealthy man with many attendants, had a more luxurious conveyance. In any case there was room for Philip to sit in the car with him, and to speak as they travelled.[2] It is to be noticed that in the three reliefs where the attendant sits behind, he is represented as looking towards the rear (in the same fashion

---

"Inscr. Lat. Select.," 2378. Two similar scenes on Gallic tombstones may be found in Daremberg and Saglio, "Dict. des Antiq.," I. p. 928, no. 1197, and III. p. 862, no. 5939.

[1] The nearest equivalent for "speculator" would probably be "gendarme"; but no term is exact : see p. 317.

[2] In Daremberg and Saglio, on the same page as above quoted, the following figure shows a car of similar, but more elaborate, character with two people sitting side by side : the travellers are represented in a higher position than the driver, who sits on the front of the car with his feet on the pole.

PLATE II.—Blassius Nigellio, a speculator of the Legion VII. Claudia, travelling with his servant. A third horse is loosely harnessed to the car to ensure speed (Belgrad).

FIG. 7.—A Roman Courier travelling with his servant (Belgrad).

as on the back seat of a modern dogcart); and his seat seems to be only a bundle of baggage.

The courier's horses are represented galloping. In the other reliefs the progress is quieter. We have to remember that the courier was bound to travel faster. In my calculations with regard to rates of travel,[1] I have supposed that ordinary travellers went regularly 25 miles a day, and couriers at double that rate; and that the stages and equipment of travel were arranged accordingly. Foot travellers on a journey did between 16 and 17 miles per day. These rates are very slow in comparison with what Friedländer and other German scholars suppose; but they have done their travelling in the study; and I have quoted considerable evidence to prove that these rates are likely to be correct, and are not too slow for truth. Mr. Hunter, in the last number of the "Journal of Roman Studies," 1913, has an article on Cicero's journeys in Asia Minor, based on the Roman governor's letters and dates: and he finds that Cicero travelled 25 miles a day until he reached the army, but very much slower after that; yet Cicero was hurrying to his army.

(2) Not merely was Avircius, in composing his epitaph, mindful of the scene in Acts VIII.: he could feel confident that his Christian readers (to whom the symbolism and the cryptic language used in his epitaph were intelligible) would be able to understand the allusion. He travelled and read Paul, as the Ethiopian travelled and read Isaiah. The incidents described in the Acts were therefore familiar to the congregations of the Phrygian Pentapolis in the latter part of the second century (which might be taken for granted, though a confirmation is always welcome). See also p. 84.

---

[1] " Roads and Travel in New Testament Times," in Hastings' " Dictionary of the Bible," Vol. V.

(3) In these two episodes all the details are different, and characteristic of different countries and occasions. Yet the general analogy is unmistakable to the unprejudiced and unbiassed reader.

(4) It will illustrate what has been said above, especially in Chapter VI., if we describe the character of this scene more fully. The speculatores were part of the officium or special service-staff of the governor of a province. One of their principal duties was to act as gendarmerie or armed police. They officiated as executioners, and Domaszewski seems to regard this—perhaps in rather too narrow a view —as their most characteristic duty, for he calls them "gerichtsofficialen": it is, however, often a not unfair rendering of the conception that has been entertained in central and south-eastern Europe regarding gendarmerie, and a not unjust expression of the work of the modern gendarmerie in the Balkan provinces, to call them torturers and executioners. The speculatores also acted as couriers, but perhaps only in urgent business, as when Caligula announced his victories to Rome (Suetonius Calig. 44), and when the Syrian armies' oath to Vespasian was reported to Vitellius (Tacitus, "Hist." II. 73). They were all legionary soldiers (ten were in each legion) ; and in a very rough way they may be said to correspond to a humble grade, but not the lowest grade, of non-commissioned officers in our army —so far as mere rank is concerned, though the duties are wholly different.

Even on their police-duties they had often to travel from the governor's headquarters to outlying parts of the province. Both on such missions, and when acting as couriers, they were of course empowered to use the Imperial postal service, and the cars in which they are represented as travelling belonged to that equipment, and in one case are represented as bearing the Imperial insignia ; these insignia (heads of Emperors) are usually omitted, as the reliefs are on too small a scale to show such slight details.

Their conduct to the provincials is described as generally tyrannical, unjust, greedy and domineering. A stick is the mark of their rank, but it seems on the rude reliefs (in which it is regularly carried by the attendant, as a magistrate's fasces by his attendant lictors) to be more like a heavy spear or even an axe. They had the right to commandeer on the public service any of the possessions, even the ploughing cattle, of the peasantry, and complaints are rife in the inscriptions that their requisitions were often illegal : we learn of these complaints, because they were inscribed by cultivators of Imperial estates who had brought their case successfully to the knowledge of their Imperial Lord and God ; had ti r prayer to him been unsuccessful, it would not have been permitted to be inscribed. Such was the Imperial " Salvation " (described [1] from another point of view in Ch. xv.).

[1] On the speculatores see also Domaszewski, Rangordnung d. roem. Heeres, pp. 32 and 63 f., and in Rhein. Museum, xlv. pp. 209 f. ; Mommsen, Strafrecht, p. 924 f. ; Marquardt, Handbuch d. roem. Staatsverw., i. p. 560, ii. p. 547 f.

CHAPTER XXIII

"YOUR POETS HAVE SAID"

AT every point in the early history of Christianity we find that the relation to the Roman autocracy has to be taken into account as a factor in the problem. The Church and the Empire, the Imperial and the Christian "Salvation," stood over against one another. The Empire was striving to solve the same problems that the new religion was attacking. Its spirit, on the whole, setting aside some degenerate Emperors, was good. Its aims were noble. It sought to benefit the whole population of the world, and to raise the provincials and the outer people on the fringe of the Empire to the level of the Roman civilization. It was satisfied that Roman culture was perfect, that the civilized world was the Roman world, and that the best thing for every nation was that it should be initiated into the Roman culture, and brought into the Empire as soon as it was worthy of that privilege.

In Christian opinion Rome knew not that it was wretched and miserable and poor and blind and naked : it thought that it was rich and had need of nothing.[1] Rome flattered herself that she sat a Queen ; but her sins reached even unto heaven.[2] Her culture was vicious at the heart. The religion that she created to strengthen and maintain the Imperial patriotism was the worship of Satan, sitting in the temple of God, setting himself forth as God :[3] it deified the

[1] Rev. III. 17.   [2] Rev. XVIII. 7 and 5.   [3] Rev. II. 13 ; 2 Thess. II. 4.

State and the Emperor as embodying the majesty of the State.

Yet it is not enough to look at the Empire as painted by its enemy. We must look at it as it presented itself to the world. The Imperial " Salvation " was a great idea : it was a restraining power,[1] averting anarchy and bestowing on the nations a certain order and quiet, as Paul and Luke knew. Here we can only take the Imperial idea at its birth, and show how it appeared to those poets who saw its origin and knew by experience what it was doing for the " civilized world " : they had " looked before and after" its birth. They did not know, or did not care that the paternal government of the Emperor was the antithesis of freedom, and must, as it developed, destroy liberty in the Roman world. We have seen in Chap. XV. something of that line of development.[2] We now look for a moment at its beginnings.

The first perception of what Virgil and Horace saw in the Roman Imperial idea was the opening of a new world to me. The expression of that idea in plain and sober prose in an inscription of Asia Minor about the time when Christ was born shows marvellously close analogy to the Christian ideas regarding the coming of Christ into the world. Some scholars, who apparently had never noticed the poetic expression in the great Augustan poets, were so struck with the statement in prose as to imagine that the language of the New Testament had been influenced by the words of an inscription of the year 9 B.C., and that the story of the Birth of Jesus was modelled on the pagan conception of the holiness of Augustus's birthday.[3]

---

[1] 2 Thess. II. 7.   [2] See also Chap. XX.

[3] One inscription was in my mind while writing " The Church in the Roman Empire," after I had copied parts of it at Apameia in 1886 and 1887; another is quoted by Deissmann, " Bibelstudien," p. 277, with unjustifiable inferences.

The striking analogy in language arises from the existence of a general belief that only the coming of God into
the world could save it. The fact that such a belief was
generally entertained seemed to Paul to prove that the
"fulness of the times had come," and that the world
was now ripe for and expectant of a Saviour; and he
declared to men the true nature of the salvation which
they were groping after.[1] This fact is important and arresting; but only a very prosaic mind could suppose that it
either created or affected the Christian idea of a Saviour
and of salvation. There was an analogy between the Imperial and the Christian conceptions of " Salvation," because
the Empire was seeking some cure for the same evils that
the new religion wished to heal; but the analogy grew
weaker as time passed and as the worse side of Imperialism
became more pronounced. As Virgil saw it and described
it, the Roman idea was capable of a higher future than it
ever attained.

The Fourth Eclogue of Virgil, with its hope and confident
prophecy of a better age which had already surely begun,
was only one indication, though the most striking one, of
a dawning hope, which was spreading in the Roman Empire.
This poem was also the first clear and articulate expression
of that hope; and indubitably exercised considerable influence in giving form and definition to the vague emotion
which was stirring in the popular mind, felt by many, and
expressed by one great writer.

The Fourth Eclogue had its origin in an interesting
episode of literary history; and, if it were regarded solely
from the literary point of view, it might almost be called
an occasional poem. But what might have been a mere

---

[1] " The Teaching of Paul in Terms of the Present Day," pp. 94, 285.

occasional poem in the hands of a lesser poet, became, in passing through the mind of Virgil, a work of far wider and higher character. It is, however, essential to a right comprehension of this Eclogue that it should be studied in its origin. Only in this way can its relation to the popular conceptions of the time be understood.

It was through the relations between Virgil and Horace, so friendly and for the latter so important, that this poem of Virgil's took its actual form.[1] Horace was an officer, who served in the army of Brutus and Cassius, and took part in the disastrous battle of Philippi, which wrecked the aristocratic and republican party, late in the year 42 B.C. He fled from the rout of Philippi and returned to Italy, where he found that the landed property, which he had inherited from his father, had been confiscated and assigned (like many other Italian estates) to the soldiers of the victorious armies. He came to Rome, where, as he says,

> Bereft of property, impaired in purse,
> Sheer penury drove me into scribbling verse.

The metropolis was the only place which offered at that time a career to a young man conscious of literary power, and compelled to seek a living thereby. Horace had now neither property nor patron nor influential friend. As an adherent of the defeated and unpopular party, the young poet's career was doubly difficult ; and we could not suppose that his republican and aristocratic sentiments were blazoned by him in Rome when he settled there. That these sentiments were now concealed by him is proved by the fact that he found employment as a clerk in one of the

---

[1] The thought must have been simmering in the mind of Virgil, but the form was suggested as a reply to a poem of Horace. My own personal view is that the two poems inaugurated the personal relations and intimate friendship of the two poets.

government offices : a pronounced aristocrat would not have received, and would hardly have asked, such a position.

Horace's mind was not that of a zealot or an extremist. He had fought for the side which he believed in, and he accepted the result of the fight. The question for him was settled, and he now accommodated himself unreservedly to the new situation. Moreover, he had unquestionably lost his faith in his former party, from causes at which the historian can guess without any difficulty. He recognized that it was incapable and dead, and that Rome had nothing to hope from it, even if it had been successful in the fight. Every reader of his works knows that such was his feeling, and such was the widespread feeling of the Roman world. Men recognized that the degeneration of the Mediterranean world had proceeded one stage further, and that the republican party had failed decisively to govern the Empire which it had conquered. Horace represents the general opinion of the pagan world. He stands in the world of men, not above it (as Virgil did); he expresses the sentiments of the world from a sane, common-sense point of view ; and, as he emerged from penury, he attained a high level of wisdom, propriety, and self-respect in his outlook on the world, and a singularly lofty level of easy and graceful yet dignified expression of popular philosophy and worldly experience. From him we gather the best side of popular sentiment and popular philosophy, as they were trained in the stern school of life.

In one of Horace's poems the popular estimate of the situation in which the Roman world was placed found full expression. This poem is the Sixteenth Epode, which stands at the end of the first period of his literary activity and prepares the entrance on his second period. In the first period he was the hungry wolf, the impoverished and disappointed writer, who had felt the injustice of the world and was embittered by his experience. In the Sixteenth Epode he pours forth unreservedly the disappointment which he and the people generally felt about the existing situation of the Roman world. The long civil wars had sickened and disgusted the popular mind, except in so far as they had brutalized it into positive enjoyment of the apparently endless series of intestine wars and massacres, each more bloody than its predecessor. The Roman Empire and Roman society were drifting steadily towards ruin, and their motion onwards towards the abyss was becoming ever more rapid.

This consciousness of degeneration and approaching ruin generally turned to utter despair. No hope was apparent. The Roman people had outgrown its old religion, and had found no new religion to take its place. Hence there was no religious consolation for it, no God to whom it could look for help and salvation. To which of the deities should the Roman people turn: what prayer would avail to importune Vesta and the old Divine patrons of the State and compel them to help the city and the Empire in their need? So asks Horace in the second Ode of the first book, a poem written at a considerably later date, when he thought he had found a new god and a present help. But in the first period of his literary work he had no hope. He had not even a political party to which he could join himself and for which he could fight. He had lost his old faith in the Republican party, and found nothing to replace it; the mind of man craved for the help of God, and there was no God known to it. So Horace consoled himself by an excursion into the land of fancy and of dreams. The Romans, as he says, had now only one chance left. They could abandon their country, and go far away from Italy

into the Western Ocean, to find that happy land of which
legend tells and poets sing, where the Golden Age of quiet
and peace and plenty is always present, because there the
degeneration which had affected the whole Mediterranean
world had never begun. And so the poet calls upon all
true men and good patriots to abandon their country, to
desert Rome, and sail far away into the Atlantic Ocean,
seeking a " new world to redress the balance of the old
world," to dwell in

> The rich and happy isles
> Where Ceres year by year crowns all the untill'd land with sheaves,
> And the vine with purple clusters droops, unpruned of all her leaves ;
> Where the olive buds and burgeons, to its promise ne'er untrue,
> And the russet fig adorns the tree, that graffshoot never knew ;
> Where honey from the hollow oak doth ooze, and crystal rills
> Come dancing down with tinkling feet from the sky-dividing hills ;
> There to the pails the she-goats come, without a master's word,
> And home with udders brimming broad returns the friendly herd.
>
> . . . .
>
> For Jupiter, when he with brass the Golden Age alloy'd,
> That blissful region set apart by the good to be enjoy'd ;
> With brass and then with iron he the ages sear'd, but ye,
> Good men and true, to that bright home arise and follow me ! [1]

Evidently, this fanciful description of the Golden Age
in the Western Isles, with the advice of the Romans to
take refuge there, does not express any serious belief.
Horace and the popular mind generally had no cure to suggest for the malady of the State. To them the world of
reality had sunk beyond salvation, and human life had degenerated into a riot of bloodshed and strife. Only in
dreamland was there any refuge from the evils of actual
life. Horace is here only " the idle singer of an empty
day," singing in the brief interval between the last massacre and the next one. There is no faith, no belief, no
reality in the poem, because the poet had no religion, while

[1] From the translation of Sir Theodore Martin.

the popular mind knew in a vague fashion that God alone could help now. Despair was seeking a moment's oblivion, and cheating itself with the false words of hope in this poem.

But, while there is no reality in the proposed remedy, no one can doubt, or has ever doubted, that the poem is political, and touches on the real facts of the Roman situation. This was what the people thought and felt and vaguely said. The old Rome could not stand : the Republican and aristocratic party, which had fought to maintain the old Rome, was mistaken and practically dead, and its policy had utterly failed. The poem is really the expression of a despairing acquiescence in the tyranny of the triumvirate and the autocracy of the coming Empire. This was the reluctant and hopeless view with which Tacitus a century later (and many for whom Tacitus speaks) regarded the government of the Flavian Emperors : a republican constitution, though the best, was too good for the Roman people, and autocracy was the only government that was practically possible. And, after a similar fashion, in the Sixteenth Epode Horace abandoned definitely his Republican views, to dream about freedom, and to acquiesce in the slavery of Imperialism.

For our purpose the most important feature of the Epode is its expression of the general opinion that no salvation could be hoped for except through some superhuman aid. Man, left to himself, had degenerated and must degenerate. The almost universal pagan view was to that effect ; and history confirms it. Paul makes this view the starting-point for his philosophy of history : God alone can give help and preserve true civilization. In this the Apostle of the Gentiles agrees with the almost universal Gentile thought. What he adds to it is the evangel of the Way, revealed first to the Hebrews imperfectly, now perfectly to all men.

The opinion of Virgil stands by itself, practically solitary in pagan literature. In his mind there sprang into existence a new idea, the hope of an immediate and present salvation through a new-born child.

It may be assumed, for the moment, that chronology and general conditions permit the supposition that Virgil's poem started from and gave the answer to Horace's.[1] The late Professor Kiessling, of Berlin, pointed out that Virgil in this poem caught up and echoed two of Horace's phrases. It seems beyond doubt that

nec magnos metuent armenta leones

is not independent of Horace's

nec ravos timeant armenta leones ;

and similarly that Virgil's

ipsae lacte domum referent distenta capellae ubera

has some connexion with Horace's

illic iniussae venient ad mulctra capellae
refertque tenta grex amicus ubera.

Two contemporary poets, known to one another, each (as we may be certain) familiar with the other's work, do not write in this way by accident. The resemblance is intentional, and was regarded, both by themselves and by the world, as a compliment paid by the imitator to the imitated. The question might be raised, however, which was the imitator ; and there is a certain probability, *a priori*, that Horace, as the younger and less distinguished, was the imitator ; for we know of other places in which beyond doubt that was the case. But in this instance Kiessling concludes that Virgil was the one who echoed

[1] The Book of Epodes was not published collectively till 30 B.C. ; but it is a well-established fact that important single poems like this were known.

Horace ; and his reasoning from internal evidence seems conclusive.[1]   Moreover, Virgil's poem was written in the year 40 B.C., and (as is universally accepted) in the latter part of the year, whereas Horace's poem, which arose through the horrors and suffering of the bloody Perusian war and expresses the feeling of repulsion excited thereby in the poet's mind, can hardly be placed later than the early months of 40 or the end of 41 B.C.   The imitation is a graceful compliment paid by the older and more famous poet to his young and as yet little known contemporary. We can appreciate how much the compliment meant to Horace ; and we can understand how the language of his Ode addressed to Virgil is not hyperbolic, but perfectly sincere and well deserved.   It was the kindness and courtesy which Virgil showed to Horace when he was still struggling with poverty that endeared him to the latter ; and this spirit of kindness and courtesy prompted Virgil to pay this graceful compliment, which may be regarded as the beginning of the friendship between the two poets.   That friendship opened the door of society to Horace.   After a time Virgil introduced him to Maecenas, who became his patron and intimate friend.   In the sunshine of moderate prosperity his character expanded and blossomed into the genial temper of his maturer work.   A deep gulf, caused by a profound difference of tone and spirit, separates that maturer work from his earliest work.   While he was struggling amid hard fortune, he was bitter and narrow.   What he quickly became after he met Virgil, the world knows and appreciates.

Now, looking at the Fourth Eclogue from this point of view, let us place it beside the Sixteenth Epode, and see

---

[1] I write without recurring to books ; and it is many years since I read Kiessling, but I think the above statement is correct.

what meaning it gathers from the collocation. Horace had said that no hope for the Romans existed, except that they should abandon Italy and Rome, to seek a happy life in the islands of the Western Ocean. Virgil replies that the better age of which Horace dreams is here in Italy present with them, now just beginning. The very words in which Horace had described a fabulous island and a legendary Golden Age are applied by Virgil to describe Italy as it will soon be, as the child already born in Italy will see it. What are mere fanciful marvels when told about an unknown isle of the Ocean become real in the imaginative vision of Virgil, for they are being now realized in Italy under the new order, through the power of the peace and good order and wise administration, settled government and security of property, which have been established in the country.

Reading the two poems together, and remembering that they were written within a year of one another by two friends, one cannot doubt that they were companion and contrasted pieces, responding one to the other. They say to Rome respectively : " Seek your happiness by fleeing far into the Western Ocean "; and " Your happiness is now being wrought out before your eyes in Italy". A glance suffices to show the intention to anyone who has eyes to see. But in literary criticism inability to see more than one has been taught and habituated to see is a striking characteristic of some very learned scholars. Wagner, the learned and devoted and dull pupil of a great master, who can understand only what his teacher put before him and into him, is regarded by Goethe as a typical German professor, but he has analogies among us.

Virgil is the prophet of the new age of Italy. He was always thinking about Italy and imagining what it might be made by the application of prudence, forethought, and true knowledge. The subject of the Georgics is to describe what Italy might become, if agriculture were wisely and thoroughly carried out. "You have all you need in Italy, the most beautiful and the best country of the whole world, if you will only use it right." The intention of the poem is to force this lesson home to the Roman mind.

The practical and skilful administration of Augustus appealed to Virgil. He saw that Augustus had wise plans, and skill to carry them into effect. He was a convinced adherent and apostle of the Emperor. The union of science and government had made the Mediterranean world fertile. The science had originally been supplied by the theocratic order, when the accumulated experience and growing wisdom of a people was concentrated at the hieron of each district, where the Goddess educated and guided, nourished and tended her people. The union of science and government was now beginning to make Italy perfect under the new Empire ; that union would soon destroy every noxious plant and animal, produce all useful things in abundance from the soil, tame all that was wild, improve nature to an infinite degree, make the thorn-tree laugh and bloom with flowers : it would naturalize in Italy all that was best in foreign lands, and thus render Italy independent of imports, and so perfectly self-sufficient that navigation would be unnecessary. This was the imperial salvation, on which see Chap. XV.

In this last detail we have one of those startingly modern touches, which so often surprise us in Roman literature. Virgil would have no free trade. The ideal he aimed at was that Italy should depend on itself alone, and not on sea borne products. His ideal is here different from and narrower than the Imperial. He does not think of binding the lands of the whole Empire into a unity, as the Emperors desired ; he wishes only that Italy should learn to produce everything for itself and that thereafter the "estranging sea" should once more separate the lands, and navigation should cease. He probably had not thought of all that was implied in this ideal ; but the modern form would be that the single Empire should be self-sufficient within its own limits, and not that Italy alone should produce all that it needs.

That the Fourth Eclogue stands in close relation with the new Empire is obvious. It is the wise new system of rule that is to produce these blessed results for Italy. But there is as yet no trace of the autocratic idea in the poem. Augustus is neither named nor directly alluded to.

Virgil thinks of the continuance, in an improved form, of the old Roman system of constitutional government by magistrates (*honores*), of the political career open to all Romans in the old way, and of the military training which was the foundation and an essential part of the Roman education. War must continue for a time, in order that the young Roman may be educated in the true Roman fashion. But it will be foreign war, carried on in the East ; new Argonauts must explore and conquer and bring under the Roman peace the distant Orient ; a new Achilles was sailing for another Troy in the person of Antony, who was charged with the government of the whole East and the conduct of the Parthian war. The triumvirate, Antony, Augustus,[1] and Lepidus, was not in appearance an autocracy ; it was, in name at least, a board of three commissioners

---

[1] For convenient reference we may use by anticipation this title, which was not bestowed till January, 27 B.C. ; it marked a great step forward in the personal and autocratic rule of Augustus, and a noteworthy step in the way towards his deification.

for establishing the Republic, professedly a temporary ex-
pedient to cure the troubles of the state. To speak or
think of a single Emperor, or to connect the salvation of
Rome with any single human being, was treason to the
triumvirate, and was specially out of place at the moment
when Virgil was writing, shortly after the peace of
Brundisium had established concord and equality between
Antony and Augustus. In the Eclogue a more obvious
allusion is, in fact, made to Antony than to Augustus, for
every one at the time recognized Antony in the new Achilles
who was starting for an eastern war : the Provinces east
of the Adriatic Sea were under Antony's charge, and a
Parthian war was in progress.

But, while Antony is more directly alluded to, the
thought that incites the poem and warms the poet's
enthusiasm is the wise and prudent administration of Italy
by Augustus. That is the real subject. The enlightened
forethought of Augustus and Agrippa made their rule the
beginning of a new era in Italy ; and Virgil looked forward
to a continuous growth in the country.

Still less is there any dynastic thought in the Fourth
Eclogue. The idea that an expected son of Augustus, or
the son of any other distinguished Roman, is alluded to, is
anachronistic and simply impossible. Every attempt to
identify the young child mentioned in the poem with any
actual child born or to be born has been an utter failure,
and takes this Eclogue from a false point of view.

Least of all is there any idea in the Fourth Eclogue of
deifying either Augustus personally or a son of his who
might hereafter be born.[1] That view is not merely untrue

---

[1] The idea of some literary critics is that the poem celebrates the birth
of an expected son, who unfortunately for the poet turned out to be a
daughter. This idea is really too absurd for anyone but a confirmed

to the existing facts of the conjoint government and the
union of Augustus and Antony ; it misunderstands and
misrepresents the development of the Imperial idea and the
growth (or growing perversion) of thought in Rome ; it
places Virgil on a plane of feeling far too low ; it is a hopeless anachronism in every point of view. Schaper, in a
very interesting paper, pointed out many years ago that
the deification of Augustus and his son and his dynasty was
wholly inconsistent with the composition of the Eclogue
so early as 40 B.C. The paper was convincing and, in a
certain way, conclusive. But instead of drawing the inference that the deification of the dynasty is a false idea,
read into the poem under the prejudice caused by the
development of history in the years following after A.D. 40,
he propounded the impossible theory that the poem was
composed at a later time, viz. in the period ending June,
23 B.C., when Augustus was governing no longer as triumvir,
but as consul, and was practically sole master of the Empire,
though maintaining the Republican forms and the nominal
election of another consul along with himself. To support
this theory, Schaper eliminated the illusion to Polio's
consulship, which fixes the composition to the year 40 B.C.,
reading *Solis* instead of *Polio.*[1] To make this theory
possible chronologically, and reconcile it with the date of
publication of the Eclogues not very long after 40 B.C.,
Schaper supposed that the Fourth Eclogue was composed
at a later date, and inserted in a revised second edition of
the Eclogues.[2]

literary and " Higher " Critic. A poet does not work so ; even a " poet
laureate " could not work under such conditions.

[1] As he pointed out, the correct spelling of the name was Polio, and not
Pollio.

[2] Two others, the Sixth and the Tenth, were also supposed by Schaper
to have been composed for the enlarged second edition.

These impossible buttresses of Schaper's theory were universally rejected; the faults of his paper distracted attention from its real merits; and the perfectly unanswerable argument from which he started was tacitly set aside, as if it shared in the error of the theory which he had superimposed upon it.

The truth is that the poem belongs to an earlier stage of thought than the worship of Augustus; and the Divine idea in it was still so vague that it was readily capable of being developed in accordance with subsequent history. But it was equally capable of being developed in a different direction and in a nobler and truer style. Had the Pauline idea of Christianity as the religion of the Empire been successfully wrought out during the first century, the Fourth Eclogue would have seemed equally suitable to that line of development. The later popular instinct, which regarded the poem as a prophecy of the birth of Christ, was not wholly incorrect. The poem contained an inchoate idea, unformed and vague, enshrining and embodying that universal need which indicated "the fulness of time" and the world's craving for a Saviour. The Roman world needed a Saviour; it was conscious of its need; it was convinced that only Divine intervention could furnish a Saviour for it. Paul was fully aware that this universal craving and unrest and pain existed in the Roman world; and he saw therein the presage of the birth of Divine truth. "The whole creation groaneth and travaileth in pain until now."

The political side of the Fourth Eclogue is emphatically marked, and was indubitably recognized universally at the time. It suited the situation, and it glorified the wise policy of Augustus. We are not blind to it. But the significance of this aspect should not blind us to the fact that this alone is quite insufficient to explain the genesis and the full meaning of the poem. Professor Mayor[1] here seems to us to be in the right, as has been argued from additional reasons in the later part of this paper. Virgil had learned something from Hebrew poetry and especially from Isaiah.

The Hebrew idea of a growth towards a happier future through the birth of a Divine child was simmering in his mind, when Horace's despairing poem declaring that no happiness for Rome could be found except in voluntary exile to the Islands of the West caught his attention, and drew from him a reply. As a convinced and enthusiastic supporter of Augustus, he declared that peace and happiness was being realized in Italy by the wise rule of the triumvir. With this he interwove the almost universal thought of his contemporaries that Divine aid alone could afford real and permanent improvement in the condition of the state ; and this Divine aid expressed itself to him in the form that he had caught from the Hebrew poetry.

Whom then did he think of as the child ? He must have had some idea in his mind. There can be no doubt as to this, if we simply look at the genesis of the Imperial cult. The power of that cult lay in a certain real fact, the majesty and dignity and character of the Roman people, which was assumed to be represented by the Emperor as the head of the state. Augustus permitted worship of himself only in the form of a cult of " Rome and Augustus ". To a Roman like Virgil in 40 B.C., the Divine child, who embodies the future of Rome, who has to go through the education of war and magistracies (as the poem declares), could only be " Rome," i.e. the Roman people collectively, the new generation of Rome, born under happier auspices and destined to glory and advancement in power and in happiness. As

[1] See his paper in the " Expositor," April, 1907.

Virgil elsewhere apostrophizes the one Roman as typical of the race and its destiny,[1] and as Macaulay, imitating him, uses the same figurative speech, " Thine, Roman, is the pilum," to paint the Roman racial character, so here the Latin poet, with the Hebrew thought of a child in his mind, can describe the birth and infancy of the child as really taking place with the natural concomitants.[2]

There was more than this in Virgil's poem, more than he was fully conscious of; but this he had in his mind. He did not see, what we can now see, that there was placed before the Empire a dilemma and a necessity. It was a necessity that a new religion should arise for the consolidation of the Empire. There was proposed for the Empire by Paul the new religion of Christ. The Emperors, in refusing the proposal, were inevitably driven to lay stress more and more upon the Imperial religion and the Imperial God. It is not always fully realized that this cult was not very much insisted on until the reign of Domitian, under whom the opposition to Christianity was first developed fully to its logical consequences. Augustus, who instituted the Imperial cult as a support of the state, was always a little ashamed of it; and his successors[3] had something of the same feeling, until Domitian began to take a real pleasure and pride in it.

It seems to the present writer, as it does to Professor J. B. Mayor,[4] impossible to understand the Fourth Eclogue without the supposition that Virgil had experienced a certain influence from Hebrew poetry; and other reasons for this

---

[1] In the famous line, often quoted, *tu regere imperio populos, Romane memento.*

[2] As in lines 60 f.

[3] It is difficult to make up one's mind whether Caligula did not regard it as all a joke, when he talked of his brother Jupiter.

[4] " Expositor," April, 1907.

opinion besides those mentioned by Professor Mayor will be mentioned in the following pages.

But, whereas Professor Mayor is inclined to reject the supposition that this influence came direct to Virgil from the works of Isaiah as translated (we must, of course, understand a Greek, not a Latin, translation), and argues that the Roman poet knew no more of the Hebrew poet than what filtered through the poor medium of the Sibylline Books, I confess that this appears to me an inadequate hypothesis, and that there seems no difficulty to prevent us from believing Virgil to have been acquainted with a Greek translation of Isaiah. It is mentioned by ancient authorities that he had read widely in remote regions of philosophy ; and as Isaiah had certainly been translated into Greek, and as the lofty religious thought of the Jews had certainly exercised a strong influence over many Roman minds and over the popular imagination of the ancient Roman world, it seems quite a fair supposition that he had become acquainted with Isaiah in Greek.

I shall not, however, enter on this question, except to remark that the influence on Virgil's metre in this poem (which will be pointed out in the sequel) seems inconsistent with the idea that he was indebted to the Sibylline verses alone. I am not concerned to deny or to affirm anything about his having seen the Sibylline poems ; but it seems quite safe to assert, in the first place, that no such commonplace lines as make up those poems could have any influence on Virgil's metrical form—one might as soon imagine that Shelley was influenced in his metrical form by Shadwell or Pye ; and, in the second place, that only the original expression of the ideas in the suitable metrical form by a great poet could have determined Virgil to make this unique experiment in Latin metre—an experiment which he never

repeated—or could have inspired him to express the antici-
pations of the champions of the New Empire in so Hebraic
and un-Roman a form.

We may assume all that Professor Mayor has so well said
about the relation of Virgil's details and words to Isaiah.
I shall add some remarks on the Hebrew and non-Roman
character of the main subject and of the metre, and on the
form in which Virgil develops an idea which was floating
before the minds of many in Italy at the time. To show
how naturally our results rise from the facts, I shall use the
statement which I made on the subject many years ago to
a meeting of the Franco-Scottish Society, only slightly
modifying the form, but leaving the thoughts unchanged.

There are two facts which determine the evolution of
this ideal picture in Virgil's poem. Virgil is perfectly
sure that the glorified and idealized Italy of his vision is
being realized in their own time and before their own eyes,
and he connects that realization with a new-born child.
These are two ideas to which no real parallel can be found
in preceding Greek or Roman literature. The Better Age
had been conceived by the Greeks as lying in the past, and
the world's history as a progress towards decay. Even
where a cycle of ages was spoken of by the Greek philosophers, it was taken rather as a proof that no good thing
could last, than as an encouragement to look forward to
a better future. Moreover, Virgil's new age, though spoken
of in his opening lines as a part of a recurring cycle, is not
pictured before his view as evanescent ; it is coming, but
its end is not seen and not thought of by him.

How does Virgil arrive at his firm conviction that the
best is last, and that the best is surely coming, nay that
it now is ? We cannot regard it as arising entirely from
his own inspiration, springing mature and full-grown,

like Athena from the head of Zeus. Rather we must agree with Professor Mayor that we ought to trace the stages in its development to the perfect form which it has in this poem.

Again, the association of a young child with this coming age is something entirely alien to Greek and Roman thought. It springs from a sense of a divine purpose, developing in the growth of the race and working itself out in the life of other new generations, a thought not in itself foreign to the philosophical speculation of Greece, but taking here a form so unusual that it imperatively demands our recognition and explanation. It was too delicate for the philosophers, though one finds it to a certain degree in the poets. Nowhere can we find any previous philosophy or religion that had grasped the thought firmly and unhesitatingly, except among the Hebrew race. To the Hebrew prophets, and to them alone, the Better Age lay always in the future :—

> The best is yet to be,
> The last of life, for which the first was made.

The Hebrews always recognized that the divine purpose reserved for them a future better than the past, and they alone associated the coming of the Better Age with the birth of a child. We must, I think, look to the East and to Hebrew poetry for the germ from which Virgil's poem developed, though in the process of development nourishment from many other sides determined its growth and affected its character.

Looking at the poem from another point of view, we recognize that it is a metrical experiment, which Virgil tried in this one case and never repeated. Its metrical character seemed to him appropriate to his treatment of this one subject ; but he found no other subject which it suited, and he considered that the true development of the heroic verse lay in another direction.

Landor, in his criticisms on Catullus's twelfth ode, has the following remarks on the metrical character of this Eclogue. "The worst, but most admired, of Virgil's Eclogues, was composed to celebrate the birth of Pollio's son in his consulate. In this Eclogue, and in this alone, his versification fails him utterly. The lines afford one another no support. For instance this sequence (lines 4-6) :—

> Ultima Cumæi venit jam carminis ætas.
> Magnus ab integro sæclorum nascitur ordo.
> Jam redit et Virgo, redeunt Saturnia regna.

Toss them in a bag and throw them out, and they will fall as rightly in one place as another. Any one of them may come first ; any one of them come last ; any one of them may come immediately ; better that any one should never come at all." But in this criticism (apart from the fact that the force of the lines would suffer seriously if they were transposed, though grammar and metre might be uninjured), Landor has not observed that Virgil is deliberately trying an experiment in order to obtain a special effect. We do not maintain that the ruling metrical form would be suitable for ordinary Latin use, but its employment in this case is obviously intentional and dictated by the subject ; it is no case of accidental failure in versification.

The two most distinguishing and salient metrical characteristics of this Eclogue are, first, that the stops coincide more regularly with the ends of lines than in any other passage of Virgil, so that to a large extent each single verse gives a distinct sense ; and, secondly, that in a number of cases the second half of the line repeats with slight

variation the meaning of the first half, or, when the sense
is enclosed in two hexameters, the second repeats the meaning of the first. These characteristics are unlike any previous treatment of the hexameter. As to the first, it is
true that in the earliest stages of Virgil's metre the stops
are placed at the ends of lines to a much greater extent
than in its later stages. But there is a general agreement
among Latin scholars that the fourth Eclogue is not the
earliest ; and even compared with the earliest, its metre is
seen to be something peculiar and apart.

These characteristics are distinctly those of Hebrew
poetry ; and it appears to me that the metrical treatment
of this Eclogue can hardly be explained except as an experiment made in imitation of the same original, from which
sprang the central conception of the Better Age surely
approaching, and inaugurated by the birth of a child.
Virgil found the idea and the metrical form together ;
that is to say, he did not gather the idea from a secondary
source, but had read it (in translation) as expressed by a
great writer, whose poetic form dominated his mind for the
moment. Only a writer of the loftiest poetic power could
have so affected the mind of Virgil. We notice, too, that
the peculiar metrical form is most marked where the expression approaches the prophetic type, while in the descriptive parts the metre is closer to the form common in
the Eclogues.

That such an origin for Virgil's idea is possible, will be
doubted by no one who takes properly into account both
the width of his reading, and the influence which the strange
and unique character of the Jewish nation and religion
(and here the religion made and was the nation) already
had exerted and was exerting on the Græco-Roman world.
That is a subject over which there hangs, and must always

hang, a thick veil; but enough is known to give us increasing certainty, as time goes on, that the fascination which Judaism exerted on a certain class of minds was very strong, and its influence on Roman society far greater than is apparent in the superficial view which alone is permitted us in the dearth of authorities.

Finally, the often quoted analogies with several passages of the prophet Isaiah afford some indication as to the identity of the great poet whose words, either in a Greek translation or in extracts, had come before Virgil, and influenced the development of his thought. It is true that there are numerous points in this Eclogue which go back to Greek models. The ideas taken up by Virgil from a Semitic source are developed in a mind rich with Hellenic knowledge and strong with a vigorous Italian life. Virgil is never a mere imitator except in his most juvenile work; he reforms and transforms everything that he has learned from his great instructors. It is an Italian idyll that he has given us, not a mere transplantation of a foreign idea, or of any number of foreign ideas.

The aim of the writer is rather to add to what Professor Mayor has said than to differ from him. The process of adding, however, may sometimes change the point of view, though it does not really express any essential difference of opinion, but merely builds on what he has said already very well. Thus, though I think that mere knowledge of Sibylline verses is not sufficient to explain the origin of the Fourth Eclogue, I should entirely agree in thinking that most probably Virgil was acquainted with those verses.[1] In all that Professor Mayor has said on this curious subject I must

---

[1] Most of the Sibylline books, as we have them, are later, but some are earlier, than Virgil, and there were almost certainly more in his time that have been lost.

be taken as agreeing cordially ; and I quite admit that Virgil may have ideas from them and have been directed in his reading by them ; but I cannot consider that they are the sole or the chief foundation of the Fourth Eclogue.

Professor Mayor sees quite clearly and rightly that the Fourth Eclogue must be studied as simply one moment in the long evolution of pagan thought. He sees that ancient thought and philosophy always turned on the idea of a steady degeneration in human life and in the history of the world. Even where there was among the ancients some conception of a cycle in mundane affairs, the cycle consisted of a degeneration culminating in total destruction, following by a fresh beginning on a better scale. This is not really anything more than a degeneration and a recreation by divine power. We have here nothing in any degree corresponding to the modern idea of development and growth and steady improvement.

Now the modern theory of human history, and especially of the history of religion, is that it is a continuous evolution from the savage state to the civilized, from cruelty to kindliness, from ignorance to knowledge. Is the modern theory based on a true assumption, or on a false one? It is certainly based on a very big assumption ; and I cannot see that any real attempt is ever made to establish the assumption on a firm basis. We are now all devotees of the theory of evolution ; it is no longer to us a theory, it has become the foundation and guiding principle of all our thought. We must find some principle of development everywhere and in all things ; and we arrange our view of history accordingly. But this is all very good, if we get hold of the right principle of development in history : then it is a truly scientific process that we are following. But what if we have got hold of a false principle? Then our whole procedure is pseudo-scientific, and only leads further and further away from the truth.

The ancient view was diametrically the opposite of the modern. To the ancient all history was a progress towards decay, a degeneration from good to bad. We are too apt to set aside this old view without a thought as pure prejudice and as the ancient fashion; all people used to think so. We remember the usual tendency of old persons to moralize on the better state of the world in their youth, and on the decay of good conduct and good manners. But is that all that lies underneath the ancient view? When we remember the practical universality of that view, and the way in which it colours all ancient literature, I cannot think that this is a sufficient explanation of the phenomenon. It was not merely the conscious expression of philosophers or of popular moralists: it was the deep, almost unconscious, hardly articulate view of all men. It caused that undertone of sadness which one hears in all Greek and Roman poetry, a certain note of hopelessness which makes itself felt everywhere. Every person who has to lecture on ancient poetry, and especially Roman poetry, to young students must often call their attention to this deep-seated feeling. It is the same that every one who lives in Constantinople at the present day [1] becomes conscious of. It arises from the inevitable perception that one is in an atmosphere of decay, degeneration, degradation, and that there is no improvement to be hoped for. The contemplation of and living among the degenerate aspects of modern civilization, as seen in great cities, produces something of the same feeling; but the sense of hopelessness is here not so strong; the evil and the decay are equally conspicuous, but there is also a correcting

---

[1] This was first written 20 years ago. It is true in 1914, though in the period of hope, 1908 onwards, it ceased for a time to be the case.

impression of error that may be rectified and fault that must be struggled against.

But that hopelessness was the almost universal feeling in the world of Greek and Roman paganism. To regard it as mere popular fallacy, and lightly to set it aside as of no account, as the modern writers generally do, is neither scientific nor justifiable. That the professional philosophers should have erred is not impossible or even improbable ; but the universal deep-lying feeling of the people, underlying all their poetry and guiding their half-articulate expression of thought, cannot be wrong, and must be accounted for. To one who looks at ancient history in the Mediterranean lands it must seem to rise from a perception of the truth and the facts.

It was patent to every observer in late Greek and Roman times that the history of the Mediterranean lands had on the whole been a process of degeneration and decay ; and as we now look back over that history we must come to the same opinion. In the sphere of agriculture we can trace in outline the peaceful conquest in remote time of a naturally rocky and barren land for the use of man. We can recover through recent research some faint idea of the way in which prosperity, civilization, and well-being in the Mediterranean lands were built up in early time—of the knowledge, accumulated experience, wisdom and forethought which were applied in order to lay the foundations of that prosperity—of the order, peace, settled government and security of property which made that slow, laborious process possible. Of this subject the present writer has published a brief study in his " Luke the Physician and other Studies," p. 171, entitled " The Peasant God ".

And to take just one example in the intellectual sphere, we now know that the art of writing was well known and familiarly practised at a very early time in the Mediterranean world (especially the East Mediterranean) ; and that practical administration presupposed the existence of that knowledge and familiar use of writing.   The processes of government and law were based on the principle that everything must be written down at the moment, e.g. that all sales and conveyance of important property must be registered in writing. But this inestimably important fact we have learned only in quite recent times from the discovery of the writings themselves : a process of discovery in which this University has played the leading part.   We know that people wrote at a very early time, because we have found the documents which they wrote—on stone, on bronze, on pottery, partly incised or in relief, partly in ink.   The use of ink is an extremely important fact, because ink was never invented for use on materials of that kind ; it was invented for the purpose of writing on more perishable materials, such as paper or skins or parchment ; ink-written pottery implies the previous and contemporary use of those less durable materials.[1]   But Egypt is the only country which is dry enough to preserve such perishable substances ; and the wider knowledge and use of ink furnishes the proof that similar perishable materials for writing were used in other countries besides Egypt.

In this way we are beginning to elaborate an outline of the ancient Mediterranean civilization, and to trace the steps of its history and its gradual decay.

Its decay arose from inner weakness ; and the inroads of eastern barbarians, which finally destroyed it, became dangerous only when its weakness increased.   There is always going on the same historic conflict between civilization

---

[1] See " The Letters to the Seven Churches," chap. i.

and barbarism ; and so long as civilization is true to itself, healthy in its construction, or, as Paul would say, so long as it listens to God, it can resist and overcome the forces of barbarism. Paul, in his brief way, sums up the stages of decay as the stages in the degeneration of human sympathy with and knowledge of the Divine nature, i.e. in the growth of idolatry. We may work them out in more detail, and show the precise changes in circumstance and outward form by which the decay proceeded. We may trace how the inner weakness showed itself first in one region, then in another. We may see that Sicily and Greece were already a prey to ruin, when some other parts of the Mediterranean world were still growing and healthy. We can delight ourselves with the picture which Statius draws, as late as A.D. 92, of the improvement effected by wisely planned operations on the bare rocky headland of Surrentum (Sorrento), on the southern horn of the Gulf of Naples, where the barren expanse of stone was subdued to the use of man and became docile to his hand, where the projecting rocks were cut down to the level, and the soil brought and laid down, so that groves of trees could grow, where no soil, but only bare stone, formerly was seen ; where a marvel greater than the fables of Orpheus and of Amphion was taking place before the sight of living men, under the orders of a wise owner, who made the rocks move and the tall forests follow after him. In that picture you have an account which may be applied all round the Mediterranean Sea in ancient times, and which still applies to a few regions like Malta (naturally a bare rock, where almost all the soil has been introduced by man).

Not merely was this idea of a continuous degeneration of the Mediterranean world practically universal in Greek and Roman thought, it is also a fundamental principle in the view of the Apostle Paul.   There was only this one mighty difference: the pagan opinion was hopeless and despairing—with one remarkable exception, which we must proceed to study in its character and extent—whereas Paul made this opinion the foundation on which to base his argument that all nature and all men were eagerly looking for a Saviour from this impending ruin and death, and that the Saviour was before them, and offered to them, if they would only recognize and believe.

In this way Paul presented his doctrine to the men of the Græco-Roman world as the completion and culmination of their own philosophy and their own experience. He did not denounce their philosophical or religious views as wholly wrong. He maintained that in their original opinions there was contained some true knowledge about the nature of God and about His relation to mankind; but that there had been a degeneration from this fair beginning. The reason of the degeneration lay in the growth of false ideas about the nature of God, i.e. in idolatry. Yet man, as Paul says, never becomes so wholly corrupt that it is impossible for him to recover his lost advantages and return to the truth. Some of the Gentiles, knowing not the higher truth of the Law as revealed to the Jews, are a Law unto themselves; but in most of them this instinct towards the truth has become so obscured by wrong-doing that they have lost all consciousness of it, and cannot and will not hear the voice of God in their hearts. Still in the most utterly vitiated pagan man there remains a sense of misconduct, a feeling of pain, and a consciousness that he is wrong. This remnant of the original power of apprehending the Divine truth is traceable in the sorrow and the pain and regret from which no man is free entirely. So long as this pain lasts, hope exists that the man may return to God. The pain is an accompaniment of the coming birth of higher ideas, of regeneration and redemption.

This Pauline view, as stated in Romans I. 19 ff., II. 14 f., VIII. 19 ff., has been described more fully in the " Teaching of Paul in Terms of the Present Day," pp. 132, etc.

The Pauline theory of degeneration is simply the application to human history of the ultimate fact from which he begins, and on which his whole mind and being rests—his consciousness that the Divine alone is real, and that all else is mere error and false appearance. From this initial fact it follows that a serious error as to the nature of God distorts and vitiates the nature of man. If the error goes on increasing and deepening, the distortion and vitiation of man's nature becomes worse and worse : in other words, the history of man and of society, in a state of idolatry and thorough misconception of the Divine nature, must be a process of steady, continuous degeneration. There can be no standing still in human life. The mind which sees God and hears His voice must move towards Him, and comprehend His nature better and better. The mind which is closed against the Divine voice is necessarily involved in a process of hardening, of increasing blindness, and of progressive degradation.

Thus the universal pagan view about the history of the Mediterranean lands seemed to Paul merely the correct perception of the facts of life, a proof of the original affinity that united human nature to truth and the Divine ; and the tone of melancholy in pagan literature was to him a symptom of the pain which afforded some hope that the Græco-Roman world might awaken to the consciousness and true perception of God.

The degeneration of the pagan world had worked itself out by certain stages, which it is the business of the historian to trace in detail. Paul's business was only to insist on the fact of this degeneration, to prove it from the universal consciousness of men, to insist on the one and only possible remedy, and to point out that this remedy was open and ready and certain for the whole world.

Now, as we have said, there was one exception to this universal hopelessness in the pagan world; and this exception was born out of the most desperate straits to which the Mediterranean world had yet been reduced, viz. the Civil Wars of Italy, and the apparently imminent ruin of the one great remaining power of order in the Mediterranean. The terrible suffering entailed by those wars and disorder proved, just as the Pauline view declared, the birth-pangs of a new hope. It was in this situation that the Fourth Eclogue sprang into being, the announcement by a great poet of the hope which was coming into being in the minds of many at this crisis.

PART III.

ASSOCIATED QUESTIONS

CHAPTER XXIV

THE OLD TESTAMENT IN THE ROMAN PHRYGIA

THE position and numbers and influence of the Jews under the Roman Empire outside of Palestine is an interesting and obscure subject which has been discussed (to mention only moderns) by many scholars, such as Reinach, Lévy, etc., since Schürer's great collection of the statistics appeared. Even more interesting is the question as to the character, the religious feelings and beliefs, the conduct and moral standard of action of the extra-Palestinian Jews.

At present we are concerned only with those Jews so far as they are set before us in the Acts, and mainly in the Pauline provinces of Asia Minor, viz. Asia and Galatia ; and even there we have only to publish a new document and to show what important light it throws on other memorials already known, and hardly suspected[1] to be Jewish. The present writer has had something to say from time to time on this subject, especially on the character and conduct of the extra-Palestinian Jews. One most important fact is the following : yet his attempts to draw attention to it have failed ("Pauline and other Studies," p. 347).

So long as the Jews were living in a small country like Palestine, it would be possible, in the disposition of the calendar and fixing of the proper full moon for the Passover,

---

[1] My suggestion that they were perhaps Jewish (which is mentioned in the sequel) was received with scepticism ; and it was considered that I was suspecting Jewish influence without any justification or sound reason.

to be guided by local conditions and actual experience of the first visible appearance of the new moon; but when Jews were coming to the Passover from distant parts of the Mediterranean world, and even sometimes from places outside of the Mediterranean basin, it was necessary that the calendar should be fixed long beforehand, so that travellers to Palestine should know whether to expect the Passover in March or thirty days later. Thus the sacred month had to be fixed at least in the previous year and published then through the Jewish world. For this purpose astronomical considerations alone could be taken into account; and there was abundant astronomical knowledge available at the time.

It is, of course, highly probable that the local conditions were observed in the traditional sacred fashion, and the first appearance of the new moon duly reported to the high-priest, who then put out the proper advertisement of the approaching feast: but it was already known that the moon was there, and the day of the feast had been unofficially advertised in the calendar a year or several years previously. Without this admission of scientific knowledge, the problem of keeping the distant Jews true to the holy custom of the holy city would have been far harder. After A.D. 70, when the city was destroyed and the feast no longer drew the Jews to Jerusalem, the whole situation changed.

That there were large settlements of Jews in the Phrygian cities is well known. On one single occasion, about 200 B.C., Antiochus king of Syria brought two thousand Jewish families from Babylonia, and settled them in the cities which he and his predecessors had found in Phrygia; and the statements of Cicero in his oration on behalf of Flaccus, the governor of the Roman province Asia, show that there was a population of very many thousands of Jews there in the lsat century before Christ.

Those Jews were placed there as supporters and trusted upholders of the power of the Greek kings, the successors of Alexander the Great, helping to maintain their hold of the country. Every foreign power ruling the country found the Jews useful and trustworthy. They were servants of foreign rulers, and therefore they were an aristocratic, conservative, dominant caste. This position powerfully influenced their character and history, and not wholly for the better ("Cities of St. Paul," Part II).

The correct understanding of the position and character of the Hellenist Jews in Asia Minor and Syria is of extreme importance for the proper appreciation of Luke's history. Paul's work lay among them largely at his first entry into any of the great cities of Asia and Galatia; and the impression is forced on us by the narrative that they were present in large numbers everywhere he went, and that they exercised great influence. In Europe, on the contrary, they were less important, and had evidently a struggle to maintain their position : in Philippi they were apparently not more than a mere handful.

The work of Paul in the Anatolian cities starts from the Jews, is conditioned by their attitude to him, and is often brought to an end through their opposition. They can move the magistrates or the mob to take action against the new teaching, finding various charges under which they can mask their religious hatred and wear the guise of vindicators of the Roman law. That law depended always on voluntary prosecutors to set it in motion ; and the Jews appeared as *delatores* in the Roman courts.[1]   See Chapter VI.

[1] The term delator was in the first century applied almost exclusively to one class of prosecutors, viz. those who brought charges under the law of treason in the interest of the Emperor. The Jews at Thessalonica appear in this guise, so familiar to us in the pages of Tacitus. But all voluntary accusers are equally entitled to be called delators.

This character ought to be recognized more clearly and definitely than is usually the case in the commentaries on the Acts. The Jews had to appear in the courts either as Roman citizens, if they possessed the *civitas*, or as ordinary provincials. They possessed certain limited powers in their relation to members of their own race, and could in that way act through the synagogue against them as Jews ; but they desired to inflict on Paul and his companions more serious penalties than their Jewish powers were capable of ; and they had to subject themselves to Roman regulations in order to secure Paul's expulsion or any severer punishment. As Romans or provincials they appeared under Roman or Greek names, which they bore in the city ; but they had another aspect in which they appeared to Paul and to their compatriots in the synagogues. That double character has to be clearly understood. In the case of Paul it corresponds to his double name, " Saul otherwise called Paul ".[1]

An interesting discovery fell to our lot in 1914, when my wife and I passed through Ushak on our way to Antioch the Pisidian. It throws some light on this subject, both directly and indirectly.

Those Jews of Asia Minor for the most part either died out, or melted gradually into the surrounding population, a unique fact in Jewish history. They were too favourably situated. First the kings of Syria, then Julius Cæsar, then the Roman Emperors, regarded them as faithful friends and subjects, and granted or confirmed many privileges in their

---

[1] It goes without saying that Paul had a complete Roman name, as to which our Hellenic historian does not inform us. Perhaps he was " C. Julius Paullus otherwise called Shaoul ". See " St. Paul the Traveller," p. 31. The frequent conjunction of the names Julius Paullus (or feminine) in Lycaonia gives some ground for this conjecture.

favour. There can be little doubt that the Jews married into the dominant families. The case of Timothy's mother in the Acts XVI. 2 f., may be safely regarded as typical ; it is an incidental example of the flood of light which the rational study of and trust in that great historical work throws on Roman social history in the Eastern Provinces.

So much is necessary to explain the importance of the new discovery. A great deal more may be found in the three chapters on the Jews in Tarsus and in Antioch, and on Hellenism and Hebraism in my "Cities of St. Paul" ; and also in the chapter XV. on the Jews in Phrygia in the " Cities and Bishoprics of Phrygia," Vol. II. Here it need only be said that discovery has been gradually proving the view there maintained regarding the large number of Jews and their influential position in the provinces of Galatia and Asia under the Roman Empire. The task of tracing these Jews is very difficult, because they adopted Greek or Roman names, and avoided anything distinctive in outward appearance. Even in their epitaphs they are hard to detect.

Critics of those books have sometimes expressed distrust or disbelief in these statements, and have doubted whether Jews would hide their nationality so persistently. These critics apparently hold that the Jews (whose existence in those regions can hardly be denied) have hardly left any known memorials of themselves, because these were probably buried in separate cemeteries which have not yet been discovered.

They can point to the existence of separate Jewish cemeteries in Rome. There is, however, this difference between Rome and Phrygia. The Jewish cemeteries in Rome are the burying-place of a humble and despised caste ; but the Phrygian Jews were largely the nobles and the rich (as I have maintained). A humble and poor population clings to its distinctive religion, whereas a rich or aristocratic caste adapts itself to circumstances and refrains from blazoning the distinguishing marks of religion, even when it still retains the religion.

In May, 1914, we found at Ushak two gravestones, about five feet high, in shape tall square altars, surmounted by a pointed ornament like a conventionalized pine-cone. One of these was unimportant in every respect, except as proving that the same form of gravestone was common at the place of origin (which, as will be stated, was Blaundos) in the period A.D. 220-50.[1]

I. One of these gravestones was inscribed on two sides : on the principal side there is a long epitaph of the ordinary type, stating the name and family of the maker of the grave and its purpose, and finishing with a curse against any violator of the sepulchre : on the other side is a recital of the honours in the state which had been held by the maker of the tomb. At the top of the principal side is the date, equivalent to A.D. 248-9. Then follows the epitaph :—

" Aurelius Phrougianos, son of Menokritos, and Aurelia Juliana (his) wife, to Makaria (his) mother and to Alexandria (their) sweetest daughter, constructed (the sepulchre) while still living, in remembrance. And if any one after their burial, if any one (*so !*) shall inter another corpse or do injury in the way of purchase, there shall be on him the curses which are written in Deuteronomy." [2]

---

[1] A third was found with the other two, more ornate than the others, but of similar form and arrangement of lettering. See a later footnote.

[2] In July, 1914, I received from Mrs. Wingate of Cæsarea in Cappadocia another copy (sent through Miss Dodd). The copy is correct except in some small details, especially the last word of the longer inscription.

The texts of the two sides of this stone are as follows :—

(a) ἔτους τλγ' (anno 333 of the Phrygian era = A.D. 248-9). Αὐρήλιος Φρουγιανὸς Μηνοκρίτου καὶ Αὐρ. Ἰουλιανὴ γυνὴ αὐτοῦ Μακαρίᾳ μητρὶ καὶ Ἀλεξ-

PLATE III.—Two gravestones from Blaundos, now at Ushak. The epitaph of Aur. Phrougianos is engraved on two sides of the upright stone. Weather prevented a photograph of the inscribed sides.

ΕΤΟΥΣ ΤΛΓ

ΑΥΡ·ΦΡΟΥΓΙΑΝΟϹ
ΜΗΝΟΚΡΙΤΟΥΚΑΙΑΥΡ
ΙΟΥΛΙΑΝΗΓΥΝΗΑΥΤΟΥ
ΜΑΚΑΡΙΑΜΗΤΡΙΚΑΙΑ
ΛΕΖΑ   ΝΔΡΙ
ΑΘΥ   ΓΑ   ΤΡΙ
ΓΛΥ ΚΥΤΑΤΗ ΖΩΝ
ΤΕϹ ΚΑΤΕϹϹ ΚΕΥ
ΑϹΑ   ΝΜΝ   ΗΜΙϹ
ΧΑ   ΡΙΝ

ΕΙΔΕΤΙϹΜΕΤΑΤΟΤΕΘΗΝΑΙ
ΑΥΤΟΥϹΕΙΤΙϹΘΑΥΕΙΕΤΕΡΟΝ
ΝΕΚΡΟΝΗΑΔΙΚΗϹΕΙΛΟΓΩ
ΑΓΟΡΑϹΙΑϹΕϹΤΑΙΑΥΤΩΑΙΑΡΑΙ
ΗΓΕΡΑΜΜΕΝΑΙΕΝΤΩΔΕΥΤΕΡΟ
ΝΟΜΩ

Fig. 8.—Jewish epitaph from Blaundos, dated in the year 233, corresponding to A.D. 248-9. Square altar-stone with rounded top. On one side is the second part of the epitaph: on the back is a hand-mirror in a sunk panel: the fourth side is blank.

On the other side are inscribed the honours :—

'Stewardship of the market-place, corn-purchasing, guardianship of order, having filled all municipal offices and duties and having held the post of strategos or commander." [1]

We were informed by a good authority that the two gravestones with some other stones had been brought from Blaundos, a city on the frontiers of Lydia and Phrygia, about eight hours south of Ushak. Marbles are brought in large numbers from the ancient sites for building purposes to the large modern towns like Ushak ; but statements of the provenance of such monuments always require to be scrutinized. In this case the authority is good. My informant, one of the richest and most respected Turks in Ushak, had nothing to gain from false information ; when he had no information he said so plainly : he was aware that digging had recently been going on to a considerable extent at Blaundos, and wished to take us there to see all that had been discovered. Moreover, the stones, though of a type similar to the Phrygian altar-stones, differ in form from the strictly Phrygian character (such as occurs at Akmonia) ; and an origin from Blaundos would suit well.[2]

ανδρίᾳ θυγατρὶ γλυκυτάτῃ ζῶντες κατεσκεύασαν μνήμης χάριν. εἰ δέ τις μετὰ τὸ τεθῆναι αὐτοὺς, εἴ τις θάψει ἕτερον νεκρὸν, ἢ ἀδικήσει λόγῳ ἀγορασίας, ἔσται αὐτῷ αἱ ἀραὶ ἡ γεγραμμέναι ἐν τῷ δευτερονόμῳ.

(*b*) ἀγορανομίᾳ, σειτωνείᾳ, παραφυλακείᾳ, πάσας ἀρχὰς καὶ λειτουργίας τελέσας, καὶ στρατηγήσαντα. The construction is so confused and ungrammatical that it is difficult to tell whether the first three offices are to be treated as nominatives, or as datives with κοσμηθείς or some similar word understood, " honoured with stewardship," etc.

[1] The enumeration is stated in the most illogical way and in total defiance of grammar ; the participles are ἄρξας and στρατηγήσαντα, nom. and accus.

[2] The stone published by Director Th. Wiegand, " Athen. Mitth.," 1911, p. 393, as found at Thyatira, was made by the same hand as the two which we saw at Ushak, and must be attributed also to Blaundos. We saw it in Berlin, and recognized its provenance instantly. Mr. Buckler tells me that it bears no resemblance to the stones of Thyatira, of which he has made a careful study.

This is perhaps the earliest writing that has come down to us stating the name of a book in the Old Testament. Older references to some of those books occur, but the handwriting in which the references were originally inscribed has perished.

The allusion at the end of the principal inscription is to the great chapters of curses, Deuteronomy XXVII.-XXIX. The curses there written are not specifically against violators of graves ; but the same curses as are there written are here invoked against violation. Aurelius Phrougianos, son of Menokritos, therefore, was a Jew, and probably his wife also.

The same custom of appealing to the curses in Deuteronomy can now be recognized in a number of other Phrygian epitaphs, found in widely separate cities of central Phrygia.[1]

The invariable Greek form of the name Deuteronomy is Δευτερονόμιον. Here the ι is omitted. This is, as we may feel certain, due only to local pronunciation, in which ι before a vowel was pronounced as *y* and left unexpressed in the writing. There is not the smallest reason to think that the name was in Phrygian Jewish circles Δευτερόνομος, or Δευτερονόμος.[2] We should really read in the inscription ἐν τῷ Δευτερονόμγῳ, leaving the accent as in the nominative and accusative of the name.

II. (564 in " Cities and Bishoprics of Phrygia ") was found

---

[1] The complete Greek text of them all except VIII. is published in the " Cities and Bishoprics of Phrygia," under the numbers mentioned. I give here only the English translation of the part that bears on our purpose.

[2] I thought at first that the form intended was δευτέρο (for δευτέρῳ) νόμῳ, but although the spelling is very bad, yet I hesitate to think that *o* could be used for ῳ in the dative termination at such an early date as this. Such misspelling might occur in the seventh or ninth century after Christ, but hardly in A.D. 249. I should add that Mrs. Wingate's copy has δευτέρῳ νομίῳ, but I took special note of *o* in δευτερο, and doubt if my eye (though sometimes failing to see small lines) could have omitted iota here.

at Ushak : I have not seen it : it is dated A.D. 243-4.   The
inscription contains a curse strikingly similar in character
to the epitaph of Phrougianos ; after which comes a legal
penalty in the form of a fine :—

" And after the burial of me Alexander and my wife
Gaiana, if any one shall open the tomb, there shall be upon
him the curses as many as are written in (the book), on his
sight and his whole body and his children and his life ; and
if any one shall attempt to open (the grave), he shall pay
to the treasury in the way of fine 500 denarii."

This inscription was brought from Akmonia to Ushak (as
is the case with a large number of the inscriptions , at
Ushak).   It is described by MM. Legrand and Chamonard,
as being engraved on a quadrangular altar, a form very common in Phrygia generally and at Akmonia : the ornamental
top which is the distinguishing feature at Blaundos (see no.
1) is here absent.   Accordingly, though the real bearing of
the curse can be understood only through the epitaph from
Blaundos, there can be no doubt that they belong to different
cities.   So in no. 9 we shall find an Apamean epitaph
whose meaning was misapprehended, until the inscription of
Blaundos threw an unexpected light on it.

The reference to the curses in Deuteronomy is therefore
a general feature in the Jewish custom of Central Phrygia,
and not a special feature of one family or one city.
The Phrygian Jews were in the habit of adapting to the
sepulchral purpose that part of the Law of Moses, which
they found convenient for their purpose without any regard
to its force in its own context.   Such procedure is in accord
with the Jewish way of using the words of the Bible.   In this
curse ἀυγεγραμμέναι[1] means written in (the Book of Deuter-

---

[1] ἀυγεγραμμέναι : ἀναγράφειν is used to indicate the careful entry in a
book or on a stele, of laws, etc.

onomy, or the Law of Moses). "It is written" is a usual way of referring to the Scriptures.[1]

III. Akmonia (465, 466). I have hesitated much whether to assign Jewish or Christian character to this tomb; and I conclude "probably this epitaph marked the grave of a Jewish Christian; but it would appear that the Church here was of a debased type, much infected by non-Christian elements" (p. 566). The doubt would now appear to be decided; the inscription is Jewish; the part that bears on our subject is as follows :—

"And if any one shall attempt after Amerimnos has been buried to intrude any other corpse, he shall have [to reckon with the most high God]"; the end is lost. On another side of the stone :—

"[If any of them] shall bury any other, may they receive the unexpected stroke which their brother Amerimnos [received]; and if any of them shall not fear these curses, may the sickle of curse enter into their houses and leave no survivor."

This epitaph belongs to Akmonia, and the following also is from the same city; each helps to complete the other.

IV. Akmonia (563). "[If any one shall intrude another corpse], he shall have to reckon with the most high God; and may the sickle of curse [enter] into his house [and leave no survivor]."

V. Akmonia (565). "Ammia, daughter of Eutyches, prepared the tomb for Salimachos her husband and herself from her own dowry; and there shall be a curse extending to children's children prohibiting any other from being (here) buried except my son Eutyches and his wife."

VI. Akmonia (566). "Gaius [son of —] in his lifetime

---

[1] γέγραπται is the form in the New Testament.

made [the tomb for himself and his wife? and after] the burial of these two whoever shall open or destroy or sell the grave, there shall be a curse on him extending to his house and children's children."

VII. Akmonia (567). "Ammia [made the tomb] for Gaius Vibius Crispus and Tyche her foster-parents during their lifetime in remembrance: after the burial of the two whosoever shall dig up the grave may an iron broom raze his house?: and [the same] to any accomplice."

VIII. At Ushak: probably from Akmonia; published by J. Keil & A. von Premerstein, "Zweite Reise in Lydien," p. 137:—

"Tiberius Claudius Julianus [made the tomb] for himself and his wife in remembrance, and Chelidon for her own foster-parents in remembrance; and whosoever shall do harm to this grave, children's children shall have the curse."[1]

The suggestion which was made in publishing this group of inscriptions (see my "Cities and Bishoprics," p. 652 f.), that the curses in them "distinguish them from the ordinary Phrygian type," and "may all arise through Jewish influence," must now be unhesitatingly accepted.

IX. Apameia (399 *bis*). This epitaph must now be interpreted in a different fashion :—

"Aurelius Rufus, son and grandson of Julianus, made the heroön for myself and my wife Aurelia Tatiana : and into it another shall not be intruded ; and if any one shall bury, he knows the Law of the Jews."

---

[1] ἕξει τέκνα τέκνων ἀράν : the change of subject is awkward, and one might interpret on the hypothesis that this is an ungrammatical condensation of the usual fuller form, " he shall have the curse [extending to] children's children "; but this involves too great a violation of elementary Greek usage, though these epitaphs are very ungrammatical (see a later paragraph).

On this I suggested that the law which is meant must be some special law of the municipality of Apameia for the protection of the graves of the Jews of that city : my reason was that the Mosaic law makes no provision of this kind, and therefore cannot be intended here. This view must now be rejected. We have here a reference to the Mosaic Law, and the passage specially in the mind of Aurelius Rufus was Deuteronomy XXVII.-XXIX. The fact that those chapters have no bearing on impiety towards sepulchres was a serious argument, when this epitaph seemed to stand alone ; but now that it is established that the Phrygian Jews in their epitaphs appealed to those chapters, the bearing of the safeguard in this case is unquestionable.

In few of these epitaphs are there any names that demonstrate religious character or racial affinity. Even the names of women are pure Greek or Roman,[1] though, owing to the character of Oriental society, the names of women are generally more typical than those of men ; for example at the present day in some villages of the Hermus valley, where the men have for several centuries conformed to Islam and bear always Moslem names, the women use Christian names still. Only in I Makaria has the look of being, not Jewish, but Christian : the adjective μακάριος, " blessed," had become by the time to which these epitaphs belong typically Christian. Amerimnos, too, " who takes no thought for the morrow," though it has a certain look of Christian nomenclature, is quoted as a pagan name (C. I. Att., 194).

Yet among the names certain tendencies can be observed :

---

[1] Makarios is a personal name in the fifth century B.C. ; see Thucydides, III. 100, and Makaria occurs both in mythology and in ordinary pagan life : see Pape-Benseler : but in the third century one would expect that Makaria should be Christian.

Alexander and Alexandria are common among the Hellenist Jews, and it will probably be found that names taken from the Seleucid kings were also common. This may seem strange to those who think only of the Palestinian Jews and their hatred for those kings. But the Hellenist Jews of Asia Minor and Syria were friends of the kings. The kings trusted them, employed them as trusty colonists and adherents in their garrison cities of those lands, and bestowed many favours on them. The old-fashioned Palestinian Jews, who made the Maccabean revolt, were disposed to look down on the Hellenist Jews as too liberal and too much affected by foreign customs and Gentile ways.

Again, the names Eutyches (and Tyche)[1] point to the Hebrew Naaman ; and Herzog in " Philologus," LVI. p. 50 ff. regards Eutyches as a translation of the Semitic name.

At Sala in Phrygia on the Lydian frontier near Blaundos, there occur frequently on coins the names of Meliton Salamon and C. Valerius Androneikos Salamon, perhaps father and son. These are probably Roman citizens, with a Greek cognomen and they often add their Hebrew name as a second cognomen.[2] As the names are all in the genitive, some might understand " of Meliton, son of Salamon," and " of C. Valerius Andronicus, son of Salamon " ; but Meliton and Androneikos cannot reasonably be regarded as brothers on account of the dates (Meliton 100-117 ;

---

[1] Tyche is a shortened form of Eutychia, " she who is fortunate ".

[2] Meliton never mentions his Latin names, but either the Greek alone, or the Greek and Hebrew names. It is only through C. Valerius Androneikos that we learn of the Roman citizenship and Roman name of Meliton. Androneikos sometimes omits the Hebrew name, and sometimes calls himself only by the Greek name : sometimes he has the Greek and Hebrew names without the Latin names. This case throws much light on the case of Paul otherwise called Saul.

Androneikos 130-65).[1]   The Hebrew name was an additional cognomen used by both those Jews; and we may infer that in many other cases the additional cognomen or alternative name was omitted amid the Greek and Roman surroundings in which the inscription was placed.

There is some probability, then, that those Phrygian Jews still kept Hebrew names in their home life and the relations of the Synagogue as late as the third century : certainly this can be proved for the second century.   There is a possibility that in V the strange name Salimachos may be a transformation of some Hebrew name : it would then be connected with Salem, " peace ".   The analogy of L. Julius Pius Salamallianus, in which an old Carthaginian name, Salam-Allah, " the peace of God," survived late in the Imperial period, suggests that here in Phrygia the name should be understood, Salem-malchos, " Peace of the King ". The loss of the *l* before *ch* can be paralleled in the dialect of Greek spoken in Phrygia.[2]

Debbora is known at Antioch the Pisidian.[3]

Thus the use of Hebrew names at least as alternative and occasionally perhaps as the sole name [4] is established as probable or certain as late as towards A.D. 200.   The Hebrew tradition was still alive at that date ; and the general character of the Hebrew people would suggest that

---

[1] Moreover, the form ἐπὶ ᾽Ανδρο Σαλαμῶνος is hardly reconcilable with the interpretation that A. was son of S.

[2] See the explanation of the forms χακώματα, καχείτης, for χαλκώματα, καλχείτης (dialectic for χαλκείτης) in Phrygia Galatica, in my article in " Journal of Hellenic Studies," 1912, p. 160, with note by Mr. G. F. Hill.

[3] On Debbora, Deborah, see " Cities of St. Paul," p. 256.   The tendency to retain women's names was naturally stronger, as has been said.

[4] Though Salimachos is the only name mentioned, the example of Androneikos Salamon proves that a strictly Greek name also may have been used in civic surroundings by this person.

these few facts may be taken as signs of more far-reaching conditions.

On the other hand these facts are all associated with burial, and the tombstones are without exception devoid of any Hebrew characteristic,[1] and almost all markedly Phrygian in type. It is evident that the Phrygian Jews had adopted in regard to sepulture the custom of the country, and refrained from placing anything markedly national on the gravestone. They were therefore becoming to some extent assimilated to the people among whom they lived. The inscribing of a curse against violation of the tomb was probably borrowed from Phrygian usage; and, while a certain difference of cast is given to the curse, yet this is recognizable as Hebrew only in the two cases I and IX. Yet there is no sign that there was any danger to the family in the confession of Hebrew origin: besides I and IX, there is a case where the maker of the tomb is "Alexander a Jew".[2] These Jews were a powerful body, and as a whole they enjoyed Imperial favour. They had much to gain by living like their neighbours, and they did so.

It has been pointed out in the book already quoted that the Jews probably so far conformed to Imperial custom as to become high-priests in the worship of the Emperors. This statement depends on the evidence of coins; and neither of the Jewish inscriptions in which the offices held by the maker of the tomb are mentioned alludes to a priesthood. Few, however, could be of such rank and wealth as to hold a high-priesthood, and perhaps also those who had held one would not like to blazon this on their tombs; for

---

[1] Only in one case have I seen a seven-branched candlestick on a gravestone in Phrygia: " Cities and Bishoprics of Phrygia," II. p. 651 f., no. 561.

[2] " Cities and Bishoprics," II. p. 652, no. 562.

the fact would have been an outrage on the Book which they quoted, or had in mind, in the epitaph.

The discovery confirms some of the most typical details in the picture given elsewhere of the Phrygian Jews.

The incorrectness of the Greek in almost all these epitaphs is very marked. The Greek of the Christians was bad :[1] that of the Jews is quite as bad, and yet some of those who sin most were persons of high rank in their cities.[2]

---

[1] This is noteworthy in their epitaphs, and is animadverted on by Aristides : see " Church in the Roman Empire," p. 351 f.

[2] In I κατεσσκεύασαν : generally the spelling is more correct than in any other of these epitaphs : εἴ τις is repeated unnecessarily : ἔσται has the plural ἀραί as subject ; ἡ is written for αἱ. Three of the offices are in the nominative (or dative), ἀγορανομία, etc., then follow ἀρχὰς . . . τελέσας, but στρατηγήσαντα. I do not admit δευτέρο as dative for δευτέρῳ.

In II λοιπήσας (οι for υ), ἀνύξῃ (υ for οι), μνημιὸν, ὅσε, [ἰ]σίν : the construction εἰς ὅρασιν etc., is rather mixed.

In III εἰσέλθοιτο (middle for active, was loved in Phrygia : see examples quoted in my papers in " Philologus," Neue Folge, I. p. 755, and Zft. f. vgl. Sprachforschung, N, F., VIII. p. 389) : so also ἐνκαταλείψετο (ε for αι) : μηδίναν is doubly wrong.

In IV ὕκον for οἶκον.

In V the construction of the curse is loose : γυναικί for accusative.

In VI πολήσει and γουτάριον (on the latter see under VIII).

In VII ξάναιτο (see under III) : [ο]ἴχωνα, if I rightly take it for οἶκον, is a *monstrum.* (Compare τούνβονα for τύμβον in a Graeco-Phrygian epitaph : Ramsay in Oesterr. Jahreshefte, 1905, Beib. pp. 79-120, no. XXXI.)

In VIII Κλύδιος (υ for αυ) : τίς for ὅστις : ποίσει : the curse has an unusual form (see footnote on the text). The word γούντη (compare VI) is not Greek. The words γούντη and γουτάριον are evidently names indicating the grave or some part or accessory of it. The latter is a formation from the former, in which ν expresses probably a slight nasalization of τ (a use of ν of which many examples occur in the country). The word may perhaps be Phrygian in origin : it is not Hebrew or Semitic (as Prof. A. R. S. Kennedy tells me), nor is it either Greek or Latin. Keil and Premerstein quote from an inscription of North Italy the word guntha (with guntharii), and if this is connected, it must have been brought to Italy by natives of Asia Minor.

In XI οὐ τεθῇ (conjunctive apparently) : the construction of conditional sentences is always a difficulty in these and in very many Phrygian epitaphs.

CHAPTER XXV

THE NAME OF THE EVANGELIST LUKE

THE origin of the name Loukas has always presented difficulty, and has roused a good deal of discussion. The name belongs to the class of familiar or pet names (called in German *Kosenamen*), which are usually shortened [1] from a longer original form.

Loukas is a Greek and not a Latin name. In Latin the prenomen Lucius could not produce a *Kosenamen* Loukas; and those scholars who are thinking of the Latin name Lucius cannot recognize any connexion between it and this Greek name Loukas.

The difficulty presented itself at an early period: what is the full, proper, legal name of which the popular and familiar corresponding form was Loukas? Several manuscripts of the Old-Latin (which must, as Professor A. Souter says, be attributed to the fifth century) give the name of the Evangelist as Lucanus. There was therefore as early as Cyprian a certain school or group in the West, where the Latin Bible was used, which believed that Lucanus was the correct name. Did this belief rest on an old tradition, or was it the result of educated speculation about the name? If it rested on a really ancient tradition, it would have great weight; but this is improbable; there is

[1] Some are made by adding a suffix of the proper kind, and the name is thereby lengthened, so for example Iulia, Kosenamen Iulitta.

no reason to think that such a tradition would be preserved in one small part of the West alone. The Latin manuscripts have, as a rule, elsewhere the reading *secundum Lucam.* The reading *secundum Lucanum* must therefore be due to learned speculation and discussion about the origin of the form, and has only the authority that attaches to the education and philological knowledge of the school. The form was strange ; it was Greek, not Latin ; and they asked how it originated. We also must put the same question, and seek for evidence. Philological speculation among the ancients had not much value, because it was not guided by authority and method, but largely by fancy ; and we are perfectly free to set aside their philological speculation as of no real value.

How should the question be put ? The right formulation of the problem is scientifically of the highest importance. We ought not to ask what Latin name would be most likely to become Loukas ; such a way of putting the question is unscientific. The matter belongs to Greek usage, not Latin. The name Loukas is Greek, and doubtless originated in the mouths of Greek-speaking persons, treating names according to Greek tendencies and fashions. Moreover, it is certain on other grounds that the great writer and historian in the New Testament who bore the name Loukas, was a Hellene, living in Hellenic society. We have to ask whether or not the Greek name Loukios, borrowed from the Latin Lucius, could according to Greek custom have as a familiar by-form the *Kosenamen* Loukas.

This question must be treated as a matter of evidence. Are there any examples of the equivalence Loukios = Loukas ? If such examples exist, then there ceases to be any question, for it would be evident that people who spoke of Loukas knew that they were speaking of one whose more ceremonious and proper name was Loukios.[1] If no examples of the equivalence occur, there would be a certain presumption that the two forms were not equivalent; and this presumption would increase in proportion to the extent of our knowledge of colloquial and familiar forms in Greek.

Hitherto no proof could be given that the two names were used as equivalents in the East. No case was known in which any individual was called indifferently Loukios and Loukas; and without some proof of the equivalence it seemed unsafe to maintain that the fuller Loukios ever degenerated into Loukas. Accordingly there came to be among modern scholars a growing strength of opinion that Lucanus was the proper Latin form of the name of the Evangelist.[2]

Professor V. Schultze,[3] however, thought otherwise, and unhesitatingly maintained the opinion that Loukas, the familiar name, implied a more formal Loukios as the proper name of the historian. As for the present writer, he could not go with Schultze, but held that the balance of evidence accessible was against the equivalence.

We have not a large store of evidence about the equivalence of full names and corresponding familiar names among the Greek-speaking peoples; and, therefore, the recent dis-

---

[1] Similarly in English custom those who speak to or of Charlie or Willie or Johnnie know that the person so mentioned bears the name Charles or William or John in more ceremonious style. The occasional giving of a diminutive name to a child as his proper name is due to individual freaks of taste, and is not proved to have been common in the early Imperial age.

[2] I think that I have somewhere stated this opinion, but new evidence has convinced me of my error.

[3] Professor Deissmann reminded me of his view. Schultze had kindly sent me his article, when it appeared; but I am at present not able to find the copy.

covery at Pisidian Antioch of a considerable number of inscriptions expressed in popular colloquial style, and containing names of the *Kosenamen* type, presents some interest.

Parts of the south-west and north-west walls of the peribolos, which surrounded the sanctuary of the god of Antioch, Men Askaênos, one of the wealthiest and most powerful gods of Asia Minor, are covered with dedicatory inscriptions recording vows to the god. These all belong to the Roman period, and a certain number of them are expressed in Latin. The Latin vows are, in general, the oldest; and some of them are perhaps as early as the time of Augustus and his immediate successors. The vast majority, however, of them are the work of Greek-speaking people, who bore Roman names.

The dedications in the Greek language were therefore made, as a rule, not by the original Latin-speaking colonists of Antioch, a sort of aristocracy in the town, but either by the Greek-speaking population, who sprang from the pre-Roman inhabitants of Antioch, or by the descendants of the old Roman colonists, who gradually degenerated from the Roman standard and were merged in the Greek-speaking people. These Greek-speaking inhabitants (*incolae*) were gradually elevated to the Roman citizenship; and it is proved in a paper by Mrs. Hasluck (" Journal of Hellenic Studies," 1912, pp. 144 ff.) that there exists among the dedications an overwhelming majority of Roman names. Some are slave-names, others are the names of freedmen (*liberti*) or of *incolae*,[1] and a few are probably names of de-

---

[1] *Incolae* were distinguished from the *coloni* in a colonia like Antioch. They were the older non-Roman population in the colonia, but they had a share in the privileges of a colonia, and they were gradually advanced to the dignity of Roman citizens and took Roman names.

scendants of the original Roman colonists. The dedications are often expressed in the familiar speech, and give some interesting evidence about the Greek usage in respect of Latin names.

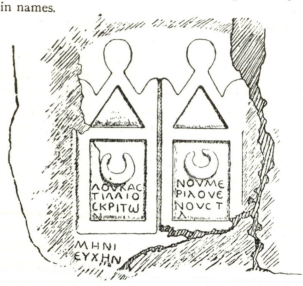

Fig. 9.—Dedication to the God Mên by L. Tillius Crito and his wife, engraved on a buttress of the outer wall of the Sanctuary at Pisidian Antioch.

1. Copied by Mr. J. G. C. Anderson, Mr. W. M. Calder, and myself in 1912.

In very rough and rude lettering on the south-west wall of the sanctuary of Mên : letters small and hard to read :—

Λουκᾶς	Νουμε-	Loukas Tillios
Τίλλιο-	ρία Οὐε-	Kriton (and)
ς Κρίτω-	νοῦστ-	Noumeria Ve-
ν	a	nousta
Μηνὶ		to Men
εὐχην		a vow

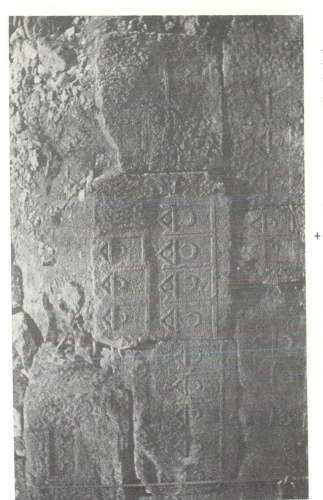

+

PLATE IV.—Part of the outer wall of the Sanctuary on the mountain over Pisidian Antioch.

(Fig. 8 is indicated by a cross.)

The names of the man and woman are inscribed in two spaces marked off by lines as *aediculae* of the type usual in these vows to the god of Antioch. The name of the god and the statement of the vow written beneath was intended to be common to the two *aediculae*. The two names are therefore a pair, i.e. husband and wife.

Although the name of the god and the vow are written only at one corner [1] under the two *aediculae* there can be no doubt that the *aediculae* are a connected pair, and that the vow is common to both. The *aediculae* are often grouped in this way at the Sanctuary, sometimes as many as five being connected together. In the accompanying photograph of a small part of the Sanctuary wall there are groups of two, three, four, and five *aediculae*, and also single *aediculae*. The general appearance rarely leaves any doubt whether a group or a single *aedicula* is intended. The surface generally was smoothed to receive the carving, and the shape of the cutting is usually sufficient indication of the grouping (as in this case), while other signs also conspire. *Aediculae* of different groups vary in shape and size, and grouping is indicated by placing the members of the group close together and making them identical in shape and size.

This, therefore, is a joint dedication by L. Tillius Crito (and his wife) Numeria Venusta to the god of the sanctuary. Both bear Latin names (except the Greek cognomen of the husband): both are *cives Romani*. Yet they are a Greek-speaking family to whom Greek comes more naturally than Latin.

There cannot be the slightest doubt that Loukas Tillios Kriton was a Roman citizen, whose name in Latin must

---

[1] A crack running across the stone compels this arrangement of the letters.

have been Lucius Tillius Crito. In the Greek that was spoken at Antioch Loukios and Loukas were evidently felt to be equivalent; and Crito writes himself in Greek as Loukas. His third name suggests that he was perhaps a freedman; but it is (as Mrs. Hasluck says)[1] difficult or even impossible to distinguish the names of freedmen from the names of *incolae* who had received the Roman citizenship and had assumed the full name of the *civis Romanus.*

This single case would be sufficient and conclusive : one clear example is legally as strong as a hundred. The equivalence was accepted at Antioch ; and there can be no reason for thinking that Antiochian custom differed from that of other Greek-speaking towns of Asia Minor and the Roman East generally : Loukas was a Greek *Kosenamen* of Loukios.

This case does not stand alone. There are several examples among these Antiochian dedications, in which the same individual or family repeats the inscription, usually with some variations. In one of these pairs the same person is mentioned once as Loukios and once as Loukas. The two dedications in question, which are engraved very near one another, are seen on pp. 378-9.

2. On the sixth buttress from west corner of S.W. wall of the Great Sanctuary :—

Μηνὶ	To Men
εὐχ[ήν	a vow
Γάμος 'Αβασκάν[τ-	Gamos (son) of Abas-
ου μὲ [γ]υν[αικός.	kantos with his wife.
Λούκιος υἱός.	Loukios a son.
Πουμπούλιος υἱός	Pompilius a son.

[1] "Journal of Hellenic Studies," 1912, p. 145, note 67.

3. On the wall close to the same buttress :—

Μηνὶ εὐχήν	To Men a vow
Γάμος 'Αβάσκάντου	Gamos son of Abas-
υός, καὶ Αουκᾶς καὶ	kantos, and Loukas, and
Πουμπούμλιος (*sic !*)	Pompilius
καὶ Εὔδοξος.	and Eudoxos.

The second of this pair of dedications was correctly read by Mrs. Hasluck, Mr. Calder, and myself in 1911, and published by Mrs. Hasluck in the "Journal of Hellenic Studies," 1912, p. 130, with one slight difference.[1]

The other we failed to read completely in 1911 : part of it is published by Mrs. Hasluck on p. 127. In 1912 [2] we deciphered it entirely, and then found that the two are almost duplicates.

The modern Greek form $\mu\epsilon$ for $\mu\epsilon\tau\acute{a}$ is here used, and is a good example and proof of the colloquialism of the dedications. Other examples of $\mu\epsilon$ occur in the epigraphy of central Anatolia in the fourth century ; but the complete form is far more common.

In the second dedication, which is apparently later than the first, Eudoxos is mentioned : in the first the wife of the dedicant Gamos occurs.

This difference must be carefully noted. Probably

---

[1] She gives the name as Gallos, not Gamos ; but states in her commentary that Gamos is quite possible. I appended in a footnote to her paper that my reading was unhesitatingly Gamos, and quoted a Bithynian example of this name. Re-examination in 1912 by Mr. Anderson, Mr. Calder, and myself, confirmed this reading. It is often difficult to distinguish λλ from μ in these dedications.

[2] When we first uncovered them in 1911, the letters were filled with soil, of the same colour as the stone, being decomposed from it. During the winter of 1911-12 the stones were washed clean by rain : the cleansing made them easier to read, but even in 1912 this and many others of the dedications were difficult. This one was read by Mr. J. G. C. Anderson, Mr. Calder, and myself.

FIG. 10.—Dedication to Mên by Gamos and his family, engraved on the outer wall of the Sanctuary at Pisidian Antioch.

ΜΗΝΙ ΕΥΧΗΝ

ΓΑΜΟΣ ΑΒΑΣΚΑΝΤΟΥ
ΝΟΣ ΚΑΙ ΛΟΥΚΑΣ ΚΑΙ
ΠΟΥΜΠΟΥΜΛΙΟΣ
ΚΑΙ ΕΥΔΟΞΟΣ

FIG. 11.—Dedication to Mên by Gamos and his family, engraved on the outer wall of the Sanctuary at Pisidian Antioch. The line on the left represents the edge of the buttress on which the other dedication by Gamos is incised.

Eudoxos is a son born since the earlier dedication, while the mother is now left out. It is a plausible, and even highly probable interpretation of the facts, that the vows were both made by the family in a season of danger. The whole family, father, mother and two sons, made the first dedication : the father and three sons made the second : the mother had passed away in the interval. The period of childbirth was a dangerous one, when doctors were few and medical practice in an elementary condition. Dr. W. R. Macdonell has established by a wide survey of the evidence,[1] that under the Empire the expectation of life for young women was less than for men, and for elderly and old women greater. The reason obviously lies in that one supreme danger. In the family of Gamos we have an individual case of the general principle.

It follows, then, that Loukios in the first vow is the same as Loukas in the second : he was the eldest son of the dedicant Gamos.

Two witnesses suffice. An accumulation of other examples would not really strengthen the argument. Loukios and Loukas were felt as equivalent names by the Antiochian Greeks, one formal and the other familiar.

It has often been pointed out, and is a familiar fact, that the two names, the polite and the familiar, are known in the case of several persons mentioned in the New Testament, Apollôs and Apollônios, Priscilla and Prisca, Silas and Silvanus. Of these Apollônios is found only in the Bezan Codex ; but its presence there is a sufficient proof.[2] By its form Apollôs is proved to be a *Kosenamen ;* and Apollônios is the full name. The same man was called Apollônios in formal and polite speech, Apollôs in familiar usage.

[1] See his paper in " Biometrika," 1913, IX., pp. 366-386.
[2] " Church in the Roman Empire before 170," p. 152.

It happens that Loukios is not attested in any document as the formal name of the Evangelist; but we now have the proof that in Antioch, and therefore generally, Loukas was known to be the familiar form of Loukios.

Another point also has to be observed, as indicative of popular custom at Antioch. The wife and mother is alluded to, but not named: and the omission of the wife's name is very common at this Sanctuary. Among the vows there are others where the mother is named with her children; and there we may conclude that she is the head of the family, either because she survived her husband or for some other reason. The omission of the wife's name puts her in a secondary position as a mere adjunct, and this is hardly in accordance with Anatolian custom, in which the position of women was important and influential.[1] In this case it may be accounted for by the character of the cult of Mên; the personality of the god in the Antiochian religion gradually became more and more dominant, while that of the goddess associated with him sank into the background (as Mr. Anderson has shown clearly).[2]

In these three inscriptions there occur two different usages. In no. 1 Loukios or Loukas is a Roman *prænomen:* Lucius Tillius Crito was a Roman citizen with a proper Roman name. His *cognomen* Crito, however, shows that he was a Hellene by race, who had been promoted to the citizenship:[3] either he was libertine in origin, or he was an *incola* who had attained the Roman citizenship.

In nos. 2, 3, Loukios seems to be used as the full and sole name of a Hellene. *Prænomina* were often taken over

---

[1] " Church in Roman Empire," pp. 67, 161.

[2] See his article in the " Journal of Roman Studies," 1913, p. 272.

[3] Possibly his family had been promoted to citizenship and he inherited *civitas* (like Paul).

into Greek usage and employed as the full and sole name of Hellenes.[1]   The mixture of Roman and Greek names in the same family is characteristic of a colonia.

With regard to the name of the evangelist, there are two possibilities open.   On the one hand Lucius may have been his *prænomen* as a Roman citizen; and in that case it would follow almost certainly that the physican Loukios was a freedman, who acquired the full Roman name when he was set free; for the custom of society would make it probable that this physician, who led for many years the life of a companion of Paul, was not born a Roman citizen (as perhaps Silvanus was).   Physicians were often freedmen; and freedmen were frequently addressed by their *prænomen*, which marked their rank.[2]

On the other hand the evangelist might have been a Hellene bearing the simple name Loukios, which was often adopted in Greek from the Latin as an individual name. Loukios was in such cases not a *prænomen*, and did not imply Roman citizenship; in fact this usage was a complete proof that the man whose name in full was simply Loukios, without *nomen* or *cognomen*,[3] was not a Roman citizen.   We may also infer with equal certainty that a person named Loukios simply was not a slave; the Roman name could not be degraded to a slave name in that age.   Such a Loukios would be an ordinary free Hellene.

---

[1] A number of examples are mentioned in an article published by the present writer in " Journal of Hellenic Studies," 1883, p. 36 : Lucius, Gaius, Marcus, Quintus, are all found in use, single and complete, as names of Hellenes.

[2] See Horace, " Satires," III. 5, 32 : and the commentators thereon : " Quinte," *puta, aut* " Publi ": *gaudent prænomine molles auriculæ.*

[3] This does not apply to cases where in casual mention a man is spoken of by his *prænomen* alone.   I refer only to cases where the full legal name was Loukios.

No evidence is known sufficient to prove which of these alternatives applied to the Evangelist Luke. The former would suit specially well with the profession of a doctor ; but a *libertus* usually remained in close relation to his former master, who continued to be his *patronus*. Luke was perfectly free to go about the world in Paul's company, and has no appearance of being in connexion with a patron. Exceptional cases might, however, occur. Perhaps some unnoticed detail may yet furnish a decisive argument.

The correspondence of the Latin Lucius through the Greek Loukios with Loukas can be established by other similar cases which I quote from the excellent article and list of examples published by M. Lambertz in "Glotta," 1913, Vol. IV, pp. 78-143, and W. Schulze, "Graeca Latina," p. 12. From the Latin name Geminus comes the form Geminas, "which," as Lambertz says, " is in itself interesting on account of the vivification of the Latin stem Geminus with the common Greek abbreviation-suffix as ". He then quotes from Schulze the following similar examples :—

Longinas (from Longinus), Rufas (from Rufus), Tiberas (from Tiberius), and Loukas.[1]

The last case is the one with which we have been dealing. Schulze and Lambertz, both scientific philologists, assume its character and origin as obvious. We have now furnished two clear examples from ordinary life in the Eastern provinces.

The conclusion may now be called certain. The name of the Evangelist Loukas implies an original form Lucius,[2]

---

[1] Tiberas is a perfect parallel to Lucas ; the latter occurs in a Roman name C. Julius Lucas (Lepsius, *Monum. aegypt. inscr.*, VI. 17685).

[2] Lambertz's exact words are added, " Γεμινᾶς, der an sich interessant ist durch die Verquickung des lat Namenstammes (Geminus = Δίδυμος) mit der häufigen griech. Kurzformendung-ᾶς ". This sentence states in the brief terms of philological science exactly what is printed in the text in full. I did

but this original Latin name was used in the corresponding Greek form.

The evidence is convincing and beyond doubt that the Evangelist was named Loukios or Loukas. Professor Deissmann has an article in preparation on this subject, to which I hoped to refer; but the war of 1914 has probably postponed this and many other studies by many scholars. It would have contained the inscriptions here republished, with Deissmann's comments, which are in perfect agreement, as I understand, with the view taken in this paper (reprinted from the "Expositor").[1]

I understand from Dr. Deissmann that he has other views to propound with regard to the personality of Loukios, which I leave it to him to state at his own time and in his own way. As stated in brief they did not convince me, but his full argument may be more effective.

not see Lambertz's article until this chapter was in type, as "Glotta" does not come to any library accessible to me except that of the University of Aberdeen. Brouttaras is also quoted as derived through the Greek from a Latin original by another Greek suffix.

[1] It is here enlarged, but the opinion maintained and the line of argument are the same. The confirmation from "Glotta" came to my knowledge by chance in September, 1914.

CHAPTER XXVI

THE FIRSTFRUITS OF ACHAIA

A GOOD deal of difficulty has been found in this description, which is applied by St. Paul in 1 Corinthians XVI. 15 to the household of Stephanas of Corinth. It has been understood to imply that Stephanas was the first convert from the province of Achaia. How is this to be reconciled with Luke's statement about Paul's work in Athens, Acts XVII. 34 : " certain men also clave unto him and believed, among whom was Dionysius the Areopagite, and Damaris," etc. ?

In the first place the view of the present writer may be stated, as this can be done very briefly. Both Luke and Paul are perfectly correct. All that is needed is to understand their words. The remarks that have been made in an earlier chapter about the meaning of the word " believe " in the Acts must be kept in mind.[1]

The evident meaning of Luke is that in Athens there was produced on a few persons an effect genuine and deep : " they believed ". Paul, however, did not remain at Athens to follow it up. No Church was formed there, and in all probability no baptism was administered.

It is, on the other hand, most likely that the brief reference to Dionysius and Damaris was very significant to Luke's readers : they knew what was implied in the naming of Dionysius : the " woman named Damaris " carried with

[1] See Chapter XII.

her many memories to the Christians of the first century. This is one of the passages in the Acts where the thought is present in the author's mind that he was writing for readers who knew a great deal.   He wrote in advanced life about A.D. 77-81, while Titus was ruling the Roman Empire;[1] and his plan and purpose were calculated for the Church as it was after the religion had been proscribed by the Imperial policy; but he wrote with the vivid memory of all that he had seen and heard as the events occurred.   He had seen much. He had heard Paul's own description of the earliest missionary journeys.   He had listened to Rhoda telling how she, in her glad and eager haste to tell the good news, had forgotten to open the door to Peter, and how her news was disbelieved until they opened and saw him standing in the street.   He had known Mark and Philip.   He made abundant use of Mark's Gospel.   His excellent sources of information, " as they delivered them to me, who were eye-witnesses and ministers of the Word," were utilized to meet the situation produced by the Imperial action; and the narrative was in a very advanced stage (Book I, the Gospel, being complete and perfect already, and Book II needing only the final touches) about A.D. 80.

Now consider the case of Sergius Paullus, as discussed in Chapter XII.   Evidently he did not become a member of a Christian congregation at Paphos; the supposition is irreconcilable with all our conceptions of Roman and Græco-Roman society.   When a Church was formed at Paphos or elsewhere in Cyprus, the first baptized and received member of the congregation would be called, rightly and fairly, " the firstfruits of Cyprus ".

After the same analogy, it is not Dionysius or Damaris,

---

[1] " St. Paul the Traveller," p. 387.

but Stephanas with his household to whom belongs the title "firstfruits of Achaia". In his case, as in those of Lydia and the jailer at Philippi, it may safely be assumed that the household consisted of persons who were fully under the authority[1] of the head; in other words, the children were young. Slaves were attached and obedient members of the household, and custom was that the head should think for them, and that they should lovingly and trustfully follow his advice in such matters. Children, as they grew up, thought for themselves according to Greek custom. The jailer at Philippi was not likely to have a household of slaves; but he would be likely to have a family. See p. 193 and note on p. 186.

It is hardly reconcilable with Greek or Græco-Asiatic custom that grown-up children should change their religion at a moment's notice and at the order even of a parent; nor is it reconcilable with the spirit of freedom which belongs to Christianity that grown persons should be received for baptism except on their own free and deliberate choice. There is no rational and sufficient explanation of those cases, except that they are examples of the baptism of infants and young children or slaves, for whom the parents or master can act as the responsible parties.

Stephanas, therefore, being baptized with his young children and probably his slaves, was "the firstfruits of Achaia," in spite of the existence of people at Athens who believed, even if we take that word in the full sense of being converted to Christianity.

---

[1] There was in the Greek world nothing comparable to the *patria potestas*, the absolute authority extending even to power of life and death, which belonged to Roman custom and which also existed among the three Gaulish tribes of North Galatia (see "Historical Comment. on Galatians," p. 131). This Roman power was valid over fully grown children, even married sons.

In the next place, we may examine some other opinions that have been advanced on this question.

It has been maintained that if Luke's statement is true, Dionysius or Damaris or some Athenian must have been the first convert in the province, and therefore either Luke's narrative is inconsistent with Paul's words and therefore incorrect, or the phrase "firstfruits of Achaia" has not the meaning that has usually been taken from it.

The former supposition we must forthwith dismiss : we hold that Luke is trustworthy and that his account is necessarily in perfect agreement with Paul's words, provided that both are correctly translated and understood. The latter opinion is followed by Dr. Steinmann, formerly a *Privatdocent* in the University of Breslau.[1] He holds that Achaia as the province did not include Athens, and he draws from this a number of inferences which I have not succeeded in properly understanding (as they seem mutually contradictory), but which have the appearance of being far from consistent with our opinion of the high value of both Luke's and Paul's evidence.

Dr. Steinmann[2] maintains that Athens was not a city of the province Achaia, but, as a free and allied city, it was outside the province and outside of the Roman Empire, an *externa civitas*, i.e. a foreign and non-Roman city. If this were so, many interesting questions would arise, on which we need not enter. The previous question is whether Dr. Steinmann's statement, that in Roman usage Athens was not part of Achaia, can be accepted as correct : he admits,

---

[1] I sent a copy of an article on the same subject, less complete than the chapter here printed, to his address in the University ; but the packet was returned after some time to me, marked " Unbekannt " and " Adresse nicht ermittelt ".

[2] " Leserkreis des Galaterbriefes," pp. 88-94.

of course, that popular Greek usage might have loosely
called Athens a city of the province, but infers that, if St.
Paul spoke in that way, he followed, not proper Roman,
but loose and inaccurate Greek custom.

This matter, if considered at all, must be treated on a
considerable scale. It opens up questions of Roman administration in the East, and of the varying rights of different
classes of cities and bodies of population in the provinces,
which are rather complicated. The Roman task of governing a number of cities possessing very diverse privileges was
not a simple one, but required great freedom and variety in
the practical application of the fundamental Roman principles. If the matter is opened up at all, the character of
that complicated system has to be indicated. It might
perhaps be better to leave it to a more convenient occasion;
but, on the whole, there are advantages in treating it here,
in order to form some picture of the relation in which the
provinces stood to Rome in the Imperial system.

As was stated in Chap. XV. the keystone of the Imperial
system was the worship of the Emperor (in the strict and
original usage, of Rome and the Emperor as the embodiment
of the majesty of Rome). The unity of the province lay in
the association of all the units composing the province in
this worship. The province was thus made into a single
organism; all the parts met together in this ritual. Similarly, as has been pointed out in Chap. XV., the population of a great Imperial estate was united in an association or religious fraternity for the worship of the Lord
Emperor.

Ancient thought demanded inexorably a religious bond
to hold together every association, as has been repeatedly
shown. None of the old national religions could be of any
service in this case. All were national and separatist, though

only two carried their separatist principles to such a degree
as to involve a hostile relation to the Imperial unity; these
were Druidism, which was proscribed by Claudius as hostile,[1]
and Judaism, which obtained a peculiar toleration and was
allowed to continue as a separatist cult.[2]   Still all confined
themselves to narrow circles of worshippers.   None had any
positive idea to impart, except Judaism and the shadowy and
barely animate pretensions of the Mysteries.   None could
in any way be made into a bond to hold together the unity
of each individual province and of the Empire as a whole.
The Emperor Augustus caught the idea that the majesty,
the wisdom, and the beneficent power of Rome might form
the unifying bond; and the people first of the East and then
of the West insisted on giving personality to this idea by
regarding it as embodied in the reigning monarch.   Thus
the system grew.[3]

A national and racial character for the province was
aimed at in the East, where the Greek term " Nation "
(ἔθνος) was applied to the provincial unity.   Asia, with its
numerous races and stocks and once separate countries,
was " the Nation Asia " (ἡ Ἀσία τὸ ἔθνος): so Lycia,
Galatia, etc. ; and τὰ σύνεγγυς ἔθνη was used as the official
translation of *adiacentes provinciae*, " the neighbouring provinces ".   This use, however, though common in epigraphy
and found even in historians, is really only an extension of
the " genealogical fiction ".

---

[1] Christianity was proscribed *de iure* by Vespasian, but not *de facto* in the
fullest way till Decius and again by Diocletian.

[2] Hence " the nation of the Jews " was permitted to continue as a separate
body in the great cities, so to say outside of the Empire and yet in the Empire.   The very term " nation " was anti-Roman and hostile (see p. 56), but
it was permitted to the Jews to preserve the term and the legal fact ; and yet
they were treated as subjects.   Nothing is more wonderful than the position
and treatment of the Jews under the Empire.

[3] " Church in the Roman Empire," pp. 191, 323, 354, etc.

In passing it may be mentioned that friends have asked why I did not reply to Dr. Steinmann's book on the Galatian question, which is written to a large extent in polemic against my views. I waited till time and fresh discoveries should make their reply on my behalf. The constitution of the province Galatia has been gradually revealed, and many difficulties have been cleared away. The subject, however, is an extremely complicated one, and can never be understood properly without a great deal of careful and minute study and a considerable knowledge of Roman provincial administration.

In respect of such matters I regret to be obliged to say that Dr. Steinmann's book leaves much to be desired; and I cannot find in it any argument to which I could reply without a long and detailed discussion of Roman law in the Eastern provinces generally and in Galatia specially. On one page after another I find in his book statements at which I can only wonder. It is unprofitable to carry on a discussion when there is so little in which we are agreed. In regard to the most fundamental facts and principles of Roman administration in the East I should have to express my dissent from him. If discussion is to be profitable, there must be some common foundation on which we could build up, detail by detail, a serviceable structure of reasoned knowledge. Otherwise nothing can be gained by controversy. Argument should be constructive, and should leave the reader wiser and more able to appreciate ancient life than he was.

Of this hopeless disagreement about the facts of Roman administration examples occur broadcast. At present we shall take one which has no connexion with the Galatian question: Athens and the province Achaia and the meaning of "firstfruits of Achaia". To discuss this needs much consideration of elementary principles.

Here we are entirely outside of the province Galatia. Dr. Steinmann, however, cannot shake off the thought of Galatia. He goes into the question, not for its own sake, but in order to bang the South-Galatian theory. With this idea his mind is prepossessed, and consequently he has not been so careful about matters of Roman history and antiquities as he otherwise doubtless would have been.

Dr. Steinmann's conclusion, p. 94, seems to amount to this, that, if Paul used the term Achaia to include Athens, he was not in accordance with Roman ideas and custom, because the Roman usage of the term Achaia, as he thinks, excluded Athens.[1] Accordingly, he considers that Achaia meant the country of Greece, and that this was an old Greek pre-Roman usage, but he quotes no proof of such Greek usage, and it is contrary to everything that I know or have been taught from childhood.[2]

What I have always learned and understood to be the accepted teaching is that to the Greeks of pre-Roman time Achaia was the strip of land on the north coast of the Peloponnesus, between Arcadia and the Gulf of Corinth, and that Corinth itself was not a part of Achaia in the Greek sense. The use of "Achaia" for Greece as a whole is Roman, due to popular inaccurate usage, like the Roman use of "Asia" for the kingdom of the Attalids and thereafter for the Roman province: the Romans spoke of Greece as "Achaia," because the Achæan League included most of Greece, and they gave this name to the province.

Dr. Steinmann simply assumes without any proof, con-

---

[1] "Athen von der roemischen Provinz Achaja ausgeschlossen war."

[2] He actually quotes Pausanias's express statement, vii. 16, 7, that the Romans used the name Achaia in the sense in which the Greeks used Hellas, and Pausanias's correct explanation of the origin of this Roman usage. He does not realize that Pausanias is denying what he is asserting about the Greek sense of the name Achaia.

trary to all modern teaching, that this wide use of the term Achaia was "beyond all doubt a very ancient" (Greek) custom.[1] From every statement in this conclusion and every step in the argument I would dissent : and, especially, the method of substituting a "beyond doubt" for the quotation of ancient authorities is unscientific.

On p. 108 Dr. Steinmann says that in Pauline usage "Achaia is equivalent either to Corinth or to the whole of Greece, including Athens"—a pretty wide choice, destructive of any belief that the learned scholar has reached any clear geographical view—"and therefore is in no case fully coincident with the Roman official circuit of the province".

Now Dr. Steinmann proves at considerable length that Athens was a "free" and "allied" city (*libera* and *fœderata*). This proof was unnecessary ; every one admits the fact, which is a matter of the most rudimentary knowledge. Here, where all text-books agree and give the ancient evidence, Dr. Steinmann repeats the proof. Where he differs from the accepted opinion, he merely says "doubtless," and quotes no evidence.

The question which really matters is whether such "free" and "allied" cities were or were not reckoned as cities of the province. That concerns not Athens alone, but a number of other "free" and "allied" cities. It is no answer to the question to quote at length the privileges of such cities. Those privileges were honourable and highly esteemed. Governors of the province dismissed their lictors when they entered a free city. The citizens did not pay tribute.[2] The lawsuits in a free city were decided according to its own laws by the elected magistrates.

This whole subject requires retreatment, and a well-in-

[1] "Ohne Zweifel sehr alt war."
[2] We assume that all *liberæ civitates* were also *immunes.*

formed discussion would have been welcome.   Dr. Steinmann, however, follows mainly Marquardt's "Handbuch," and quotes none of the more recent investigations on constitutional and legal points.   He uses Mommsen's History, but not his later articles.   These later studies, along with Liebenam's "Städteverwaltung im roem. Kaiserreiche," and Mitteis' works, etc., are the basis for the following remarks.

The privileges granted to the free cities, according to a common Roman method of governing its subjects, had a great show of honour, but the Government set them aside as often as it chose.   Contributions and taxes were frequently imposed on the free cities, at the discretion of the governor or of the central administration.   Free cities were degraded at any time when it suited Government to do so.[1]

This "freedom" was, after all, little more than nominal. Holm, IV. 147, remarks that modern ideas of independence should not be introduced into the *libertas* of the "free" cities.   It was absolutely inconsistent with Roman system to have a state within a state.   The "free" state could exercise its freedom and use its laws only in so far as conduced to the well-being of the Empire.[2]   "Even in the East, where Roman favour allowed many privileges to exist, it was evident that this 'freedom' meant really nothing, since the word of any Roman governor could nullify it."[3] When Maximus was sent to govern Achaia, Pliny wrote to him, VIII. 14, urging him not to deprive Athens and Sparta of that nominal and shadowy freedom which they had possessed.

The right of "free" cities to govern according to their

---

[1] See Liebenam, p. 466.
[2] "Ein Staat im Staate war undenkbar," Liebenam, p. 472.
[3] Liebenam, p. 473.

own laws caused after all no very great practical difference. True, the ordinary cities of the province had to accept the Roman law, but in practice Rome allowed great influence to local custom in the civilized Eastern provinces. Hence the law as administered in these provinces was a sort of compromise between strict Roman law and native custom. In some notable cases extraordinary care was taken to act according to the usage of the city. On this subject see Mitteis' "Reichsrecht und Volksrecht" and later works; also Liebenam, p. 466 ff., and the authorities quoted by him. I have followed Mitteis in my "Historical Commentary on Galatians" (see the Preface).

As a proof that Athens and other allied cities were outside the province, Dr. Steinmann quotes the fact that the Areopagus Court decided a criminal case in the reign of Tiberius. Doubtless it did so; but that was the privilege of all free cities: we know it at Amisos in the province of Bithynia-Pontus, from Pliny's correspondence with the Emperor Trajan, while he was acting as governor. It is certainly wholly inconsistent with Pliny's conception of his duties and power to say that Amisos was outside of his province: he had distinct duties there, but these were narrower than in the ordinary cities of the province (*civitates stipendiariæ*). The question as to the limit of his power in Amisos exercised his mind a little, but there was no question that he had power there. He was doubtful whether he should prohibit the continuance of clubs (*eranoi*) in Amisos, and consulted Trajan on this point. The Emperor's reply was that Amisos should be allowed to keep its clubs, if they were in accordance with its own laws. A hint, however, is appended that the proconsul should keep himself informed whether the clubs tended to encourage riotous conduct and unlawful assemblies. The

Emperors always reserved the power of annulling the rights of a *civitas fœderata*, if this seemed advisable for Imperial interests ;[1] and, if clubs in Amisos were found conducive to disorder, the analogy of Imperial policy in other cases shows that the governor would be directed to interfere and probably to do away with the agreement (*fœdus*). But Amisos was one of the Pontic cities associated in the cult of the Emperors by the province ; and no more conclusive proof can be given that it ranked officially as part of the province : see p. 389.

Dr. Steinmann tries to demonstrate that "*Athen gehöre gar nicht zur Provinz Achaia*". There is, of course, a pedantic sense, almost a legal fiction, in which this statement is true under the Empire.[2] In certain matters of courtesy and form the fiction of independence of the "allied" and the "free" cities (*civitates fœderatæ* and *liberæ*) was maintained. Marquardt points out that their autonomy was rather shadowy—I need not go into details—but he did not know, what is now proved, that, although the free city administered its own law there was always allowed an appeal from the judgment of the city to the Roman governor of the province, and that even if an appeal were made

---

[1] As Marquardt says, p. 74, Augustus deprived several *civitates fœderatæ* of their *libertas*, because they were using it in a way dangerous to public peace, Suet., "Aug.," 47. Byzantium was originally *fœderata* (Tac. "Ann.," xii. 62) : after the province Macedonia was formed, Byzantium was subject to the governor on the footing not of *fœderata* but of *libera civitas* (Cic. "in Pis.," iii. 6). In A.D. 53 it was subject to Bithynia and was *stipendiaria* (Tacitus, l.c.) ; but Pliny then calls it *libera* ("Nat. Hist.," iv. 11). Vespasian deprived it of *libertas* (Suet., "Vesp.," 8), which it regained and kept till Severus punished the city for a short time (Dio., lxxiv. 14).

[2] Dr. Steinmann applies facts and principles of the Republican period respecting the allied and the free cities too directly to the Imperial time. It has now become clear that the Imperial administration interfered very freely with the rights of these cities, whenever there was any occasion ; the tendency of discovery is to illustrate this truth.

within the allied or free city to the Emperor, it could only take effect through the governor and with his sanction. This is known for both Achaia and Asia; and is doubtless true of all provinces. I quote Mommsen in " Zft. der Savigny-St. f. Rechtsgesch.," 1890, pl. 36 f. : " *es ist für die Stellung der freien Städte von Wichtigkeit dass sowohl von Athen wie von Kos nicht bloss an den Kaiser sondern selbst an den Proconsul appellirt werden kann. . . . Nicht minder bemerkenswerth aber ist es, was Ramsay mit Recht der Inschrift entnahm, dass der Staathalter danach der Appellation an der Kaiser und überhaupt wohl der Beschickung des Kaisers aus seiner Provinz Folge zu geben wohl berechtigt, aber nicht verpflichtet ist."* [1] Why did not Dr. Steinmann quote this important fact, which puts a very different aspect on the whole question?

I do not fancy that even Dr. Steinmann would press the fiction of the freedom of allied cities to the extent of maintaining that they as allies of Rome (*fœderatæ civitates*), and standing outside of the Empire (*externæ*), were independent of the Emperor. The Emperor was the ultimate fountain of law for them; and any matter could be appealed from the Athenian courts to him. The governor of Achaia is an intermediate power; appeal to him is made from the city courts; and even an appeal to the Emperor, as already said, must be sanctioned by the governor of the province before it can go forward to Rome.

To talk about Athens, or Kos, or Amisos, or Tarsus, or Mopsouestia in Cilicia, or Sagalassos, or Ephesus, or Smyrna, or a host of other cities, as being in any real sense outside of the province in which they were situated, is mere trifling. Many of them were outside the Roman Empire

---

[1] Reprinted in his collected papers on legal subjects, Vol. III, p. 388.

in the legal sense that an exile from Rome might live there; they administered their own affairs, indeed, but according to a *lex civitatis* which was fixed by Rome; their rights could be diminished or taken away by the Emperor, when he thought advisable; and, although the governor of the province did not interfere in their suits, yet any suit could be carried before him by appeal. The last is a decisive criterion: the governor of the province is the higher power in all law-cases, while the city officials are the subordinate power. The advantage of being free (*libera et immunis*) was in some respects great,[1] but in other respects this freedom would have been positively prejudicial, if it had not been in practice completely disregarded.

Moreover, a grave misconception pervades the whole of Dr. Steinmann's reasoning on this subject. He seems never to have taken into consideration the great variety of privilege and honour and standing which existed among the cities and other units out of which a province was built up. This inequality of rights is a general feature of Roman administration at all periods. Cities were not treated all after the same fashion: their civic rights varied greatly according to their individual character and services to Rome, or according to historical circumstances. As in Italy in the period from 270 to 89 B.C.,[2] so in the Eastern provinces in the first and second centuries,

---

[1] Marquardt points out that the privilege of sheltering a Roman exile, while an apparent honour as implying independence, sometimes meant that the exiled Roman noble made himself a tyrant in the city where he settled.

[2] The differences of name persisted long after the Social War, 90-89 B.C., but the persistence was merely a historical survival: there were still the old names and classes, coloniæ, municipia, præfecturæ, and so on, and the old names of local town magistrates continued, but there was no real distinction of rights.

there was a wide diversity of rights and standing among the cities. The most privileged and honourable class was the Colonies : in Greece these were Corinth and Patrae, in Macedonia Philippi, in Asia Parium and Troas, in Galatia Antioch and the Pisidian colonies. Next came the allied cities (*fœderatæ*) which were also free and immune from tribute. After them came the cities which were free and exempt from tribute (*liberæ et immunes*) without having a treaty with Rome.[1] After them came the ordinary cities, which were subject to tribute (*stipendiariæ*). Then the *dêmoi* or peoples which did not possess the Hellenic city constitution, but apparently were organized on the Anatolian village system (though we really possess hardly any quite trustworthy knowledge about them).[2] Last of all come the *ethnê*, in which Rostowzew recognizes the population of the great Imperial estates, whose position approximated to that of serfs (though technically they were free), and whose organization continued to be as in the pre-Roman period with the Emperor substituted for the ancient lord, whether priest or king or noble.[3] The *ethnos* of a single estate lived in villages, each of which had its own headman and

[1] Practically they had the same rights as the *fœderatæ*, but the rights of the latter were perhaps a little more permanently certain, and the former could not with the same legal right call themselves " friends ".

[2] What we can say about them is largely reconstruction from general considerations, and, though it is highly probable and approximates in part to confident assurance, still is not free from hypothesis.

[3] These estates had in many cases belonged to one or other of the great Sanctuaries, whose gods were often extremely wealthy as owners of lands and lords over the cultivators. Brandis on " Asia " (Pauly-Wissowa, " Realencyclop.," p. 1556 f.) gives a different explanation of ἔθνη in this usage ; but Rostowzew rejects it in his " Studien zur Gesch. des röm. Kolonats," p. 262. I go with Rostowzew, though acknowledging that the matter remains uncertain and hypothetical : but Rostowzew's view seems to me the most reasonable and probable. See above, ch. xv.

officers ;[1] its administrative arrangements approximated in character to the village system of the *dêmoi*, though on an apparently less favourable footing, as the *dêmos* was evidently freer and was called by a Greek constitutional name, while the *ethnê* are mentioned last in the list and bear a name which was reckoned more alien to Roman character and system.

In such a province as Asia all these various classes of states were brought together as the body politic of the province.   The *ethnê* were hardly perhaps honourable enough to be ranked along with the really free peoples.   They were the private property of the Emperor and looked to him, not to the governor of the province.   The Emperor's procurator and slaves managed their affairs.   So far as they were outside of the province it was because they were unworthy of that honour : they corresponded in status rather to the people of client-kingdoms, not yet worthy of admission to the rank of provincials.   Yet these *ethnê* are in certain inscriptions ranked as members of the Commune [2] of the province Asia, and this is the absolute proof that they enter into the ultimate and fundamental being of the province.

In the province of Achaia there were some differences from Asia ; but the general principle remains the same.

Now why should the free and allied cities be deemed by Dr. Steinmann too honourable to be degraded into the pro-

[1] The best known estate is that large block of Phrygian land near Pisidian Antioch on the north, where a considerable amount of information has been found; this is published and discussed by the writer in " Studies in the History of the Eastern Provinces," pp. 304 ff. (the account there given has been entirely approved by Rostowzew).   Some additional details have been found and published in " Journal of Hellenic Studies," 1912, pp. 151 ff. and in " Annual of British School Athens," 1912.

[2] The Commune of Asia is the union of the whole province in the worship of Rome and the Emperors: at its head are the Asiarchs or High-priests of Asia.

vince, when the *Coloniae*, whose burgesses were all Roman citizens,[1] and which were, so to say, outlying portions of Rome itself, serving as garrisons in the province, are ranked by him as parts of the province? That he does so rank them, though he never actually says so, is proved by the fact that his whole argument is directed to show that, while the *Colonia* Corinth was part of the province, Athens was not.

There is, of course, a sense in which the *Coloniae* were outside the province; all its citizens, as Romans, were even more completely emancipated from subjection to the provincial governor than the citizens of free and allied cities.

Yet Corinth was the capital and official residence of the proconsul of Achaia : Lugudunum (Lyon) occupied the same position in the Three Gauls : Pisidian Antioch was the military centre and a sort of secondary capital of the southern part of the province Galatia. It was a special honour to a province to contain one or more *Coloniae* which represented the full Roman qualification as the ideal in front of the province. The province, ideally speaking, was a sort of imperfect Rome, i.e. it was a foreign nation in the process of being made fully Roman : the *Colonia* was the perfect Rome in visible and material form within the province. It would be false to the Roman idea of the province to put the *Colonia* outside of it : the *Colonia* was the visible soul.

Next, let us look at a closely analogous case. Smyrna offers an excellent parallel to Athens. Smyrna is given by Marquardt as only a free, but not an allied city. He has,

---

[1] The *incolae*, who had not Roman citizenship in a *colonia*, were not burgesses and had no place in the popular assembly : they were mere residents, yet they had privileges of their own.

however, omitted the evidence of Cicero in his Eleventh Philippic, II. 5 (which is quite conclusive), "a city which ranks as one of our most faithful and most ancient allies". The account of the Asian War and the treaty that ended it in Livy, XXXVII. f., must be understood as implying a treaty, though the treaty (being of older date) is not actually mentioned there.

As an allied state Smyrna had the right of sheltering exiles from Rome, i.e. exiles who were expelled from the Roman Empire could go to live there and had the right of being received as citizens. This constituted it a *civitas extera*, i.e. legally outside the Roman Empire.[1] The same right belonged to Thessalonica and Cyzicus and Patrae;[2] but no one, so far as I am aware, has ever thought or argued that these were not parts of the provinces Macedonia and Asia and Achaia, or not parts of the Empire.

As regards Smyrna, Tacitus has preserved the report of the argument which it laid before the Senate in support of its claim to construct a provincial temple dedicated to Tiberius and Livia and the Senate.[3]   Now Smyrna was the oldest ally and the most faithful friend of Rome in the East,[4] occupying an honourable position corresponding to Marseilles (Massalia) in the West.   Its chief glory and its special characteristic as a city of the Empire was its faithfulness. It laid its case before the Senate, because it was a city of the province.   It had no standing in this matter except as a city of the province.   The Commune of the province[5] had resolved to have this temple as a new seat of the Imperial cult, and eleven cities of the province claimed the honour

---

[1] Marquardt, p. 80, with note 1.

[2] Marquardt, loc. cit.   [3] "Annals," IV. 55.

[4] See the chapter on Smyrna in "Letters to the Seven Churches".

[5] On the Commune see note above on p. 400.

of being chosen as seat of the new temple. Smyrna was one of these. It assumes to have the right to compete for the privilege : other ten cities claim to be preferred : all the eleven present their claim as cities of the province. If Smyrna had been *extra provinciam*, it would not have sought an honour which was reserved for the province. If other cities had thought that Smyrna was not a city of the Province, they would have argued that Smyrna was disqualified as being outside the province. The right to compete is accorded to Smyrna by universal consent.

The argument in this case is the most perfect proof that Smyrna was a city of the province Asia, accepted and honoured as such by the Senate and by the whole province. Yet, if there were any city which was pre-eminent in the East as the friend and ally of Rome, the conspicuous " free and allied city " in the fullest sense, that city was Smyrna. Athens had massacred its Roman inhabitants, joined Mithradates, and been besieged and captured by Sulla. In that same war Smyrna's sympathy and loyalty to Rome had been conspicuous. In the public Assembly the citizens, hearing of the sufferings of Sulla's soldiers from the winter cold, stripped themselves of their outer garments (which were of thicker material), and sent them to the shivering Romans. Any honour and privilege that attached to a *civitas fœderata* belonged above all others to Smyrna ; yet it claimed the title " first and fairest (city) of (the province) Asia,"[1] and engraved this on its coins and embodied it in its official inscriptions.

It is instructive to read the earlier chapter (IV. 15) in which Tacitus describes the nature of the case. The Commune of Asia was the expression of the provincial unity and

---

[1] 'Ασία means the province Asia.

loyalty : it was the association of all the cities of the province in the common worship of the Imperial god and his
divine ancestors.   To be a member of the Commune was
to be a member of the province.

It would be valueless to argue that Smyrna in its case
before the Senate appeals to its conduct in 195 B.C., when
it dedicated the first temple to Rome long before a Roman
province existed, and to infer that the construction of a
temple to Tiberius did not prove it to be a city of the province.   The point, however, is this.   Smyrna might have
built its own special temple to the Emperor, and this would
not prove any provincial connexion ; but the temple, which
it was finally selected by the Senate to build, was a temple
of (the province) Asia, and only cities of the province could
have such a temple.   A special legate of the proconsul of
Asia was appointed to superintend the building.

Dr. Steinmann, p. 94, is possessed with the strange idea
that Achaia could not acquire a Roman name until A.D. 44,
because it had previously been classed with Macedonia
under the same governor, and was only in that year separated
from Macedonia and given to the senate as a province.[1]
But even when it was under the same governor as Macedonia
it was the Roman province Achaia, and not merely a part
of Macedonia.   The province was *Macedonia et Achaia*[2]
(Tac. Ann. I. 80, V. 10 ; Dio Cass. LVIII. 25) : Cicero often
speaks of Achaia, meaning the Roman province.

Again, if free cities were outside the province, not merely

---

[1] He forgets that it was made a separate province in 27 B.C.   He also
forgets that the constitution of Achaia was regulated by the *lex Mummia*,
imposed by its conqueror in 146 B.C. (Liebenam, p. 469), whereas Macedoni
was regulated by the *lex Aemilia*, 167 B.C.

[2] Like Lycia et Pamphylia, two provinces under one governor : so the
united Galatia and Cappadocia between A.D. 74 and 106 or later, and the
Tres Eparchiae.

Athens, but also Sparta, all the Eleutherolacones, Delphi, Thespiae, Tanagra, Abae, Pharsalus, Elatea, Patrae, Nicopolis, Mothone, Pale and Pallantion, also the Ozolian Locrians and Amphissa,[1] were so. Brandis in Pauly-Wissowa, I. 191, adds Thyrreion (an allied city), and Plataea (a free city), and states that it is false to think that Achaia did not become a province until 27 B.C. : it had been a province from 146 B.C.

In A.D. 67 Nero made all Greece free. The freedom released the country from taxation, but it would be absurd to suppose that this took Greece out of the Empire : moreover this act was a freak and not a sober Roman device for government.

The nature of that sham freedom appears from the fact that the democratic constitution was suppressed in the free cities, and a timocratic and oligarchic organization was substituted by Rome.

In C.I.L. VIII. 7059 an official is mentioned who was acting as governor in Athens, Thespiae, Plataeae, and Thessaly simultaneously, and Dr. Brandis infers from this that Thessaly belonged to the same province as Athens, Thespiae and Plataeae, i.e. he takes those cities as being all included in the province of Achaia.

The criticism to which Dr. Steinmann's argument about Athens exposes itself is this. Whereas Marquardt's account of Achaia accommodates itself naturally to the new evidence (of which a brief outline has been given in these pages), Steinmann's assertions are in contradiction with it; and yet the latter founds his argument solely on Marquardt, and quotes hardly any other authority. The reason for this is that Marquardt confines himself to stating

---

[1] Marquardt gives two inconsistent lists, p. 325, 10, and p. 328, 2.

facts and their necessary implication, and therefore the recently discovered facts come in to complete the picture which he draws in bare outline ; Steinmann, on the contrary, selects certain facts from Marquardt to suit a preconceived purpose ; he groups them to produce a certain effect ; he slurs over the facts stated by Marquardt which tell against him, mentioning some of them without pointing out their bearing on his case ; and his apparently most telling arguments are really unproved assertions regarding matters of which we have no knowledge (owing to the lack of data), which is false and unscientific method. The consequence is that the newly discovered facts are absolutely inconsistent with Steinmann's opinion. Let any person read through Marquardt's non-partisan statement in the light of the new knowledge, and he will see for himself that this is so.

While Marquardt mentions that, so far as the right of sheltering Roman exiles was concerned, certain cities in the provinces were *externæ*, he never applies this survival of ancient right as a proof that those cities were outside of the province. In practice he always treats these provincial allied cities under their province, showing his opinion that they after all belonged to it ; and he lays little stress on their special standing, but calls it a mere shadow of freedom. He expressly calls Amisus the most easterly city of the province Bithynia (p. 350), and gives its municipal custom as a proof of Roman behaviour towards provincial cities (p. 143); and so on. Only with regard to Athens does he use an expression that might be misinterpreted in too sweeping a sense about the shadowy liberty[1] that was left to it, and says that it was exempt from the authority of

---

[1] Pliny, " Epist.," VIII. 24 ; Dio. Chrys., II. p. 200 R. ; Plutarch, " præc. ger. reip.," 32, § 8 (quoted by Marquardt, p. 86).

the proconsul : the authorities on whom he relies are not
sufficiently clear to prove this in its full sense, and Mommsen
(quoted by Steinmann) expresses the fact more carefully :
"Athens was not under the fasces of the proconsul," i.e.
when he entered the city the proconsul was not preceded
by axe-bearing lictors.   The fact that cases were carried on
appeal from courts in Athens to the hearing of the proconsul
proves that the city was not really exempt from his authority.

Marquardt mentions that Athens differed from the rest
of the province Achaia in never using the provincial era ;
and Steinmann religiously follows him, quoting this as a
very weighty proof that Athens was exempt from the provincial Roman system of dating.   There is nothing in this
antiquated fallacy.   (1) There prevailed extreme and
capricious variety in regard to chronology in Hellenistic
and Hellenic cities; and Athens, like many other Greek
cities, dated by its own magistrates.   (2) No provincial era
was used in Achaia,[1] and neither Athens nor any other city
of the province dated by a provincial era.[2]   This piece of
evidence is worse than valueless ; it is fictitious.   A more
careful study of discoveries regarding Achaian facts is needed
before writing about the province.

Even in regard to the chief glory of Athens, the University
and its administration, the Emperor interfered as he pleased.
It was required that the four masters of the Schools should
be Roman citizens ; and this regulation, according to
Mommsen, must certainly have been made early in the
Empire and probably by Augustus.[3]   The regulation was

---

[1] Some rare cases are known in which a provincial era seemed to be used
by a city of Achaia, but these are now better explained ; the dating is not
from the foundation of the province, but from a different era.

[2] Kaestner *de Aeris*, 66 f., Kubitschek *Aera* in Pauly-Wissowa, *Real-Enc.*

[3] Mommsen in " Zft. d. Savigny St. f. Rechtsgesch.," 1891, p. 152 f.

relaxed by Hadrian, who permitted the head of the Epicurean School (and probably the others on the same principle) to be chosen from all, whether Roman citizens or non-Romans. This we learn from his rescript, which was discovered and first published in 1890, and immediately commented on by Diels, Mommsen, and others.[1]

Dr. Steinmann's long discussion of the rank of Athens, and its relation to the province, therefore, is vitiated by neglect of important facts. The neglect was, of course, unintentional : he would not willingly have passed over any fact bearing on his subject, as his whole intention is to be judicial and complete. But he simply follows a book published in 1881, taking it as his final statement of the law, though anyone who studied Roman law or Roman history or the Eastern provincial administration, would have put him on the line of modern investigation, if he had sought to learn what is known on the subject.

Other considerations of a general character point to the same conclusion. It was a great source of wealth to any city that the governor should reside, or should even hold the assizes, in it,[2] and any free or allied city which had the opportunity would not have wasted it by vainly pleading that it was outside the province. Many free and allied cities were seats of *conventus :* Thessalonica and Antioch were always the residence of the governors of Macedonia and Syria, Ephesus and Tarsus of the governors of Asia and Cilicia. Ephesus and Tarsus and Smyrna and

---

[1] " Archiv f. Gesch. d. Philosophie," iv. 487 f. ; " Zft. d. Savigny St. f. Rechtsgesch.," 1891, p. 152 f. It is an interesting fact that the students of the School co-operated in the selection of a Scholarch (as was previously known), and were even empowered to depose an unworthy Professor and appoint a successor to him (which was revealed by the newly discovered inscription containing this rescript).

[2] On this enrichment see, for example, " Cities of St. Paul," p. 273.

Laodiceia on the Lycus were *conventus* from the beginning.
In Ephesus (Acts XIX.) the Secretary (γραμματεύς) warned
the people in the theatre that if they did not dissolve this
irregular assembly (one which was not permitted in the
charter of the city),[1] the city would be called to account
(obviously before the proconsul, whom the Secretary has
just previously mentioned as the fountain of justice).

Dr. Steinmann admits that several allied and free cities
of this class were the residence of the governor of the province, and that in others the Roman assizes (*conventus*) were
held by the governor. These admitted facts give away his
case. What meaning can be attached to his statement that
those free cities were outside of the province, if these facts
are true? It was the basis of provincial administration
that a governor could not reside outside his province, or
exercise his power legally anywhere except in his province.
Now at the *conventus* the governor exercised the full and
absolute authority over the provinces; he represented the
judicial dignity and the power of Rome. If Athens or
Smyrna or any of the other free and allied cities were outside the province, the governor could not possibly exercise
his supreme judicial authority or fix his residence permanently in any of them. To be the residence of the governor
of the province, a city must be in the province.

It is vain to attempt to bolster up the case by pleading
that Thessalonica and the other cities which we have mentioned were not allied, but belonged to the lower class of
free cities. The rights of the two classes, however, were
the same;[2] the superiority of the allied cities lay in the
more assured permanence of the rights. The question that

---

[1] νόμος in the Acts: *lex civitatis* was the technical Roman term.

[2] Marquardt asserts this quite positively, p. 80: see also Mommsen,
" Saattsrecht," III. p. 654, *n.* 4, and 658.

concerns us is whether these rights caused the city that possessed them to be ranked outside the province or not; and although Ephesus or Tarsus might lose its rights more easily than Athens or Amisos, yet so long as it possessed those rights, the effect on status was the same. In fact, allied cities are frequently described simply as " free " (for example, so always by Pliny); and the occurrence of a city in a list of *liberæ civitates* does not prove that it did not belong to the other and higher class of *fœderatæ*.[1]

Except in certain quite unimportant details, therefore, the free and allied cities were regularly counted as cities of the province. They ranked along with the other cities as members of the Commune or Association of provincial cities. Ordinary usage and, so far as is known, Roman custom ranked them as provincial cities; they were places into which the governor of the province entered in performance of his duty, although he respected the rights which they possessed. Paul and Luke thought and spoke of Athens and Smyrna and other free cities as cities of Achaia or Asia, and they were justified by Roman custom. When Paul speaks of a Corinthian as the " firstfruits of Achaia," he is thinking of the province, and his expression is in perfect agreement with Roman and general custom. The meaning of the words must be sought in the direction indicated at the beginning of the chapter.

Note (p. 387).—The nature of the household, and the relation of slaves to the master, come up constantly from many points of view in our study of Christianity amid its social surroundings under the early Empire; and correct conceptions on this subject are essential to a correct view of early Christian history. As to slavery we must always

---

[1] See Mommsen, loc. cit.

remember that in Rome a man's most trusted and faithful servants were his slaves; and that there was a strong prejudice against all paid labour in every department as untrustworthy. Paid servants were "hirelings,"[1] who had no personal interest in their duty, but looked to get money alone. We are now-a-days accustomed to hate slavery as barbarous and degrading to all concerned, alike owners and slaves; and in the state in which the institution of slavery has been practised in modern times, this hatred was fully justified. So also in the Roman system the application of slave labour in great gangs to the cultivation of large estates, a custom learned from the Carthaginians, was an unmingled evil, and produced many permanent and increasing disorders and diseases in the body politic. Household slavery, however, was a different and a comparatively humane institution; and the faithfulness of slaves to a master, and the general custom of trusting them with the most important and confidential business, bear witness to this. The whole body of slaves of the Emperor formed the "household of Caesar" (Philippians IV. 22); and, as we have seen on the Imperial estates (see Chap. XV.), their Imperial master was their God and they were his people.

The dislike of the Romans for "hired workers" may be illustrated in modern times by the German feeling that an army raised by voluntary enlistment is a mere force of mercenaries, while an army raised by conscription and national service stands on a far higher level of duty. So Naaman's Hebrew slave girl was genuinely interested in his welfare, 2 Kings V. 3.

[1] Mercennarii.

CHAPTER XXVII

THE PAULINE CHURCHES IN THE THIRD CENTURY

THE great importance of the Churches of the Two Regions
(as Luke would probably have called them), i.e. the
Churches of Galatia, stands out more and more impress-
ively as we comprehend better the Acts and the Epistles of
Paul. Paul gives a brief account of his work in founding
those Churches of Phrygia and Lycaonia, when he writes
to Timothy: "Thou didst follow my teaching, conduct,
purpose, faith, long-suffering, love, patience, persecutions,
sufferings: what things befell me at Antioch, at Iconium,
at Lystra: and out of them all the Lord delivered me.
Yea, and all that would live godly in Christ Jesus shall
suffer persecution."

This passage to Timothy is a résumé of the teaching of
Paul's second visit to those three cities, as described in the
Acts: "They returned to Lystra, and to Iconium and
Antioch,[1] confirming the souls of the disciples, exhorting
them to continue in the faith, and that through many
tribulations we must enter into the kingdom of God".

Here are two brief statements of the same period of
teaching in the same three stages: (1) confirmatory in-
struction; (2) the inevitableness of persecution for all
Christians without exception; (3) the final deliverance.
Both statements come from Paul. One is written by him

[1] Acts XIV. 21-3. See p. 422.

direct to Timothy. The other comes to us indirectly through Luke from Paul's mouth; and Luke associates himself with the statement of the second and third stages by using the pronoun "we". This is not a case similar to the later "we-passages," which are incidental to travel and indicate the personal presence of the historian. In this place the historian identifies himself in spirit and experience with the teaching of Paul as regards persecution. It is pointed out elsewhere[1] how much importance belongs to this phrase, in which the deep emotion of Luke breaks through his usual self-suppression.

That this teaching, as summarized in 2 Timothy III. 10-12, belongs to the second visit of Paul to the Galatian Churches, is clear from the omission of Derbe. Paul turned back from Derbe to revisit Lystra and Iconium and Antioch after a considerable absence. In this passage Paul recurs to that visit, and to the teaching then given. That is the occasion that rose to his memory in the last message to Timothy, when he knew he was near the gate of death. It is not so much the first visit and the conversion, as the second visit and the confirmation, that suits his present purpose. He had not been in Derbe the second time on that journey, and his teaching there had been of the order of conversion combined with farewell messages. Hence Derbe is omitted at this moment.

Paul also recalls to Timothy's memory that he had forewarned the three Churches against " evil men and impostors," who " shall wax worse and worse deceiving and being deceived ". In his letter to the Galatians, also, he says that he had by word of mouth forewarned the Galatians against evil men—"that they who practise such things shall not

---

[1] " St. Paul the Traveller," p. 123.

inherit the kingdom of God"—and against false teachers (i.e. impostors)—" as we said before, so say I now again : if any man preacheth unto you any Gospel other than that which ye received, let him be anathema ".[1]

The striking agreement between the words to Timothy, to the Galatians, and to Luke, constitutes a proof of real value that the same mind lies behind them all as the common source and origin.

We see how largely those Churches bulked in the mind of Paul and of Luke. We observe the great space which Luke allots to them in his highly compressed history. We notice that Paul's feet turn back again and again to the cities, and his memory recalls them in the imminence of death. Now what became of those Churches? What was their future history? How did they die out? This question must arise in every mind. Was all Paul's care and anxiety for them lavished on a niggardly and grudging soil? or did their future deeds repay his toil? Did they desert his Gospel " so quickly " (Gal. I. 6), or were they recalled by his Epistle to a right mind?

If there is any historic value in the second letter to Timothy, the four Churches[2] were Paul's to the end of his life. His letter to them was successful. Apart from any other argument, this reference alone furnishes conclusive testimony.[3] Later a veil falls over them. History has almost forgotten them.

Only in recent years archæological evidence is restoring to us some slight outline of their fate. The number of

---

[1] Galatians v. 21, I. 9, 10.

[2] I add Derbe, though Paul's purpose omits it to Timothy.

[3] Even those critics who do not accept the three Pastoral Epistles as Paul's composition, are almost all agreed that at least Second Timothy is in part genuine, and that its historical testimony is trustworthy.

inscriptions which remain in those regions and the close adjoining districts is very large: they begin in the second century, and become numerous in the third and in Lycaonia still more so in the fourth.

Their history was one of "tribulation," ending in death. The Churches were almost exterminated by Diocletian's soldiers. Paul's last word about them was prophetic of their fate. They did not recover from the persecution, but new people took their place, and a new tone. It is not suitable to our present purpose to write the story; but I add one single memorial, which has been discovered since I attempted to sketch the fortunes of the four Pauline Churches.[1]

The memorials of their existence have been recognized by the use of certain formulæ, and by far the most common of these is the appeal to the Judgment of God.[2]

At Synnada, a small but important city of Phrygia, metropolis in the Byzantine period of the province Phrygia Pacatiana, there was found in June, 1907, and sent to the Museum of Broussa, one of the most remarkable of the early Christian monuments that are now being slowly discovered, year after year, one here and one there, in Asia Minor (chiefly in Phrygia and Lycaonia). I have not seen it, but take all the description that is here given from the excellent Catalogue of the Museum, published by Monsieur G. Mendel, formerly of the French School of Athens.

This monument is a small box of marble, about six inches long in its largest part (where the moulding projects most prominently); and it has the form of a tiny sarcophagus, differing only in being higher than its length, whereas

[1] "The Cities and Bishoprics of Phrygia," ch. XII. (last sections).

[2] ἔσται αὐτῷ πρὸς τὸν θεόν: δώσει λόγον θεῷ: and several variations of the formula occur.

sarcophagi generally are longer than they measure in height.[1]
With the box, and apparently inside it, though the account
is not quite clear and explicit on this detail, there were found
fragments of a skull.   On the body and on the lid of the
sarcophagus are inscriptions :—

(1) On the body :—

ὧδε ἕνα Τρο-
φίμου τοῦ μ-
άρτυρος ὀστέ-
α

Within are Tro-
phimus the M-
artyr's bones.

(2) On the lid :—

τίς ἂν δὲ ταῦ-
τα τὰ ὀστέα
ἐκβάλῃ ποτέ,
ἔσται αὐτῷ
πρὸς τ[ὸν] θεό-
ν[2]

And whosoever
shall these bones
ever cast out,
he shall have to
reckon with God.

M. Mendel and Monsieur H. Grégoire, whose opinion
he quotes, are agreed in regarding this box as having been
intended to contain part of the remains of Trophimus from
Pisidian Antioch, who suffered at Synnada in the short persecution under the Emperor Probus, A.D. 276-82.   There
are no two scholars whose opinion on a matter of Christian
antiquities in Asia Minor ranks higher ; and their agreement
may be taken as very strong, though, as M. Mendel states,
Mgr. Duchesne regards the box and the inscriptions as later
than the fourth century.[3]

---

[1] I speak of the height including the lid or cover (which is a separate piece
both in the large sarcophagi and in this small box).

[2] Grammatically the only difficulty lies in ἕνα, apparently a vulgarism for
ἔνεστι or ἔνι, a relic of local Phrygian Greek.

[3] I had always understood that Mgr. Duchesne was one of the first to re-
cognize that this formula was Christian and belonged to the third century.
Many occurrences of the formula are on the stones dated in that century.
None are dated later.

MM. Mendel's and Grégoire's arguments are (as they both recognize) founded largely on the criteria of the dating of Christian inscriptions in Phrygia, which are laid down in my "Cities and Bishoprics of Phrygia," II, chapter XII. I have sometimes feared that my views might be considered to exaggerate the antiquity of Christian monuments in Phrygia; and it is a great encouragement to find that the same reasons which in 1894 appeared conclusive to me are still regarded by two such excellent scholars as decisive. The discoveries of the intervening sixteen years have distinctly tended to confirm the main lines of my chronological system.[1] In our view the formula "he shall have to reckon with God" belongs to the third century, when Christianity, in its public appearance, was still concealing itself under cryptic symbols and language. After the triumph of Christianity, in the epoch to which Mgr. Duchesne assigns this monument, one can hardly suppose it possible that no cross or other open sign of religious character should appear in the epitaph or on some other part of the box. The use of the cross in Christian epitaphs, or of some equivalent symbol, became almost universal soon after A.D. 340.[2]

The inscriptions, brief as they are, are marked not merely by the presence of an early formula, but by the absence of any late and stereotyped Christian expressions. At the date to which Mgr. Duchesne assigns the monument, we

---

[1] The character of the Lycaonian Christian inscriptions of the late third, fourth, and fifth centuries, and the principles on which they should be tentatively placed in chronological periods, are described in "Luke the Physician" (concluding paper).

[2] The usage had not been established when Bishop Eugenius of Laodicea of Lycaonia prepared his sarcophagus in A.D. 341 ("Expositor," November, 1908).

should expect a term like the Holy Martyr.[1]   The public
cult of the holy martyrs was fully established by that time,
and an adjective of respect could hardly be omitted.   In
that later period this monument would naturally have to
be regarded as a reliquary made to contain relics (supposed or real) of the Saint, and preserved in a Church for
general reverence and worship.   We can hardly suppose
that a tomb, with a sepulchral inscription, was made for
the bones of a person who had died a century and a half
or even more, previously.   But this monument is marked
as sepulchral, for that character is guaranteed by scores of
similar examples.   The form of the inscription cannot be
mistaken.

Had this box been a reliquary, much greater horror would
have been expressed at the thought of the bones being
thrown out, and a more definite and severe punishment
would probably have been denounced against sacrilege.
The whole style of the epitaph is early, and has nothing in
it that recalls the thought or expression characteristic of the
fifth century or later.

M. Mendel also points out that the form of the letters in
the epitaph favours a date distinctly earlier than the fifth
century: but (as he says) this consideration could not be
relied on as a quite conclusive proof of date.

The small size of the box must be explained by the
supposition that the Christians did not obtain the corpse
from the Roman authorities.   They only succeeded in
getting a part which they buried.   The words which I have
used in the " Cities and Bishoprics of Phrygia," II. p. 730,
" Rome did not war against the dead ; and the remains
of the martyrs were allowed to be buried by their friends "

---

[1] τοῦ ἁγίου μάρτυρος.

—while true of the case there mentioned and of many others—are too absolutely expressed ; and exceptions must be admitted even in the earlier persecutions, still more in the later. The Roman officials observed the eagerness of the Christians to get possession of the corpses of the martyrs, or even parts of them, and probably dreaded lest some mystic or magical power might be imparted by the relics of the dead.[1] Accordingly, as early as the martyrdom of Polycarp (probably A.D. 155), the body was refused to the Church. The high respect and veneration for the martyrs, which began quite early, passed gradually into a public cult, and gave rise to some abuses as early as the time of Diocletian.

Each new fact regarding the state of Christianity in Asia Minor during the third century has its distinct value ; and we are gradually collecting the materials out of which a clearer idea of the beginnings of the Eastern Church can be formed. M. Grégoire accepts the early date assigned to Paul the Martyr of Derbe (whose tombstone was published by Miss Ramsay in " Studies in the History of the Eastern Provinces," p. 62), remarking that a commonplace sepulchral formula, such as is employed in the epitaph, is not the sort of inscription that would have been placed over a martyr in the time following the triumph of the Church. He here recognizes fully and confirms by his authority our principle that those simple forms of sepulchral inscription, which are either common to pagans and Christians, or only slightly modified in Christian usage from pagan phraseology, belong to the period before Constantine, and disappear with the generation which was living at the time when the peace of the Church was finally assured.

The same scholar also accepts my interpretation of the

---

[1] On the magical powers attributed in pagan circles to the Christians in the early centuries, see above, ch. VIII.-X.

epitaph of the five Phrygian "children, who on one single occasion gained the lot of life ": they are five martyrs, who suffered at Hieropolis, not far from Synnada, probably in the persecution of Decius A.D. 249-51, and were buried by their spiritual father, doubtless the Bishop of the Church.[1]

On the other hand M. Grégoire is not convinced by the conjecture advanced by Mr. Anderson and myself in the "Studies in the Eastern Provinces," pp. 125, 201, that Bishop Akylas (Aquila), whose epitaph we have published, was a martyr. The language of the epitaph is obscure, and the text is not complete. For my own part I still believe that the view taken by Mr. Anderson is highly probable, and that further discovery is likely to confirm it. In any case it is a gain to have three assured and generally accepted graves and epitaphs of martyrs belonging to the third century.

The Acta of the martyrs Trophimus and his companions are published in "Acta Sanctorum," of September, VI. pp. 12 ff., and in Migne's "Patrol. Gr.," CXV. pp. 733 ff. See also Harnack, "Gesch. d. altchr. Litt.," II. 2, p. 481 note; Goerres, "Jahrb. f. protestant. Theol.," XVI. 1890, pp. 616 f. (who denies the authenticity of the "Acta"); Allard, "Hist. des Persecutions," III. p. 279, 4; and Aubé, "L'Église et l'État," p. 52 f. (who both maintain the authenticity).[2] My impression has always been that the "Acta," which are extremely interesting and well deserve a special publication, are of the fourth century, and pro-

---

[1] "Cities and Bishoprics of Phrygia," II. p. 730 ff.

[2] See also Mercati, "Studi et testi," 5, "Note di letterature biblica e cristiana antica," XV. pp. 206-26; "Un apologia antiellenica sotto forma di martirio". On the formula "he shall have to reckon with God," see "Monumenta Ecclesiæ liturgica," by Cabrol and Leclerc, I., "relliq. liturg.," section I., "relliq. epigraph.," p. 12*, no. 2798.

bably quite trustworthy in the main outlines, though they give a later view of the situation.

The discovery of this monument now gives assurance to the rather bold series of inferences which have been drawn from the study of the whole group of inscriptions marked by the concluding formula, that any violator of the grave "shall have to reckon with God". These inferences are stated at length in the chapter already mentioned.[1] Given on the one hand the narrative of Paul's work founding the original Churches in the provinces Asia and Phrygia, and on the other hand their character in the third century, there stands out the story of an early and forgotten Christian society, which was destroyed with fire and sword, and practically extirpated, by Diocletian. Nothing of it has remained except those epitaphs. It produced no great writers, whose works might form its memorial. The very names of its bishops and leaders have perished. Men, women and children perished, as Eusebius says, "calling on the God Who is the power over all".[2] The story of the great central atrocity in the Phrygian churches has been discredited by some with irrational scepticism. It rests on the authority of two practically contemporary historians, Eusebius and Lactantius. They differ only in the slight detail that Eusebius says an entire city with all its people was destroyed, while Lactantius states only that the whole population with their church were destroyed, implying that they assembled at the church and were burned there. To one who has by the patient toil of years tracked out those Christian communities by their formula of appealing to "the God," it comes as one of those startling and convincing

---

[1] "Cities and Bishoprics of Phrygia," ch. xii.

[2] Eusebius, "Hist. Eccl.," viii. 11. Compare Lactantius, "Inst. Div.," v. 11.

details of real life and truth that the only thing recorded in history regarding that destroyed people is that they died "appealing to the God Who is over all". Unconsciously Eusebius writes as the epitaph over the ashes of the destroyed people the thought and almost the very words by which we have recognized the epitaphs which they used to place on the graves of their families.[1]

These are the fruit of Paul's work. They perished and a different class of Phrygian or Lycaonian Christians succeeded them. The Church was now taken under the protection of the State, and in gratitude to the Constantinian dynasty condoned and accepted many of the false principles which were knit into the fabric and constitution of the Roman Empire. The Pauline Churches were practically destroyed in central Asia Minor, where they had been almost universally dominant during the third century among the population.

Note (p. 412).—The reading which Westcott and Hort print as secondary, resting on good early authority, must be preferred in Acts XIV. 21 : εἰς is omitted before Ἀντιόχειαν, making Iconium and Antioch a pair of cities in the same region, while Lystra is kept apart as a city of a different region.

---

[1] "Cities and Bishoprics of Phrygia," II. p. 507 f.

INDEX

(423)